JAPAN
A Documentary History

D1564732

JAPAN
A Documentary History

Volume II

The Late Tokugawa Period
to the Present

David J. Lu

An East Gate Book

M.E. Sharpe
Armonk, New York
London, England

An East Gate Book

Library of Congress Cataloging-in-Publication Data

Japan : a documentary history / Vol. II: The Late Tokugawa Period to the Present /
edited by David J. Lu.
p.   cm.
"An East Gate book."
Includes bibliographical references and index.
ISBN 0-7656-0036-6 (pbk. : alk. paper)
1. Japan—History
I. Lu, David John, 1928–.
DS835.J37   1996
952—dc20
96-24433
CIP

Printed in the United States of America

The paper used in this publication meets the minimum requirements of the
American National Standard for Information Sciences—
Permanence of Paper for Printed Library Materials,
ANSI Z 39.48-1984.

BM (p)   10   9

To

Kevin, Brian, Annamaria, Olivia, Naomi, and another little one on her way

Contents

Japan: A Documentary History is being published simultaneously in one clothbound edition, which includes the complete text, and two paperback editions: Vol. I: *The Dawn of History to the Late Tokugawa Period*, and Vol. II: *The Late Tokugawa Period to the Present*. The complete table of contents and the complete index appear in all three, and the pagination of the paperbacks is sequential.

Preface

The history of mankind is full of joy and vicissitude, and the history of Japan is no exception. "Man," to paraphrase Leopold von Ranke, "is a creature so good and at the same time so evil, so noble and at the same time so animal-like, so polished and at the same time so uncouth who, while seeking eternity, is bound by the fleeting moment." This book is a narrative of Japanese history as rendered by the Japanese people themselves at the time they lived. It shows their foibles and triumphs with their tears and laughter. There is a thread of common experience that they share with the rest of the world. As such, a documentary history has the power of immediacy not enjoyed by an interpretive history. It speaks directly to its readers beyond the constraints of time and space.

This book is intended not just for college students but has a broader audience in mind, including businessmen, diplomats, policymakers, and anyone interested in Japan. With that supposition, the following criteria are used in selecting the documents: (1) a given document must adequately reflect the spirit of the times and the lifestyle of the people of that age; (2) the emphasis must be placed on the development of social, economic, and political institutions, without neglecting important cultural attainments; and (3) some key documents must be studied in depth from different perspectives. Among the key documents so identified are Prince Shōtuku's seventeen-article constitution (604), Goseibai Shikimoku (1232), laws for military households (1615), Charter Oath (1868), Meiji constitution (1889), Shōwa constitution (1946) and the U.S.–Japan security pact (1960). In each case, the text is accompanied by commentaries. In the case of the Charter Oath, three different versions are reproduced, thus allowing us to study its drafting process. In the case of the Shōwa constitution, committee deliberations as well as comments by Japanese and American participants are reproduced. Many of these documents are not available in English elsewhere. As much as possible, duplication with existing sources in English is avoided. Close to three-quarters of the documents contained in this volume are original translations by this writer.

Some alert readers will find that this book is a successor to my two-volume *Sources of Japanese History* published in 1974. The first part of the present volume retains much of the 1974 edition, but a number of documents are added to show business practices in the Tokugawa period. The second part has extensive revisions and totally new chapters. Again serious consideration is given to Japan's economic might, which has resulted in a new chapter on Japan's emergence as an economic superpower.

I have been fortunate in being able to visit and observe the workings of more than 120 Japanese companies since the early 1980s. That experience is reflected in this new chapter. The debates extended by contemporary Japanese writers contained in Chapters 17 and 18 of this volume are refreshingly relevant to contemporary America, as these writers cope with many of the same problems facing us today. For close to a quarter of a century, I have been a contributor to the Japanese weekly *Sekai to Nippon* (The World and Japan). Through the pages of this paper, I too have been a participant in these ongoing debates.

In preparing the 1974 edition, I benefited greatly from the massive compilation of historical documents that the Japanese undertook to commemorate the centennial of the Meiji Restoration. In preparing the current edition, I benefited from disclosure of official documents made in commemoration of the fiftieth anniversary of the end of World War II. For example, Japan's right to self-defense and obligation to engage in peacekeeping operations under the U.N. Charter can now be definitely established. Documents made public in the fall of 1995 and winter of 1996 show clearly how the provisions of Article 9 are to be interpreted. These are contained in the documents added to Chapter 15, "Japan under Occupation."

There is no right or wrong way of using this book, but I would like to make one suggestion: Please read a chapter in one sitting instead of reading only one document. In this way you will not only be able to get the sense of the *zeitgeist* that governed the era but also discern the meaning of each individual document more clearly. Please do not hesitate to question statements and assumptions made by the writers. From whatever eras they come, treat them as if they were your contemporaries and engage them in a lively conversation.

Do not be discouraged if some of the *shōen* documents in Chapter 4 seem to recite various rights (*shiki*) endlessly like a litany. They are documents that defined the functions and entitlements for each inhabitant of a *shōen*. Not satisfied with merely reading and translating *shōen* documents, I diligently sought original documents. One day, I came upon a number of them on exhibit in the Osaka Municipal Museum. One of the documents had three lines drawn after the name of a peasant. The three lines represented the lengths between his fingertip to the first joint and to the knuckle of his right pointing finger. In an age when there was no way of identifying fingerprints and no other means of identification, this was a clever way to let an illiterate person "sign" his name. With this fashion, the document assumed the quality of a living document. There is a phrase in Japan called *"seikatsu no chie,"* the wisdom that is gained from the experience of living. The documents contained in this book represent the sum total of Japan's *seikatsu no chie* over the ages.

Today we often hear of the excellence of Japanese management. One of its most frequently discussed features is their ability to reach a consensus. That ability can be traced back to the Goseibai Shikimoku of 1232. History is a continuing process. What is past is also prologue. This volume allows us to probe deeply into the roots of contemporary Japanese civilization.

Many Japanese friends have kept me informed of events in Japan and have supplied me with books and articles that have been of interest to them. They have filled the gap between my visits to Japan. These friends include Hirose Hideo, Kiyomiya Ryū, Shibata Yūzō, Shiina Takeo, Sumitomo Yoshiteru, and Takayama Michio. I thank them for giving me a chance to be in constant touch with Japan, which is an indispensable ingredient in preparing this new volume. Professors Ardath Burks, Marius Jansen, John Hall, Harry Harootunian, and Bernard Susser read part or all of the 1974 edition before it was published. I wish to thank them again for their encouragement and friendship.

I have had the privilege of meeting a number of contributors to this volume in person. It was good to renew acquaintance with some of them and make new friends in the summer of 1996 as this volume was readied for press. Conversations with them were akin to an old CBS program "You Were There." I hope that sense of participation in history is recaptured in the pages of this book. My gratitude for Japanese authors extends to Japanese publishers who have gone to an extraordinary length to make my contacts with the authors possible. Matsui Kaoru of the Edo Tokyo Museum was most gracious in helping select the illustrations from the Museum collection which now grace this volume.

I also wish to thank my former students at Bucknell University and at the Associated Kyoto Program. Their approving smiles, disapproving frowns, and intelligent questions have helped to shape and reshape the book. Because of them, this volume, in fact, is a far better book than the 1974 edition. This book, however, would have never taken its present shape without the gentle prodding of Douglas Merwin of M. E. Sharpe. Born in China and trained at Columbia in East Asian studies, he is a partaker of the true wisdom of the East. Angela Piliouras, the project editor, has been a delightful, cheerful, and enthusiastic co-worker. The staff of the Bertrand Library at Bucknell as always has been courteous and helpful. Finally, with love and affection, I wish to thank my wife, Annabelle, my constant companion for more than forty years, for her *naijo-no-kō* (help from within). We have jointly decided to dedicate this book to our grandchildren, and with it symbolically to express our hope for the coming century and for the new generation of scholars of Japan.

David J. Lu

Note on Japanese and Chinese Names and Terms

Japanese names are given in this book in the Japanese order, that is, the surname precedes the given name. In the case of Americans of Japanese descent, however, the conventional order is maintained, that is, the given name precedes the surname. Macrons are employed to distinguish long vowels from short vowels. The Hepburn-Reischauer system of romanization is used, but the preference of the individual cited is observed, thus Konoye and not Konoe.

Chinese names are also given in the traditional order, that is, the surname precedes the given name. The *pinyin* Romanization system, with a few exceptions, is utilized throughout this volume.

JAPAN
A Documentary History

CHAPTER X

The End of the Tokugawa Rule

Tokugawa society contained within itself seeds of its own destruction. Commercialization and urbanization brought about unprecedented riches among certain groups, but in their wake also left trails of corruption. By the nineteenth century, the Tokugawa government found itself suffering from many setbacks. The gold that it once held in abundance dwindled quickly, and with the exception of the *tenryō*, or the territory directly held by the *bakufu*, it lacked a means of direct taxation. Social unrest was compounded by the frequent peasant uprisings and urban riots. While the merchants prospered at the expense of the *daimyō* and samurai, the latter became restive and sought changes in the status quo (Documents 1–7).

Two major reforms were attempted near the end of the Tokugawa era. They were the Kansei reforms (1787–1793) and Tempō reforms (1841–1843). The former did not last beyond the tenure of *rōju* Matsudaira Sadanobu, and the latter was abruptly terminated with the removal from office of its chief instigator Mizuno Tadakuni (1793–1851). The Tempō reforms encouraged the samurai to return to the pursuit of learning and military arts, and decreed general austerity for all classes of people. Farmers were ordered to remain in the villages, and those who went to the cities were forced to return. Trade associations (*kabunakama*) were disbanded, and the prices of certain merchandise were forcibly reduced. In this fashion, the *bakufu* attempted to exercise direct control over commercial activities, but it failed because it could not cope with the concerted power wielded by the merchants in Osaka and Edo. Its effort to consolidate private domains and lands around Osaka and Edo, to incorporate them into the *tenryō*, also failed, due to the objection of Tokugawa retainers and peasants who

273

would stand to lose if the measures went into effect. Finally the powerful *shimpan* of Kii intervened to bring an end to the reforms. The failure of the Tempō reforms underscored the inherent weaknesses of the *bakufu* as the ruling power. At the same time, some of the Western *han* had modest success in their own reform attempts, which in turn paved the way for their entry into national politics.

Near its end the Tokugawa *bakufu* was also beset by the lack of effective leadership at the top, especially in the person of the *shōgun*. The succession disputes divided the *daimyō* into two contending parties (Document 13). And when Commodore Perry came to force open the door of Japan, it further divided the country into the camps of *jōi* (expel the barbarians) and *kaikoku* (opening the country) groups (Documents 8 and 9, see also Document 10).

The domestic and external problems gave some of the great *tozama han* opportunities to challenge the supremacy of the *bakufu*. The *han*, unlike the *bakufu*, were successful in their internal reforms, which included financial reforms and effective use of able lower samurai within their own *han* irrespective of the lineage (Document 14). Some of them also employed a system of monopoly to enhance their own financial position. In first contesting and later supplanting the power of the *bakufu*, the *han* and their samurai employed as their shibboleth *Sonnō Jōi* (Revere the Emperor and Expel the Barbarians). The *sonnō* thought had its origin in the Confucian ideal of rectification of names, such as that expressed by the Mito school of thought. Initially the proponent of this thought did not seek to overthrow the *baku-han* or feudal system as such, but simply attempted to utilize the catalytic force of the Imperial Court to infuse new life into the old system and institutions. It was in this spirit that men like Sakamoto Ryōma worked diligently to effect a compromise between the contending forces of Satsuma-Chōshū and *bakufu* (Document 16). And in a similar vein, Yamanouchi Yōdō, former Lord of Tosa, also attempted at the last moment to forestall the complete overthrow of the *bakufu* as an institution. Yet in the end the idea of the supremacy of the imperial house, as advocated by Yoshida Shōin (Document 15), was to triumph, and along with the dictate of *Realpolitik* (Document 17), ushered in the Meiji Restoration.

DECAY OF THE TOKUGAWA SYSTEM

The samurai class had been the backbone of Tokugawa society. However, after two and a half centuries of peace they hardly resembled their forefathers who had won the country for Tokugawa Ieyasu. The long periods of residence in Edo and in the castle towns made them "soft," less given to martial arts and more to the fine things of life. Documents 1 and 2 show the luxurious modes of life they adopted for themselves and the resulting corruption. However, their incomes remained on a meager scale (Document 3), and their morale was generally low (Document 4).

The declining economic conditions of the country are described by Honda Toshiaki (1744–1821) (Document 5). Aside from accepting new knowledge from the West, he found part of the solution in the adoption of an enlightened agricultural policy that could prevent the practice of infanticide and encourage farmers to remain on their lands.

As the daimyō *went deeper into debt, they exacted a larger amount of taxes from the peasants in their domains. This condition is described by Matsudaira Sadanobu (1758–1829), the lord of the Shirakawa-han who became the First Councillor (*rojū shuza*) to the eleventh* shōgun, *Ienari. Sadanobu was responsible for the so-called Kansei reforms while in office (1787–1793) (Document 6).*

*In spite of many attempts to reform, economic conditions continued to deteriorate, and tax exactions went unabated. In the first part of the nineteenth century, peasant uprisings (*hyakushō ikki*) and urban riots (*uchikowashi, *literally destroying stores) became frequent. One of the most unusual uprisings was led by one Ōshio Heihachirō (1793–1837) who was an official in the Osaka Town Commissioner's Office (Osaka* Machi-bugyō*). After a great famine in 1836, he first petitioned for general relief of the dispossessed. When this was not approved, he sold his personal belongings and gave the proceeds to the poor. In 1837 he resorted to an armed uprising, and attempted to take food and money away from rich merchants in Osaka to distribute them to the poor. He was suppressed within a day, but because of his scholarly reputation and of his former official position, the uprising attracted nationwide attention. Document 7 is his manifesto calling for direct action.*

1 Luxurious Living of Samurai, 1816[1]

Concerning the clothes worn by the samurai, here is a story coming from the time of the Keichō era (1596–1615) when Lord Ieyasu was still living. A samurai in attendance to Lord Ieyasu appeared before his Lordship attired in a *hakama* (divided shirt) made of *sendaihira* silk. His Lordship was angered and brandished his long sword to expel the samurai, saying that not long after the attainment of peace the man had already indulged in a taste of luxury. However, nowadays, not only those unimportant vassals but also those lower-ranking samurai, foot soldiers (*ashigaru*), merchants (*chōnin*) and farmers all wear *sendaihira* silk. The extravagance in clothing can be readily seen by this.

Concerning food and drink, when *rōju* Doi Toshikatsu (1573–1644) visited Sakai Tadakatsu (1587–1662, who later became *tairō* under Iemitsu) at the latter's home, he was treated with cold soup. In those days people had a habit of saving, and if a host invited his guests, the guests brought their own food, and the

---

[1]Buyō Inshi, *Seiji Kenbunroku (What I Witness in This World)* (1816) as quoted in Ishin Shiryō Hensan Jimukyoku, *Ishinshi (A History of the Meiji Restoration)*, Vol. 1 (Tokyo: Meiji Shoin, 1939), p. 322.

host provided the hot soup (*siruko*). If *sake* was also added, it was considered quite a treat. Nowadays, people are so extravagant in their consumption of *sake* and food, and their pastries contain all sorts of delicacies. For example, the price of an elegant meal for one person is anywhere from two to three bags (*hyō*) to four to five bags of rice. And a pastry may cost as much as one quart (*shō*) to two or three quarts of rice. When *sake* is served, it now requires soup and other side dishes. And nowadays even those lowly people who live in insignificant town houses and back alleys refuse to eat cold soup.

2 Corruption of Samurai, 1855[2]

Many *han* samurai on duty in Edo indulge in dissipation. In most instances, they are led into this habit by those samurai who are on regular attendance in Edo. The Edo samurai cannot make a living on their regular income. From their youthful days, they are accustomed to supplementing their income by outside work. They freely spend their pocket money and grow up without becoming literate. Many of them consider riotous living the fashion of Edo. They treat those who are fresh from the country as bumpkins, and the latter are anxious to become men of the world like the Edo samurai. In this way, the Edo samurai lead their country cousins into a life of dissipation.

3 Family Budget of a Hatamoto, 1845[3]

When one compares the income of a *chōnin* (townsman or merchant) with that of a samurai, one hundred *ryō* of coin is equivalent to three hundred *koku* of rice. In the household of a *hatamoto* (bannerman)[4] with a stipend of 300 *koku*, in accordance with the law of 1633, the *hatamoto* must keep two samurai, one armor carrier, one spear carrier, one traveling-box carrier, two stablemen, one carrier of sandals, and two porters for military services. At the current scale, the salaries of two samurai are eight *ryō* and the salaries of eight others are twenty *ryō*. It costs nine *ryō* to feed a horse. And fifty bags (*hyō*) of rice must be given to ten retainers as their stipends. In this way the *hatamoto* has 139 bags of rice left for himself. However, he must appropriate an additional thirteen *ryō* for food (other than rice) for his ten retainers. For his own service for the *shōgun* and for the maintenance of his own armor and furniture, he must budget six or seven *ryō*. Then the living expenses of the family of four or five, including a maid servant, require an additional thirty *ryō*.

---

[2]Fujimori Taiga, *Shinseidan (A New Treatise on Politics)* as quoted in *Ishinshi, op. cit.*, p. 323.

[3]Kuwabara Nobumitsu, *Ryugō Zappitsu (Essays)* in *Ishinshi, op. cit.*, pp. 328–329.

[4]The *Hatamoto* were enfeoffed vassals of the *shōgun* who received an annual stipend of less than 10,000 *koku*, but had the privilege of having audience with the *shōgun*. Those vassals who were below them and did not have the privilege of audience were called *gokenin*.

Altogether he must count on spending fifty *ryō* a year. When he sells his 139 bags of rice, he can gain a little over forty-six *ryō*. This means that annually he runs a deficit of a little over three *ryō*. Thus the cumulative deficit from the year 1633 through 1845 comes to a total of 636 *ryō*. If a *hatamoto* with an annual stipend of 300 *koku* owes 600 *ryō*, his annual net income is reduced to an equivalent of seventeen *ryō*, since he must pay an annual interest of thirty *ryō* for his debt. In this manner he cannot keep his ten retainers and he spends his days without being able to secure their services.

4 **Decline in Samurai Morale, 1796**[5] They may be called the samurai, but it is hard to keep up the samurai spirit. Their regular income is constantly inadequate, and without meaning to, they bow and kneel down even to merchants and farmers. They engage in handicraft and sell their products in order to get over their financial difficulty. As a result, they lose their self-respect, and the samurai spirit is constantly on a downward trend, as if pushing a cart downhill. It goes down day after day, month after month.

5 **Economic Conditions in Edo and in the Countryside, 1798**[6] The system of keeping the *daimyō* and their families in Edo in alternate years, and letting them report on the governing of their domains, came into being through the profound wisdom and thought of the great founder of the *bakufu*. A *daimyō* must instruct the samurai and common people of his domain to enrich the soil and be diligent in their study of literature and practice of military arts. If a *daimyō* is not remiss in accomplishing these tasks during the year he is at his domain, he fulfills his duties as the protector of the domain. The *daimyō* of different domains have imitated the system of residence in Edo, and have required their retainers to reside in the castle towns of their domains. If the samurai reside in castle towns, they meet their colleagues frequently. If they can remember that their basic functions are the study of literature and practice of military arts, and diligently pursue them, and if they can refrain from luxury and live frugally, treating the farmers well and sincerely nurturing them, then there will be no poverty. . . .

However, nowadays, it is common to see a debt incurred by a *daimyō* increasing instead of decreasing even when he continuously reduces the stipends due his retainers to pay for his debt to the merchants. There was an example of a *daimyō* with a stipend of 60,000 *koku* whose debts multiplied and finally reached an

---

[5]Takano Tsunemichi, *Shōheiyawa (Evening Talks on the Peaceful Condition of Our Times)* in *Ishinshi, op. cit.*, p. 329.

[6]*Keisei Hisaku (Secret Plans for Governing the Country)* in *Honda Toshiaki*, in Iwanami Shoten, *Nihon Shisō Taikei (Major Compendium of Japanese Thought)*, Vol. 44 (Tokyo: Iwanami Shoten, 1970), pp. 26–28.

aggregate of 1,180,000 *ryō* in gold. When he was not able to repay, a public suit ensued. In this case, if the *daimyō* assigned all of his income from the 60,000 *koku* for the repayment of his debts, it would still take fifty to sixty years to complete the full payment. I doubt if all the *daimyō* are in this kind of financial difficulty. However, there is not a single *daimyō* who is not in debt with one or more merchants. How pitiful this is. In the eyes of the merchants, the *daimyō* must look like birds or fish caught by a net cast by a hunter or a fisherman. All the *daimyō* select officials who impose extra burdens on farmers in an attempt to repay their debts, but these debts do not decrease, and instead they increase year after year. Many officials are replaced for incompetence. Under their successors, farmers are again placed under enormous exactions, but the debts continue to grow. This being the case, even those of stout heart give up their positions and money to retire. Some of them feign illness and refuse to leave home, others lose their rational minds and die early. No matter how much thought they put into the matter to alleviate the difficulties, neither the *daimyō* nor their officials can find alternatives. As the popular saying goes, when one sinks to the depth of the abyss of debts, even children and grandchildren cannot have a chance to surface. Some of them may allow the merchants to take free rein, give up their domains, place them under the merchants' control, and receive the latter's remittance to meet their official and private expenses. They can no longer give thought to keeping the functions ordained by heaven (*tenshoku*) under the grace of the deities and Buddha, and to protecting and nurturing the farmers.

Since the great famine of 1783, many of the fields and gardens previously owned by the victims of starvation have been abandoned. In the olden days, between the regions of Kantō and Ōu, there were so-and-so villages here, and so-and-so districts there. But nowadays, many of them are reduced to ghost villages without any harvest, and especially in the province of Ōshiū[7] five districts can count practically no harvest with their fields and gardens abandoned. Within the three-year period starting in 1783, bad crop years and famine continued, and within the one province of Ōshiū alone, the number of those starved to death exceeded two million.[8] The number of farmers had always been scarce. With this large-scale starvation, abandonment of fields and gardens occurred in many places. Furthermore, if the evil custom of infanticide does not stop, the number of farmers may be reduced further and eventually they may become extinct. Therefore unless the *daimyō* treat the farmers kindly and protect them and nurture them, this evil custom cannot easily be eradicated. We look for the coming of an enlightened ruler who will establish a system of government based on the great mercy and compassion of the Buddha. Then after so many years, that evil custom may stop, and again bring about rich crops and prosperity to the country.

---

[7]Covering the present-day Fukushima, Miyagi, Iwate, Aomori and part of Akita prefectures.

[8]This is an obvious exaggeration. The actual figure was probably closer to 200,000.

I can only ask for great mercy and compassion. If an extremely poor woman becomes pregnant, send an inspector to find out, and give two bags of rice each year to the mother from the birth of the child until he is ten years of age. In this way the evil custom of infanticide can be stopped immediately. In ten years, the *daimyō* expends only twenty bags of rice. This is a secret plan which will not only gain for the *daimyō* a capable farmer, but will also eradicate hostilities toward him. I have spoken of hostilities. How would a mother feel when she is forced to kill her own child born in this realm of humanity. The love between parents and children exists even among the animals. How much greater is it among human beings? Many Confucian scholars, past and present, speak of humanity and compassion (*jin-ji*) without having these feelings in their hearts. Officials and administrators speak of benevolent rule (*jinsei*) without meaning what they say. Whose fault will it be if farmers die of hunger and good fields and gardens are abandoned? It must be ascribed to the fault of the *daimyō*. If that happens, he is indeed a disloyal and unprincipled person. When I ponder on this, my mind creates uncontrollable rage with a feeling that even the punishment of heaven comes too late for him.

6 **Tax Burdens Suffered by the Farmers, 1781**[9] Nowadays, we have taxes in the range of 50 percent, 60 percent and 70 percent, and it is difficult to recite the different types of taxes and miscellaneous exactions in existence. There is a tax on vacant lots and gardens, a tax on buildings, a tax on doors and windows, and there is even a tax on girls who have reached a certain age. Taxes are also imposed on cloth, *sake*, herbs, and sesame seeds. . . .

If a person adds a room to his house, he pays tax on it. . . . If a child is born to him he pays tax. . . . At the harvest time tens and hundreds of officials come to inspect. If they come from a distance, they stay overnight at the farmers' homes. If in any small degree the farmers are remiss in treating the officials, they can expect an increase in their taxes, or imposition of [additional] *corvée* labor. Farmers fear officials like tigers and foxes. They make new roads and bridges and prostrate in the mud to show their respect for the coming of the officials. They also serve the best food and drink, and provide the prettiest clothing and bedding items for the use of the officials. They do so because they are fearful of being persecuted by them. When *corvée* labor is imposed on them, they build highways, bridges and dikes, and send off travellers (by first providing them accommodations, or providing relay horses). Even during the farming season, if they are ordered to engage in *corvée* labor, they must discard their plows, leave their horses, carry their own provisions and travel five, six or even more than ten *ri* to go to the city. They work all day without getting a cent. Instead they are hit

---

[9]Matsudaira Sadanobu, *Kokuhonron (On the Basic Matters of the Nation)* in *Ishinshi, op. cit.*, pp. 342–343.

and lashed, scolded and abused. When they return to their own fields, the weeds may have overtaken the fields and they become unmanageable. . . . There are many other instances of severe exactions and oppressive rules which I do not have time to enumerate.

7 Ōshio Heihachirō's Manifesto, 1837[10]

If the four seas suffer destitution, the beneficence of heaven cannot long survive. If a man of small stature governs the country, calamities become inevitable. These are the teachings bequeathed by the sage of old to the later generations of rulers and subjects. The Deity enshrined in Tōshōgu [Ieyasu] decreed that to show compassion for the widows, widowers and the lonely is the foundation of benevolent government (*jinsei*). However, during the past 240 to 250 years of peace, those who were above gradually became accustomed to luxury and they now live in sheer extravagance. Those officials who are entrusted with important political affairs openly give and receive bribes. Some of them who lack virtue and righteousness still attain high positions as a result of connections they have through the ladies in waiting in the inner palace. They devote their efforts and intelligence to enrich their private coffers. They levy an excessive amount of money from common people and farmers in their own domains or administrative districts. These are the people who have suffered over the years the severe exactions of annual taxes and various types of *corvée* labor. Now they propose such nonsensical demands. As the needs of those officials increase, the poverty of the four seas is compounded. . . .

The excessive rise in the price of rice today does not deter the commissioner (*bugyō*) in Osaka and his officials from engaging in their arbitrary handling of policies, forgetting that everything under the sun is one in the way of human heartedness (*jin*). They transport rice to Edo, but fail to make any provision for delivery of rice to Kyoto where the Emperor resides. Instead they even arrest those people from Kyoto who come to buy rice in the amount of five to ten quarts (*shō*). . . .

The rich in Osaka have over the years made profitable loans to the *daimyō* and seized a large sum of gold, silver and stipend rice in interest. They now enjoy unprecedented riches, and even though they are *chōnin* they are treated and appointed to positions comparable to elders (*karō*) in the households of the *daimyō*. They own numerous fields and gardens and newly cultivated fields and live in plenteous comfort. They observe the natural calamities and punishments of heaven occurring now, but are not afraid. They see the poor and beggars starve to death, but do not lift their fingers to help them. . . . Meanwhile they continue to indulge in their pastime, and act as if nothing has ever happened.

---

[10]Fujimoto Kunihiko, ed., *Nihonshi: Shiryō Enshū (A Japanese History: Documentary Exercises)* (Tokyo: Tokyo University Press, 1956), pp. 289–291.

This is not different from King Zhou's[11] long night's feast. The commissioner and his officials have the power to control the actions of the above mentioned people and help the lowly. But they do not do this, and day after day deal in commodities. They are bandits stealing the beneficence of heaven, whose actions cannot be condoned by the Way of Heaven or by the will of the sage.

We who are confined to our homes find it is no longer possible to tolerate these conditions. We lack the power of King Tang and King Wu.[12] We do not have the virtue of Confucius or Mencius. For the sake of all under heaven, knowing that we have no one to depend on and that we may impute the punishments to our families, those of us who are of like mind are resolved to do the following: First we shall execute those officials who torment and harass those who are lowly. Next we shall execute those rich merchants in the city of Osaka who are accustomed to the life of luxury. Then we shall uncover gold and silver coins and other valuables they hoard as well as bags of rice kept hidden in their storage houses. They will be distributed to those who do not own fields or gardens in the domains of Settsu, Kawachi, Izumi and Harima, and to those who may own lands, but have a hard time supporting fathers, mothers, wives and other members of the family. The above money and rice will be distributed. Thereafter as soon as you hear that there is a disturbance in the city of Osaka, mind not the distance you must travel, come immediately to Osaka.

What we do is to follow the command of heaven to render the punishments of heaven.

Eighth year of Tempō [1837]   month,   day.

To the village officials (*shōya*), elders (*toshiyori*), farmers (*hyakushō*), peasants and tenant farmers (*komae hyakushō*) in the domains of Settsu, Kawachi, Izumi, and Harima.

DEBATES OVER THE OPENING OF JAPAN

When Commodore Matthew Perry anchored off the shores of Uraga in 1853, his action was to precipitate one of the greatest debates to occur in Tokugawa Japan. In an unprecedented move, the bakufu *solicited the opinions of the* daimyō, *and they were divided. At issue were the questions of* jōi *(expelling the barbarians) or* kaikoku *(opening the country), and of acquiescence to the foreign demands or preservation of the two-century-old tradition of seclusion. In the background were such issues as the declining power of the* bakufu, *and the pending succession disputes.*

---

[11]The last king of the Shang dynasty, known for his cruelty and unrighteous acts.
[12]Respectively, the founder of the Shang dynasty and of the Zhou dynasty.

In the following selections, Tokugawa Nariaki (1800–1860), former Lord of Mito, represents the policy of jōi *(Document 8) and Ii Naosuke (1815–1860), Lord of Hikone who was to become the* tairō *in 1858, represents the policy of* kaikoku *(Document 9). While they started from different premises and arrived at differing conclusions, there were also some common denominators, such as the desire to preserve Japan's national power, and the realization that importation of Western guns and books was inevitable and necessary.*

8 Tokugawa Nariaki to Bakufu, 14 August 1853[13]

Observations on coastal defense:

It is my belief that the first and most urgent of our tasks is for the *bakufu* to make its choice between peace and war, and having determined its policy to pursue it unwaveringly thereafter. When we consider the respective advantages and disadvantages of war and peace, we find that if we put our trust in war, the whole country's morale will be increased and even if we sustain an initial defeat we will in the end expel the foreigner; while if we put our trust in peace, even though things may seem tranquil for a time, the morale of the country will be greatly lowered and we will come in the end to complete collapse. This has been amply demonstrated in the history of China and is a fact that men of intelligence, both past and present, have always known. . . . However, I propose to give here in outline the ten reasons why in my view we must never choose the policy of peace.

1. Although our country's territory is not extensive, foreigners both fear and respect us. That, after all, is because our resoluteness and military prowess have been clearly demonstrated to the world outside by such events as the conquest of Korea by the Empress Jingō in early ancient times; by the repulse of the Mongols in the Kōan period (1278–1288) during the middle ages; and in the recent past by the invasion of Korea in the Bunroku period (1592–1596) and the suppression of Christianity in the Keichō (1596–1615) and Kanei (1624–1644) periods. Despite this, the Americans who arrived recently, though fully aware of *bakufu*'s prohibition, entered Uraga displaying a white flag as a symbol of peace and insisted on presenting their written requests. Moreover they entered Edo Bay, fired heavy guns in salute and even went so far as to conduct surveys without permission. They were arrogant and discourteous, their actions an outrage. Indeed, this was the greatest disgrace we have suffered since the dawn of our history. The saying is that if the enemy dictates terms in one's own capital one's country is disgraced. The foreigners, having thus ignored our prohibition and penetrated our waters even to the vicinity of the capital, threatening us and making demands upon us, should it happen not only that the *bakufu* fails to expel

[13]From *Select Documents on Japanese Foreign Policy 1853–1868*, translated and edited by W. G. Beasley and published by Oxford University Press, pp. 102–107. Reprinted by permission of Oxford University Press.

them but also that it concludes an agreement in accordance with their requests, then I fear it would be impossible to maintain our national polity (*kokutai*). That is the first reason why we must never choose the policy of peace.

2. The prohibition of Christianity is the first rule of the Tokugawa house. Public notices concerning it are posted everywhere, even to the remotest corner of every province. It is said that even so, during the Bunsei period (1818–1830), men have been executed for propagating this religion secretly in Osaka. The *bakufu* can never ignore or overlook the evils of Christianity. Yet if the Americans are allowed to come again this religion will inevitably raise its head once more, however strict the prohibition; and this, I fear, is something we could never justify to the spirits of our ancestors. That is the second reason why we must never choose the policy of peace.

3. To exchange our valuable articles like gold, silver, copper, and iron for useless foreign goods like woolens and satin is to incur great loss while acquiring not the smallest benefit. The best course of all would be for the *bakufu* to put a stop to the trade with Holland. By contrast to open such valueless trade with others besides the Dutch would, I believe, inflict the greatest possible harm on our country. That is the third reason why we must never choose the policy of peace.

4. For some years Russia, England, and others have sought trade with us, but the *bakufu* has not permitted it. Should permission be granted to the Americans, on what ground would it be possible to refuse if Russia and the others [again] request it? That is the fourth reason why we must never choose the policy of peace.

5. It is widely stated that [apart from trade] the foreigners have no other evil designs and that if only the *bakufu* will permit trade there will be no further difficulty. However, it is their practice first to seek a foothold by means of trade and then to go on to propagate Christianity and make other unreasonable demands. Thus we would be repeating the blunders of others, seen remotely in the Christianity incidents of the Kanei period (1624–1644) and before [in Japan] and more recently in the Opium War in China. That is the fifth reason why we must never choose the policy of peace.

6. Though the *Rangakusha* (scholars of Dutch studies) group may argue secretly that world conditions are much changed from what they were, Japan alone clinging to ideas of seclusion in isolation amidst the seas, that this is a constant source of danger to us and that our best course would therefore be to communicate with foreign countries and open an extensive trade; yet, to my mind, if the people of Japan stand firmly united, if we complete our military preparations and return to the state of society that existed before the middle ages [when the emperor ruled the country directly], then we will even be able to go out against foreign countries and spread abroad our fame and prestige. But if we open trade at the demand of the foreigners, for no better reason than that, our habits today being those of peace and indolence, men have shown fear merely at the coming

of a handful of foreign warships, then it would truly be a vain illusion to think of evolving any long-range plan for going out against foreign countries. That is the sixth reason why we must never choose the policy of peace.

7. The *bakufu* entrusted the defense of the Uraga district to the Hikone and Wakamatsu *han*, and I hear that the Aizu retainers [from Wakamatsu] have already gone there, travelling night and day for some 170 miles or more despite the heat. I also hear that in addition to this the *daimyō* ordered to defend Edo Bay are sending troops at once. All this is admirable. But if we ignore the fact that the foreigners went so far as to enter Edo Bay and carry out surveys without permission, if we do not take action to expel them, this will be to allow the men of all provinces to exhaust themselves in activity that is but vain and wasted effort, and in the end our people will be brought to a state of complete collapse. That is the seventh reason why we must never choose the policy of peace.

8. When Kuroda (lord of Fukuoka) and Nabeshima (lord of Saga) were made responsible for the coast defense of Nagasaki it was not intended that this be directed solely against the Dutch and Chinese. It was a measure directed against all foreigners. But by agreeing to receive written requests from the foreigners at Uraga—and still more were the *bakufu* to conclude an agreement there in accordance with those requests—would we not, as it were, be allowing the foreigners to enter by the back door, thus rendering futile the guard-duties entrusted to those two families and arousing their resentment? That is the eighth reason why we must never choose the policy of peace.

9. I hear that all, even though they be commoners, who have witnessed the recent actions of the foreigners, think them abominable; and if the *bakufu* does not expel these insolent foreigners root and branch there may be some who will complain in secret, asking to what purpose have been all the preparations of gun-emplacements. It is inevitable that men should think in this way when they have seen how arrogantly the foreigners acted at Uraga. That, I believe, is because even the humblest are conscious of the debt they owe their country, and it is indeed a promising sign. Since even ignorant commoners are talking in this way, I fear that if the *bakufu* does not decide to carry out expulsion, if its handling of the matter shows nothing but excess of leniency and appeasement of the foreigners, then the lower orders may fail to understand its ideas and hence opposition might arise from evil men who have lost their respect for *bakufu* authority. It might even be that *bakufu* control of the great lords would itself be endangered. That is the ninth reason why we must never choose the policy of peace.

10. There are those who say that since the expulsion of foreigners is the ancient law of the *shōgun*'s ancestors, reissued and reaffirmed in the Bunsei period (1825), the *bakufu* has in fact always been firmly resolved to fight, but that even so one must recognize that peace has now lasted so long our armaments are inadequate, and one cannot therefore tell what harm might be done if we too recklessly arouse the anger of the foreigners. In that event, they say, the *bakufu* would be forced to conclude a peace settlement and so its prestige would

suffer still further damage. Hence [it is argued], the *bakufu* should show itself compliant at this time and should placate the foreigners, meanwhile exerting all its efforts in military preparations, so that when these preparations have been completed it can more strictly enforce the ancient laws. This argument sounds reasonable enough. However, to my mind the people here [in Edo] are temporizing and half-hearted; and even though the *shōgun* exhorts them day and night he cannot make them resolute. Now there is not the slightest chance that the feudal lords will complete military preparations, however many years may pass, unless they are set an example in military matters by the *bakufu*. There have already been clashes in Ezo (Hokkaidō) during the Kansei (1789–1801) and Bunka (1804–1818) periods [against the Russians], but despite the *bakufu*'s efforts to effect military preparations they have not yet been completed. Again, relaxation of the expulsion laws was ordered in 1842, with the apparent object of first placating the foreigners and then using the respite to complete military preparations, but here, too, I do not think the various lords have made any particular progress in rearming in the twelve years that have since elapsed. On the arrival of the foreign ships recently, all fell into a panic. Some take matters very seriously while foreign ships are actually at anchor here, but once the ships leave and orders are given for them to revert to normal, they all relax once more into idleness and immediately disperse the military equipment which they had hurriedly assembled. It is just as if, regardless of the fire burning beneath the floor of one's house, one neglected all fire-fighting precautions. Indeed, it shows a shameful spirit. I therefore believe that if there be any sign of the *bakufu* pursuing the policy of peace, morale will never rise though preparations be pressed forward daily; and the gun-batteries and other preparations made will accordingly be so much ornament, never put to effective use. But if the *bakufu*, now and henceforward, shows itself resolute for expulsion, the immediate effect will be to increase ten-fold the morale of the country and to bring about the completion of military preparations without even the necessity for issuing orders. Hesitant as I am to say so, only by so doing will the *shōgun* be able to fulfill his 'barbarian-expelling' duty and unite the men of every province in carrying out their proper military functions. That is the tenth reason why we must never choose the policy of peace, and it is by far the most urgent and important of them all.

I have tried to explain above in general terms the relative advantages and disadvantages of the war and peace policies. However, this [policy I recommend] is something that is easy to understand but difficult to carry out. In these feeble days men tend to cling to peace; they are not fond of defending their country by war. They slander those of us who are determined to fight, calling us lovers of war, men who enjoy conflict. If matters become desperate they might, in their enormous folly, try to overthrow those of us who are determined to fight, offering excuses to the enemy and concluding a peace agreement with him. They would thus in the end bring total destruction upon us. In view of our country's tradition of military courage, however, it is probable that once the *bakufu* has taken a firm decision we shall find no such cowards among us. But good advice is as hard to accept as good medicine is unpleasing to the palate. A temporizing and time-serving policy is the one easiest for men to adopt. It is therefore my belief that in this question of coastal defense it is of the first importance that the *bakufu* pay due heed [to these matters] and that having once reached a decision it should never waver from it thereafter. . . .[14]

9   **Ii Naosuke to Bakufu, 1 October 1853**[15]   Before the year 1635 there were nine government-licensed trading vessels belonging to Nagasaki, Sakai, Kyoto, etc., but with the prohibition of Christianity in the time of the *Shōgun* Iemitsu the *bakufu* put an end to the voyages of these nine ships and laid down laws closing the country. Commerce was entirely limited to the Dutch and Chinese, no others being allowed to participate in it. Careful consideration of conditions as they are today, however, leads me to believe that despite the constant differences and debates into which men of patriotism and foresight have been led in recent years by their perception of the danger of foreign aggression, it is impossible in the crisis we now face to ensure the safety and tranquillity of our country merely by an insistence on the seclusion laws as we did in former times. Moreover, time is essential if we are to complete our coast defenses. Since 1609, when warships of over 500 *koku* were forbidden, we have had no warships capable of opposing foreign attack on our coasts with heavy guns. Thus I am much afraid that were the foreigners now to seize as bases such outlying islands as Hachijō-jima and Ōshima, it would be impossible for us to remain inactive, though without warships we should have no effective means of driving them off. There is a saying that when one is besieged in a castle, to raise the drawbridge is to imprison oneself and make it impossible to hold out indefinitely; and again, that when opposing forces face each other across a river, victory is obtained by those who cross the river and attack. It seems clear throughout history that he who takes action is in a position to advance, while he who remains inactive must retreat. Even though the *shōgun*'s ancestors set up seclusion laws, they left the Dutch and the Chinese to act as a bridge [to the outside world]. Might not this bridge now be of advantage to us in handling foreign affairs, providing us with the means whereby we may for a time avert the outbreak of hostilities and then, after some time has elapsed, gain a complete victory?

I understand that the coal for which the Americans have expressed a desire is

---

[14]In the remaining pages of this memorandum, in which he deals with the specific military steps to be taken, Nariaki recommends encouragement of training with sword and spear (for, armed with them, no soldier will fear warship or cannon); the purchase of ships and cannon with the proceeds of the Dutch trade, using the Dutch as agents; the granting of permission to *daimyō* to build modern ships and guns; and the construction of the defense works along the coast. (Beasley's footnote.)

[15]Beasley, *op. cit.*, pp. 117–119.

to be found in quantity in Kyushu. We should first tell them, as a matter of expediency, that we also have need of coal, but that should their need of it arise urgently and unexpectedly during a voyage, they may ask for coal at Nagasaki and if we have any to spare we will provide it. Nor will we grudge them wood and water. As for foodstuffs, the supply varies from province to province, but we can agree to provide food for the shipwrecked and unfortunate. Again, we can tell them, of recent years we have treated kindly those wrecked on our coasts and have sent them all home. There is no need for further discussion of this subject, and all requests concerning it should be made through the Dutch. Then, too, there is the question of trade. Although there is a national prohibition of it, conditions are not the same as they were. The exchange of goods is a universal practice. This we should explain to the spirits of our ancestors. And we should then tell the foreigners that we mean in the future to send trading vessels to the Dutch company's factory at Batavia to engage in trade; that we will allocate some of our trading goods to America, some to Russia, and so on, using the Dutch to trade for us as our agents; but that there will be a delay of one or two years because we must [first] construct new ships for these voyages. By replying in this way we will take the Americans by surprise in offering to treat them generally in the same way as the Dutch.

We must revive the licensed trading vessels that existed before the Kanei period (1624–1644), ordering the rich merchants of such places as Osaka, Hyōgo, and Sakai to take shares in the enterprise. We must construct new steamships, especially powerful warships, and these we will load with goods not needed in Japan. For a time we will have to employ Dutchmen as masters and mariners, but we will put on board with them Japanese of ability and integrity who must study the use of large guns, the handling of ships, and the rules of navigation. Openly these will be called merchant vessels, but they will in fact have the secret purpose of training a navy. As we increase the number of ships and our mastery of technique, Japanese will be able to sail the oceans freely and gain direct knowledge of conditions abroad without relying on the secret reports of the Dutch. Thus we will eventually complete the organization of a navy. Moreover, we must shake off the panic and apprehensions that have beset us and abandon our habits of luxury and wasteful spending. Our defenses thus strengthened, and all being arranged at home, we can act so as to make our courage and prestige resound beyond the seas. By so doing, we will not in the future be imprisoning ourselves; indeed, we will be able, I believe, so to accomplish matters at home and abroad as to achieve national security. Forestalling the foreigners in this way, I believe, is the best method of ensuring that the *bakufu* will at some future time find opportunity to reimpose its ban and forbid foreigners to come to Japan, as was done in the Kanei period. Moreover, it would make possible the strictest prohibition of Christianity. And since I understand that the Americans and Russians themselves have only recently become skilled in navigation, I do not see how the people of our country, who are clever and quick-witted, should prove inferior to Westerners if we begin training at once.

The national situation being what it is, if the *bakufu* protects our coasts peacefully without bringing upon us permanent foreign difficulties, then even if that entails complete or partial change in the laws of our ancestors I do not believe such action could really be regarded as contrary to the wishes of those ancestors. However, I think it is essential to win the support of the country for *bakufu* policy on this occasion, so the *bakufu* should first notify the [Imperial] Court and then arrange to send Imperial messengers to the Ise, Iwashimizu, and Kashima shrines and a Tokugawa messenger to the Nikkō shrine, announcing there its resolve to secure tranquillity at home and security for the country. Trust in the will of the gods, after all, is the ancient custom of our land; and I believe, moreover, that by so doing the *bakufu* may be able to unite national opinion.

It is now no easy matter, by means of orders concerning the defense of Edo and the nearby coast, to ensure that all will be fully prepared for any sudden emergency, so not a moment must be wasted. However many firm walls we construct, they will certainly not be as effective as unity of mind if the unforeseen happens. The urgent task of the moment, therefore, is for the *bakufu* to resolve on relieving the nation's anxieties and issue the appropriate orders.

I am conscious of my temerity in putting forward views that conflict with the existing [seclusion] laws, but I have so reported in accordance with your orders that I was to do so fully and without reserve.

THE HARRIS TREATY OF 1858

To complete the work begun by Commodore Perry, Townsend Harris was sent to Japan as the first Consul General of the United States. At first an unwelcome guest in the small fishing village of Shimoda, he slowly gained the confidence of Japanese officials. With consummate diplomatic skill, he signed a convention in June 1857 that was followed by an unprecedented audience with the shōgun *in the Edo Castle on December 7 of the same year. A prolonged negotiation in Edo later resulted in a Treaty of Amity and Commerce, which was concluded on July 29, 1858 (Document 10). It promised, among other things, "friendly aid" to Japan by American ships and consular representatives (Art. II) and providing technical experts to work for Japan (Art. X).*

However, in many other respects, the treaty was an unequal one. It included a provision for trials by consular courts (Art. VI), and another depriving Japan of her tariff autonomy (Art. IV, and Regulation 7). Harris' insistence on the right to reside, lease property and construct buildings for Americans in Edo, Osaka and in the ports to be opened (Art. III) created grave domestic problems for the Tokugawa government. Furnishing Japanese coins to foreign traders for coins of equal weights (Art. V) caused a serious gold drain for Japan, whose dual currency system of gold and silver assigned a relatively lower value of gold in relation to the world price.

In the text of the treaty, Harris wisely stipulated that the ratification "shall be exchanged at the City of Washington," thus creating an opportunity for Japan to send her envoys overseas for the first time since the closing of the country in the early seventeenth century.

That first Embassy left Japan for Washington in February 1860 aboard the U.S. frigate Powhatan. *To accompany the Embassy, the Tokugawa government also sent its own warship* Kanrin maru, *purchased from the Netherlands a few years earlier. The ship was manned by a Japanese crew (very discreetly the captain of the* Powhatan *placed some American officers and seamen aboard), and was captained by one Katsu Rintarō, who later became Minister of Navy. Thus the* Kanrin maru *became the first Japanese ship manned by a Japanese crew to cross the Pacific.*

Document 11 is an eye-witness account of America by Lord Muragaki Norimasa (1813–1880), the Deputy Ambassador. He was not easily dazzled by the might of the United States, and was pleased to rediscover that he was "born in that divine country of ours." To this view, Tamamushi Sadaifu's diary serves as a necessary antidote. Tamamushi (1823–1869) was an intellectual, and a perceptive observer of the West. His diary records in minute detail his observation of the technology, economic conditions, weather, customs, flora and fauna of America. Unlike Ambassador Muragaki, the virtue of the egalitarian concept in the American life did not escape his scrutinizing eyes (Document 12).

10 The Treaty of Amity and Commerce Between the United States and Japan, 1858[16]

ARTICLE I. There shall henceforth be perpetual peace and friendship between the United States of America and His Majesty the Ty-Coon [i.e., *shōgun*] of Japan and his successors.

ARTICLE II. The President of the United States, at the request of the Japanese Government, will act as a friendly mediator in such matters of difference as may arise between the Government of Japan and any European Power.

The ships-of-war of the United States shall render friendly aid and assistance to such Japanese vessels as they may meet on the high seas, so far as can be done without a breach of neutrality; and all American Consuls residing at ports visited by Japanese vessels shall also give them such friendly aid as may be permitted by the laws of the respective countries in which they reside.

ARTICLE III. In addition to the ports of Simoda [Shimoda] and Hakodade [Hokodate], the following ports and towns shall be opened on the dates respectively appended to them, that is to say: Kanagawa, on the 4th of July, 1859,

---

[16]Hunter Miller, ed., *Treaties and Other International Acts of the United States of America*, Vol. 7 (Washington: U.S. Government Printing Office, 1934), pp. 947–973. Original in English, Japanese, and Dutch.

Nagasaki, on the 4th of July, 1859; Nee-e-gata [Niigata], on the 1st of January, 1860; Hiogo [Hyogo], on the 1st of January, 1863.

. . . Six months after the opening of Kanagawa, the port of Simoda [Shimoda] shall be closed as a place of residence and trade for American citizens. In all the foregoing ports and towns American citizens may permanently reside; they shall have the right to lease ground, and purchase the buildings thereon, and may erect dwellings and warehouses. . . .

No wall, fence, or gate shall be erected by the Japanese around the place of residence of the Americans, or anything done which may prevent a free egress and ingress to the same.

From the 1st of January, 1862, Americans shall be allowed to reside in the City of Yedo; and from the 1st of January, 1863, in the City of Osaca [Osaka], for the purposes of trade only. In each of these two cities a suitable place within which they may hire houses, and the distance they may go, shall be arranged by the American Diplomatic Agent and the Government of Japan. . . .

The Japanese Government will cause this clause to be made public in every part of the Empire as soon as the ratifications of this Treaty shall be exchanged.

Munitions of war shall only be sold to the Japanese Government and for-eigners. . . .

ARTICLE IV. Duties shall be paid to the Government of Japan on all goods landed in the country, and on all articles of Japanese production that are exported as cargo, according to the tariff hereunto appended. . . .

The importation of opium is prohibited; and, any American vessel coming to Japan for the purposes of trade having more than three catties (four pounds avoirdupois) weight of opium on board, such surplus quantity shall be seized and destroyed by the Japanese authorities. All goods imported into Japan, and which have paid the duty fixed by this Treaty, may be transported by the Japanese into any part of the empire without the payment of any tax, excise, or transit duty whatever.

No higher duties shall be paid by Americans on goods imported into Japan than are fixed by this Treaty, nor shall any higher duties be paid by Americans than are levied on the same description of goods if imported in Japanese vessels, or the vessels of any other nation.

ARTICLE V. All foreign coin shall be current in Japan and pass for its corre-sponding weight of Japanese coin of the same description. Americans and Japan-ese may freely use foreign coin in making payments to each other.

As some time will elapse before the Japanese will be acquainted with the value of foreign coins, the Japanese Government will, for the period of one year after the opening of each harbor, furnish the Americans with Japanese coin in exchange for theirs, equal weights being given and no discount taken for re-coin-age. Coins of all description (with the exception of Japanese copper coin) may be exported from Japan, and foreign gold and silver uncoined.

ARTICLE VI. Americans committing offenses against Japanese shall be tried in American Consular courts, and, when guilty, shall be punished according to

American law. Japanese committing offenses against Americans shall be tried by the Japanese authorities and punished according to Japanese law. The Consular courts shall be open to Japanese creditors, to enable them to recover their just claims against American citizens; and the Japanese courts shall in like manner be open to American citizens for the recovery of their just claims against Japanese. . . .

ARTICLE VIII. Americans in Japan shall be allowed the free exercise of their religion, and for this purpose shall have the right to erect suitable places of worship. No injury shall be done to such buildings, nor any insult be offered to the religious worship of the Americans. American citizens shall not injure any Japanese temple or *mia* (shrine), or offer any insult or injury to Japanese religious ceremonies, or to the objects of their worship.

The Americans and Japanese shall not do anything that may be calculated to excite religious animosity. The Government of Japan has already abolished the practice of trampling on religious emblems.

ARTICLE X. The Japanese Government may purchase or construct in the United States ships-of-war, steamers, merchant ships, whale ships, cannon, munitions of war, and arms of all kinds, and any other things it may require. It shall have the right to engage in the United States scientific, naval and military men, artisans of all kind, and mariners to enter into its service. All purchases made for the Government of Japan may be exported from the United States, and all persons engaged for its service may freely depart from the United States: provided that no articles that are contraband of war shall be exported, nor any persons engaged to act in a naval or military capacity, while Japan shall be at war with any Power in amity with the United States.

ARTICLE XIII. After the 4th of July, 1872, upon the desire of either the American or Japanese Governments, and on one year's notice given by either party, this Treaty, and such portions of the Treaty of Kanagawa as remain unrevoked by this Treaty, together with the regulations of trade hereunto annexed, or those that may be hereafter introduced, shall be subject to revision by Commissioners appointed on both sides for this purpose, who will be empowered to decide and insert therein, such amendments as experience shall prove to be desirable.

ARTICLE XIV. This Treaty shall go into effect on the 4th of July, 1859, on or before which day the ratifications of the same shall be exchanged at the City of Washington; but if, for any unforeseen cause, the ratifications cannot be exchanged by that time, the Treaty shall still go into effect at the date above mentioned. . . .

This Treaty is executed in quadruplicate, each copy being written in English, Japanese, and Dutch languages, all the versions having the same meaning and intention, but the Dutch version shall be considered as being the original. . . .

Regulations under Which American Trade
Is to Be Conducted in Japan

REGULATION 7. Duties shall be paid to the Japanese Government on all goods landed in the country according to the following tariff:

Class 1. All articles in this class shall be free of duty. Gold and silver, coined or uncoined; Wearing apparel in actual use; Household furniture and printed books not intended for sale, but the property of persons who come to reside in Japan.

Class 2. A duty of 5 percent shall be paid on the following articles:

All articles used for the purpose of building, rigging, repairing, or fitting out of ships; Whaling gear of all kinds; Timber for building houses; Rice; Paddy; Steam machinery; Salted provisions of all kinds; Bread and breadstuffs; Living animals of all kinds; Coal, Zinc; Lead, Tin; Raw Silk.

Class 3. A duty of 35 percent shall be paid on all intoxicating liquors, whether prepared by distillation, fermentation, or in any other manner.

Class 4. All goods not included in any of the preceding classes shall pay a duty of 20 percent.

11   Excerpts from the Overseas Diary of Lord Muragaki, 1860[17]

May 17, 1860. Our audience with the President was scheduled for twelve o'clock. Each of us prepared himself befitting the occasion. The principal ambassador wore his *kariginu* (formal court robe) and his samurai sword, and I did likewise. The third ambassador attired similarly, and each of us also wore our ceremonial cap (*eboshi*). . . . We rode in four open carriages, and the principal ambassador, myself, and the third ambassador (who concurrently served as the censor) were each accompanied by a suite of three footmen, one spear-bearer, and three samurai.

. . . The main avenue was congested by the coaches of curious onlookers. There were also a countless number of pedestrians, both men and women. I thought that my formal attire was strange to the eyes of the beholders, . . . but felt that I was showing the glory of our imperial country by coming to this barbarian country. So I forgot for a moment who I was and enjoyed the public display. . . .

We arrived at the President's house. . . . Lewis Cass (the Secretary of State) greeted us and then withdrew. . . . We were then shown to the audience chamber. . . . As we approached the chamber (East Room), the double doors to its entrance swung open. In the center of the room, there stood the President, whose name was Buchanan (1791–1868). He was flanked by many civil and military officers. Behind them were ladies, and old and young alike were all attired in beautiful dresses. Masaoki (the principal ambassador), I (the deputy ambassador) and Tadamasa (the third ambassador and censor) entered the room. We made an obeisance and advanced to the center of the room. We made another obeisance

---

[17]Muragaki Norimasa, *Kōkai Nikki (Overseas Diary)* as contained in *Gendai Nihon Kiroku Zenshū (A Series on Modern Japanese Records)*, Vol. 1 (Tokyo: Chikuma Shobō, 1969), pp. 117–119, 126–127. The author was then the deputy ambassador and was age forty-seven. He was Commissioner of Foreign Affairs (*gaikoku bugyō*) from 1858 to 1863.

and approached where the President stood. Masaoki then delivered an address conveying to him the wishes of the *Shōgun*, in a distinct and strong voice. It was translated by Namura Goyarō. . . .

After the audience was over, the President held our hands and expressed his pleasure in having us sent as Ambassadors to ratify the treaty of amity between the two countries for the first time since Japan's seclusion. He also conveyed to us the boundless joy felt by the entire nation . . . and gave us an oral statement written in English. Five or six high ranking officials also greeted us by shaking our hands. However, it could become endless, so I bowed and took leave of them. . . .

The President is an old man over seventy years old. He has silvery hair and is gentle and dignified. However, today he was attired in drawers and a jacket [sic] made of black woolen which is no different from what the merchants wear. He had neither decorations nor the two swords. . . .

The United States is the largest or the second largest country in the world. However, the President is essentially a governor general who must be elected by the people every four years. (I understand that such an election is to be held October 1 this year. There is no way of knowing who is to become the next President before such an election is held. It must be the karmic conditions of our past lives which led us into meeting this President. In any event, I seriously doubt if this American system [of election] is going to last for a long time.) The President was not a sovereign of a nation. However, we came to this country to deliver a state paper from our sovereign, so we treated him with the courtesy due that of a king. It was probably a useless gesture on our part to have worn our *kariginu*, when we discovered that the Americans attach little significance to class distinction and that all manners of decorum cease to exist in this country. However, the President was exceedingly pleased with this mission, and took pride in showing this occasion to other nations. I also understand that the pictures of us in our *kariginu* appeared in many newspapers. This is the first time that I have been an ambassador to a foreign land. There is no greater joy than to know that I have accomplished our mission well. It was an achievement worthy of a man:

> Arise all ye aliens,
> Look up with awe
> The light that shineth from the East,
> The Land of the Rising Sun.

May 23. Clear sky. Our schedule called for a visit to Congress in the morning. Our usual guide came and took us by carriage for seven or eight blocks eastward to the Capitol building. It was about two city blocks in length and one block in width and three stories high. Everything was made of white marble. Over the roof was to be erected a dome which was only half completed and still under construction. . . . We were led into a chamber where people deliberated. . . . On the raised platform in the center sat the Vice President. Slightly below him also on the platform were two clerks. There were desks and chairs forming semi-circles on the floor. Many books were placed on the desks. There were forty or fifty people sitting on their chairs. One person stood up and shouted very loudly. His wild gesticulation was more like that of a crazy man. After he finished saying something, another one stood up and behaved exactly in the same manner. I was told that the affairs of state were to be deliberated by the people, and everyone would have to say what he thought without any reservation. After hearing the debates, the Vice President would render his decision.

We were asked to ascend to the second floor (to the visitors' gallery) to get a better view of the chambers. We sat on the bench to observe the proceedings. Obviously they were discussing some matters of state. But as we saw that they were clad in their regular drawers and jackets with tight sleeves, we could not help but compare them to our fish market in Nihonbashi. We talked to each other privately of the similarities as we observed how they shouted loudly to each other, and how the Vice President sat on the raised platform. . . . I understand that all matters of state were handled within the confines of this building. There were many officials. The President as a custom does not come to Congress. He hears from the Vice President after the matters have been decided. . . .

12 Recollection of Tamamushi Sadaifu, 1860[18]

May 6, 1860. We are scheduled to leave San Francisco for Washington tomorrow, and there was a roll call [of American sailors] on board our ship. . . . The roll call [which included a medical examination] was strictly enforced.

However, with regard to decorum, there was hardly any observance. A sailor might remove his cap, but did not bow to his captain. As I reflected on this matter more closely, I discovered that not only at a time like the formal roll call, but also on any other day, there is really no distinction between the captain and his first mate. The high and low alike work together closely, and even plain sailors do not pay undue deference to the captain. As to the captain, he is not arrogant, and treats his men like his colleagues. They are personally close to each other. In an emergency they do their best to help one another, and if there is a moment of sorrow, it is shared by everyone with tears.

In our country, the observance of decorum is very strict. Even a close retainer cannot readily have an audience with a commissioner (*bugyō*). The latter's ostentatious display of power and position is everywhere. And those who are below him, who hold inconsequential ranks, imitate him by looking down on those who

---

[18]Tamamushi Sadaifu, *Kōbei Nichiroku (Diary of a Voyage to America)* in *Gendai Nihon Kiroku Zenshū, op. cit.*, pp. 226–227. His work contains careful drawings of trains, wheels, bathroom fixtures, etc.

are lower in rank than themselves, treating the latter with utter contempt. The regulations governing our social intercourse are very strict, but our personal relations get worse day after day. In a moment of sorrow, those who are above may make a superficial show of condolence. That is the way those who are above and below are treating each other. In an emergency, can anyone expect anyone else to come to his rescue? Is this another of our social ills created by a long period of peace? How dreadful it is! Can we somehow combine the best of the two systems—e.g., by strictly enforcing our decorum so that we may not be scorned by those who adhere to barbaric customs, but at the same time finding a way to have friendship like the foreigners have?

THE SUCCESSION DISPUTES

In the year when Commodore Perry arrived in Japan, Iesada became the thir-teenth shōgun. *He was sickly, and at the age of twenty-nine was given very little chance of living much longer. He had no heir, and the issue of succession became one of the most difficult problems. Under normal circumstances, Tokugawa Yoshitomi (later Iemochi), the Lord of Kii, would have been chosen because of his closer blood relationship to Iesada. However, he was only eight years of age, and many* daimyō, *including Shimazu of Satsuma and Matsudaira of Echizen supported the candidacy of Hitotsubashi Yoshinobu (also known as Tokugawa Keiki, 1837–1913, a son of Nariaki, Lord of Mito) who was then age seventeen and was known for his great ability.*

The candidacy of Yoshinobu looked bright until 1857 when one of the chief supporters, rōju *Abe Masahiro, died. Then in the early summer of 1858, Ii Naosuke was appointed* tairō, *and the balance radically shifted in favor of the candidacy of the Lord of Kii. The Hitotsubashi group tried unsuccessfully to have the Imperial Court intervene in its favor. The disputes also involved the questions of reform of the Tokugawa government, the position of the* fudai daimyō, *and the preference of* ōoku, *or the Ladies' Quarters in the Edo castle.*

The following account is given by Nakane Yukie (1807–1877), a scribe in the service of Matsudaira Yoshinaga, Lord of Echizen (1828–1890).

13 The Succession Dispute, Yoshinobu vs. Iemochi, 1858[19] [Fifth year of Ansei (1858), fourth month, 27th day, the author Nakane Yukie was ordered to interview Date Munenari (1817–1892), Lord of Uwajima-*han*, after the latter

[19]Nakane Yukie, *Sakumu Kiji (Records of the Dreams of the Past)* in *Nihon Shiseki Kyōkai Sōsho (Japanese Historical Document Society Series)*, Vols. 119 and 120 (Tokyo: Tokyo University Press, reissue, 1968); Vol. 3 (Ser. Vol. 119), pp. 394–396; Vol. 4 (Ser. Vol. 120), pp. 10–11.

met Ii Naosuke, the *tairō*. Nakane then recorded the conversation that took place between Ii and Lord of Uwajima as reported to him by the latter.]

In discussing the matter of a treaty with America, I (Date Munenari) mentioned that "lately so many things are happening that it is no longer possible to follow tradition by blindly obeying whatever the *tairō* has commanded of us (*daimyō*). . . ."

Tairō Ii replied: "With the great crisis facing our nation, it is imperative to make the foundation of the government secure, and for that reason, the selection of a right heir to the position of *shōgun* is of utmost urgency. On this matter, the opinion of the Imperial Court, the opinions of the *daimyō* as well as the feelings of the populace must be taken into account. I believe there is no one who can enjoy a higher reputation than Lord Hitotsubashi Yoshinobu as a candidate. However, Iemochi, Lord of Kii, is closer in blood relations to the present *shōgun*, and the wishes of the founding father of the *bakufu* (Ieyasu) must be carefully weighed. Therefore there can be no other candidate except the Lord of Kii. I have heard Lord Hitotsubashi Yoshinobu is a capable person, but not all information is on the positive side. Furthermore, his real father, the Lord of Mito is a dangerous person, and if Yoshinobu is selected, there is no telling what kind of subversive plans the Lord of Mito may entertain. Therefore it has to be the Lord of Kii who must become the heir."

I (Date Munenari) then responded: "If the country is peaceful, it is perfectly legitimate to place in the position a youngster because of his closer blood relationship. However, at a time of crisis public confidence can be gained only by the appointment of a mature person. The reputation of Lord Yoshinobu in Kyoto is excellent. If you appoint an immature person over Lord Yoshinobu, our relations with Kyoto will become worsened. . . ."

[On the second day of the fifth month, Nakane's master Matsudaira Yoshinaga met Ii Naosuke for the first time. Again the following is Nakane's record.]

[Yoshinaga said to Lord Ii:] ". . . One could assert that if the founder of the *bakufu* were alive today, he would be disposed to make an immature person the heir, because of the latter's closer blood relationship. But such an argument takes into account only the private affairs of the Tokugawa family. We are arguing that for the sake of all people under heaven, an older and abler person must be appointed the heir. However, Lord Ii is said to have slandered Lord Yoshinobu by saying that the latter lacks respect for those who are above him. . . . My Lord, the important thing is to see what is good for the country, and the consensus reached (*kōron*) [in support of Lord Yoshinobu] must be accepted. . . ."

TOWARD RESTORATION

Where the bakufu *failed, in administrative reforms, economic changes, and military reorganization, some of the* han *succeeded, and the most notable examples can be found in the two* tozama han *of Chōshū and Satsuma. They were able to*

reorganize their governments, refurbish their treasury, and gain popular accep-
tance and support for their new vision for Japan.

In the summer of 1858, Lord Tadamasa of Chōshū returned from Edo to Hagi
and ordered administrative reorganization of the han *government. This included*
elimination of sinecure positions, and was intended to prepare Chōshū for a
place in national politics. In his speech to his retainers, Tadamasa employed the
words "imperial country" several times, showing clearly his leaning toward the
Imperial Court as against the bakufu *in the* bakumatsu *(end of the* bakufu*)*
period politics. In response to Lord Tadamasa's command Masuda Danjō
(1833–1864), the han *resident elder (*tōeki*) drafted a series of recommendations*
(Document 14). Not all of these measures were enacted. However, they did serve
to end a period of Chōshū's inertia.

Chōshū's preeminence in national politics was enhanced by many of its capa-
ble young shishi *(concerned samurai), who were taught by Yoshida Shōin (1830–*
1859) in the virtue of loyalty, even to the point of complete subjugation and blind
obedience. Document 15 is one of Shōin's prison letters to his learned friend,
Mokurin, which shows his abiding faith in the imperial institution. Words such
as, "the sincerity of one single man touches the hearts of millions," gave encour-
agement to men like Takasugi Shinsaku (1839–1867), Kido Kōin (1833–1877),
and Itō Hirobumi (1841–1909) who studied under him and became prominent
leaders of the Meiji Restoration.

Sakamoto Ryōma (1835–1867) was a Tosa loyalist who helped bring about
the Satsuma-Chōshū alliance. He was also a perceptive political thinker, who
while traveling with Gotō Shōjirō drafted on shipboard an eight-point program for
Japan (Document 16). It contained a vision for a new Japan that would have a
broadly based government. It was also intended to serve as a program for reconcili-
ation between Satsuma and Chōshū on the one hand, and the bakufu *on the other.*

The Satsuma and Chōshū loyalists were, however, not given to a notion of
rapprochement with the bakufu. *They were practitioners of* Realpolitik, *and their*
views are articulated in a joint letter written by Saigō Takamori (1828–1877)
and Ōkubo Toshimichi (1830–1878) and addressed to Iwakura Tomomi (1825–
1883) on the eve of the Imperial Court's proclamation of imperial restoration
(Document 17).

14 Chōshū-han's Reforms of the Ansei Period, 1858[20]

(a) On Matters Relating to Military Administration

3. On the peasant soldiers.

The two provinces [of Nagato and Suō, which made up the *han* of Chōshū]

---

[20]Suematsu Kenshō, *Bōchō Kaiten-shi (A History of Chōshū in Changing the Man-*
date) (Tokyo: Kashi Shobō, reissue, 1967), Vol. 1, pp. 177–185.

are endowed with long coast lines, and in an emergency, the defense may not be effectively handled by the samurai residing in various areas alone. Therefore it is imperative that peasant soldiers be drafted into such services. . . .

4. Expansion in the military administration.

There have been repeated discussions of the military administration, but they have remained merely academic, and have lacked the actual measures which could be applied in a real situation. In view of the contemporary conditions, may I implore your Lordship to investigate the matter thoroughly and order your *hatamoto* (bannermen) and all the regiments to engage in military drills on a regular basis. Order them also to become familiar with the order of battle and with line formation. In this way, they will not be thrown into confusion when facing the enemy and will be useful to your Lordship. Furthermore steps must be taken to replete our military provisions and ammunition. As to the weapons, frivolous ornamentation must be avoided in favor of practical use, and this matter must be carefully looked into. . . .

Additional Note: The order of battle and line formation can be established after due deliberation.

After ordering the amount by which annual production of weapons and ammunition can be increased, the financial commitment can be discussed. It is suggested that the needed silver pieces are to be provided by the Household Office (*shotaigata*) of your Lordship.

As to the storage of grains, the Household Office and Buikugata[21] be ordered to investigate the matter.

(b) On Matters Relating to Encouragement of Learning and Military Arts

1. If your Lordship encourages learning and military arts, the people will become harmonious and the morale will be enhanced. . . .

2. It is of primary importance not to be tardy in administering rewards or punishments for meritorious or lazy work in drills and exercises.

3. . . . With regard to the entrance requirements to the *han*-school, Meirinkan, if we maintain the status quo and only admit those who are from a certain rank and above, the most able may be denied admission because they come from the lower-rank samurai class. Thereafter order the school to admit its students on the basis of ability without regard to gradations in rank. Within the dormitory, or even when your Lordship appears before the lecture hall, the seating order is to be determined by the student's abilities and achievements. This is consistent with the purpose for which this school is built. In this manner resorting to gradations may gradually disappear, and the public morale will be restored. . . .

---

[21]A special bureau created for the purpose of savings and investments, which maintained a separate account, and whose assets could not be touched except in emergencies.

(c) Articles on Government and Close Relations
Among the Retainers

4. Rumors concerning the actions the Imperial Court is going to take toward the *bakufu* cannot be adopted by this *han* as its policy. Matters such as these must be discussed privately and must be kept secret. . . .

13. Beginning with clothing, food and housing, all extravagance must be strictly forbidden. This prohibition includes use of fine tableware and furniture and other luxury items. . . .

17. A number of years ago, an order was issued to investigate a means of simplifying procedures at governmental offices. At which time it was also ordered that unnecessary fees ought to be suspended. It is hereby recommended that a new order to the same effect be given to different bureaus and district offices. . . .

22. Practicing frugality and changing bad customs.

If one desires to reform the bad custom of extravagance, the first thing to do is practice true austerity. Your subject, with trembling, begs of your Lordship to set a good example in this matter. Thus, your Lordship's ministers and others of like mind will each in turn adopt frugal manners, and their actions will set the standards for the domain. . . .

(d) On Civil Administration

2. To emphasize agricultural administration in order to strengthen the power of our provinces.

There is no denying that to put priority on the agricultural administration constitutes the basis of a rich country and strong army (*fukoku kyohei*). Therefore when true austerity is implemented, and when there are only a few who seek after the trivia, and a large number who engages in the basic [works], the provinces will prosper. A system which will bring about such results must be established. To encourage agriculture, taxes must be reduced and *corvée* labor must be eliminated. In appointing district magistrates, select those who will be diligent in performing their duties, in order to spread the benevolence of your Lordship [to the people].

15 **Yoshida Shōin's Prison Letter, 1856**[22]   I am a subject of the house of Mōri. Therefore I bind myself day and night to the service of the house of Mōri. The house of Mōri is subject to the Emperor. When we are loyal to our Lord, then we are loyal to the Emperor. For over 600 years our Lords have not bound themselves completely to the service of the Emperor. This crime is evident. It is my intention to let him expiate his guilt. But because I am condemned to confinement in the house, I can neither write nor speak with him directly. I can only speak about this with my brother and my parents and I await with

---

[22]H. van Straelen, *Yoshida Shōin: Forerunner of the Meiji Restoration* (Leiden: Brill, 1952), pp. 102–105.

patience the occasion to speak about this with the samurai and the loyalists. This opportunity will occur, when—pardoned—I can freely visit those who have the same opinion as I. Then I shall undertake with them: (1) to show to the *shōgun* his crime committed during more than 600 years and to show him his actual duty; (2) to show also to our *daimyō* and all the other *daimyō* their crimes, and (3) to show to the whole *bakufu* all their crimes[23] in order to make them serve the Emperor. If I am condemned to death before I can realize these things, I cannot help it. If I die in prison, after me another will execute this intention and certainly there will be an occasion for my successors to do this. I should like to write this to you with the following words: The sincerity of one single man touches the hearts of millions. I hope that you will understand me. By nature, it is repugnant to me to speak lightly about things that touch my innermost heart, but to you alone I confide by thoughts. Observe well how I dedicate my life to it. I know only too well that the Emperor is just as Yao and Shun[24] and that the *shōgun* is just as Mang and Cao.[25] Because I know this, therefore I give myself up to study and cultivate my spirit in order to accomplish someday something grand. I have a reason for not speaking night and day about the crimes of the *shōgun*. Namely it is in vain when I accuse him, because I am imprisoned. And because I live here without speaking openly of the crimes of the *shōgun*, therefore I can say that—in a sense—I take part in his crimes. This is also the case with my Lord. Never—even if I should have to die for it—shall I disclose the crimes of others, unless I have corrected my own fault. Therefore, until such an occasion arises—as I have told you above—I am satisfied to ponder over these things in my thoughts or to give advice to my acquaintances. If one day I explain the wrongs to my Lord and he does not listen, I shall sacrifice my life in order that he might repent. Among the three virtuous Chinese, Pi Gan, Jizi, and Weizi, only Pi Gan is my master.[26] I shall not leave my Lord in order to go to another province, when my Lord does not listen. I hope, that also my descendants may share this same conviction and do like Pi Gan. Those who would not act like Pi Gan but rather like Jizi and Weizi, I do not consider as my descendants. I swear this from the bottom of my soul before the Gods of Heaven and

---

[23]Yoritomo became *shōgun* in 1192. Shōin regarded the encroachment upon the prerogatives of the Imperial Throne by the successive *shōgun* wrong, and the *daimyō* who served these *shōgun* equally culpable.

[24]Yao and Shun were mythical Chinese emperors known for their virtue.

[25]Wang Mang usurped the Han throne in 8 A.D. to establish his own Xin dynasty which collapsed in 23 A.D. Cao Cao (155–220), one of the generals who rendered the coup de grace to the decaying Later Han dynasty, was regarded as a type of cunning and unscrupulous rebel.

[26]Pi Gan, twelfth century B.C., uncle of the tyrant Zhou Xin, the last ruler of the Shang dynasty, killed by Zhou Xin when remonstrating with him. Jizi, another uncle of Zhou Hsin, imprisoned by him but left the country afterwards, and believed to have founded the kingdom of Korea. Weizi, a brother of Zhou Xin, who went over to King Wu of Zhou and received from him in fief the dukedom of Song.

Earth. When my Lord listens to me and sees clearly the crimes he committed during more than 600 years, then he shall be in a position to correct the wrongs of the other *daimyō* and those of the *bakufu* as well. Although my Lord is supposed to be independent of the *shōgun*, we must grant that the Mōri family has obtained from the *shōgun* many favors (*ongi*) during more than 200 years. It would be a very good thing for my Lord to admonish the *shōgun* frequently about his abuses, so that eventually he might correct them. But if the *shōgun* does not correct his wrongs—and all the *daimyō* agree on the point—my Lord must bring the case before the Emperor and obtain a commission to prosecute their plan.

If, however, he will not listen, we may compare the *shōgun* with Jie and Zhou[27] or even call him so. Yet, although we may call the *shōgun* Jie or Zhou, we have in fact no right to accuse him of his crimes, because my Lord and myself are lacking in loyalty and devotion toward the Emperor. The first thing therefore we have to do, is to recognize our own defects.

There is a point about which I hold an opinion which differs from yours. It is that you think that "an unjust power can be killed by the pen." This is indeed the idea of Confucius who wrote the *Spring and Autumn Annuals (Chun chiu)*[28] and I cannot see that this was a bad thing. However, today the country is menaced by thousands of dangers and in this case we cannot expect very much from our writings.

If you consider the *shōgun* like Jie or Zhou, then my Lord is like Feilian or Olai.[29] It is your practice never to admonish people like Jie and Zhou. You think that even today those who make a plot, are traitors of the State. Again, there is for you—apart from the brush—no other way. This idea of yours I regret very much indeed. This attitude impedes us in correcting a man of his wrongs to make him better. If a man does not correct himself, if he does not become better, what use is it to say: "An unjust power can be killed by the pen."

If you take the trouble to ponder thoroughly on the opinion which I dare to present to you, not only myself, but also the souls of my ancestors will be very happy. I should very much like to speak with you about it personally, but unfortunately, I am deprived of my liberty, because the warders have bound me with cords.

16 Sakamoto Ryōma's Eight-Point Program, 1867[30]

1. Political power of the entire country should be returned to the Imperial Court, and all decrees should be issued by the Court.

2. There should be established an Upper and a Lower Legislative House

---

[27]Jie Gui, the last Emperor of the Xia dynasty. He is said to have indulged in cruelty and lust almost unparalleled in history. Similar accusations are raised against Zhou Xin, the last Emperor of the Shang dynasty.

[28]Supposedly to criticize and expose the wicked deeds of rulers and their ministers.

[29]Bad ministers of the last emperor of the Shang dynasty, Chou.

[30]Iwasaki Hideshige, *Sakamoto Ryōma Kankei Monjo (Documents Relating to Sakamoto Ryōma)* (Tokyo, 1925), Vol. 1, pp. 297–298.

which should participate in making decisions pertaining to all governmental policies. All governmental policies should be decided on the basis of deliberation openly arrived at (*kōgi*).

3. Men of ability among the court nobles, *daimyō* and people at large should be appointed as councillors and receive appropriate offices and titles. Those sinecure positions of the past should be abolished.

4. In dealing with foreign countries, appropriate regulations should be newly established which would take into account broadly the deliberation openly arrived at.

5. The laws and regulations (*ritsu-ryō*) of earlier times should be scrutinized [to preserve only those provisions which are still applicable], and a great new code to last forever should be promulgated.

6. The navy should be properly expanded.

7. An Imperial Guard [directly controlled by the Imperial Court, and not dependent on the *bakufu* or various *han*] should be set up to defend the capital.

8. There should be a law established to equalize the value of gold, silver and goods with those of foreign countries.

The above eight-point program is proposed after due consideration of the present state of affairs in the nation. When this is proclaimed both internally and externally to all the countries, it becomes inconceivable to think of engaging in the urgent talk of alleviating the current crisis outside of this program. If with determination these policies are carried out, the fortunes of His Majesty will be restored, national strength will increase, and it will not be difficult to attain the position of equality with all other nations. We pray that based on the enlightened and righteous reason (*dōri*), the Imperial Government will act decisively to undertake the path of renewal and reform of the country.

17 Letter of Saigō and Ōkubo on the Imperial Restoration, 1867[31]

When with great resolve, a policy of establishing the foundation for the imperial restoration is proclaimed, there is bound to be a great deal of confusion. People have been contaminated by the old habit of settling down into the more than two hundred years of peace. If we decide to resort to arms, it can conversely have the salutary effect of renewing the spirit of all people under heaven, and pacifying the central regions of the country. Therefore we deem it the most urgent task to decide for war, and to find victory in the most difficult situation.

It is a well established principle that one must not take up arms because he loves warfare. However, if everything is allowed to proceed as it is, and the great issue of how to govern the country is delegated merely to the hard work of the Imperial Court and to the consensus (*koron*) reached by the three highest posi-

---

[31]*Saigō Takamori Monjo (Saigō Takamori Documents)* in *Nihon Shiseki Kyōkai Sōsho, op. cit.*, Vol. 102 (Tokyo: Tokyo University Press, reissue, 1967), pp. 208–210.

tions within the Council of State (*Dajōkan*), then war is to be preferred. In the olden days, when great works were begun, how to conserve such great works was hardly decided by debates. Even those [debaters] who were exceptionally well endowed did not escape criticism from later generations of scholars. The situation is even more critical today with the deteriorating conditions. We urge you to think through the matter carefully and consider all the alternatives. It is most important that the first step in the new government is not a mistaken one.

On the important matter of how to deal with the Tokugawa family, we have been informed of the outline of a secret decision. We heartily concur with your decision through a secret edict to order the [former] Lords of Owari (Tokugawa Yoshikatsu, 1824–1883) and Echizen (Matsudaira Yoshinaga, 1828–1890) to become intermediaries in arranging for the *shōgun*'s immediate repentance and restitution. This is indeed an appropriate and magnanimous gesture.

The danger which has befallen our imperial country today is due to the great crime committed by the *bakufu*. This fact is very well established, and two months earlier, on the thirteenth day, you did reach a decision to impose certain penalties. At the present time, regardless of whatever arguments may be advanced, it is necessary to demote the *shōgun* to the position of a mere *daimyō*, reduce his official rank by one degree, let him return his domains, and let him ask for the pardon of his sins.[32] Unless these measures are followed, whatever we do will be contrary to the consensus (*kōron*, or broadly public opinion) and there is no way the public can be satisfied. These secret understandings which we reached previously must not be changed in any manner.

If the mediation through the Lords of Owari and Echizen does not succeed, it shows very clearly that the *shōgun* fails to appreciate the magnanimity of the Imperial Court, works against the consensus, and is not truly penitent. In that event an imperial command must be given immediately and resolutely to implement the above measure. . . .

If we fail to take these appropriate measures, we will be acting contrary to the principle and consensus at the initial phase of the imperial restoration. Then the fortunes of the imperial power will suffer, and the great ills of the past years will re-surface. . . . May we beg you to consider the matter carefully, and also consult with the three ministers to arrive at a resolute decision. . . .

Eighth day of the twelfth month, 1867

> Iwashita Sajiuemon
> Saigo Kichinosuke (Takamori)
> Okubo Ichizō (Toshimichi)

To: Lord Iwakura Tomomi

---

[32]Saigō originally favored death for *Shōgun* Yoshinobu, but British Minister Harry Parkes advised Saigō that in such an event all foreign powers might side with the *bakufu*.

CHAPTER **XI**

Early Meiji Political Development

With the accession to the throne of the young Emperor Meiji, the task of starting everything *de novo* (*goisshin*) began. It meant not only restoration of power to the Imperial Court, but also commencement of a series of reforms calculated to create a unified modern nation.

The leadership for this restoration was supplied by the former samurai who occupied positions of consequence in the Meiji government. They were shrewd practitioners of *Realpolitik*, and could profess as their ideals the Five-Article Charter Oath, and at the same time continue to suppress the populace through the measures contained in the five notice boards (Documents 1–3). The West provided several models for emulation, and the Iwakura mission that was sent to the U.S. and to Europe brought home more clearly than ever the necessity for modernization. *Fukoku kyōhei* (Rich Nation, Strong Army) and *bummei kaika* (Civilization and Enlightenment) became the watchwords for those who ruled.

In practical terms, the Meiji oligarchs instituted land tax reform and conscription to fortify the bases of the government. To strengthen the nation, subsidies were given to fledgling industries, and steps toward compulsory education were taken. Japanese students accepted new knowledge without questioning. They provided skilled workers for the industries and also through the network of higher education, managerial and bureaucratic manpower for the nation. *Shokusan kōgyō* or encouragement of industries became another basic policy and slogan for the new government.

This chapter covers the period from 1868 through 1890, from the issuance of the Charter Oath to the promulgation of the Constitution and of the rescript on education. It was a period when Japan's newly acquired skills and institutions remained largely untested, and there was an element of uncertainty throughout this period. It is true that the Meiji leaders were able to resolve many of the problems confronting them successfully and in relatively short order. However, this is merely a retrospective view. At the time of the issuance of the Charter Oath, the Korean question (*seikanrōn*), or the crisis of 1881, the government was unstable and one false move would have invariably led to a civil war. It was a government that had to contend with lack of financial resources, and with divisive mistrust among its many constituent elements. The fact that they ultimately succeeded does not in any way minimize the danger they had to face or the pressure under which they had to work. The differing opinions expressed or consensus reached as contained in the documents in this chapter must be read in this light.

Even the extreme of adulation for the Emperor, as expressed in Itō's commentaries on the Constitution (Document 19) or in the rescript on education (Document 20), must not be taken at their face value. As Erwin Baelz, a German doctor and Emperor Meiji's personal physician observed, the victory by Japan over China in 1895 was the turning point in the people's attitude toward their Emperor.[1] Prior to that the nation remained skeptical. And this mood of uncertainty characterized the early Meiji period under discussion.

FOUNDATIONS OF EARLY MEIJI GOVERNMENT

On April 6, 1868, the new Meiji government announced its basic policies in a document called the five-article oath (Sec. 1, Document 2). The Charter Oath was based on a draft submitted by Kido Kōin (Document 1c), who in turn was influenced by the drafts given by Yuri Kimimasa (1829–1909), a samurai of Echizen (Document 1a) and by Fukuoka Takachika (1835–1919), a samurai of Tosa (Document 1b). These drafts shared in common a desire to have public matters discussed openly (kōron), and to have an assembly of all daimyō formed. Initially the intent seemed to be that all the domains, not just Satsuma and Chōshū, were to share in the power of decision-making.

To implement the provisions of the Charter Oath, on June 11, the government issued a Document on the Form of Government (Seitaisho) (Document 2). It announced the restoration of power to the Council of State (Dajōkan), and the division of power into legislative, executive and judicial branches. There was also a provision for selecting qualified men to serve as assemblymen. These were forward-looking measures emulating the governmental systems of the Western world. However, in actual practice, common people were controlled as before. The orders given in the five notice boards bear witness to this (Document 3).

[1]Toku Baelz, ed., *Awakening Japan: The Diary of a German Doctor*, tr. from the German by Eden and Cedar Paul (New York: Viking Press, 1932), pp. 115–116.

Note also that these orders were given the same day the Charter Oath was announced.

The leadership for the early Meiji government was provided by a number of court nobles, lords of Satsuma, Chōshū, Tosa, Hizen, and other powerful daimyō, *and samurai from these domains, most notably from Chōshū and Satsuma. To them, to unify the country and broaden the base of support for the government was the most important task. Kido Kōin (1833–1877) was most instrumental in effecting the return of feudal domains and census registers to the imperial government, and his reminiscence is included as Document 5. The memorial of the* daimyō *of Chōshū, Satsuma, Tosa, and Hizen returning their feudal domains is given in Document 4. This move in effect took away the former* daimyō's *right to rule their respective* han, *but they were "appointed" as governors of their former domains. The true step toward centralization was accomplished when the* han *system was abolished in favor of a prefecture system (*fu-ken sei*) (Document 6).*

1 Three Drafts of the Charter Oath, 1868[2]

(a) Draft by Yuri Kimimasa

General Outline on Legislative Matters

1. It is requested that a system be established under which common people may be permitted to pursue their respective callings so that there may be no discontent.

2. It is necessary for the samurai and common people to unite in carrying out vigorously the administration of economic and financial affairs (*keirin*).[3]

3. Knowledge shall be sought throughout the world so as to widen and strengthen the foundations of imperial rule.

4. The term of office held by qualified men [selected by the *han*] (*kōshi*) must be limited. Thereafter they must yield their positions to talented men.

5. All matters of state must be decided by open discussion (*kōron*) [with the participation of all factions on *han* concerned] and must not be discussed privately.

The intent of the [proposed] League of the *Daimyō* (*Shokō Kaimei*) may be

---

[2]Ōkubo Toshiaki et al., *Kindaishi Shiryō (Documents on Modern History)* (Tokyo: Yoshikawa Kōbunkan, 1965), pp. 50–51. A highly useful discussion of these three versions and the final version of the Charter Oath is contained in Robert M. Spaulding, Jr., "The Intent of the Charter Oath" in Richard K. Beardsley, *Studies in Japanese History and Politics*, University of Michigan Center for Japanese Studies, Occasional Papers No. 10 (1967), pp. 3–29.

[3]Yuri Kimimasa attempted to carry out financial reforms in his native Echizen-*han*. His reform failed because of lack of support from rich farmers and rich merchants. In writing this draft, he was recalling that specific incident.

announced along the lines discussed above.[4] [It is further recommended that] general amnesty be announced concurrently.

(b) Amended Draft by Fukuoka Takachika

A Compact

1. An assembly consisting of *daimyō* shall be established, and all matters of state shall be decided by open discussion.

2. It is requested that a system be established under which not only the civil and military officials, but also the common people may be permitted to pursue their respective callings so that there may be no discontent.

3. The high and low shall all unite in carrying out vigorously the administration of economic and financial affairs.

4. Knowledge shall be sought throughout the world so as to broaden and strengthen the foundations of imperial rule.

5. The term of office of those appointed [by the imperial government] must be limited. Thereafter they must yield their positions to talented men.

The above may be announced as the intents. When the League [of the *Daimyō*] is formed, it is suggested that general amnesty be announced concurrently.

(c) Draft by Kido Kōin

Oath

1. An assembly consisting of *daimyō* shall be established, and all matters of state shall be decided by open discussion.

2. The high and low shall all unite in carrying out the administration of economic and financial affairs.

3. It is requested that a system be established under which not only the civil and military officials, but also the common people may be permitted to pursue their respective callings so that there may be no discontent.

4. Evil practices of the past[5] shall be discarded and [all our actions] shall follow the accepted practices of the world.

5. Knowledge shall be sought throughout the world so as to broaden and strengthen the foundations of imperial rule.

2   Excerpts from the Document on the Form of Government (Seitaisho), 1868[6]

1. In determining the national policy and establishing a new system of government and regulations, the text of the Charter Oath shall become the guide.

---

[4]Yuri was primarily interested in the cooperation between the *kuge* (court nobles) and *shokō (daimyō)*, which accounts for the phrase *kanbu itto* (unity of civil and military officials) when explaining the intent of his draft.

[5]E.g., the practice of *jōi*, or expelling barbarians.

[6]Ōkubo, *op. cit.*, pp. 51–52. For another translation, see Walter W. McLaren, "Japanese Government Documents," in *TASJ*, 1st ser. Vol. 42, part 1 (1914), pp. 8–10. Section 1

(1) A deliberative assembly shall be convoked on a broad basis, and all matters of state shall be decided by open discussion.

(2) The high and low shall all unite in carrying out vigorously the administration of economic and financial affairs.

(3) It is necessary to have a system under which not only the civil and military officials, but also the common people may be permitted to pursue their respective callings so that there may be no discontent.

(4) Evil practices of the past shall be discarded and [all our actions] shall follow the just way of the world [i.e., international law].

(5) Knowledge shall be sought throughout the world so as to broaden and strengthen the foundations of imperial rule.

The intent of this document is not to go contrary to the conditions set forth in the above oath.

2. All the power of the government shall be restored to the Council of State (*Dajōkan*), so as to eliminate the ills of having two separate authorities issuing orders.[7] The power of the Council of State shall be divided threefold into legislative, executive and judicial powers. In this way, the lack of checks and balances shall be avoided.

3. No legislator shall become concurrently an administrator. Nor can an administrator be concurrently a legislator. However, legislators may be given such tasks as serving on temporary tours of inspection of cities or entertaining foreign envoys.

5. Each great city, *han*, prefecture (*ken*) shall select qualified men (*kōshi*) to serve as assemblymen. The purpose of establishing a system of deliberation [in this manner] is to enable the opinion of the public to be aired openly.

8. All officers shall be altered after four years of service. Their positions shall be filled by means of election through balloting. However, at the first expiration of terms hereafter, one-half of the officials shall remain in office for two additional years. In this way the working of the government shall not suffer interruption. If a particular official is so well accepted by the public and it is difficult to replace him, a few additional years may be added to his term of office.

10. A system shall be established under which those from the *daimyō* down to farmers, artisans and merchants, shall each contribute to the sustenance of the government. In this way governmental expenditures can be reimbursed, armaments can be strengthened, and public security can be maintained. Therefore even those who hold ranks or positions shall be levied a tax equal to one-thirtieth of their income or salaries.

---

contains the final version of the Charter Oath. Here following Spaulding, *op. cit.*, I am translating the term *kaigi* in a singular form.

[7]Meaning the Imperial Court and the *bakufu*.

3   Five Notice Boards, April 6, 1868[8]

(a) The First Notice

Order

1. As a human being, man must observe the five cardinal rules (*gorin*) [of Confucianism].
2. Be compassionate toward widows, widowers, those who are alone and those who are disabled.
3. Do not commit the crimes of murder, arson, robbery and the like.

(b) The Second Notice

Order

For whatever reason when a large number of people agree to band together to engage in nefarious activities, that group is called a group of conspirators (*totō*). When a group of conspirators presents a direct petition, it is called an appeal by force (*gōso*). When people agree to leave the town or village in which they have been residing, it is called an act of absconding. All of the above acts are strictly forbidden. If anyone among you knows of others who are engaged in the above acts, report immediately to the governmental offices which have jurisdiction. There will be a reward for informing.

(c) The Third Notice

Order

[The practice and propagation of] Christianity [are] strictly forbidden. If there is anyone acting suspiciously, report to the governmental offices which have jurisdiction for a reward.

(d) The Fourth Notice

Memorandum

With the coming of the imperial restoration, the Imperial Court has made known its desire to maintain friendly relations with foreign countries. All such matters relating to foreign countries are to be handled by the Imperial Court, which is determined to abide by the provisions of the existing treaties consistent with international law. Therefore in obedience to His Majesty's wishes, the people in the entire country must not in any way act imprudently.

Hereafter, if a willful murder of a foreigner or an indiscreet act is committed, it will be deemed an act against this specific imperial command, calculated to bring about a national crisis. Furthermore, if such an act is committed, this imperial country, which has entered into friendly intercourse with foreign nations, will suffer a loss of prestige. Deplorable indeed is such an act.

In the event anyone commits such an act, depending on the severity of the

---

[8]Ōkubo, *op. cit.*, pp. 53–54.

crime, a samurai may be removed from his samurai registry, and an appropriate punishment will be meted out. Therefore it is ordered that each of you must follow this imperial command, and must not engage in any unwarranted act of violence.

(e) The Fifth Notice

With the coming of the imperial restoration, His Imperial Majesty has been concerned with a quick return to peaceful conditions, relief for all the people, and finding a way to enable everyone to engage in his own profession. Unfortunately, there are so many vagabonds in the country. Some samurai and common people may take advantage of today's [unsettled] conditions, and flee from their home provinces. This must be stopped without fail. In the event a person who flees his home domain commits a crime, his crime will be imputed to his original master.

At a time like this, if there is anyone, irrespective of his position, who wishes to make a recommendation for the sake of our imperial country or for his master's house, he may do so. He must utilize the existing channels, and with a righteous mind, articulate all that must be said. He may also petition the officers of the Council of State (*Dajōkan-dai*) to enable him to make the recommendations.

However, hereafter anyone who hires samurai or even farmers and merchants must investigate the place of origin of his prospective employees. If an employer hires a person who has fled from another place of origin, and if that person commits a misdeed or causes other disturbances, it goes without saying that such misdeeds will be imputed to the new master.

4 **Memorial on the Return of Feudal Domains and Census Registers, March 5, 1869**[9] Your servants venture to address Your Majesty with profound reverence. There must be one central body of government and one sovereign authority, both of which are indispensable to the Imperial Court. Since the Imperial Ancestor founded this country and established a basis of government, all things in the wide expanse of heaven and all things on earth to its farthest limits have belonged to one imperial line from generation to generation, and all people therein have been its subjects. This is what is meant by "one central government." The power of granting and withholding ranks and fiefs or stipends to sustain those who are below also belongs to the imperial line exclusively. Thus no one can occupy a foot of ground or subjugate another subject [of the Emperor] for his own private gains. This is what is understood by the term "one sovereign authority. . . ."

---

[9]Ōkubo, *op. cit.*, pp. 56–57. Walter W. McLaren, "Japanese Government Documents," in *TASJ*, 1st ser. Vol. 42, part 1 (1914), pp. 29–32.

When the Tokugawa family rose in power, half of the country was held by old families and clans. Some new families also sprang up. These numerous families took no heed of the question as to whether their lands and subjects had been received in grant from the Imperial Court, and kept them simply by virtue of age-old evil customs. It was commonly said [by members of these families]: "These possessions of ours were gained by the military power of our ancestors." However, is there any difference between raising an army to seize [the imperial land and subjects] and defying the death penalty by plundering the imperial storehouses and stealing their treasures? Those who break into storehouses are commonly termed robbers, but no suspicion is cast by the nation on those who seize upon the imperial land and subjects. This confusion between right and wrong is terrible indeed.

Now that we are about to establish an entirely new form of government, it is incumbent on us to preserve intact both one central body of government and one sovereign authority. Wherever your servants reside are Your Majesty's lands, and whomever they shepherd are Your Majesty's subjects, none of which can be privately owned by anyone of us. Your servants accordingly beg respectfully to surrender to Your Majesty the feudal domains and census registers. They ask the Imperial Court to deal with everything as it may see fit, giving what should be given and taking away what should be taken away. They entreat Your Majesty to issue edicts to redispose of the enfeoffed lands of our clans. Furthermore, they ask that the court lay down regulations governing all things from the administration of troops to military uniform and equipment. In this way, all matters of state, great and small, may be decided by one and the same authority. Thus, both in name and in fact, our country may be placed upon a footing of equality with foreign powers. . . .

5   Kido Kōin's Recollection of Return of Feudal Domains, 1868[10]   In the

year 1868, after the battle of Toba-Fushimi, a large number of people from *han* converged in Kyoto and there were many different opinions expressed. Some spoke of *jōi*, or explusion of barbarians, others spoke of *kaikoku*, or opening the country, and still others preferred continuation of *sakoku* or the policy of seclusion. Within these three major points of view were formed many factions, and each faction claimed that it represented the view of the nation or of its particular *han*. The diversity of opinion easily created a great deal of confusion. After the battle in the Northeastern region was over, people from different *han* returned to their respective domains, each *han* persisting in its own view and continuing to foster its own military power. Thus Chōshū vied supremacy with Satsuma, and

---

[10]*Kido Kōin Monjo* in Ōkubo Toshiaki et al., *Shiryō ni yoru Nihon no Ayumi (Japanese History through Documents), Kindaihen (Modern Period)* (Tokyo: Yoshikawa Kōbunkan, 1951), p. 35.

Tosa competed against Hizen. Each of the *han* occupied one corner of the country, and was concerned with only what was happening in Japan. They were unaware that a great crisis could emanate from overseas. There were some within the Imperial Court who had a rational approach to the entire problem, but they could not change the existing tide. This could have brought to this imperial country and to its millions of people an unprecedented calamity.

Unless we could discuss the danger inherent at that time, formulate general policies to be followed, destroy the evil customs prevailing in the past seven hundred years, and unify this imperial country, we could not possibly expect to preserve our nation and give security to its millions of people. I could not rest at ease for a moment with this perturbing prospect, and secretly started a discussion leading to the return of feudal domains and census registers (*hanseki hōkan*). I was especially anxious to clarify and rectify the way of the subjects, and in so doing guide the country to the logical solutions of this urgent issue. I also wanted to have our own Chōshū *han* take a leading role in order to maintain its own existence. However within our *han*, many difficulties were encountered. And such problems were multiplied and compounded in the entire nation, which were hard to describe.

I was aware that if we failed to take advantage of an opportune moment, the country might find itself in utter confusion. So I made up my mind and secretly had an audience with our Lord Tadamasa (Lord of Chōshū). I discussed major trends in the country and shared with him my fear of a great calamity which could take place in the near future. Lord Tadamasa agreed with me and gave me permission to enter into secret conversation with the Satsuma *han*. In this way there was a hopeful beginning. There were many indescribable difficulties in bringing about the return of feudal domains. And, without Lord Tadamasa this difficult task could not have been accomplished.

6 Replacing Han with Prefectures, Letter of Kido Kōin, 1871[11] . . .

After the imperial restoration, I initiated the discussion of the return of feudal domains and census registers, and did my utmost to carry through the project. It led to the voluntary return of the domains by the Lords of Satsuma, Chōshū, Tosa, and Hizen, and it became the official policy of the Imperial Court. At that time those who were inside and outside the Chōshū *han* all considered me an extremely dangerous person. Those who never held a grudge against me became angry with me, and all the anger of the world was centered on me. When initiating that policy, I was prepared to die for the cause. However, I was careful in avoiding danger and have survived until this day.

Since that time the conditions of the country have substantially changed.

---

[11]Ōkubo, *Kindaishi Shiryō, op. cit.*, p. 59. This letter was dated October 14, 1871. Hereafter all references to the Ōkubo work in this chapter are from *Kindaishi Shiryō*.

During the spring and summer of this year, not an insignificant number of *han* suggested that large, middle and small size *han* ought to be abolished to form a combined prefecture. Others suggested that a distinct geographical unit, *shū*, should become a prefecture. Now that the abolition of *han* is ordered, no one seems to be surprised. When I compare this with the time of the return of feudal domains and census registers, I can detect a change in the times and in people's way of thinking. People's perception changes, and those who were angry yesterday are enlightened today, enabling us to bring about the coming of this event. I consider this most fortunate for our imperial country. . . .

Lately from Satsuma, Saigō Takamori came to serve in the Imperial Court. I am delighted for the sake of our imperial country. In this manner, the suspicions people hold against the new measures will melt away like snow, and any view in support of feudalism will dissipate. We can confidently expect progress to come at a much faster pace. This being the case, there is no need to divide the large *han* like Satsuma and Kaga into three new prefectures, or Chōshū into two prefectures. If this is not done, the smaller *han* will be forced to combine with other *han* to form a new prefecture. The details can be worked out and then an order can be issued. In any event, we can now see our way clear. Some of the *han* may regard our new measures as a means of transferring their debts to the Imperial Court. This view is not supported by facts. However, nowadays, the *han* no longer maintain separate budgets. As the military establishments and other matters are unified under the national government, I am confident that within ten years, our general policy will be so well entrenched that no deviation from it will become possible.

CENTRALIZATION AND STATE POWER

With the abolition of the han *system, the samurai from the four* han *of Satsuma, Chōshū, Tosa and Hizen stepped into positions of authority both in name and in reality, and with this newly acquired strength, adopted many measures intended to strengthen the position of the central government.*

Military conscription was suggested as early as 1868 by Ōmura Masujirō (1824–1869), who held the position of Vice Minister of Military Affairs. However, its adoption had to wait until after the abolition of the han *system, and the recommendations submitted by Yamagata Aritomo (1838–1922) and others were subsequently adopted (Document 7). Here, Yamagata cited the danger of encroachment by the Russians as one of the prime reasons for the necessity of having a standing army. The early conscription was criticized as a blood tax and there were many loopholes (Document 8). However, such a conscript army did show its prowess against Saigō's samurai army in the Satsuma rebellion.*

The Land Tax Reform of 1873 was a monumental achievement. Traditionally land tax was collected in kind, and the tax yields were subject to fluctuation, inconveniencing both the taxpayers and the government. With the reform, it was decided to assess the tax according to the value of land and to collect it in specie, and in this way the national treasury was guaranteed a predictable amount of funds each year (Document 9).

The Meiji government also encouraged growth of indigenous industries. It called for governmental subsidy and other encouragement. Just how such policies suited Japan's current needs was presented by Ōkubo Toshimichi (1830–1878), one of the ablest leaders of the early Meiji period (Document 10).

The contribution that education had made in every modernized state was well recognized by the Meiji leaders. One example of such a view was represented by Ōki Takatō (1832–1899), Minister of Education in 1872 (Document 11).

7 **Opinion on Military Affairs and Conscription, 1872**[12] A military force is required to defend the country and protect its people. Previous laws of this country inculcated in the minds of the samurai these basic functions, and there was no separation between civilian and military affairs. Nowadays civilian officials and military officials have separate functions, and the practice of having the samurai serve both functions has been abandoned. It is now necessary to select and train those who can serve the military functions, and herein lies the change in our military system. . . .

As your subjects carefully consider this matter, we discover that we are now maintaining the Ministry of Military Affairs (*hyōbu*) to serve domestic purposes, but in the future it will be required to serve foreign purposes. When we probe the matter further, we find that foreign and domestic considerations are essentially one and cannot be separated. This is so because, if our defense establishment is organized sufficiently to defend ourselves against threat from foreign countries, we shall have no fear of our inability to cope with domestic situations.

The status of our armed forces today is as follows: We have the so-called Imperial Guards whose functions are nothing more than to protect the sacred person of His Majesty and to guard the Imperial Palace. We have altogether more than twenty battalions manning the four military garrisons who are deployed to maintain domestic tranquility, and are not equipped to fight against any foreign threat. As to our navy, we have a few battleships yet to be completed. How can they be sufficient to counteract foreign threats?

Since the time of the Restoration, day after day and month after month, we have made significant progress. The governing of the districts (*gun*) and prefectures (*ken*) has been in the hands of the imperial government. Soldiers maintained by the *han* have been disbanded and all the armaments have been returned to the central government. In this way the domestic conditions have

---

[12]Ōyama Azusa, ed., *Yamagata Aritomo Ikensho (Opinions of Yamagata Aritomo)* (Tokyo: Hara Shobō, 1966), pp. 43–46.

been completely altered. This is the time to establish a firm national policy, and to adopt as our purpose the defense of our country against foreign threats.

The first concern of the Ministry of Military Affairs is to set up a system to defend our homeland. For this purpose two categories of soldiers are required: a standing army and those on the reserve list. The number of troops differ from country to country. Of the major countries, Russia maintains the largest number of troops and the United States the smallest. The reason for this discrepancy comes from the fact that the governmental system differs from one country to another. Consequently the regulations governing each of the countries also differ. The Netherlands and Belgium are among the smallest countries, but they are located between large countries, and in order to avoid contempt and scorn from their neighbors, they diligently go about the business of defending their countries. Even though one of these countries has a total area not exceeding one-third of the area of our country, it maintains a standing army numbering not less than forty to fifty thousand. If we apply the existing standards prevailing in our country to judge these two countries, they may appear to be concerned only with military affairs to the neglect of other matters. However, they do attend to hundreds of other affairs of state and do not abandon them. This is possible because their national goals are already set, and they can act accordingly to implement them.

Therefore the creation of a standing army for our country is a task which cannot be delayed. It is recommended that a certain number of strong and courageous young men be selected from each of the prefectures in accordance with the size of the prefectures, and that such young men be trained in the Western-type military science and placed under rigorous drills, so that they may be deployed as occasion demands.

The so-called reservists do not normally remain within the military barracks. During peacetime they remain in their homes, and in an emergency they are called to service. All of the countries in Europe have reservists, and amongst them Prussia has most of them. There is not a single able-bodied man in Prussia who is not trained in military affairs. Recently Prussia and France fought each other and the former won handily. This is due in large measure to the strength of its reservists.

It is recommended that our country adopt a system under which any able-bodied man twenty years of age be drafted into military service, unless his absence from home will create undue hardship for his family. There shall be no distinction made between the common man and one who is of the samurai class. They shall all be formed into ranks, and after completion of a period of service, they shall be returned to their homes [to become reservists]. In this way every man will become a soldier, and not a single region in the country will be without defense. Thus our defense will become complete.

The second concern of the Ministry is coastal defense. This includes building of warships and constructing coastal batteries. Actually, battleships are movable batteries. Our country has thousands of miles of coastline, and any mobile corner of our country can become the advance post of our enemy. However, since it is not possible to construct batteries along the coastline everywhere, it is imperative to expand our navy and construct the largest warships. The latter can cover the areas that cannot be reached by the batteries and protect our homeland. The topography which is formed by nature cannot be changed by man. Every time there is war, the important strategic points will suffer the consequences of warfare. Therefore, a defense line must be predetermined during peacetime, and a line must be drawn clearly which must be strictly guarded, and people must be told to evacuate.

The third concern of the Military is to create resources for the navy and the army. There are three items under consideration, namely, military academies, a bureau of military supplies, and a bureau of munitions depots. It is not difficult to have one million soldiers in a short time, but it is difficult to gain one good officer during the same span of time. Military academies are intended to train officers for these two services. If we pay little attention to this need today, we shall not be able to have the services of capable officers for another day. Therefore, without delay military academies must be created and be allowed to prosper. Students shall be adequately trained by the faculty consisting of experts from several countries. There shall be established a set of regulations in the teaching of military drills and other subjects. The goal is to gain a supply of capable officers in a number larger than needed. The bureau of military supplies shall be in charge of procuring military provisions and manufacturing weapons of war for the two services. The bureau of munitions depots shall store such provisions and munitions. If we lack military provisions and weapons and our munitions depots are empty, what good will the million soldiers in the army or thousands of warships do? Therefore, well-qualified craftsmen from various countries must be hired to make necessary machines and build strong storage houses. We must make our own weapons and store them, and must become self-sufficient without relying on foreign countries. The goal is to create a sufficient amount and if there is any surplus it may be sold to other [countries].

Some people may argue that while they are aware of the urgency in the need for the Ministry of Military Affairs, they cannot permit the entire national resources to be committed to the need of one ministry alone. They further aver that from the larger perspective of the imperial government, there are so many other projects covering a wide range of things which require governmental attention. They reason that everything in the country changes continuously and everything occurs simultaneously. Therefore if military affairs advance one step, all others must advance one step. In this way everything in the country can become orderly. This argument fails to discern the fundamental issues. The recommendations herein presented by the Ministry of Military Affairs in no way asks for the stoppage of all govern-

318 JAPAN: A DOCUMENTARY HISTORY

mental activities or for the monopolization of all governmental revenues. But in a national emergency, a new set of priorities must be established. Those of us who are given the task of governing must learn from the past, discern the present, and weigh all matters carefully.

In the past there was Emperor Peter who was determined to make his country a great nation. He went overseas and studied naval sciences. After his return he built many battleships and constructed St. Petersburg. He created a standing army numbering several million, and was able to engage in the art of international politics against five or six of the strongest nations. As to domestic politics, he was satisfied to leave them to a woman. There were one or two internal quarrels, but they were eradicated almost immediately. It is to him that the credit is due for making Russia a great nation.

Those of us who govern must first of all discern the conditions prevailing in the world, set up priorities and take appropriate measures. In our opinion Russia has been acting very arrogantly. Previously, contrary to the provisions of the Treaty of Sevastopol[13] [sic], she placed her warships in the Black Sea. Southward, she has shown her aggressive intent toward Moslem countries and toward India. Eastward, she has crossed the borders of Manchuria and has been navigating the Amur River. Her intents being thus, it is inevitable that she will move eastward sooner or later by sending troops to Hokkaido, and then taking advantage of the seasonal wind move to the warmer areas.

At a time like this, it is very clear where the priority of this country must lie. We must now have a well-trained standing army supplemented by a large number of reservists. We must build warships and construct batteries. We must train officers and soldiers. We must manufacture and store weapons and ammunitions. The nation may consider that it cannot bear the expenses. However, even if we wish to ignore it, this important matter cannot disappear from us. Even if we prefer to enter into this type of defense undertaking, we cannot do without our defense for a single day. This situation is repeated everywhere in every country. At a time when a strong enemy from the north threatens us, can we afford not to make grand preparations? As to the actual system of installations, feeding of soldiers, building of ships, and all other matters and the expenses connected with them, we shall make a detailed report at a later date. Meanwhile, the above recommendations from the Ministry of Military Affairs represent its considered judgment and show the goals it wishes to attain. We respectfully submit these for your consideration.

> Vice Minister of Military Affairs Yamagata Aritomo
> Deputy Vice Minister Kawamura Sumiyoshi
> Deputy Vice Minister Saigō Tsugumichi.

---

[13]Here Yamagata was obviously referring to the 1858 Treaty of Paris, which ended the Crimean War.

8 **Conscription System and Regulations, 1873**[14] Conscription is applicable to those who have reached the age of twenty who are to be drafted to serve in the navy or army. The army is divided into three categories. First, the standing army; second, reserve troops; and third, national guards. Also in accordance with the qualifications of the soldiers, the army is divided into five branches, namely artillery, cavalry, infantry, engineer corps, and transport corps. Soldiers for these branches of service are to be called from the prefectures and districts under the jurisdiction of a specific military garrison to serve in that garrison for a given period of time. They are to be assigned to the defense of that locality.

1. The standing army is formed by those soldiers who are selected by lot from those who are eligible for that given year, and are to serve three years. . . .

2. The reserve troops are formed by those who have completed their three-year term of service with the standing army, and are allowed to return home to engage in their own occupations. They are further divided into two categories, the first reserve and the second reserve.

The first reservists are to serve two years, and in time of war will immediately be called upon to become part of the standing army. They must be prepared for such emergencies, and therefore must be called to the military barracks once a year to review the military skills they learned previously. . . .

3. In addition to the standing army and the reserve troops, all men between the ages of seventeen through forty are to be placed in the military registry, and when there is a nationwide, large-scale war, they are to be incorporated into the ranks, and be assigned the task of defending the territories covered by the garrison.

ARTICLE 3. Exemption from service in the standing army.[15]

1. Those whose height is less than five feet (*shaku*) one inch (*sun*).

2. Those who cannot serve on account of infirmity, chronic illness or deformity.

3. Those who are officials of the Council of State, Ministries, special cities, or prefectures.

4. Those who are students at the naval and military academies.

5. Those who have graduated with special skills from schools publicly maintained by the Ministries of Education, Industry, Development and other bureaus. Those who are studying overseas and those who are studying medicine and veterinary science. However, proof from their professors, and certificates showing their specialization are required.

6. Those who are head of the household.

---

[14]Ōkubo, *op. cit.*, pp. 85–86.

[15]Article 1, dealing with the officers in charge of conscription and their functions, and Article 2, dealing with supervision of the conscription system, are omitted.

7. Those who are the heir, or the appointed heir, of a grandfather.

8. Those who are the only child or the only grandchild.

10. Those whose father and elder brother may still be living but are incapacitated, and thus are assuming the responsibility for the household.

11. Those who are adopted to become the legitimate heir. However, this provision is not applicable to those who are still at the homes of their natural parents.

12. Those who have a brother currently serving in the standing army.

ARTICLE 6. Regulations.[16]

15. At the year when his turn for the conscription comes, the eligible young man may be exempt from service in the standing army and in the reserve troops by remitting a sum of two hundred and seventy yen as a substitutionary fee. Such substitutionary fees are to be submitted to the head of the lesser district (*ku*), transmitted to the offices of special cities or prefectures, and then remitted to the Ministry of Army headquarters during the month of May.

9 Land Tax Reform Regulations, 1873[17]

1. The land tax reform which is to be promulgated is not an easy task, and a thorough investigation based on a careful review of the tax potential is required. Some lands can be readily and easily classified while others can only be slowly and painstakingly classified. It is therefore not necessary to implement the reform simultaneously in all the regions. Nor is it necessary to work toward a quick success of the reform. The old tax law can be abrogated and the new law implemented only after permission is given by the Ministry of Finance. Such permission is granted on the basis of an application which indicates that a firm estimate on the detailed classification of the lands is possible. Addendum: When the classification in a given region is not completed, the law may be put into effect in a single district (*gun*) or lesser district (*ku*) where the investigation is completed.

2. When the land tax reform is implemented, a tax shall be levied on the basis of land value, and there shall be no additional tax levied in the year of good harvest, or a reduction in the tax in the year of crop failures.

3. In the event of natural disasters which cause changes in the land, tax immunity may be granted for the year, or for a period of years until the land can be returned to cultivation. Such immunity may be granted after an on-the-spot inspection.

4. After the implementation of the land tax, the distinction between paddy fields and dry fields (or gardens) shall be discarded, and all shall be designated as arable land. All other lands shall be classified as pasture, forest or wasteland, depending on the use accorded them.

---

[16]Article 4 on physical examinations, and Article 5 on written examinations and methods of drawing the lot, are omitted.

[17]Ōkubo, *op. cit.*, p. 93.

5. Where the land is used for residential purposes, it may continue to be called residential land.

6. Previously the land tax included commodity and house taxes. With the implementation of the land tax reform, such taxes must be clearly differentiated. The land tax may eventually be fixed at one percent of land value. However, since no separate commodity or other taxes are established the land tax at present is to be determined at three percent of land value. Hereafter, with the introduction of taxes on tea, tobacco, lumber and other commodities, and when revenue for this source exceeds two million yen, a proportionate reduction in the land tax is to be effected which is to be confined to those areas in which the land tax reform is already implemented. The land tax may be reduced gradually and finally reach one percent.

7. Until the land tax reform is implemented, the old laws shall continue to govern. No grievances concerning heavy tax impositions, under the old laws, except in extreme cases, may be given hearings. However, those fields which have been subjected to preharvest inspection (*kemi*) and whose taxes have been fixed on the basis of average yields of the fields irrespective of the actual amount of harvest in a given year (*jōmen*), may be granted a tax immunity (*hamen*) after a petition for relief is submitted in accordance with the old established custom [of the Tokugawa period].

10 Ōkubo Toshimichi's Opinion on Encouragement of Industries, 1874[18]

Generally speaking, the strength or weakness of a country is dependent on the wealth or poverty of its people, and the people's wealth or poverty derives from the amount of available products. The diligence of the people is a major factor in determining the amount of products available, but in the final analysis, it can all be traced to the guidance and encouragement given by the government and its officials. . . .

We have come to a point where all the internal conflicts have ceased, and the people can now enjoy peace and can securely engage in their respective callings. This is the most opportune time for the government and its officials to adopt a protective policy which has as its goal the enhancement of people's livelihood. . . .

Anyone who is responsible for a nation or its people must give careful consideration to the matters which can enhance the livelihood of the people, including the benefits to be gained from industrial production and the convenience derived from maritime and land transportation. He must set up a system suitable to the country's natural features and convention, taking into account the characteristics and intelligence of its people. Once that system is established it must be made the pivot of the

---

[18]*Ōkubo Toshimichi Monjo (Ōkubo Toshimichi Documents)*, Vol. 5, in *Nihon Shiseki Kyōkai Sōsho (Japanese Historical Document Society Series)*, Vol. 32 (Tokyo: Tokyo University Press, reissue, 1968), pp. 561–566.

country's administrative policies. Those industries which are already developed must be preserved, and those which are not in existence must be brought into being.

An example can be found in England which is a very small country. However, she is an island nation and has excellent harbors. She is also richly endowed with mineral resources. Her government and its officials have considered it the greatest fulfillment of their duties when they have made full use of their natural advantages, and have brought about maximum [industrial] development. In this endeavor the Queen and her subjects have put together their ingenuity and created an unprecedented maritime law in order to monopolize the maritime transportation of the world and to enhance her national industries. . . .

In this way her industries have prospered, and there has always been a surplus after providing the necessary commodities to her people. . . .

It is true that time, location, natural features and convention are not the same for each country, and one must not always be dazzled by the accomplishments of England and seek to imitate her ability. . . .

However, our topography and natural conditions show similarities to those of England. What differs most is the feebleness in the temperament of our people. It is the responsibility of those who are in the administrative positions in the government to guide and importune those who are weak in spirit to work diligently in the industries and to endure them. Your subject respectfully recommends that a clear-cut plan be established to find the natural advantages we enjoy, to measure the amount by which production can be increased, and to determine the priorities under which industries may be encouraged [e.g., subsidized]. It is further recommended that the characteristics of our people and the degree of their intelligence may be taken into account in establishing legislation aimed at encouraging development of industries. Let there not be a person who is derelict in performing his work. Let there not be a fear of anyone unable to have his occupation. If these goals can be attained the people can reach a position of adequate wealth. If the people are adequately wealthy, it follows naturally that the country will become strong and wealthy. . . . If so, it will not be difficult for us to compete effectively against major powers. This has always been your subject's sincere desire. He is even more convinced of the necessity of its implementation today, and is therefore submitting humbly his recommendations for Your Majesty's august decision.

11 **An Opinion on Education, 1872**[19] As your subject reflects on the matter of education, he discovers that behind the wealth, power, security and well-being of a nation there lies invariably an advance in the talents of a civilized people. Therefore it is necessary to build schools and establish educational meth-

---

[19]An opinion by Ōki Takatō, Ōkubo, *op. cit.*, pp. 97–98.

ods which enable us to attain similar goals. It is recommended that educational laws and regulations be uniformly established to eliminate useless miscellaneous studies. In their place there shall be created an educational system consisting of universities, middle schools and primary schools, and a trend toward the development of arts shall be introduced. To attain these goals, we shall adopt the best educational law in the world, and take into account the facilities available in and out of the country. The country shall be divided into seven or eight educational regions which will be formulated on the basis of population and land area. In each of these regions, there shall be a university, and a number of middle schools and grade schools. Furthermore there shall be established a detailed system of inspection to make it certain that the standards will not be violated. As to the admission, the wealthy and the poor shall be differentiated, and there shall be no indiscriminate acceptance of pupils and students. As to the order of implementation, all the existing educational systems shall be abolished, and a new law and regulations be established. New textbooks shall be issued, and new educational materials be supplied. The method of teaching as well as the regulations governing those who receive instruction shall be newly formulated. Once the above described regulations come into effect, even village schools and private schools shall be governed by their provisions. Detailed recommendations will be submitted at a later date. . . .

February 12, 1872

Minister of Education, Ōki Takatō

THE IWAKURA MISSION AND REJECTION OF SEIKANRON

The Iwakura mission that visited the United States and Europe in 1871–1873, in retrospect, was one of the most significant governmental undertakings. It exposed some of the most important leaders of the new government to the progress enjoyed in the Western countries. It thus inculcated in their minds the necessity for Japan to modernize. The letter of Emperor Meiji to President Grant shows the firm resolve of the Japanese people "to stand upon a similar footing with the most enlightened nations" (Document 12). Members of the mission were perceptive observers. For example, Ambassador Iwakura Tomomi (1825–1883) wrote home suggesting the advantage of utilizing American methods instead of European ones in the building of railways in Japan. The welcome given by the American public so overwhelmed the mission that its members thought that the time was ripe for beginning a negotiation for revising the existing unequal treaties. On this they did not succeed, but the quest for equitable treaty revision would continue to be one of the major problems for early Meiji Japan.

The knowledge of the West gained through the mission was also instrumental in enabling the mission members to reject a grandiose scheme of foreign expansion, as advocated by Saigō Takamori and his followers. Ōkubo Toshimichi articulated his objection to the Korean expedition in Document 13.

12 Emperor Meiji's Letter to President Grant on Iwakura Mission, 1871[20]

Mutsuhito, Emperor of Japan, etc., to the President of the United States of America, our good brother and faithful friend, greeting:

Mr. President: Whereas since our accession by the blessing of heaven to the sacred throne on which our ancestors reigned from time immemorial, we have not dispatched any embassy to the Courts and Governments of friendly countries. We have thought fit to select our trusted and honored minister, Iwakura Tomomi, the Junior Prime Minister (*udaijin*), as Ambassador Extraordinary and have associated with him Kido Takayoshi, member of the Privy Council; Ōkubo Toshimichi, Minister of Finance; Itō Hirobumi, Acting Minister of Public Works; and Yamaguchi Masanao, Assistant Minister for Foreign Affairs as Associate Ambassadors Extraordinary, and invested them with full powers to proceed to the Government of the United States, as well as to other Governments, in order to declare our cordial friendship, and to place the peaceful relations between our respective nations on a firmer and broader basis. The period for revising the treaties now existing between ourselves and the United States is less than one year distant. We expect and intend to reform and improve the same so as to stand upon a similar footing with the most enlightened nations, and to attain the full development of public rights and interest. The civilization and institutions of Japan are so different from those of other countries that we cannot expect to reach the declared end at once. It is our purpose to select from the various institutions prevailing among enlightened nations such as are best suited to our present conditions, and adapt them in gradual reforms and improvements of our policy and customs so as to be upon an equality with them. With this object we desire to fully disclose to the United States Government the condition of affairs in our Empire, and to consult upon the means of giving greater efficiency to our institutions at present and in the future, and as soon as the said Embassy returns home we will consider the revision of the treaties and accomplish what we have expected and intended. The Ministers who compose this Embassy have our confidence and esteem. We request you to favor them with full credence and due regard, and we earnestly pray for your continued health and happiness, and for the peace and prosperity of your great Republic.

In witness whereof we have hereunto set our hand and the great seal of our Empire, at our palace in the city of Tokyo, this fourth day of eleventh month, of fourth year of Meiji.

Your affectionate brother and friend,

Signed   Mutsuhito

Countersigned   Sanjō Sanetomi, Prime Minister

---

[20]Adopted from the official translation as reproduced in *The New York Times*, March 5, 1872.

13   Ōkubo Toshimichi's Opinion Against Korean Expedition, October

1873[21]   In order to govern the country and protect the people it is necessary to have a flexible policy and to watch [the world situation]; always watching the situation as we go forward or retreat. If the situation is bad we simply stop. The reasons *why I say that it is too early to send a mission to Korea are as follows:*

1. . . . The basis of our government is not yet firmly established. We have made remarkable progress in abolishing the *han*, etc., and if we look at the central part of Japan, everything seems accomplished, but if we look at the countryside, many people who oppose this will be seen. We have established a fortress and have good military equipment, so they dare not rise up against us. But if we reveal some weak point, they will be quick to take advantage. There is no special problem now, but we must look to the future. With the restoration many new laws have been promulgated, but people are not yet at ease and they fear our government. In the last two years there have been many misunderstandings and these led to uprisings. It is a truly difficult situation. This is one reason why I am opposed to making war on Korea.

2. Today government expenditures are tremendous, and income is below expense. Thus if we open fire and send several tens of thousands of men abroad we will incur enormous expense. This will require heavy taxes or foreign loans or the issuance of paper notes and will lead to higher prices, social unrest and uprisings. Already we have 5,000,000 [yen] in foreign loans; even this is difficult to pay.

3. Our government has started to stimulate industries, but it will be several years before we get results. . . . If we now begin an unnecessary war, spend a huge amount of money, shed blood, and worsen the daily life of people, all these government works will break like a bubble and lose several decades of time. We will regret it.

4. Regarding the foreign trade situation, each year there is a one million yen deficit . . . and our gold reserve decreases. Thus our international credit worsens, leading to inflation and our people's livelihood becoming hard. Also the export of our products faces difficulties. If we open fire without thinking of our economic and military power, our soldiers will have a bad time and their parents will be in difficulty; they will cease to work well and our national productivity will decrease. Such things as weapons must be purchased from foreign countries; our foreign trade deficit will become worse and worse.

5. In regard to the diplomatic situation, the most important countries for us are Russia and Britain. . . . Relations with them are uncertain. I fear that Russia will interfere unless we secure our independence. If we open fire on Korea,

---

[21]Hilary Conroy, *The Japanese Seizure of Korea: 1868–1910* (Philadelphia: University of Pennsylvania Press, 1960), pp. 47–49. The full text is in *Ōkubo Toshimichi Monjo*, Vol. 5, *op. cit.*, pp. 53–64.

Russia will fish out both the clam and the bird and get a fisherman's profit. Thus we should not begin a war in Korea now.

6. In regard to the Asian situation, Britain is especially powerful, watching with a tiger's eye. Our foreign loans depend on Britain. If there is trouble and we become poor, Britain will surely interfere in our internal affairs on that pretext. Look at India ... observe carefully the process by which India became a colony. We must build our industry, our exports, etc. It is our most urgent business.

7. The Japanese treaties with Europe and America are not equal. This is harmful for our independence. Therefore we must do our best to revise them, or England and France will send armies on the pretext of an insecure internal situation.... The first thing is to revise the treaties, the Korean business after that.

Conclusion. As I have said above we must not hurry to begin war. Of course, we cannot overlook the arrogant attitude of Korea, but we have no clear reason to attack Korea. Now it is argued, send the envoy and depending on his reception open fire or not. But we may be sure from experience that his reception will be cold, so this automatically means open fire. Thus we must decide about sending an army before we send the envoy. If there is war we must have more than 100,000 soldiers, laborers, ships, etc. It will cost many time 10,000 yen. Even though we are victorious, the expense will be far beyond the profit. Also after the victory there will be uprisings over there. Even though we get all kinds of goods in Korea, they will amount to less than the expense. Also it is said that neither China nor Russia will intervene, but there is no proof. It is said that we cannot endure Korean arrogance, but this is an insufficient reason and it would be very bad to open fire without thinking of our security and our people's welfare. Therefore I oppose....

POLITICAL EQUALITY AND PEOPLE'S RIGHTS

The search for political equality was conducted by former samurai of Tosa (Kōchi) and Hizen (Saga), who unlike their counterparts from Satsuma and Chōshū, were not first among equals in the Meiji oligarchy. They started the people's rights movement, which was supported by rich farmers and former samurai who sided with the Tokugawa bakufu. As a means of gaining power for themselves, and taking it away from their former colleagues in the Meiji oligarchy, the Tosa-Hizen group advocated some form of representative government. Itagaki Taisuke (1837–1919) of Tosa was among the signers of a memorial (Document 14) urging the establishment of a representative assembly. His "progressive stance" was enunciated in January 1874, shortly after his resignation from the government. Ōkuma Shigenobu (1838–1922) of Hizen, who intermittently was a member of the oligarchy and a progressive when ejected from power, wrote a well-reasoned opinion on the necessity of establishing represen-

tative government (Document 15). The document included a provision seeking the establishment of a British-type party government. Its content was hidden from his colleagues for three months, and precipitated another infighting within the oligarchy. In the end Itō Hirobumi outmaneuvered Ōkuma, forcing the latter again to resign from his post. This incident, known as the crisis of 1881, had a serious repercussion on the making of the constitution. Those liberal thinkers, who were detested by Itō Hirobumi, are represented by Nakae Chōmin in Document 16. Nakae studied in France and was deeply influenced by Jean Jacques Rousseau's liberalism and Auguste Comte's positivism. His translation of Rousseau's Contrat Social *was widely read, and profoundly influenced the leaders of the popular rights movement.*

14 Memorial on the Establishment of a Representative Assembly,

1874[22]   As your subjects humbly reflect upon the quarter in which the governing power lies, we discover that it does not lie with the Throne above, nor with the people below, but with the officials alone. This is not to suggest that the officials are disrespectful of the Throne, yet the Throne is gradually losing its prestige. Nor do we suggest that the officials fail to protect people, yet the manifold decrees of the government appear in the morning only to be changed in the evening. The administration is conducted in an arbitrary manner, rewards and punishments are meted out with partiality, the channel of communication is blocked, and people have no way of stating their grievances. How can the country be governed peacefully in this manner? Even an infant knows that it is impossible. We fear, if the evil practices are not altered, they may bring about the ruin of the nation. Unable to restrain the promptings of our patriotic feelings, we have sought a way to rescue our nation from this danger, and have found that it consists in the promotion of public discussion of issues in the empire. The only means of promoting public discussion is to establish a representative assembly elected by the people. In this way a limit will be placed on the power of the officials, and those who are above and below will obtain peace and happiness. We therefore beg your indulgence in allowing us to express our opinion on this matter.

The people who have the duty to pay taxes to the government concurrently possess the rights to be informed of the affairs of the government and to approve or reject such governmental matters. This is the principle universally accepted in the world, which requires no further elaboration on our part. We therefore humbly request that the officials do not resist this great truth. Those who now oppose the establishment of a popularly-elected representative assembly assert: "Our

[22]Ōkubo, *op. cit.,* pp. 145–147. For a full text in English translation, see W. W. McLaren, *op. cit.,* part 2, pp. 26–33. Those who signed this memorial were Soejima Taneomi (samurai of Saga), Gotō Shōjirō (Tokyo), Itagaki Taisuke (Kōchi), Etō Shimpei (Saga), Yuri Kimimasa (Tsuruga), Komuro Nobuo (Kyoto), Okamoto Kensaburō (Kōchi), and Furusawa Urō (Kōchi). The date of submission was January 17, 1874.

people lack knowledge and intelligence and have not yet reached the plateau of enlightenment. It is too early yet to have a popularly-elected representative assembly." If what they say is true, then the way to give our people knowledge and intelligence and to lead them expeditiously into the plateau of enlightenment is to establish a popularly-elected representative assembly. This is so because to give our people knowledge and intelligence and to lead them into the plateau of enlightenment, they must in the first place be made aware of the truths commonly accepted in the world and learn how to protect their rights. They must respect and value themselves, and be inspired by the spirit of sharing with the state its joys and tribulations. Such an end can only be accomplished by giving them a voice in the affairs of the state. . . . The worst argument put forth by those who are opposed to the immediate establishment of a representative assembly is that such an assembly could be convened simply by gathering all the fools in the country. How arrogant is this argument! How contemptible are they toward the people! No doubt there are among officials men who surpass others in intelligence and skills, but how can they be certain if the society does not contain men who surpass them in learning and knowledge? Therefore, the people of our country cannot be treated with such contempt. If the officials continue to think that the people deserve such contempt, one must not forget that they themselves are part of the people. In such a case we must assume that the officials are equally lacking in learning and knowledge. Between the arbitrary decisions of a few officials and the opinion of the people arrived at through public discussion, where can one find wisdom or stupidity? . . .

It is our understanding that under the pretense of being cautious, the present officials perpetuate the old evil customs and look upon those who advocate reforms as "rash progressives." They deny reforms with the two words "too early." We now wish to discuss this matter.

First of all, we do not comprehend the phrase "rash progressives." If by rash progression is meant initiation of measures carelessly, that fear can be alleviated by the careful deliberation of a popularly elected representative assembly. If by rash progression is meant the lack of harmony between different ministries, loss of perspectives with regard to priorities, and inability to coordinate works of different institutions, then again the establishment of a popularly-elected representative assembly will be desirable. This is so because the above-cited difficulties are caused by the want of a fixed law in this country, and by the capricious actions of the officials which can only be eliminated by a popularly-elected representative assembly. Progress is the most beautiful thing in the world, and everything must move forward. Therefore the officials cannot condemn the word "progress." It follows that their condemnation must be intended for the word "rash," but the word "rash" has no place in our conception of a popularly-elected representative assembly. . . .

Another argument advanced by the officials is that the parliaments now existing in Europe and America were not formed in a day, but were brought to their present status by gradual progress, [therefore they cannot be transplanted to Japan overnight]. However, gradual progress has not been the case with parliaments only. All branches of knowledge, technology and machines are subject to the same gradual development. It took the foreigners to bring them to the present status after several hundred years, because no examples existed previously and those had to be discovered through experience or through invention. If we can select examples from these foreign inventions, we can be assured of our success. Must we delay the using of steam engines until we have discovered the principles of steam ourselves, or must we wait to construct our telegraph lines until we have discovered the principles of electricity ourselves? If we work on that assumption, our government will be able to do nothing at all.

We have presented our case for the immediate establishment of a popularly-elected representative assembly, and argued also that the degree of progress among the people of our country is sufficient for the establishment of such an assembly. We have done so, not to prevent the officials from speaking against its establishment. We are, however, actuated by the desire that through the establishment of such an assembly, public discussion in our country may be developed, the truths commonly accepted in the world and the rights of the people may be respected, and l'esprit de corps prevailing in our country may be enhanced. In this way, the high and the low shall come closer to one another; the sovereign and his people shall learn to love one another; our imperial country shall be sustained and further developed; and happiness and peace shall be assured to all. With supplication, we seek your adoption of our recommendations.

15 Ōkuma Shigenobu's Memorial on a National Deliberative Assembly, 1881[23]

As your subject humbly reflects on the questions of government, he discovers that when the root is secure the branches and leaves prosper and when a general outline is established detailed plans follow. In today's politics, there must be a root and a general outline. In the council deliberations we agreed on the establishment of a national deliberative assembly, which was confirmed in the edict of 1875. Therefore your subject wishes to follow through [this general policy outline] by submitting his opinion. There is no greater joy than in having them receive Your Majesty's consideration and acceptance.

Your subject, Shigenobu, with trepidation submits the following recommendations:

1. That the date of the opening of a national deliberative assembly be publicly announced. . . .

---

[23]Text in Rōyama Masamichi, *Gendai Nihon Bummei Shi (A History of Modern Japanese Civilization)*, Vol. 2, *Seijishi (Political History)*, pp. 117–185. See George Beckmann, *The Making of the Meiji Constitution* (Lawrence: University Press of Kansas, 1957), pp. 136–142, for a full translation.

2. That the wishes of the people be taken into account in the appointment of prominent ministers of the government.

. . . In a constitutional government, where can one find an expression of the wishes of the people? They can be found only in the national deliberative assembly. What are the wishes of the people? They are expressed in a majority vote of representatives in the assembly. Who is the one endowed with the support of the populace? He is none other than the leader of the majority party. . . .

When it becomes clear that a certain party has gained a majority in the assembly, it is for your sacred majesty to call upon the leader of that party personally, and command him to form a cabinet. After receiving such a command, the leader can place other leading figures in his party in important ministries, and thereafter officially formulate a cabinet. Normally, a cabinet must be headed by the leader of a political party, but on certain occasions others in the party may be appointed to that post. However, in no event can an administrative official [without party affiliations] be appointed to that post. . . .

3. That there be a distinction between offices that can be filled by members of political parties and offices that can only be filled by career men. . . .

. . . In general, the offices that can be filled by members of political parties are: Councillors, Ministers, Vice Ministers, Chiefs of the Bureaus, lecturers in the Imperial Household, and the Grand Chamberlain. Those who fill these positions are generally selected from members of the upper and lower houses. (In general, the examples of England may be followed. . . .)

Those offices to be filled by career men are positions in the ministries with the exception of the Minister, Vice Minister, and Bureau Chiefs. They comprise officers who are appointed with the Emperor's approval (*sōnin* rank) and other subordinate officials. . . .

4. That a constitution be promulgated at the Emperor's discretion. . . .

5. That representatives be elected at the end of 1882, and that the national deliberative assembly be convoked at the beginning of 1883.

6. That policies be determined.

There are several reasons for the formation of a political party. However, in most instances those who have similar political views join together to form a political party. The success or failure of a political party depends on the acceptance or rejection of its political views by the populace. Each of the political parties can attack one another based on their respective political views to gain popular support. Thus struggles between political parties are essentially struggles between divergent political views, and the victory or defeat ultimately determines which political views must be followed. Therefore once the date for the opening of the national deliberative assembly is announced, it is urgently requested that the present cabinet determine its policies [and make them public]. On this matter, your subject Shigenobu has other opinions as well, which will be submitted for Your Majesty's consideration at a later date. . . .

16   The Awakening of Common Men, 1887[24]   A certain merchant came
to see Mr. Nakae the other day. After talking about many things, he inquired of
Mr. Nakae: "Sir, I understand that the Imperial Diet will be convoked in
1890. But what is this Diet, and what are its purposes? Please tell me."

"Well," answered Mr. Nakae, "before we discuss the Imperial Diet, we have
to consider how governments are established. There are several types of government, and they differ from one country to another. However, in general, they can
be divided into two categories, one is autocratic government and another is
representative government. Autocratic government is a government which is
ruled by the fiat of those who are in the positions of authority. Under this type of
government, important officials, such as the premier or other ministers, consult
with the monarch, decide on all matters, and issue edicts without taking into
consideration the desires of common people.... Assuming that officials are
normally just, and not given to self-serving ends, it remains that autocratic government is not a desirable one. This is so because officials are human beings like
us.... In addition, in most autocratic countries, hereditary rules call for the
children of officials to become officials, and the children of peasants and merchants to remain peasants and merchants. No matter how dumb a child may be, if
he is born as son of an official, he can become an official. Meanwhile, no matter
how bright a child may be, if he is born as son of a peasant or a merchant, he has
no other choice but to remain a peasant or a merchant. Under this kind of
condition, peasants and merchants become gradually obsequious to the officials,
and when meeting the latter, begin to feel that the officials are somehow a
different breed of people. 'Oh, they are officials, how can we ever emulate
them.' How shameful it is for them to feel this way!

". . . [After the Restoration,] we still maintain a distinction between the
samurai class and the common people. However, the distinction is only nominal,
and there are no other social classes or differentiations. If a samurai is dumb, he
has to pull a cart, and theoretically a common man who is endowed with wisdom
and learning can even become a prime minister. However, our country is still
bound by the legacy of respecting the lineage of a man. Thus the samurai class
tends to be overbearing, and the common people retain their servile attitudes.
This is a very undesirable situation.

"When 1890 comes, and the Imperial Diet is convoked, there will be no
differentiation made between the samurai and common people with regards to
the right of casting the ballot or of being elected. Don't you think you should
realize the implication of this, and start reading some translated works during
your spare time. Bear in mind that it is your responsibility to become well-in-

---

[24]Nakae Chōmin, *Heimin no Mezamashi (The Awakening of Common Men)* in *Meiji
Bunka Zenshū (A Series on Meiji Civilization)*, Vol. 7, *Seijihen (Political Science)* (Tokyo:
Nihon Hyōrōnsha, 1929), pp. 412–415.

formed on political matters, not only by reading newspapers but also by hearing speeches.

"In contrast to an autocratic government, a representative government gives the people self-rule and freedom, and the government cannot arbitrarily enforce its decrees. People elect those whom they can trust as their representatives. The Diet consists of those representatives and watches over the actions of the government. In effect, it is the same as the people themselves watching over the government. Whenever a new law or a new tax is enacted, and that fact is announced, the people will know that it is made by themselves, and will not be angered by its enactment. It is not the same as being told by the officials to do this and thus. . . . Even though an autocratic government may still conduct itself benevolently, it is still a disgrace to the people. It shows that people are fools so that they have to defer everything to those who are above them. Under a representative government, some laws injurious to the people may still be enacted, but no one is to be ashamed of that fact. This is so because these laws are made by people's elected representatives, and the people themselves are the ones who are making the mistakes. . . .

"In the Western countries, those people who can be trusted are elected to serve in their National Diets. . . . A Diet is a place where the elected representatives investigate the reasons for enacting a particular law or levying a new tax, and give their collective judgment on the desirability or adequacy of a given measure. They deliberate on state matters and create a safeguard to insure that no official can do wrong. In short, the National Diet is an organ which watches over officials in the government on behalf of the people. We call those who are elected to the Diet, 'attorneys' (*myodainin*) or 'representatives' (*daigishi*), because they represent the interests of the people when they deliberate on state matters. If the government, i.e., the Cabinet, does things which do not meet the approval of the Diet, the representatives can institute actions to change the Cabinet. . . . If a cabinet minister has committed irregularities or questionable activities, any member of the Diet may submit in writing his allegations to the Cabinet requesting that the offending minister be called in for questioning by the Diet. Unless the minister in question can successfully defend his position, he must submit his resignation. This is called the right of interpellation. There are other rights enjoyed by members of the Diet. For example, if the Diet wishes to present its views to the throne, it may take steps to do so. If the Diet desires to enact a new law, it may draft bills for deliberation by its members. These are called the rights to present addresses to the Emperor and to draft and introduce bills.

"I have given you general ideas about the Diet. You seem to entertain a notion that the Cabinet ministries are the masters, and the Diet the subjects. On the contrary, the Diet is the master, and the cabinet ministries are the subjects. All the important matters pertaining to politics must be deliberated and receive the consent of the Diet. Politics may sound like a very complicated business. But the fact is that politics affect all of us, and we must consult each other. We cannot attend to all of our business, and it becomes necessary to entrust part of the responsibilities to the officials. In fact, government is very much like our employees, and we the people are the employers. In order to prevent the employees from acting unjustly and creating situations which are irretrievable, we are asking our representatives to watch over the conduct of the government. You people are not aware of this, and in dealing with the officials always treat them with undue deference. You are so filled with awe in their presence that you can hardly speak to them. How silly can one be? It is just like an employer fearing his clerk."

CONSTITUTION IN THE MAKING

The political crisis of 1881, which saw the resignation of Ōkuma Shigenobu, made it possible for Itō Hirobumi to obtain solid support for his gradualist approach to the drafting of the constitution. While generally mindful of the necessity for placing the Imperial Household on a firm foundation, Itō did not neglect the aspect of sharing power with the people and of maintaining harmony between the government and the people. This attitude is made abundantly clear in his memorial, which is reproduced as Document 17, written before the appearance of Ōkuma's memorial, and with which Ōkuma erroneously thought that he had much in common.

While on a mission to Europe to study European constitutions, Itō became convinced that the German state with Kaiser at the helm provided the best example for Japan to emulate. He also felt that there were certain prerogatives of the Emperor, such as the selection of cabinet ministers, which must not be controlled by the parliament. A provision in the Prussian Constitution that permitted the taxes of the previous year to remain in force was eagerly accepted by Itō as of ensuring and enhancing administrative power of the government. These views were articulated by Itō's capable subordinate Inoue Kowashi (1844–1895). They were, however, issued in the name of Iwakura Tomomi, and part of which is reproduced as Document 18.

After the constitution was promulgated, Itō wrote for posterity a commentary on the Meiji constitution that gives his views succinctly. Here excerpts from the section dealing with the Emperor are given in Document 19. It was translated by Itō Miyoji (1857–1934), who collaborated with Itō Hirobumi in the writing of the constitution, and spent his later life as a self-appointed "watch dog" of the Meiji constitution.

The Meiji constitution was, at times, regarded as an absolutist document in part due to its abuse during the thirties. However, we must not forget that it also provided a means for establishing a popularly elected Diet, which was the first of its kind east of the Suez. As such it also laid the foundation for increasing popular participation and for the coming of Taishō democracy.

17 Itō Hirobumi's Memorial on Constitutional Government,

1880[25] I, Hirobumi, am most concerned and fearful to take this opportunity to express my views. Occupying an important post in government, I feel deeply that the times are critical. I, for one, am convinced that now is the time to make unprecedented reforms and that conditions are already ripe for them. However, we must not follow the increasing thoughtless opinions; at the same time, it will be difficult to maintain old practices unconditionally. In politics, it is best to adopt methods that fit changing circumstances. Unless we take suitable measures and advance properly as well as gradually, how can we hope to lay the foundations for lasting peace?

We know now that the work of the Restoration has been nearly accomplished; yet the current situation may suddenly become a crisis. There are two reasons why we cannot safely be at ease. I will first discuss these reasons and then suggest suitable measures to adopt.

1. The government of the Restoration revised the old and established the new. One of these great changes was *haihan chiken* [abolition of the *han* and establishment of the prefectures, see Document 6]. The abolition of the *han* was inevitable. At the same time, the conscription system was established. As a result, the number of those samurai who were deprived of their stipends and lost their property amounted to several hundred thousand throughout the country. None of them was happy with the Restoration government and all of them longed for the old practices. They voiced their discontent and complained bitterly. In extreme cases, they were moved to rebel and resist the government, thus intensifying political crises. This is one of the causes of the current difficulties.

The samurai had ranked higher than commoners in feudal days. Previously, they received regular stipends, had property, and were well educated. They used to take upon themselves responsibilities for state affairs; and thus today, they take pleasure in political debates. It is from among the former samurai that most of the men of spirit and argument have come. The commoners readily follow the ex-samurai. To take the human body as an analogy, the ex-samurai are the muscles and bones and the commoners are the flesh and skin. When the muscles and bones move, the flesh and skin follow. When the ex-samurai organize the various sources of discontent, they alienate the people from the government and stand in the way of the benevolent influence of the Emperor. Today, the attitude of the ex-samurai is not good for the imperial family, and a source of trouble for the whole nation is often concealed in it.

2. It is easy to control the popular sentiments of a single village, but it is

---

[25]Reproduced by permission from George M. Beckmann, *The Making of the Meiji Constitution* (Lawrence: University Press of Kansas, 1957), pp. 131–135. For the Japanese text, see Kaneko Kentarō, ed., *Itō Hirobuni den (Life of Itō Hirobuni)*, Vol. 2 (Tokyo: Tōseisha, 1940), pp. 192–200.

difficult to control the public opinion of an entire nation. Moreover, it is easy to change the conditions of a country, but it is difficult to alter worldwide trends. Today, conditions in Japan are closely related to the world situation. They are not merely the affairs of a nation or province. The European concepts of revolution, which were carried out for the first time in France about one hundred years ago, have gradually spread to various nations. By combining and complementing each other, they have become a general trend. Sooner or later, every nation will undergo changes as a result.

In this period of changes from old to new, revolution often broke out. In fact, revolution continues at present. It has not yet stopped. Elsewhere enlightened rulers, with the help of wise ministers, led and controlled these changes, thus solidifying their nations. In brief, all have had to discard absolutist ways and share political power with the people.

Now, European ideas and things are coming into our country like a tidal flow; moreover, new opinions concerning the form of government have become popular among the ex-samurai. Within a few years' time, these ideas have spread into the towns and countryside, and this trend cannot be halted immediately. Thus, there are persons who surprise the public by voicing misleading views. Their thoughtless, disorderly acts pay no attention to the considerations of the Emperor. They groan although they are not sick, and their violent acts have evil effects upon others. However, if we take a general view of causes, it appears that this experience is common to the whole world. Like the rain falling and the grass growing, it is no wonder that we, too, have been affected.

These above two factors are what the trends of the time have brought about, and human efforts cannot control them. At present, it is the responsibility of the government to follow a conciliatory policy and accommodate itself to these tendencies so that we may control but not intensify the situation, and relax our hold over government but not yield it. We must follow the path of orderly progress and take our time in order to reach proper standards. Should we not consider the following plan carefully?

A. I ask that we enlarge the *Genrōin* (i.e., Council of Elders, or Senate) and select its members from among the nobles and ex-samurai (*ka-shizoku*).

I say that we should not establish a parliament hastily. This does not mean that we [the ruling group] want to remain at the helm of state and occupy the highest posts as long as possible. Although it is very desirable to establish limited monarchy by convoking a parliament, we must not do anything that would seriously modify our national polity [the Emperor system]. We should first make the footings firm, then erect the foundation posts, and finally raise the house. This must be done in an orderly fashion. Needless to say, the above is clearly known to the intelligent mind of the Emperor.

The constitutional nations of Europe have the upper and lower houses, like the two wheels of a cart, that complement each other and are in balance. In the monarchial nations, the *Genrōin* or upper house is essential to maintain the nation. In the various nations of Europe, the members of the upper house are selected from mature statesmen, men of merit, and erudite scholars. Moreover, in monarchial nations, they are selected largely from the nobility and they protect the royal family and maintain old practices.

I think that if we now wish to carry out changes according to some gradual program and wish to enact reforms progressively, we first should enlarge the *Genrōin* and have it actually conform to its name. If we wish to make the *Genrōin* conform to its name, we should select its members from the nobles and ex-samurai (*ka-shizoku*). The *Genrōin* was established in 1875, actually the result of the Emperor's intention to advance gradually toward constitutional government. . . . Now is the time to enlarge it and extend its functions, and make it live up to its name. At present, viewing the quality of our people, we find that the ex-samurai are the only ones who can manage national affairs and who are the most enlightened. Thus, the ex-samurai must be considered as one part of the nobility, though actually they rank just below the nobles. The members of the *Genrōin* should be selected from among the nobles and ex-samurai as well as from among those persons who are eminent for their services to the country or for their scholarship. There should be one hundred members of the *Genrōin* and each member should be paid. We should convene the *Genrōin* each year for a definite length of time. If the drafts of all laws are submitted for discussion to the *Genrōin*, the following results will be obtained:

(1) We can employ ex-samurai in posts of honor, thereby enabling them to function through many ages as guardians of the imperial family.

(2) We can provide a ground on which equilibrium will be maintained between the two houses of parliament in the future.

(3) Through the *Genrōin*, we can establish and maintain harmony between the government and the people.

(4) Thus, we can continue the fine results of the past eight years, and following the plans of our forerunners, we will tread the path of gradual progress.

B. I ask that we establish an extra Board of Auditors.

I think that in addition to broadening public opinion by selecting *Genrōin* members from among the nobles and ex-samurai, we should select members of the prefectural assemblies to fill positions as extra auditor-representatives who will discuss finance publicly. This will be the initial step toward constitutional government. It is observed in every country that some people despise their government and its officials because they suspect that a great deal of money raised by heavy taxation is spent wastefully. So it is considered to be most important in all constitutional states to permit the people to participate in the management of national finance.

Since the Restoration, our country has spent a vast amount of money not only because of the expenses incurred from the many years of abuses under the Tokugawa regime, but because of successive wars, disturbances, and frequent diplomatic emergencies. However, we have raised an army and navy, reformed the law codes, extended education, made the police more efficient, constructed prisons, begun railroads and the telegraph, and opened new roads—all of which are of benefit to the people. We have used the whole strength of the nation on things for public welfare and utility. On the other hand, we have revised the land tax and enriched the farmers and encouraged various industries through loans. Everything that we have done has been at the expense of the upper classes and for the benefit of the lower classes. That is why the national treasury has been nearly exhausted during these ten years.

However, the government's finances have always been managed honestly. Nothing suspicious or dishonest was done. . . . People who do not know the facts make accusations against the authorities, and what is worse make up rumors to slander them. In the government, there is little knowledge of this talk. But the government can show the public what is has done and make the people understand how correctly it has managed the national finances.

At present, an extra Board of Auditors should be established with its members selected from among the members of prefectural assemblies. . . . Together with the regular auditors, they should engage in business of auditing finances. However, their power should be limited only to auditing, and they should not be permitted to interfere in general fiscal policies. By this method, for one thing, we can pave the way for public discussion of finance and, second, we can acquaint the people with the actual state of affairs and give them experience.

If these two proposals are carried out, we may expect that there will inevitably be some limitations on the administrative power compared with previous days. However, this will be an important responsibility for your ministers. When we develop methods of government improperly, public agitation will increase and friction will be intensified. We do not know if our mistakes will cause any disturbances. We must exercise the greatest caution. The organization, limits of power, and the method of selecting members of these bodies are the keys to tranquility. The ministers of state must not treat these matters lightly. The authority of deciding and carrying out these plans belongs only to the Emperor.

C. I ask that Your Majesty declare the goals of the nation.

If we do not decide the goals of the nation, what will stop popular sentiments from drifting? At present, there are persons who are stirring up the disorderly elements in town and country in the name of public opinion. If we fail to check such public sentiment by clearly revealing the will of the Emperor, based on some firm proposal, the people will unite to make disturbances, rising here and there like rivers overflowing their banks. Once violence bursts out like this, I fear that in the end an adjustment cannot be made. The orders of previous governments proclaimed only fundamental principles and did not give details. The uninformed would say that they did not carry out what they promised. Resentful persons would distort the Charter Oath and the Imperial Rescript of 1875 in support of their views. This is why the government should inform the people of its intentions and make them aware of actual conditions. If we wish to promote

the government plans of the past eight years and check headstrong public sentiments, I suggest the following:

Your Majesty should kindly make up his mind and show his utmost sincerity
by an imperial edict. I beg that you inform the people that the nation should
advance gradually, and make your plans clear to them. How to share the legislative power with the people is without a doubt a matter that comes under the
supreme power of the Emperor and which is beyond the right of discussion by
his humble subjects. Moreover, the timing of the decision is left to the discretion
of the Emperor, and the people are not permitted to make disturbances or put on
pressure.

The Emperor has issued a rescript gradually instituting constitutional government. It will reach fulfillment in a matter of years. In the meantime, the Emperor
will be in control of the matter, and I think that he holds himself most responsible. If an imperial rescript is issued explaining that this policy is just, those
persons who are loyal to the imperial family will be reminded of the direction in
which they should turn their sentiments. On the other hand, unenlightened people will avoid being led astray to acts of violence. These are the most ardent
desires of this humble servant of Your Majesty. . . .

18 Iwakura Tomomi's Opinion on Constitutional Government, 1881[26]

If we wish to make the selection of cabinet ministers the prerogative of
the Emperor and not be controlled by parliament, we should rely on the following three provisions:

a. There shall be a clear statement in the constitution that the Emperor has the
responsibility to select the ministers and officials of *chokunin* rank. He shall
appoint and dismiss them. When there is such a provision, actually he will
appoint persons to the post of minister who have popular support and dismiss
those who lack it. Thus, because the power of appointment and dismissal belongs
to the Emperor, the ministers depend upon the favor of the Emperor and the trust
of the nation, and they are not controlled by the opinions of the people. They
make up their minds and adopt a fixed course. Even though they obtain only a
minority vote in parliament on two or three legislative matters, the cabinet as a
whole remains intact and does not have to alter its policy. This is based on the
Prussian Constitution.

b. The constitution shall provide for the responsibilities of ministers, and
divide them into instances of collective responsibility and individual responsibility. The French Constitution of 1875 provides that ministers are collectively
responsible for the overall administration of the government and individually

---

[26]Second of his three opinions, which were actually written by Inoue Kowashi. Repro-
duced from Beckmann, *op. cit.*, pp. 146–147. The original is in Tada Kōmon, ed.,
Iwakura Kō Jikki (True Records of Lord Iwakura) (Tokyo: Hara Shobō, reissue, 1968),
Vol. 3, pp. 725–727.

responsible for their own office. If ministers are generally collectively responsible as in the example of England, whenever one minister makes a mistake and is censured by parliament, all the ministers have to resign from their posts. In this situation, the cabinet is easily attacked by parliament, and it becomes a battlefield of frequent changes. If, in theory, the mistake of a minister is the responsibility of all the ministers, the business of the administration should not be divided into separate jurisdictions and should be discussed by all the ministers. The responsibility of each will be lessened. In England, there is a system of collective responsibility, by which the cabinet ministers are regarded as a collective organ of a party and as one individual. To establish the organization of the administration by a division into ministries is not the same thing as uniting members of the legislature and forming them into a group.

c. Our constitution must copy one article of the Prussian Constitution. Article 109 of the Prussian Constitution says: "Taxes of the previous year shall remain in force." This means that if the government and parliament cannot agree on the annual budget, the budget of the previous year becomes effective. This provision is the most important element in the Prussian Constitution because it sustains administrative power. Unless this article is included, parliament may attack the cabinet and may only give minority support to its important bills. Moreover, if the cabinet relies on the protection of the Emperor and does not resign, parliament may reject tax bills to force the cabinet to adhere to its views. In this case, the national treasury will not be paid the necessary funds.

Because parliament has the power to reject taxes which are the lifeblood of the nation, party cabinets are formed according to the will of parliament in England, Belgium, and Italy. By this concession, the support of parliament is secured.

If we wish to form a cabinet with no regard for parliament on the model of Prussia, we must rely on the tax provisions of that country. If this is not the case, even though there is a provision whereby the Emperor dismisses and appoints ministers, it will not be effective. I believe that the above three items are necessary to maintain the principle of gradual development and to protect the happiness of the nation forever.

19 Commentaries on Constitutional Provisions Relating to the Emperor's Position, 1889[27]

Chapter 1. The Emperor

The Sacred Throne of Japan is inherited from Imperial Ancestors, and is to be bequeathed to posterity; in it resides the power to reign over and govern the State. . . .

---

[27]Itō Hirobumi, *Commentaries on the Constitution of The Empire of Japan*, tr. by Itō Miyoji (Tokyo: Chūo University Press, 1906), pp. 2–4, 6–10, 15–21.

ARTICLE I. *The Empire of Japan shall be reigned over and governed by a line of Emperors unbroken for ages eternal.*

Since the time when the first Imperial Ancestor opened it, the country has not been free from occasional checks in its prosperity nor from frequent disturbances of its tranquility; but the splendor of the Sacred Throne transmitted through an unbroken line of one and the same dynasty has always remained as immutable as that of the heavens and the earth. At the outset, this Article states the great principle of the Constitution of the country, and declares that the Empire of Japan shall, to the end of time, identify itself with the Imperial dynasty unbroken in lineage, and that the principle has never changed in the past, and will never change in the future, even to all eternity. It is intended thus to make clear forever the relations that shall exist between the Emperor and his subjects.

By "reigned over and governed" it meant that the Emperor on his Throne combines in himself the sovereignty of the State and the government of the country and of his subjects. An ancient record mentions a decree of the first Emperor in which he says:—"The Country of Goodly Grain is a state, over which Our descendants shall become Sovereigns: You, Our descendants, come and govern it." . . . It will thus be seen that the Imperial Ancestors regarded their Heaven-bestowed duties with great reverence. They have shown that the purpose of a monarchical government is to reign over the country and govern the people, and not to minister to the private wants of individuals or of families. Such is the fundamental basis of the present Constitution. . . .

ARTICLE III. *The Emperor is sacred and inviolable.*

"The Sacred Throne was established at the time when the heavens and the earth became separated" (*Kojiki*). The Emperor is Heaven-descended, divine and sacred; he is pre-eminent above all his subjects. He must be reverenced and is inviolable. He has indeed to pay due respect to the law, but the law has no power to hold Him accountable to it. Not only shall there be no irreverence for the Emperor's person, but also shall he neither be made a topic of derogatory comment nor one of discussion.

ARTICLE IV. *The Emperor is the head of the Empire, combining in himself the rights of sovereignty, and exercises them, according to the provisions of the present Constitution.*

The sovereign power of reigning over and of governing the State, is inherited by the Emperor from his Ancestors, and by him bequeathed to his posterity. All the different legislative as well as executive powers of State, by means of which he reigns over the country and governs the people, are united in this Most Exalted Personage, who thus holds in his hands, as it were, all the ramifying threads of the political life of the country, just as the brain, in the human body, is the primitive source of all mental activity manifested through the four limbs and the different parts of the body. For unity is just as necessary in the government of a State, as double-mindedness would be ruinous in an individual. His Imperial

Majesty has himself determined a Constitution, and has made it a fundamental law to be observed both by the Sovereign and by the people. He has further made it clear that every provision in the said Constitution shall be conformed to without failure or negligence. . . .

ARTICLE V. *The Emperor exercises the legislative power with the consent of the Imperial Diet.*

The legislative power belongs to the sovereign power of the Emperor; but this power shall always be exercised with the consent of the Diet. The Emperor will cause the Cabinet to make drafts of laws, or the Diet may initiate projects of laws; and after the concurrence of both Houses of the Diet has been obtained thereto, the Emperor will give them his sanction, and then such drafts or projects shall become law. Thus the Emperor is not only the center of the executive, but also the source and fountainhead of the legislative power. . . .

ARTICLE VIII. *The Emperor, in consequence of an urgent necessity to maintain public safety or to avert public calamities, issues, when the Imperial Diet is not sitting, Imperial Ordinances in the place of law. Such Imperial Ordinances are to be laid before the Imperial Diet at its next session, and when the Diet does not approve the said Ordinances, the Government shall declare them to be invalid for the future.*

. . . It will be seen that Article V, providing that the exercise of the legislative power requires the consent of the Diet, regards ordinary cases; while the provisions of the present Article, authorizing the issuing of Imperial Ordinances in the place of laws, refers to exceptional cases in times of emergency. This power mentioned in the present Article, is called the power of issuing "emergency Ordinances." Its legality is recognized by the Constitution, but at the same time abuse of it is strictly guarded against. Thus the Constitution limits the use of this power to the cases of urgent necessity for the maintenance of public safety and for the averting of public calamities, and prohibits its abuse on the ordinary plea of protecting the public interest and of promoting public welfare. Consequently, in issuing an emergency Ordinance, it shall be made the rule to declare that such Ordinance has been issued in accordance with the provisions of the present Article. For, should the Government make use of this power as a pretext for avoiding the public deliberation of the Diet or for destroying any existing law, the provisions of the Constitution would become dead letters having no significance whatever, and would be far from serving as a bulwark for the protection of the people. The right of control over this special power has, therefore, been given to the Diet by the present Article, making it necessary, after due examination thereof at a subsequent date, to obtain its approbation to an emergency Ordinance.

Of all the provisions of the Constitution, those of the present Article present the greatest number of doubtful points. These points will be cleared up one after the other, by presenting them in the form of questions and answers. . . . Sixthly:

When the Diet has refused its approbation, may it demand the retroactive annulment of the Imperial Ordinance in question? As the Sovereign is authorized by the Constitution to issue emergency Ordinances, in the place of law, it is a matter of course that such Ordinances should have effect as to the period of time they have been in existence. The refusal of approbation by the Diet is consequently to be regarded simply as its refusal to approve the future continued enforcement of the Ordinance as law, and such refusal cannot reach the past. Seventhly: Can the Diet amend such an Imperial Ordinance before giving its approbation to it? According to the express provisions of the present Article, there are only two alternatives open to the Diet: either to give or not to give its approbation; so that it has no power to amend such an Ordinance.

ARTICLE IX. *The Emperor issues or causes to be issued, the Ordinances necessary for the carrying out of the laws, or for the maintenance of the public peace and order, and for the promotion of the welfare of the subjects. But no Ordinance shall in any way alter any of the existing laws.*

The present Article treats of the sovereign power of the Emperor as to administrative ordinances. A law requires the consent of the Diet, while an ordinance holds good solely by decision of the Emperor. There are two occasions for the issuing of an ordinance: the first is, when it is required to regulate measures and details for the carrying out of any particular law; the second, when it is required to meet the necessity of maintaining the public peace and order and of promoting the welfare of the subjects. . . .

Emergency Ordinances mentioned in the preceding Article shall take effect within the limits of law, and although they can supply the deficiency of law, yet they shall have no power to either alter any law or to regulate those matters for which a law is required by express provision of the Constitution. . . .

ARTICLE XI. *The Emperor has the supreme command of the Army and Navy.*

. . . At the beginning of the great events that achieved the Restoration by the present August Sovereign, his Imperial Majesty issued an Ordinance, proclaiming that he assumed personal military command for the suppression of rebellion, thus manifesting that the sovereign power was centered in him. Since then, great reforms have been introduced into the military system. Innumerable evil customs, that had been long prevailing, were swept away. A General Staff Office has been established for his Imperial Majesty's personal and general direction of the Army and Navy. . . . The present Article is intended to show, that paramount authority in military and naval affairs is combined in the Most Exalted Personage as his sovereign power, and that those affairs are in subjection to the commands issued by the Emperor.

ARTICLE XII. *The Emperor determines the organization and peace standing of the Army and Navy.*

The present Article points out, that the organization and the peace standing of the Army and Navy are to be determined by the Emperor. It is true, that this power is to be exercised with the advice of responsible Ministers of State; still like the Imperial military command, it nevertheless belongs to the sovereign power of the Emperor, and no interference in it by the Diet should be allowed. The power of determining the organization of the Army and Navy, when minutely examined, embraces the organization of military divisions and of fleets, and all matters relating to military districts and sub-districts, to the storing up and distribution of arms, to the education of military and naval men, to inspections, to discipline, to modes of salutes, to styles of uniforms, to guards, to fortifications, to naval defenses, to naval ports and to preparations for military and naval expeditions. The determining of the peace standing includes also the fixing of the number of men to be recruited each year.

RESCRIPT ON EDUCATION

The imperial rescript on education was issued by Emperor Meiji on October 30, 1890. It was drafted by Motoda Eifu (1818–1891), a Confucian mentor to Emperor Meiji, and Inoue Kowashi (1844–1895) who also participated in the drafting of the constitution. Yamagata Aritomo also took an active part.

It incorporated the neo-Confucian moral precepts in the garb of modern nationalism, and attempted to make them the foundation of education. Children were taught to hark back to "the glory of the fundamental character of Our Empire," and to "render illustrious the best traditions of your forefathers." There was an unmistakable reaction to the rapid pace of Westernization, and a desire to return to the purity of "Japanism." It served to indoctrinate generations of school children, through periodic public readings of the rescript and through required memorization, but it was repudiated in 1948 by the second post-war Diet.

20 Imperial Rescript on Education, 1890[28]

Know ye, Our subjects:

Our Imperial Ancestors have founded Our Empire on a basis broad and everlasting, and have deeply and firmly implanted virtue; Our subjects ever united in loyalty and filial piety have from generation to generation illustrated the beauty thereof. This is the glory of the fundamental character of Our Empire, and herein also lies the source of Our education. Ye, Our subjects, be filial to your parents, affectionate to your brothers and sisters; as husbands and wives be harmonious, as friends true; bear yourselves in modesty and moderation; extend your benevo-

---

[28]From Hozumi Nobushige, *Ancestor-Worship and Japanese Law*, 6th rev. ed. (Tokyo: Hokuseidō, 1940), pp. 108–109.

lence to all; pursue learning and cultivate arts, and thereby develop intellectual faculties and perfect moral powers; furthermore advance public good and promote common interests; always respect the Constitution and observe the laws; should emergency arise, offer yourselves courageously to the State; and thus guard and maintain the prosperity of Our Imperial Throne coeval with heaven and earth. So shall ye not only be Our good and faithful subjects, but render illustrious the best traditions of your forefathers.

The Way here set forth is indeed the teaching bequeathed by Our Imperial Ancestors, to be observed alike by Their Descendants and the subjects, infallible for all ages and true in all places. It is Our wish to lay it to heart in all reverence, in common with you, Our subjects, that we may all attain to the same virtue.

CHAPTER XII

Social and Economic Development in the Meiji Era

Promulgation of the Meiji constitution and issuance of the imperial rescript on education were watershed events, dividing the Meiji era into early and later periods.

In the early Meiji period, there were persistent questions of how to make the government stable, how to catch up with Western nations, and how to enrich the nation through industrialization. The terms of intellectual debates reflected these concerns as seen in the slogans of *"bummei kaika"* (civilization and enlightenment), *"fukoku kyōhei"* (rich nation, strong army) and *"shokusan kōgyō"* (encouragement of industries). Industrialization was agreed upon as a necessary goal, but the means of its implementation still remained a big question. The term "encouragement of industries" would suggest that the government continue to extend its benign protection over industries, but no one was certain what form it should take. *Laissez-faire* as a policy option was never seriously discussed. On the part of industries protected by the government, there was a sense of serving the nation and demanding sacrifice from their employees in return. Most industrial leaders came from the former samurai class. They had to find justification for assuming the new profession that had been the bane of their class in earlier days.

With the victory over China in 1895, Japan began a process of establishing a colonial empire. With the victory over Russia in 1905, Japan joined the ranks of great powers. As the government became stable, concern over political issues subsided. In contrast, debates over social and economic issues intensified, reflecting the fast pace of industrialization. There was a constant search for models to follow, and the West continued to provide sources of inspiration. Some sought answers in Christianity, while others found viable alternatives in socialism, Marxism, and even anarchism.

This chapter begins with a selection from Fukuzawa Yukichi, in which he admonishes his readers to acquire a spirit of independence and academic freedom. Next comes Fukuzawa's advocation of *Datsu-a,* or saying good-bye to Asia. These are followed by a glimpse into the entrepreneur spirit of early Meiji businessmen and concludes with an antiwar editorial of Kōtoku Shūsui. In traditional Japan, society always took precedence over the individual. Signs of the changing times can be seen in the writings selected here, as one may find redefinition of an individual's place in society (as provided by Fukuzawa), his choosing a calling (as enunciated by Shibuzawa), and exercising his conscience to disobey the state power (as suggested by Kōtoku). On a separate issue, when protection is granted by the state, corporations are honor bound to do the bidding of the state, as Mitsubishi's founder clearly suggested. There was a constant search for progress and, to accommodate it, a search for changes in attitudes. All these issues were joined together to create a vibrant Meiji society.

JAPANESE ENLIGHTENMENT AND SAYING GOOD-BYE TO ASIA

In the transmission of knowledge concerning the West, no one had a greater impact than Fukuzawa Yukichi (1834–1901). Born in a lower samurai family, Fukuzawa studied in Nagasaki and became a student of Dutch studies. In 1860 when the Tokugawa bakufu *sent its first official mission to the United States, he was retained as a translator. In 1862 when a* bakufu *mission was sent to Europe, he was again asked to accompany it. In 1867, he again went to the United States to acquire new knowledge. After his return he established a private academy called Keiō Gijuku and engaged in teaching and writing to enlighten his fellow countrymen. In 1868 he moved the site of his school to Mita and concentrated on educational activities. He taught the dignity of the individual and attempted to inculcate in his students a spirit of independence. He spoke of pragmatic approaches to social issues and renounced old customs and practices. His stress on utilitarianism and political economy paved the way for Keiō graduates to advance in the business world. Fukuzawa shunned governmental service and was content with publishing his own newspaper,* Jiji Shimpō *(in 1882), as a means of persuading the public toward acceptance of his political philosophy of gradualism. He was a prolific writer with one hundred volumes to his credit. Among his major works were* Conditions of the West *(Seiyō Jijō, 1866) and* An Outline of Civilization *(Bummeiron no Gairyaku, 1875). Document 1 is taken from his* Encouragement of Learning *(Gakumon no Susume). Chapter 5, from which this selection is taken is less well known than the popular Chapter 1. In this chapter, he spoke of a spirit of independence that would insist on independence from governmental interference and on adherence to academic freedom. Broadly interpreted, it was also the spirit that could eventually make Japan equal to other civilized nations.*

In 1885, which was the eighteenth year of Meiji and nine years before the coming of the Sino-Japanese war, Fukuzawa wrote an article "Datsu-a Ron" (On Saying Good-bye to Asia, Document 2) urging his fellow countrymen to cast away the shackles of East Asian traditions. Around that time the notion of pan-Asianism became intellectually respectable, with pundits suggesting Japan assume the leadership role over other East Asian nations. It implied Japan retain much of the East Asian traditions and become aligned with China and Korea. In Fukuzawa's view, it would have presented another obstacle to the path to bummei kaika. He wanted a clean break from the past, accompanied by changes in attitudes and perspectives, so that Japan would truly become part of the civilized world of the West.

1 **Encouragement of Learning, Chapter Five, 1874**[1] From ancient times, changes have occurred in our government in accordance with the alternating cycle of peace and turmoil. We have never lost our independence because the cycle of peace and turmoil has never been concerned with foreign powers, and the nation has been able to bask in the security of closing the country from the rest of the world. Since we have been isolated from foreign countries, peace has been one of domestic peace, and turmoil has been one of domestic turmoil. We have never fought against another nation. This situation is akin to a little child who has never had any occasion to meet strangers.

Now, suddenly, intercourse with foreign nations becomes a reality, and the business of our nation becomes closely tied with foreign affairs. The trend today is to compare things in our country with those of foreign countries before taking any action. . . .

We cannot speak of any country's civilization by simply observing its outward manifestations. Schools, industries, the army, and the navy are all manifestations of a civilization. To formulate these outward manifestations is not too difficult. They can even be purchased by money. However, there is something which is invisible. It cannot be seen, cannot be heard, cannot be sold or bought, and cannot be lent or borrowed. When it is found in the midst of the citizens of a country, its power will be strongly felt, and without it, schools or any other outward manifestations of a civilization will be rendered useless. It can indeed be called the spirit of a civilization, and is its greatest and most important factor. What is it then? It is the spirit of independence among men!

---

[1]Ienaga Saburō, ed., *Fukuzawa Yukichi* in *Gendai Nihon Shisō Taikei (Great Compilation of Modern Japanese Thought)*, vol. 2 (Tokyo: Chikuma Shobō, 1963), pp. 189–93.

In recent years, our government has been undertaking the task of building schools, encouraging industries, and establishing the army and the navy. These have provided a new outlook, which is essential to the outward manifestations of a civilized nation. Among the people, however, there is no one who is willing to assert our independence from foreign countries or willing to compete against foreigners in order to get ahead of them. These people who have opportunities to learn the conditions of the West do not attempt to probe into things deeper, but only fear them. Once a person becomes fearful of another, nothing can really cure it, even though his trepidations may yet bring some benefits to our country. In the final analysis, unless the people possess a spirit of independence, the outward manifestations of a civilization will become useless appendages to our country.

The reasons for the lack of independent spirit may be found in our political system. For a thousand years, all powers resided in the government. It intervened in all sorts of things, including armament, literature, industry, and commerce, as well as in the most minute of human activities. People blindly followed directions given by the government. The country was treated as a private preserve of the government, and its people as mere parasites. Since they were parasites without abodes of their own, receiving food and shelter in an unwelcome fashion, they looked upon their country merely as their temporary dwelling, to which they had no sense of commitment. There was no opportunity of expressing their devotion, and the entire country was in a state of drift.

How about today? There is something even worse than what I have just described. When there is no progress, there is only digression, and when there is no digression, there is always progress. There is no such thing as stillness, which neither moves nor withdraws. In the present-day Japan, the outward manifestations of civilization seem to move forward, but the spirit of its people, the very essence of our civilization, definitely moves backward. Let us consider this issue for a moment. In the olden days when the Ashikaga and Tokugawa families ruled as *shōgun*, force was utilized to govern the people. If people subjected themselves to the government, that was so because they lacked power to oppose it. It was not submission willingly entered into, but it was fear that led them into taking a posture of subjugation. Today, the government possesses not only power but also craftiness. It can deal with matters in a most timely fashion. Scarcely ten years have passed since the Meiji Restoration, and we already have our school system and military completely overhauled. Railways and communication lines are constructed. Houses are built with cement, and iron bridges span over our rivers. In the decisiveness of its action, and in the beauty of its accomplishment, the government is to be commended. But these schools, military, railways, communication lines, houses built of cement, and iron bridges belong to the government. What credit is there to the people of this country? Some people may say, "The government possesses not only power but also knowledge and this is something people cannot hope to attain. The government stands on high to govern, while we as people must humbly obey. To be concerned about the affairs of state is the responsibility of those who are above us, while we the low-born shall not worry about them." In short, the old government utilized power, but today's government utilizes both power and knowledge. In olden days, the government did not possess the technique of controlling the masses, while the present government is richly endowed with it. Government in the olden days attempted to subdue the power of the masses, but today's government entices them to gain their allegiance. . . . People feared the government of the olden days as if it were the devil incarnate. They worship the present-day government as if it were god. . . . With this favorable attitude toward the government, technically it can dictate our advancement and help acquire outward manifestations of a civilization. Under such circumstances, however, people may lose their independent spirit, and the spirit of the civilization would only deteriorate. The government now has a standing army. Must we not regard it as the army to protect our nation and delight in it? Yet we fear it as a tool of suppressing the people. The government now has schools and railways. Must we not be proud of them as symbols of our civilized status? However, they are now regarded as ones established by the grace of the government, and people are inculcated with a feeling of dependence on the government. Our people already feel a sense of trembling and fear toward the government. How can our people compete against foreign nations in building our own civilization? This is the reason why I say, unless we can instill in our people a spirit of independence, the outward manifestations of our civilization become merely its vain appendages. They can be used as tools to digress the minds of men.

From what we have discussed, the civilization of a country must not be initiated by the government above, nor can it be born of people of low estate. It is the middle class that can nurture a civilization, showing the masses a way to follow. Only in this manner can it become a success vying with the government in its importance. When we study Western history, we find that not a single invention in commerce or industry was created by the government. All worthy inventions were the products of great minds of those who stood in the middle positions. The steam engine was invented by James Watt, and the railway was the brainchild of Robert and John Stevens. The one who discussed the laws of political economy and changed the way of commerce was none other than Adam Smith. All of these great men belonged to the so-called "middle class." None were men in the position of authority, nor were they manual laborers coming from the low-born class. They stood in the middle of their own people, and by their knowledge and intellect, they led their contemporaries. To utilize these outstanding techniques and inventions, these individuals often formed private associations, and through these associations bequeathed the benefits of their inventions to all the people and to their posterity. Under these circumstances, the duty of the government was a simple one. Its task was to permit these associations to undertake adequate measures for the fulfillment of their work without interference and provide protection in accordance with the wishes of the people.

From the above, we can infer that it is the task of private citizens to make a civilization meaningful, and it is the duty of the government to protect that civilization. A civilization belongs to its people who compete and fight for it and remain jealous and proud of it. If there is a significant accomplishment, the people applaud it with joy and fear only if other nations go a step further than they have been able to proceed. Anything pertaining to a civilization is a means to enhance the vitality of its people. There is nothing in it that does not assist the independence of that nation. This is a condition that is exactly the opposite of what we find in our country.

In our country, the ones who can occupy the position of the middle class are scholars who must also become protagonists for our civilization and sustainers of our independence. . . . But unfortunately, too often scholars are dissatisfied with their own positions and prefer to become bureaucrats in the government. They trade their talents away for the sake of minuscule office procedures. Laughable as their actions may be, there are many scholars who are content with this situation, and there are yet others who accept such scholars without question. In some extreme instances, people even show pleasure in the fact that no talents can be found in the private sector. These then are signs of our times, and fault does not belong to any particular individual. However, it is one of the greatest catastrophes of our civilization. If scholars, the ones whose task is to nurture our civilization, can observe without concern deterioration in their own spirit, then they are creating a lamentable and sorrowful condition for us all.

Only our group in Keiō Gijuku has been able to avoid this catastrophe. For the past several years, we have maintained our independence, and in a school that is independent, we have nurtured our spirit of independence for the entire country. However, the trends of the world can engulf us like rapids or great winds. It is not easy to stand erect against these great forces. Unless one is endowed with strong determination, he may, without being conscious of it, become a conformist to the current trend and lose his own stand. Man's determination cannot be acquired by reading books alone. Reading is one of the means of acquiring knowledge, and knowledge is a means to practical action. Unless one is faced with reality and is familiar with things surrounding him, one cannot gain determination. Those who have acquired these abilities in our group must be willing to suffer the agony of poverty and difficulties so that they may impart their wisdom in the building of our civilization. The fields in which they can function cannot be readily enumerated. There are commercial activities, legal debates, building of industries, agricultural works, as well as translation of books and publication of newspapers. Anything that pertains to our civilization must be reserved for the private sector. We must become leaders of our nation and extend our assistance to the government. We must find a way in which the powers of the government and of private citizens can be balanced, and thus contribute toward the greater strength of our nation. Let us place our independence on a firm foundation far removed from its present weak state. Let us make it possible to compete successfully against foreign nations without yielding. And several decades from now, on the same new year's day, let us look back to today's independence, not to rejoice but to take a benign pity on its insufficient state. How wonderful it will be if this will come to pass. I beseech all of you, my fellow scholars, to set your goals high and look forward to the future.

2   Good-bye Asia (Datsu-a), 1885[2] Transportation has become so convenient these days that once the wind of Western civilization blows to the East, every blade of grass and every tree in the East follow what the Western wind brings. Ancient Westerners and present-day Westerners are from the same stock and are not much different from one another. The ancient ones moved slowly, but their contemporary counterparts move vivaciously at a fast pace. This is possible because present-day Westerners take advantage of the means of transportation available to them. For those of us who live in the Orient, unless we want to prevent the coming of Western civilization with a firm resolve, it is best that we cast our lot with them. If one observes carefully what is going on in today's world, one knows the futility of trying to prevent the onslaught of Western civilization. Why not float with them in the same ocean of civilization, sail the same waves, and enjoy the fruits and endeavors of civilization?

The movement of a civilization is like the spread of measles. Measles in Tokyo start in Nagasaki and come eastward with the spring thaw. We may hate the spread of this communicable disease, but is there any effective way of preventing it? I can prove that it is not possible. In a communicable disease, people receive only damages. In a civilization, damages may accompany benefits, but benefits always far outweigh them, and their force cannot be stopped. This being the case, there is no point in trying to prevent their spread. A wise man encourages the spread and allows our people to get used to its ways.

The opening to the modern civilization of the West began in the reign of Kaei (1848–58). Our people began to discover its utility and gradually and yet actively moved toward its acceptance. However, there was an old-fashioned and bloated government that stood in the way of progress. It was a problem impossible to solve. If the government were allowed to continue, the new civilization could not enter. The modern civilization and Japan's old conventions were mutually exclusive. If we were to discard our old conventions, that government also had to be abolished. We could have prevented the entry of this civilization, but it would have meant loss of our national independence. The struggles taking place in the world civilization were such that they would not allow an Eastern island

---

[2]Fukuzawa Yukichi, "*Datsu-a Ron*" (On Saying Good-bye to Asia), reprinted in Takeuchi Yoshimi, ed., *Azia Shugi (Asianism) Gendai Nihon Shisō Taikei (Great Compilation of Modern Japanese Thought)*, vol. 8 (Tokyo: Chikuma Shobō, 1963), pp. 38–40.

nation to slumber in isolation. At that point, dedicated men (*shijin*) recognized the principle of "the country is more important than the government," relied on the dignity of the Imperial Household, and toppled the old government to establish a new one. With this, public and the private sectors alike, everyone in our country accepted the modern Western civilization. Not only were we able to cast aside Japan's old conventions, but we also succeeded in creating a new axle toward progress in Asia. Our basic assumptions could be summarized in two words: "Good-bye Asia *(Datsu-a)*."

Japan is located in the eastern extremities of Asia, but the spirit of her people have already moved away from the old conventions of Asia to the Western civilization. Unfortunately for Japan, there are two neighboring countries. One is called China and another Korea. These two peoples, like the Japanese people, have been nurtured by Asiatic political thoughts and mores. It may be that we are different races of people, or it may be due to the differences in our heredity or education; significant differences mark the three peoples. The Chinese and Koreans are more like each other and together they do not show as much similarity to the Japanese. These two peoples do not know how to progress either personally or as a nation. In this day and age with transportation becoming so convenient, they cannot be blind to the manifestations of Western civilization. But they say that what is seen or heard cannot influence the disposition of their minds. Their love affairs with ancient ways and old customs remain as strong as they were centuries ago. In this new and vibrant theater of civilization when we speak of education, they only refer back to Confucianism. As for school education, they can only cite [Mencius's] precepts of humanity, righteousness, decorum, and knowledge.[3] While professing their abhorrence to ostentation, in reality they show their ignorance of truth and principles. As for their morality, one only has to observe their unspeakable acts of cruelty and shamelessness. Yet they remain arrogant and show no sign of self-examination.

In my view, these two countries cannot survive as independent nations with the onslaught of Western civilization to the East. Their concerned citizens might yet find a way to engage in a massive reform, on the scale of our Meiji Restoration, and they could change their governments and bring about a renewal of spirit among their peoples. If that could happen they would indeed be fortunate. However, it is more likely that would never happen, and within a few short years they will be wiped out from the world with their lands divided among the civilized nations. Why is this so? Simply at a time when the spread of civilization and enlightenment (*bummei kaika*) has a force akin to that of measles, China and Korea violate the natural law of its spread. They forcibly try to avoid it by shutting off air from their rooms. Without air, they suffocate to death. It is said that neighbors must extend helping hands to one another because their relations are inseparable. Today's China and Korea have not done a thing for Japan. From

---

[3]In Japanese, *jin, gi, rei, chi,* and in Chinese *jen, i, li, chih (ren, yi, li, zhi).*

the perspectives of civilized Westerners, they may see what is happening in China and Korea and judge Japan accordingly, because of the three countries' geographical proximity. The governments of China and Korea still retain their autocratic manners and do not abide by the rule of law. Westerners may consider Japan likewise a lawless society. Natives of China and Korea are deep in their hocus pocus of nonscientific behavior. Western scholars may think that Japan still remains a country dedicated to the *yin* and *yang* and five elements. Chinese are mean-spirited and shameless, and the chivalry of the Japanese people is lost to the Westerners. Koreans punish their convicts in an atrocious manner, and that is imputed to the Japanese as heartless people. There are many more examples I can cite. It is not different from the case of a righteous man living in a neighborhood of a town known for foolishness, lawlessness, atrocity, and heartlessness. His action is so rare that it is always buried under the ugliness of his neighbors' activities. When these incidents are multiplied, that can affect our normal conduct of diplomatic affairs. How unfortunate it is for Japan.

What must we do today? We do not have time to wait for the enlightenment of our neighbors so that we can work together toward the development of Asia. It is better for us to leave the ranks of Asian nations and cast our lot with civilized nations of the West. As for the way of dealing with China and Korea, no special treatment is necessary just because they happen to be our neighbors. We simply follow the manner of the Westerners in knowing how to treat them. Any person who cherishes a bad friend cannot escape his bad notoriety. We simply erase from our minds our bad friends in Asia.

MEIJI ENTREPRENEURS

Japan's early industrialization was guided by a number of remarkable entrepreneurs. There were Shibuzawa Eiichi (1840–1931), who presided over one hundred companies, Iwasaki Yatarō (1834–85), who founded Mitsubishi, and Nakamigawa Hikojirō (1854–1901) who reformed and reorganized the Mitsui combine to give it strength for further growth. They were giants of Japanese industries who occupied positions comparable to Carnegie, Ford, and Rockefeller in American history.[4]

Were these Japanese entrepreneurs different from their Western counterparts when they stressed the goals of the state and of community first before their own profits? Did they have a different modus operandi*? How strongly were they influenced by their feudal past? What role did the government play in Japan's industrial development? What about the factor of making right connections*

---

[4]For a convenient bibliography on early Japanese entrepreneurship, see Henry Rosovsky and Kozo Yamamura, "Entrepreneurial Studies in Japan: An Introduction," in *Business History Review* 44, no. 1 (Spring 1970): 1–12.

through the web of human relations? To what extent had they influenced the behavior of present-day Japanese industrialists? While no simple answer can be given to any of these questions, the following documents may give some inkling of how these Japanese entrepreneurs operated.

Document 3 comes from the autobiography of Shibuzawa Eiichi. This selection shows Shibuzawa's decision to resign from government services to become a businessman, and his view of the social position held by businessmen. Document 4 comes from the reminiscences of Iwasaki Yatarō. It is a letter of instruction issued by Iwasaki to his employees in 1876 when his company was engaged in a deadly struggle against the British Peninsula & Oriental Steam Navigation Company to regain the right to Japan's coastal trade. The government supported Mitsubishi by issuing regulations regarding the use of foreign ships. Meanwhile, Mitsubishi halved its fares to attract passengers and customers. The salaries of Mitsubishi employees were cut by one-third for the duration of this struggle. Document 5 again comes from Iwasaki's reminiscences. It was issued in 1878 when Mitsubishi gained more than 73 percent of the total tonnage in Japan with 35,464 tons (sixty-one ships), and began its development into other fields such as insurance, banking, mining and real estate. At that time the company had more than 2,000 employees. Iwasaki's injunctions show the strong power of control he personally wielded. Document 6 comes from a memoir of Mutō Sanji (1867–1934), who subsequently became president of the Kanebō Cotton Spinning Company, a Mitsui subsidiary. He worked under the supervision of Nakamigawa Hikojirō, and from this vantage point describes Nakamiga's management style. Nakamigawa was a nephew of Fukuzawa Yukichi, the founder of Keiō University. Mutō was a graduate of Keiō, and his mention of the Mita (i.e., Keiō) group must not be overlooked.

3 **Shibuzawa Eiichi's Reasons for Becoming a Businessman, 1873**[5] The business world around 1873, the year when I resigned my post at the Ministry of Finance, was one filled with inertia. That condition is hard to imagine from the standards we hold for the business world today [1937, when Shibuzawa dictated this autobiography]. There was a tradition of respecting officials and despising common people. All talented men looked to government services as the ultimate goal in their lives, and ordinary students followed the examples set by them. There was practically no one who was interested in business. When people met, they discussed only matters relating to the affairs of state and of the world. There was no such thing as practical business education.

---

[5]From *Shibuzawa Eiichi Jijoden (Autobiography of Shibuzawa Eiichi)*, in *Zaikai Hyakunen (One Hundred Years of Japan's Financial World)*, in *Gendai Nihon Kiroku Zenshū, (A Series on Contemporary Japanese Documents)*, vol. 8 (Tokyo: Chikuma Shobō, 1969), pp. 94–96.

It was said that the Meiji Restoration was to bring about equality among the four classes of people. In practice, however, those who engaged in commerce and industry were regarded as plain townspeople as before, and were despised and had to remain subservient to government officials. I knew conditions such as this should not be allowed to persist. A rigid class structure should not be tolerated. We should be able to treat each other with respect and make no differentiation between government officials and townspeople. This was essential to our national welfare, as we looked forward to strengthening the country which required wealth to back it up. We needed commerce and industry to attain the goal of becoming a rich nation. Unworthy as I was, I thought of engaging in commerce and industry to help promote the prosperity of our nation. I might not have talent to become a good politician, but I was confident that I could make a difference in the fields of commerce and industry. . . .

As to the question of development of commerce and industry, I felt that to engage in an individually managed shop would be going against the tide of the times, and it was necessary for small business firms to join their forces together. In other words, they have to incorporate, and I decided to devote my energy to this endeavor. As to the laws governing incorporation, I thought about them while studying in France. After my return from France and before my entering into government service, I organized a chamber of commerce in Shizuoka to serve as a model for incorporation in this country. Since that time, I have consistently advocated the advantages of incorporation.

In organizing a company, the most important factor one ought to consider is to obtain the services of the right person to oversee its operation. In the early years of Meiji, the government also encouraged incorporation of companies and organized commercial firms and development companies. The government actively participated in these companies' affairs and saw to it that their various needs were met fully. However, most of these companies failed because their management was poor. To state it simply, the government failed to have the right men as their managers. I had no experience in commerce and industry, but I also prided myself on the fact that I had greater potential for success in these fields than most of the nongovernmental people at that time.

I also felt that it was necessary to raise the social standing of those who engaged in commerce and industry. By way of setting an example, I began studying and practicing the teachings of the *Analects of Confucius*. It contains teachings first enunciated more than twenty-four hundred years ago. Yet it supplies the ultimate in practical ethics for all of us to follow in our daily living. It has many golden rules for businessmen. For example, there is a saying: "Wealth and respect are what men desire, but unless a right way is followed, they cannot be obtained; poverty and lowly position are what men despise, but unless a right way is found, one cannot leave that status once reaching it."[6] It shows very

---

[6]*Analects*, IV, 5.

clearly how a businessman must act in this world. Thus, when I entered the business world, I engaged in commerce and industry in a way consistent with the teachings of the *Analects* and practiced the doctrine of unity of knowledge and action [as taught by Wang Yangming].

4   **Mitsubishi and Japanese Coastal Trade, 1876**[7] Many people have expressed differing opinions concerning the principles to be followed and advantages to be obtained in engaging foreigners or Japanese in the task of coastal trade. Granted, we may permit a dissenting voice, which suggests that in principle both foreigners and Japanese must be permitted to engage in coastal trade, but once we look into the question of advantages, we know that coastal trade is too important a matter to be given over to the control of foreigners. If we allow the right of coastal navigation to fall into the hands of foreigners in peacetime, it means a loss of business and employment opportunities for our own people, and in wartime it means yielding the vital right of gathering information to foreigners. In fact, this is not too different from abandoning the rights of our country as an independent nation.

Looking back into the past, at the time when we abandoned the policy of seclusion and entered into an era of friendly intercourse and commerce with foreign nations, we should have been prepared for this very task. However, due to the fact that our people lack knowledge and wealth, we have yet to assemble a fleet sufficient to engage in coastal navigation. Furthermore, we have neither the necessary skills for navigation nor a plan for developing a maritime transportation industry. This condition has attracted foreign shipping companies to occupy our maritime transport lines. Yet our people show not a sense of surprise at it. Some people say that our treaties with foreign powers contain an express provision allowing foreign ships to proceed from Harbor A to Harbor B, and others claim that such a provision must not be regarded as granting foreign ships the right to coastal navigation inasmuch as it is intended not to impose unduly heavy taxes on them. I am not qualified to discuss its legal merit, but the issue remains an important one.

I now propose to do my utmost, and along with my 35 million compatriots, perform my duty as a citizen of this country. That is to recover the right of coastal trade in our hands and not to delegate that task to foreigners. Unless we propose to do so, it is useless for our government to revise the unequal treaties or to change our entrenched customs. We need people who can respond, otherwise all the endeavors of the government will come to naught. This is the reason why the government protects our company, and I know that our responsibilities are even greater than the full weight of Mt. Fuji thrust upon our shoulders. There

---

[7]From Iwasaki Yatarō, *Kaiungyō o Okoshite (Promoting Maritime Industry)*, in *Zaikai Hyakunen*, pp. 191–93.

have been many who wish to hinder our progress in fulfilling our obligations. However, we have been able to eliminate one of our worst enemies, the Pacific Mail Company of the United States, from contention by applying appropriate means available to us. Now another rival has emerged. It is the Peninsula & Oriental Steam Navigation Company of Great Britain, which is setting up a new line between Yokohama and Shanghai and is attempting to claim its rights over the ports of Nagasaki, Kobe, and Yokohama. The P & O Company is backed by its massive capital, its large fleet of ships, and by its experiences of operating in Oriental countries. In competing against this giant, what methods can we employ?

I have thought about this problem very carefully and have come to one conclusion. There is no other alternative but to eliminate unnecessary positions and unnecessary expenditures. This is a time-worn solution and no new wisdom is involved. Even though it is a familiar saying, it is much easier said than done, and this indeed has been the root cause of difficulties in the past and present times. Therefore, starting immediately, I propose that we engage in this task. By eliminating unnecessary personnel from the payroll, eliminating unnecessary expenditures, and engaging in hard and arduous tasks, we shall be able to solidify the foundation of our company. If there is a will, there is a way. Through our own efforts, we shall be able to repay the government for its protection and answer our nation for its confidence shown in us. Let us work together in discharging our obligations and let us not be ashamed of ourselves. Whether we succeed or fail, whether we can gain profit or sustain loss, we cannot anticipate at this time. Hopefully, all of you will join me in a singleness of heart to attain this cherished goal, forbearing and undaunted by setbacks, to restore to our own hands the right to our own coastal trade. If we succeed it will not only be an accomplishment for our company but also a glorious event for our Japanese Empire, which shall let its light shine to all four corners of the earth. We may succeed and we may fail, and it depends on your effort or lack of it. Do your utmost in this endeavor!

5   Iwasaki Yatarō's Control of Mitsubishi, 1878[8]

ARTICLE 1. This company is named as a company and is organized as such. However, in reality it is a business enterprise of one family and is different from a group publicly subscribed and organized into a company. Therefore, anything relating to this company, including commendations and admonitions, and promotions and demotions, must be sanctioned personally by the president.

ARTICLE 2. Therefore the profit of the company shall belong to the president. Likewise, any loss sustained by the company shall be borne by the president.

ARTICLE 3. Notwithstanding the provisions of the preceding article, if the

---

[8]*Ibid.*, pp. 195–96.

company prospers and receives a large amount of profit, there may be times when the monthly salary may be increased across the board. On the other hand, if the company's enterprise suffers and there is a certain loss, then the monthly salary may be reduced across the board and employment may be terminated.

ARTICLE 4. The Tokyo company shall be the head office, and the companies located in other prefectures, China, and Okinawa shall be branch offices. As our enterprise prospers, we may establish additional offices in other places. They shall all be called branch offices.

ARTICLE 5. As to the officers of the company, and the order establishing their rank, there shall be a general manager who shall oversee general business affairs of each of the companies or branch offices. A manager is appointed to each of the sections, stores, and ships who shall be the head of his respective section, store or ship. There shall be an assistant manager appointed to assist the manager.

6   Mr. Nakamigawa and Kanebō's Development, 1889–1901[9] The Kanebō

Cotton Spinning Company was initially known as the Tokyo Cotton Company, which was established in November 1886 by a number of cotton wholesale merchants with the Mitsui Dry-Goods Store holding the major share of its stocks. At first it was a small company capitalized at 100,000 yen. In the following year, it expanded and was capitalized at one million yen and established its cotton spinning factory in Sumida village in Tokyo. The company was operated by wholesale merchants who had no prior experience in the cotton spinning industry and met failure after failure from which they could not extricate themselves. It was then decided that the company disband in the first half of 1888. . . . There was one Mr. Inanobe, who argued against the disbanding, saying that if the company were disbanded all the money invested in it would be lost, and it was far better to find someone who could rescue its operations. Mr. Inanobe sought a meeting with Marquis Inoue Kaoru (1835–1915), an adviser to the Mitsui family, and suggested the name of Mr. Nakamigawa Hikojirō for the task of reorganizing the company. Marquis Inoue agreed. Thus was begun the Mitsui family's direct involvement in the company. In August 1889, the company was reorganized to become the Kanebō Cotton Spinning Company.

In 1893, the company increased its capitalization to 2.5 million, and decided to establish a new factory in Kobe [in the prefecture of Hyogo] with 40,000 spindles for the purpose of exporting its products to China. I was hired by Kanebō to become manager of its Hyogo plant. At that time I was twenty-eight years old. The company was divided into two branches with another branch

---

[9]Mutō Sanji, *Kanebō Funtōki (Records of Kanebo's Endeavor)*, in *Zaikai Hyakunen*, pp. 206–7, 225–27. In places, a few sentences have been added from other parts of Mr. Mutō's reminiscences to make the necessary connection.

located in Tokyo. The head of the Tokyo branch was Mr. Wada Toyoji, who was only two or three years older than I. In any event both of us were around thirty at that time. As I look back I am often amazed by the fact that a man of Mr. Nakamigawa's stature was willing to entrust to young men like us such responsible positions. Yet it was a time of reform in the business world. Mr. Nakamigawa himself was a middle-aged man barely forty years of age and was asked to reorganize the Mitsui Bank at the request of Marquis Inoue. It was a time of the old giving way to the new, and naturally he sought men of youthful ardor to serve under him in responsible positions. . . .

Around the time of the Boxer Rebellion in China [1900], the company suffered greatly. . . . After this shock I was determined to do my utmost to rebuild the financial condition of my company and to relieve it from the perils of heavy debts. . . . However, there were only two ways through which such financial reconstruction could be effected. One was a positive way by simply raising the profit of the company. The other was a negative way by enriching the assets of the company. To act positively to improve the company's financial records would take time. Thus I resorted to the other course by suspending dividends. For two consecutive periods, no dividend was paid. . . .

I was engaged in an arduous advertising campaign to sell more of our products domestically, which eventually resulted in a very substantial improvement in our profit picture. However, then a very sad event occurred.

It was the death of Mr. Nakamigawa on October 7, 1901. At that time he was forty-eight years of age. At the age of forty-eight a man is at his prime, and even though we all knew that he was ill, he was of strong constitution, and we never thought he would pass away. It was a great shock to those of us belonging to the Mita group [meaning Keiō graduates] who worked under Mr. Nakamigawa. We were quite apprehensive because we knew that the relationship between Mr. Nakamigawa and Marquis Inoue had been cold for some time. Mr. Nakamigawa was once a protégé of Marquis Inoue, and it was through Marquis Inoue's recommendation that he became the man responsible for reorganizing the Mitsui Bank. In common parlance, their relationship was one of *oyabun-kobun* (patron and underling), and from the very beginning it was not one of equality. Thus there should have never been room for misunderstanding. However, as in a relationship between father and son, as the son grows older, there may be times when their feelings are not necessarily cordial, so was the relationship between the two. As the reorganization of the Mitsui bank progressed, and as Mr. Nakamigawa actively extended his business ventures, Marquis Inoue, who tended to be conservative and believed in entrenchment, found that the former's business activities were not in his style. At times like that, it was common to have slanders and malicious gossips. I was not in Tokyo and thus did not know what took place exactly. However, I could surmise that gradually there developed a misunderstanding between Mr. Nakamigawa and Marquis Inoue, and about a year before Mr. Nakamigawa's death it became intensified. It was rumored that Marquis Inoue's personality was such that he would take radical steps against all of us who belonged to the Mita group once Mr. Nakamigawa died. . . .

Fortunately, through the effort of Mr. Masuda Takashi [1848–1938, manager of the Mitsui combine after Nakamigawa's death] and others, no significant change in personnel was effected. However, the retrenchment policy of Marquis Inoue was implemented step by step, which resulted in abandoning many business activities planned and implemented by Mr. Nakamigawa. The first to fall victim to this retrenchment policy was our silk industry, and plants erected in different parts of the country were all sold. I recall Mr. Nakamigawa's intention to have the Industrial Division of the Mitsui family operate silk mills. Wealthy families did not look upon the silk industry favorably, and as a result its operations were left in the hands of minor entrepreneurs. Their lack of capital made them highly vulnerable in this fluctuating industry. He proposed that this important industry, with its high rate of fluctuation, be supported by men of wealth like the Mitsui family for the sake of the nation. This kind of thinking was diametrically opposed to that of Marquis Inoue. Shortly after the death of Mr. Nakamigawa, on strict orders from Marquis Inoue, everything connected with the silk industry was sold, and it was divorced from the Mitsui management. It was regrettable, but under the circumstances, we could not do otherwise.

The Kanebō company for which I was responsible was incorporated and was technically not directly controlled by the Mitsui family. However, Mr. Nakamigawa devoted much of his effort in this particular company, and it was almost regarded as a monopoly undertaken by the Mitsui family. I feared that the same fate suffered by the silk industry would soon be visited upon us. . . .One day Mr. Masuda Takashi said that he wanted to see me and I went to Tokyo. Mr. Masuda said: "I hear that you are advocating very enthusiastically mergers of cotton spinning industries. I agree with you and wish to give you my support." . . . With Mr. Masuda's encouragement in 1902, Kanebō effected a merger with the Kyushu, Nakatsu, and Hakata cotton spinning companies, and the cotton spinning industry around Kyushu came under the control of Kanebō. . . .

CHRISTIANITY AND THE NONCHURCH MOVEMENT

Uchimura Kanzō (1861–1930) was the son of a samurai, and after an agonizing period of conversion experience, transferred his fierce samurai spirit of devotion to his newly found faith. He was attracted to Christianity because of the purity of its faith and of its ethical teachings. However, as he witnessed Christianity in action with all of its imperfections, he sought a return to primitive Christianity. This he found through denunciation of sectarian practices. To him, foreign missionaries erred by insisting on the acceptance of their denominational doctrines, which were contrary to the concept of "One Lord, one faith, one baptism." Thus his nonchurch movement assumed characteristics both of purifying the faith and of establishing a new brand of Japanese Christianity.

The anomaly that existed in Japan, according to Uchimura, was her inability to accept Christianity, on which Western civilization was deeply rooted. To him it was impossible to retain Oriental religions as the basis of one's own civilization and at the same time accept Western civilization in a superficial manner. For the sake of two Js, Jesus and Japan, he urged his compatriots to accept Christianity. Document 7, which follows, can also be considered as an attack on the uncritical acceptance of Western civilization prevalent in the Meiji period.

7 Great Difficulty Facing Japan, 1903[10]

Japan faces one great difficulty today. It does not stem from a lack of wealth or from a lack of scholarship. It is not found in the disorganized state of our laws, nor is it in the sluggishness of our agriculture, commerce, or industry. The difficulty is a much deeper and fundamental one. It is because of this difficulty that our society is showing such a strange state of affairs. Most Japanese do not attempt to investigate the difficulty at its source, but instead bemoan the lack of capital, grieve over the deterioration in morality, and show anger toward depravity and corruption in politicians and educators. This in itself is very much to be lamented.

What is this great difficulty, nay, the greatest difficulty that confronts Japan today? May I speak candidly? It is the fact that the Japanese adopted a civilization based on Christianity without accepting Christianity. This is at the root of all our difficulties today. It is because of this anomaly that many difficulties, hard to enumerate, besiege us today.

Christian civilization is a civilization that has its origin in Christianity. . . . In other words, no one can understand that civilization without studying Christianity. The Japanese people have adopted a Christian civilization, but refuse to accept Christianity which is its very base, origin, and the spirit and life-giver of that civilization. This is almost like a man who receives a gift from another and does not thank him for the gift because he does not wish to investigate the identity of the donor. The Japanese people are placing themselves in an unethical and ungrateful position. It is no wonder that they are now finding themselves in difficulties that know no bounds.

Let me illustrate with two or three examples. Many Japanese feel that the present-day arts and sciences are not the products of Christianity but developed in spite of the opposition by Christianity. This is the logic advanced by those who do not understand Western history. I shall not speak about the fact that many great scientists were also devout Christians. I shall not elaborate on the

---

[10]Kamei Katsuichirō, ed., *Uchimura Kanzō,* in *Gendai Nihon Shiso Taikei,* vol. 5, pp. 395–403. The original of this article, entitled *"Nihonkoku no Daikonnan"* was first published in *Seisho no Kenkyū* or *Studies of the Bible,* a journal founded by Uchimura to propagate his ideas.

fact that those scientists who observed phenomena in this universe against over-whelming odds during the infancy of modern science—such as Sir Isaac Newton, John Dalton,[11] Sir William Hershel,[12] and Michael Faraday[13]—were faithful servants of Christ. However, please consider this point. Why did science, which developed in Turkey, Egypt, Morocco, and Spain during the height of the power of the Islamic civilization, not develop in its own native surroundings, but prospered only after it was transplanted to the Christian society of Europe? Why could not science develop in the Indian Peninsula endowed with the sharp brains of the Indians? The fact is, science, like all other things, cannot develop with the appearance of great scientists alone. It is necessary to have a society that can stimulate, welcome, and encourage its growth. Scientific thoughts, like political thoughts, cannot prosper in the areas where there is suppression of freedom of thought. Science cannot develop in the countries of idol worshippers because in these countries people's minds are bound by the icons, and they cannot go beyond nature to speculate on its very essence. There is a deep and profound interrelationship between the rise of science and monotheism. Without knowing this, one tends to show his little understanding when he asserts that any nation can prosper in science by acquiring a rich reservoir of knowledge alone.

Freedom or people's rights advocated in civilized countries cannot arise without Christianity. Some people say that in the beginning there was freedom and wherever people reside there is freedom. These people show their ignorance of the history of freedom. In Rome and Greece, there was such a thing as freedom as understood by those ancient men. However, it was not the new freedom of Milton, Cromwell, Washington, and Lincoln. This was the freedom that Plato, Socrates, Cato, Seneca, and Cicero did not understand. It was the freedom first advocated by the Nazarene Jesus Christ, and without him and his disciples, this freedom would have never appeared in this world. The same thing can be said for human rights also. When we speak of rights inherent in man, we are not speaking of license for him to act in accordance with his own desires. Nor are we saying that he can freely dispose of his possessions as he sees fit, for "right" is a concept that derives its meaning from corresponding responsibility. Once responsibility disappears, the corresponding right disappears also. And the responsibility of man comes from the spiritual relationships man has toward God and Nature. If man denies the existence of God or that of the immortal soul, the concept of responsibility will collapse from its very foundation. As a result man will become only an animal endowed with knowledge in search of material profits. The concept of responsibility is a religious one and cannot be scientifi-

---

[11]English chemist and physicist (1766–1844), best known for his atomic theory.

[12]An English astronomer (1738–1822) who discovered the planet Uranus, two of its satellites, and two satellites of Saturn. Also known for his discovery of the motion of the solar system in space.

[13]Self-educated English physicist and chemist (1791–1867), whose many discoveries included that of electromagnetic induction, with far-reaching applications.

cally explained. It is not a concept invented by man in order to organize a society. If we wish to maintain the concept of responsibility, we must rely on the power of a strong religion. . . .

What are the conditions in Japan today? The Japanese people have learned from the West and drafted their constitution. They have imitated the West in arranging their legal codes and in establishing their educational system. However, they dislike Christianity, which is the source, base, and spirit of Western civilization. They claim that our country has its own religion and there is no need for borrowing one from foreign countries. Some even suggest foolishly that we can follow the West in scholarship, but abide by the virtues of the East. Fools will always remain fools, but our nation cannot long sustain itself with their foolhardiness. There is an overriding natural law, and no matter how great the Japanese people may be, they cannot overcome the work of natural law. Christianity will not punish the Japanese people, just because they do not accept Christianity. But natural law will without any hesitation punish the Japanese people for their foolhardiness, unconcern and arrogance. In fact punishment is being meted out today, and all we have to do is to look at our conditions.

We have studied Western science for the past forty years. It is being said that Japanese medicine is just as good as that of Europe or America. But let us stop for a moment to consider this point. As a result of forty years of study, has there been any great scientific discovery made in Japan? Can any of our philosophers produce a single new theory? There have been some minor inventions, some in the industrial and some in the pharmaceutical fields. But is there any single invention for which the Japanese scientists can be proud which contributes to the advance in the world of science? Why is this so? Do we lack gifted scientists? Or do we lack funds for research? No, I do not think these are the reasons. In fact, the answer is simple. Japanese scientists and philosophers lack that love for truth and knowledge. Whenever man pursues science for profit, there can be no great invention. Whenever man pursues science for prestige, there can be no great progress. And whenever man pursues science for mere pastime, there can be no science worthy of its name. If one wishes to search for truth in depth and to understand its profound meanings, one must be motivated by the love of truth and dissociate himself from self-serving motivations. . . . Yet what is the status of science in Japan today? What motivates those college students who are studying engineering? Those who know the engineering profession will sneer and say that none are like Japanese engineers in their baseness. What is the Japanese medical science like? Is it not true that the healing of patients is turned into a means of making money? What are Japanese biology and botany like? They are nothing but preparatory courses for schoolteachers, or mere avocations for dilettantes to search in order to satisfy their curiosity. And now speaking of Japanese philosophy, it has degenerated either into an apology for patriotism in a philosophical fashion or into one of dilettantism invented to appreciate the theories of great Western thinkers. Yes, Japan has sciences, and we have toyed with them and utilized them. However, Japan practically lacks the kind of science that is based on the everlasting hope that undiscovered truth can be found and that mankind's intellectual horizon can be expanded. How sad it is to observe the state of Japanese sciences!

Coming to Japanese education, it is quite a strange sight to behold. On the surface, the Japanese educational system looks excellent, and some educators boast that even in the Western nations comparable excellence cannot be found. But in reality, what the Japanese educators have done is to delete the word God as written by Herbart[14] and to replace it with the word Emperor, on the ground that the word God does not fit in our national polity. That sounds like an expression of loyalty to the Emperor, but it is an act most unfaithful to the great educator Herbart, an act that must not be committed by those who engage in the sacred profession of education. However, the great ministry of education does not find any inconsistency in this approach and forces an educational philosophy that replaces the name of God with that of Emperor as the genuine Herbartian pedagogical philosophy upon the nation.

However, nature does not condone this sin of deception. Japanese education began with deception and we must now pay the price for that deception. No teacher seriously wishes to educate the children. He regards education as another profession, and whenever he looks for a position, the first question he asks is the amount of his salary. Every year between the latter part of March to the early part of April, many normal school and middle school principals come to Tokyo to start hiring teachers, and the education world turns into a marketplace. We can hear that such and such prefecture is offering so many hundred yen less than others, or such and such prefecture is offering so many hundred yen more than others. These are discourses far removed from education itself and should not be uttered by those "education merchants." Take a look also at the publishers' campaigns to have their textbooks adopted. There is a term called "corrupters," which is reserved for salesmen from publishers who court the favor of principals, professors, teachers, and education inspectors by money, wine, or women. How terrible this term "corrupters" sounds! In order to sell textbooks on ethics which expound on the virtues of "bear yourselves in modesty and moderation; extend your benevolence to all; ... advance public good and promote common interests,"[15] these corrupters do their utmost to destroy the integrity of educators. Yet do Japanese educators avoid these corrupters with firm resolve? No, on the contrary, they are pleased to be associated with them. They devour the profits

[14]German influence on Japanese education became pronounced after 1880, and Herbartian pedagogical philosophy was expounded by the German philosopher Emil Hausknecht at Tokyo University after 1887. Johann Friedrich Herbart (1776–1841) believed that the purpose of education is the moral development of the individual who is more important than the family or the state. He also developed a method for teaching children to be "many sided" and originated the doctrine of appreciation.

[15]Direct quotation from the Imperial Rescript on Education; see Chapter XI, Document 20.

offered and conspire to help serve the interest of publishers. Where else in the world since the inception of education for children can one find a country in which well over one hundred educators are thrown into jail for receiving bribes? This is proof that Japan really does not have something that can be called education. What the Meiji government has accomplished is nothing but an education of deception. It is a deception because Japan has arbitrarily added something to the educational system developed in the West, which was a product of much prayers and supplications. And its deplorable result has been the so-called textbook incident. Where there is no God, no Christ, or no Christian-type education, the end result is the jailing of educators, as is happening in Japan today. . . .

If anyone wishes to assert that without Christianity there is still freedom, he must study closely politics in Japan today. Japan now has a constitution that guarantees the rights and freedom of its citizens. In Japanese politics, however, seldom can one find evidence of freedom. Representatives are not freely chosen. They are chosen by some personal ties from which one cannot extricate himself. There can be threats, personal considerations, or temptations. Japanese politics today is conducted essentially by these three factors. . . . In politics, as in education, everything is calculated toward one's own material gain. . . . Politicians become Diet members with the same kind of mental attitude as the people who become stockholders of companies. . . .

It is an anomaly to think of Japan having a representative government or freedom when it is not founded on Christianity. . . . A body that lacks soul, or a ship that lacks an engine, is impossible to manage, and the so-called representative government in Japan falls into this category. How sad it is!

. . . Christian civilization without Christianity will eventually destroy Japan. In this sense, China, Turkey, and Morocco are far more blessed than Japan. Their civilizations are closely tied in with their religions, and there is no danger of destroying themselves from internal conflict. Unlike them, Japan has Oriental religions and its own brand of Western civilization. This poses a great deal of difficulty for us, and unless we can rectify this anomaly, Japan will eventually be destroyed by its own internal conflict.

What must we do today? Shall we abandon Western civilization? Nay, that is not the path open to us. The only alternative is to adopt immediately the very essence of Western civilization, which is Christianity. . . . I beseech you, all the patriots of Japan, for the sake of Jesus and for the sake of Japan, devote yourselves to the propagation of Christianity.

SOCIALISM—CHRISTIANITY AND MARXISM

On May 20, 1901, Abe Isoo, Katayama Sen, Kotōku Shūsui, and three other men gathered in the small office of an iron workers union in Tokyo to form the Social Democratic Party. The six agreed to contribute five yen each (approximately

$2.50 at the then existing exchange rate) to the party coffer and issue a party declaration that was drafted by Abe Isoo, a senior member and the group's intellectual leader. The party was promptly banned, and the newspapers that published the party declaration were all indicted under the Peace Preservation Law of 1900. When found guilty, all the newspapers were required to publish the full text of the judgment, which contained the text of the party declaration in its entirety. Thus the founders of the Social Democratic Party gained a much wider audience than they had dared hope (Document 8).

The author of the declaration, Abe Isoo (1865–1949) became a socialist through the Christian concept of love and through humanitarian concerns for the welfare of his fellowmen. Katayama Sen (1859–1933) in 1901 believed in an AFL-type labor union for Japan. They were drawn to the socialist cause in part by their resentment against the enactment of the Peace Preservation Law. But they were convinced that the socialistic goals they espoused could still be accomplished through legal means. Thus the declaration makes a strong plea for universal suffrage, for equitable distribution of wealth, for extension of compulsory education, and for the workers' right to unionize. Their belief in the effectiveness of participation in the parliamentary system would be shattered later and would open the way for the more militant activist approach of Kōtoku Shūsui (1871–1911) with its renunciation of parliamentary tactics.

Kōtoku Shūsui showed his militancy by establishing a People's Weekly *(Shūkan Heimin Shimbun) during the Russo-Japanese War to propagate his antiwar stand and to introduce Marxist and sometimes anarchist doctrines. One of Kōtoku's antiwar articles, "Against the Wartime Tax," is excerpted below (Document 9).*

8   Declaration of the Social Democratic Party, 1901[16]

The means through which the gap between wealth and poverty can be bridged will indeed become one of the greatest problems facing the twentieth century. The ideals of freedom and equality, which were spread from France to the Western European countries and to America near the end of the eighteenth century, contributed greatly toward the realization of egalitarianism in political matters. However, with the immense material progress made in the past century, the social classes of aristocracy and common people have been replaced by the new classes of the rich and the poor, which are far more deplorable and fearsome social distinctions. One must not lose sight of the fact that economic equality is the root and political equality is merely its branch. Therefore people's unhappiness will remain unless economic inequality can be eradicated. This is so even if the political power is equitably distributed under a constitutional government. This is the

---

[16]Ōkōchi Kazuo, ed., *Shakai Shugi (Socialism),* in *Gendai Nihon Shisō Taikei,* vol. 15, pp. 311–21.

reason our party places its full emphasis on economic matters as solutions to political matters.

When we look at the political conditions in our country, we discover that all political agencies are operating for the benefit of the rich. Needless to say, the House of Peers represents only a minority of aristocrats and the rich. As to the House of Representatives, once we analyze its setup, we can immediately realize that it only represents the interests of the landlords and of the capitalists. We can safely say, without fear of contradiction, that our Imperial Diet today is a Diet for the rich. We must remember that the majority of the nation consists of those tenants who till the fields or those workers who sweat in the factories. Why can they not enjoy the right of suffrage? Why can they not send their own representatives to the Diet? Is it because they are ignorant, or is it because their morality is far below that of the rich? Nay, nay, it is because they lack property and thus cannot be enfranchised, and it is because they are poor and cannot receive adequate education. Should it not be the duty of the rich to give the tenants and workers adequate compensation and find a way for them to receive education? Should not the political parties provide a means to extend to them their political rights?

However, today's political parties have deteriorated into the maidservants of the rich and do not represent the will of the majority of the people.... [In contrast,] our party shall steadily work toward realizing the following ideals:

1. The wide acceptance of a philosophy that all people are brothers regardless of race or difference in politics.

2. Complete abrogation of armament as a means of peace for all nations.

3. Complete abrogation of class system.

4. Full public ownership of land and capital required for production.

5. Public ownership of transportation facilities, including railways, steamships, canals, and bridges.

6. Equitable distribution of wealth.

7. Enjoyment of equal political rights for the people.

8. Assumption by the state of the cost of education for all the people.

These are the ideals our party advocates. However, we realize that they are difficult to implement. Therefore we are submitting the following as our platform for practical action:

1. Public ownership of all railways in the country.

2. Ownership by the municipalities of city trolleys, electric and gas industries, and other industries that tend to become monopolistic.

3. Prohibition of sale of publicly owned land to private parties. The land covered under this prohibition includes that owned by the national government, prefectural governments, municipalities, townships, and villages.

4. All land within the confines of municipalities is in principle to be owned by those municipalities. If this cannot be implemented immediately, there shall be a law prohibiting speculative purchase by private parties.

5. Patent rights owned by private citizens shall be purchased by the government. In other words, inventors shall receive adequate remunerations. However, people shall be able to enjoy the fruits of their inventions inexpensively.

6. There shall be a limitation on rent, set at a certain percentage of the actual value of the house.

7. Publicly owned industries shall be operated by the government and shall not be subcontracted to individuals or private companies.

8. All excise tax on consumer goods, such as taxes on *sake* (Japanese rice wine), soy sauce, and sugar shall be abrogated. In their place, direct taxes such as inheritance and income taxes shall be imposed.

9. Compulsory education shall be extended to the eighth grade, and no tuition shall be imposed. All textbooks shall be supplied by public funds.

10. A Bureau of Labor shall be established to investigate all matters pertaining to labor.

11. No schoolchildren shall be permitted to engage in labor.

12. No women shall be permitted to engage in such occupations that shall be detrimental to their morality or health.

13. Night-shift work for women and children shall be abolished.

14. No work shall be performed on Sundays, and the working hours shall be limited to eight hours a day.

15. There shall be an employment compensation law under which the employer shall be responsible for paying adequate compensation for injuries sustained by his employees while at work.

16. There shall be a labor union law under which workers' right to organize freely shall be recognized and be given adequate protection.

17. A law for protecting tenant farmers shall be enacted.

18. All insurance industries shall be operated by the government.

19. All court costs shall be borne by the government.

20. A universal suffrage law shall be implemented.

21. A law for equitable election shall be adopted.

22. All elections shall be direct, and by secret ballot.

23. There shall be devised a method under which all important matters shall be placed under national referendum with full participation by common people.

24. Complete abrogation of the death penalty.

25. Disbanding of the House of Peers.

26. Disarmament.

27. Abrogation of the Peace Preservation Law.

28. Abrogation of the Press Law.[17]

Our party has made socialism and democracy its two cardinal principles. We

---

[17]Under the law, passed in 1875 and strengthened in 1883 and 1885, publishing an article that was inimical to the public welfare could result in suspension of publication and be subjected to the penalties of fines and imprisonments.

stand and abide by them. There may be some who do not understand these two great ideals. Some of them may regard the name Social Democratic Party too radical. Perhaps some explanations are necessary to show why this name is selected and why we are making public our principles for action. . . . Today's social organizations are based on individualistic competition. Consequently, money and political power are concentrated in the hands of one group of people, and many common people are unwittingly placed in a position akin to that of slaves. In olden days, laborers possessed their own hand tools to engage in production. They did not require help from the capitalists and lived an independent life. However, today intricate machines are invented, and unless one can invest a substantial sum, from several hundred to several tens of thousand yen, we cannot readily obtain such machines. In this way, one by one, workers are forced to leave their handicraft works at home to engage in factory work. They need machines like fish require water. Thus labor has become another commodity, having its price set in accordance with the law of supply and demand. Let us assume that one day factories will be closed because there will no longer be a need for the workers' labor. Then tens of thousands of able-bodied men will meet the fate of hunger and starvation without any recourse at hand. Isn't this inequity caused by the inadequacy in our present social organization?

The concept of free competition is a plausible one. Yet in the society we have organized there are many instances in which competition is not permitted. There is something called monopoly that will not permit others to compete against it. . . .

In short, the objectives of socialism are to guarantee to every person an occupation, to supply sufficient materials for clothing, food, and housing to everyone under an equitable law of distribution, and to provide sympathetic care in sickness and old age. Thus a society where socialism is practiced forms a great commonwealth of insured citizens. People need not save for their offsprings or for themselves for illness or old age. The society assures them a happy life if they perform their tasks in accordance with their abilities. Many people mistakenly regard socialism as an ideology that advocates confiscation of all private property and its equal distribution to the entire population. However, this is pure misunderstanding, which need not be seriously entertained. If all the property of the nation is equally divided among the entire population, the income of an individual will be unexpectedly small. Who can sustain himself with a comfortable life with that little? Socialism does not intend to redistribute land or capital in any country. It simply plans to place under public ownership the means of production, such as land and capital, and attempts to distribute equitably the wealth created by these means of production. Just how much each individual's income will be, we have no way of ascertaining. However, if one realizes how many products are wasted in the process of free competition today, there is no doubt that production will increase greatly once socialism is put into practice.

In this manner, if clothing, food, and housing—which constitute the bases of our livelihood—or wealth can be equitably and adequately distributed, the enjoyment and happiness people receive from them will be better equalized. As one of our major goals we must strive for the right to receive equal education. Our ideal is to extend the age of compulsory education to twenty, and educate all youth of school age with public funds. However, this cannot be implemented under the existing social system. Thus our party advocates that compulsory education be extended until graduation from senior grade school, and no tuition shall be imposed. Furthermore, textbooks must be supplied to them by public funds. Education is the source of human activities. Every citizen has a right to free education. It goes without saying that public funds must be committed toward the education of its citizens. We advocate equity in livelihood and education because we are convinced that the gap separating the rich and the poor emanates from these two factors.

Some people may fear that the Social Democratic Party advocates radicalism and attempts to use dangerous methods to attain its goals. While our doctrine may be radical, the methods we employ are consistently peaceful. We absolutely outlaw war as a means of international politics. How much more so do we advocate peace among individuals! To strike with a sword or to cast a bomb are acts committed only by the nihilists and anarchists. The Social Democratic Party is unalterably opposed to the use of force and shall not repeat the foolishness of the nihilists or anarchists. There were many instances in which the use of force contributed to the success of great revolutions. However, they were products of their times, and their examples cannot be emulated by us. Our party holds great and farsighted ideals. We plan to effect a basic reform of our society. Thus we must decisively reject any strong-arm tactics employed by itinerant troublemakers. We own pens and tongues that are far sharper than the edges of swords. We have a constitutional government that is far stronger than the military system. If we employ these methods to implement our avowed goals, what need is there for reverting to the foolishness of swords and bombs. We are forming a political party in order to take advantage of these civilized methods.

The Imperial Diet shall be our theater of action for the future. One day when our party gains the majority in the Diet, that day will become the day we implement our ideals. However, as described earlier, today's Diet is controlled by landlords and investors. They are misusing the Diet for their own benefits. . . . How can we accomplish equitable distribution of political power to the majority of people? There is one way. It is to reform the election law and institute with firm resolve universal suffrage. Once the majority of people are enfranchised, they pass the first hurdle toward betterment of their own welfare. In addition, if an equitable election law is adopted under which the opinion of the minority can be heard, no matter how small the membership of the Social Democratic Party may be, we can send our representatives to the Diet. Therefore as the first step toward attaining its goals, the party wishes to demand vehemently a reform in the election law.

However, there are certain dangers attendant to enfranchising people who lack education. Unless they are accustomed to self-government, they may misuse their right to vote. In today's society, where the poor are completely suppressed by the rich, the poor may follow the wishes of the rich in casting their votes. Therefore, along with our attempt to find a way of enfranchising them, we deem it as our most urgent task to provide adequate education and training for them. We not only demand that the government provide necessary protection for laborers and tenants who constitute the majority of our people, but we also desire to have a law enacted that will enable them to organize freely. Organization is the very life blood of our working men and is their only weapon. In so doing, they can not only cultivate the spirit of self-government but also receive education and training. Investors often frown upon organization by their workers, and in some extreme cases, they discharge those who join a labor union. For example, the Cotton Manufacturers Association of Kansai, while forming its own powerful organization, vehemently opposes unionization of its workers. Thus, if any worker infringes on the association's regulations, he is immediately discharged and cannot be rehired by any other member companies of the association. This system is an attempt to perpetuate the workers in their ignorant state, and to overwork them like horses and oxen. For the sake of humanity, and for the sake of economic development, we are compelled to repulse such attempts. In short, our party expects and demands enactment of a labor union law that will permit workers to organize freely, provided such an organization will not be detrimental to public safety. In this manner these workers can find a way for self-help and self-protection.

This is our platform. Our party is born with these ideals in response to the challenge of our times. Behold, socialism is against individualistic competition and ethnocentric militarism, and democracy is antipathetic to artificial aristocracy. The Social Democratic Party sets as its goals: to destroy the gap existing between the rich and the poor and to increase the welfare of all men. Are these not what the trends of the world demand, and are they not the ultimate goals of all humanity?

9 **Against the Wartime Tax, 1904**[18] The phrase "for the sake of war" is a powerful narcotic. With this phrase, the sagacious loses his sagacity, the clever loses his clarity, the wise loses his wisdom, and the courageous loses his courage. How much more will the present political parties lose who are not sagacious, clever, wise, or courageous!

All political parties in the Diet are drugged by the phrase "for the sake of war." They discard their common sense, abandon their rationality, and forget the leadership power given to them as political parties. They are now reduced to a

---

[18]Kōtoku Shūsui, *"A-a Zōzei"* (Oh, the Additional Tax!), in *Shūkan Heimin Shimbun,* no. 20, March 27, 1904.

mere machine. What kind of machine is it? It is a machine to produce more revenues. And the government skillfully manipulates this automatic machine to levy a burdensome tax of 60 million yen on us.

Oh, the additional 60 million yen tax! The heavy and burdensome additional levy! It is just "for the sake of war." . . . Wealth does not fall from heaven nor emerge from the earth. The pain that the nation must bear in paying the additional tax is still a pain. . . . Why must the nation bear this burdensome tax? Why can we not prevent this pain and misfortune from happening? Once they happen, why can we not eliminate them? Why must we obey the government blindly? They say "for the sake of war," and there is no other way. Then why must the nation fight this war? Can we somehow eliminate it as well? Why must we blindly enter into war? . . .

We organize a nation, establish a government, and in order to maintain that government, we contribute a part of the wealth produced by us. Why do we do these things? It is for no other reason than to sustain our peace, happiness, and progress! In other words, the national government provides the means and is our tool to bring about our peace, happiness, and progress, and the taxes are the price we pay for these goals. . . .

If this were true, is there any reason for allowing the existence of a national government that instead of profiting us with peace, happiness, and progress, oppresses us, restrains us and robs us of our possessions. . . .

I am not suggesting that the present-day national government is all like that, nor am I saying that the present-day Japanese government is utterly useless. However, I must clearly state that the present war, and especially the levying of excessive taxes "for the sake of war," are contrary to the basic reasons for organizing and supporting a national government.

I have said often that international wars may benefit only a small number of people, but they disturb peace, prevent progress, and create a host of miseries for the common people. It has come to pass in this manner because there were ambitious politicians who advocated war, which was pleasing to soldiers anxious for their war decorations. Sly war profiteers praised the war, and many reporters gave their support by failing to give the truth in their writing. They competed with one another to incite and urge the simple-minded common people to support the war. Behold, generals may proclaim their battle victories, but the people do not receive one extra grain of rice. Our military might may be known throughout the world, but our people do not get one extra suit of clothing. Many of our fellow countrymen are exposed to the dangers of the battlefields, and the families they left behind cry because of hunger. Our commerce and industry have to retrench, prices go up, laborers lose their jobs, and minor officials have their salaries cut. Yet we are forced to subscribe to the military bonds and to make contributions from our savings. To this end we pay an excessive amount of burdensome taxes, which injures very deeply the livelihood of the poor. . . . When we think of these little things, we question the wisdom of having a state, a government, or taxes.

I am not suggesting today that we must avoid military duties and refuse to pay taxes as taught by Tolstoy. . . . However, if the people seriously wish to eliminate unhappiness and pain, they must rise up immediately to eliminate the causes of this unhappiness and pain. What are the causes? They can be found in the unjust organization of the present-day state system. Let us change a government by politicians, war profiteers, soldiers and their families into a government by the people. Let us change a government "for the sake of war," into a government for peace. Let us change a government that oppresses, restrains and robs people into one which promotes peace, happiness, and prosperity. How can we accomplish these goals? We can begin by distributing political power to all the people and complete the task by forbidding private ownership of land and capital to ensure that the fruits of labor can be kept in the hands of producers. In other words, we must change our present military system, capitalistic system, and class system and implement a socialistic system. Once this is accomplished, we can have genuine happiness, as described in the ancient Chinese ode:

> I dig a well to drink its water,
>> I cultivate a field to produce food,
> At sunrise I go to the field,
>> At sunset I retire to my shelter.
> The power of the Emperor
>> Reacheth me not.

Is this not self-evident?

As I see our people unable to understand these simple and clear-cut facts and truth, and repressing tears to bear the pain and unhappiness "for the sake of war," more than ever, I become convinced of the important role I must play as a socialist.

XIII

Taishō Democracy

The Taishō period (1912) began with a political crisis involving the Third Katsura Cabinet, and its fall signified decline of the old order in which a handful of oligarchs dominated and manipulated Japanese politics. The new era brought a sense of popular participation and created an expanding intellectual horizon. In political theory, Yoshino Sakuzō became an advocate of *minpon shugi,* which is somewhat comparable to Lincoln's government by the people and for the people, without including government of the people. The freer air, as represented in Yoshino's pronouncements, made it possible for popular demonstrations against the government, including rice riots, and unhampered criticisms of the Terauchi Cabinet's "unconstitutional" behavior and of the Siberian expedition. It was also a motivating force in the enactment of the universal suffrage law of 1925.

Intellectually the period was dominated by the neo-Kantian school of idealism and culturalism. Immanuel Kant (1724–1804) became the philosopher most admired by the Japanese, and many of his works were translated into Japanese. With each work published came a new corps of adherents. Henri Bergson's (1859–1941) *élan vital* deeply influenced many philosophers, including Nishida Kitarō (1870–1945).

In labor relations, Yūaikai (Friendship Association) began in the spirit of conciliation. However, with the rapid changes in the industrial production caused by World War I, labor disputes became frequent. Radicalism, including left-wing socialism, Marxism, and anarchism, also became part of the intellectual tradition. It was the success of the Bolshevik revolution in Russia in 1917, along with the intensification of radical agitation, which caused the Japanese government to adopt the most stringent peace preservation law, replacing milder earlier versions. This, incidentally, was enacted in the same year as the universal suffrage law.

In the face of radicalism, some idealism also survived. Mushanokōji Saneatsu (1885–1976) and Arishima Takeo (1878–1923) established their farm communes and cooperative farms in the same humanistic spirit that influenced Leo Tolstoy (1817–75). There was also a movement toward women's liberation.

Politically, it was the formation of a Cabinet headed by a prime minister without nobility rank, Hara Takashi (1856–1921), nicknamed a *heimin saishō* (commoner prime minister), that gave a sense of progress toward democracy. It also ushered in a brief period of party government.

In foreign relations, Japan experienced participation in World War I and the Siberian expedition. There was also an imperialistic misadventure in China represented in her twenty-one demands to Yuan Shikai's government. Inclusion of the twenty-one demands in this chapter celebrating various phases of Taishō democracy may appear an oddity. However, chronologically it was part of the Taishō legacy, and the demands to China remained one of the major problems that the intellectuals had to face. Advocates of democracy at home, including Yoshino Sakuzō, did not find it inconsistent to support military expansion overseas. This intellectual ambivalence may explain why military fascism could so easily take hold in the next decade, as detailed in Chapter XIV.

The Taishō era ended with some sad notes, the infirmity of the Emperor and the catastrophe of the great Kantō earthquake of 1923. It was a brief era lasting only a little over fourteen years. It is sometimes likened to a valley between the great peaks of Meiji (1868–1912) and Shōwa (1926–89). Yet it was a period that showed significant progress toward the direction of democracy, from which post–World War II Japan continues to seek inspiration.

YOSHINO SAKUZŌ'S MINPON SHUGI

*In attempting to articulate the nature of democracy for Taishō Japan, Yoshino Sakuzō (1878–1933) had to face the problem of seemingly irreconcilable concepts of the sovereignty of the emperor, as enunciated in the Meiji constitution, and the sovereignty of the people. Yoshino resolved this problem by stating that democracy in the sense of sovereignty residing in the people (*minshu shugi)* could not apply to Japan. On the other hand, whether a country be a monarchy or a democracy, that country should have a government organized for the people, serving their welfare, and decisions reached by it should reflect the will of the people. This he called* minpon shugi, *which means an ideology having people as the base, or loosely translated, "democracy" in a more narrow and confined sense.*

After his graduation from Tokyo University, Yoshino studied in England, Germany and the United States. Upon his return he became professor of political science at Tokyo University and began contributing to the Chūo Kōron, *the prestigious journal of opinion. He organized Reimeikai, a study group, to pro-*

mote the cause of democracy and later joined the Asahi *newspapers. The following article first appeared in 1914, justifying antigovernment demonstrations and
advocating openness in the conduct of government affairs. It signaled a fit beginning for Taishō democracy.*

1 **On Demonstration, 1914**[1] Following a set pattern, there was a demonstration in Hibiya [a centrally located district of Tokyo facing the Imperial Palace] in
February of this year. The demonstration was held against the Siemens affair in
which high-ranking naval officers were alleged to have received bribes for warship construction. A subsidiary issue was the question of tax reduction. A similar
demonstration took place during the month of February in 1913. It was a more
militant one than this year's and resulted in the ouster of Prince Katsura from his
premiership. . . . Both of these demonstrations shared one thing in common. They
were staged for the purpose of effecting changes in our political system. . . .

It is a source of concern to us to see the masses assembling and creating
disturbances. On the other hand, however, some people argue that demonstrations are beneficial to the development of constitutional rule in Japan. I, for one,
welcome demonstrations if they can make the judgment of the people become
the final arbitrator in interpreting political issues or in conferring or accepting
political powers. If the will of the people can become a preponderant influence in
our politics, then demonstrations can be justified.

Of course, even in the past, the judgment of the people was not completely
ignored in politics. In most instances, people could not participate in the process
of making binding final decisions. . . . Even after the promulgation of the constitution, changes in government were never conducted in full public view and in
an aboveboard manner. For some time, it has been asserted that the Cabinet
should be a transcendental one, existing above politics and above any shift in the
balance of power within the Diet. . . . Around the time the constitution was
promulgated, changes in the Cabinet were effected in most instances by decisions made secretly by the clan oligarchs (*hanbatsu*). No one outside the
oligarchs' circle could tell why the Kuroda Cabinet had to be replaced by the Itō
Cabinet. In any event, the will of the people, or the power blocks in the Diet that
represented the will of the people, had nothing to do with changes in government. . . .

The development of political parties, especially the emergence of strong parties such as the Seiyūkai, was an occasion for hope that the government would
have to recognize the power of the people and be influenced by it in determining
changes in government. It was felt that the power of the political parties could
not be ignored. Before long, however, party executives began entering into secret

[1]Yoshino Sakuzō, "*Minshuteki Shijiundō o Ronzu* (On Democratic Demonstrations),"
reprinted in *Chūō Kōron,* November 1965, pp. 366–75.

deals with the government and started conferring or accepting political power in a manner lacking fairness. . . . This is not the way constitutional rule should develop or function. We must somehow destroy this political secrecy.

To destroy it, there is no other recourse but to rely on the power of the people. When there is a blatant abuse of power, and normal means cannot destroy it, one is forced to resort to demonstration. If demonstrations become more prevalent, they can revitalize the stale undercurrent in the political world and deepen the understanding of politics by the people. In this sense, demonstrations can contribute toward the development of a constitutional government. . . .

There are many obstinate people in this world who look with disdain on acquisition of power by the people. They somehow deem the extension of power to the people as something akin to a socialistic or subversive thought, or at times associate it with the disturbances created by the mobs in the French Revolution. . . . This type of mind set is prevalent among older people, and it is also ingrained in the so-called bureaucrats. However, when we observe the background of these people with obstinate ideas, it is not difficult to discover that they are usually fearful of losing their own power base when the power of the people is expanded. In order to maintain their present position, they have to suppress the rise in people's power. . . .

Unfortunately these people's thoughts are clouded by a one-sided view. Everything has its positive and negative aspects, and indeed democracy has certain shortcomings. If we are to speak of shortcomings, however, we must also recognize the existence of shortcomings in oligarchy. In fact, if the two are compared, oligarchy will be found to contain more shortcomings. Oligarchy by its nature stresses secrecy, and wrongdoings may not become readily apparent. In contrast, democracy is conducted in full public view, and any wrongdoing can immediately be called to the attention of the observers. Thus people tend to name the shortcomings of democracy and forget similar shortcomings existing in oligarchy. If one happens to be a member of the clan oligarchy, no matter how knowledgeable he may be, he is not likely to discover the ills of oligarchy.

Politics of a nation must first of all abide by the principles of justice, unencumbered by secrecy. . . . However, if only a few professional politicians, whose power is not based on the support of the people, can make secret deals, there is bound to be some personal considerations. . . . For example, when an officer purchases certain items, if the purchase is made in full public view, there can be no wrongdoing. However, once the purchase is made only from a certain special party, wrongdoing can occur. This was evident in the bribery case of the navy. Who would have doubted the loyalty and devotion of the officers of the imperial navy? Yet a very clear case of corruption existed because their procurement was done behind the dark screen of secrecy. If the navy could be made into a glass box open to inspection from every corner, then the corruption would not have taken place. There are many other similar instances. . . .

If we subscribe to this view, then regardless of certain merits it possesses, oligarchy cannot compare favorably with democracy. Once a person gains political power, he wishes to monopolize it. . . . To safeguard the purity of politics, we must insist on recognizing the power of the people. In this sense, I am pro-democracy, and I also applaud the recent demonstrations.

However, several rebuttals are put forward against this view. The first one states that the view just expressed is not consistent with the national polity of Japan and is contrary to the Japanese constitution. . . . The national polity of Japan does not permit the will of the people to become the final arbitrator. However, we must consider this: When the Emperor exercises his power, he invariably consults someone. He does not exercise his power alone and has an option of consulting a small number of people or a large number of people. The fact that the Emperor consults the opinion of the people in exercising his power does not go counter to the national polity. If one maintains that democracy is contrary to the national polity, then oligarchy is also contrary to the national polity. As we have indicated, the difference lies merely in the number of people the Emperor consults. . . . The Charter Oath of Emperor Meiji states that "a deliberative assembly shall be convoked on a broad basis, and all matters of state shall be decided by open discussion." If anyone denies that democracy is consistent with the national polity of Japan, it must be remembered that this thought comes from an archaic notion that the nobility must be placed between the Emperor and the people to defend the former from the latter. . . .

The notion that democracy is contrary to the constitution stems from a confusion between legality and politics. . . . The function of law is to show a certain direction, but in its application it must be entirely flexible. Thus within the framework of law, political precedents have their rightful place. For example, one of the constitutional principles states that the Emperor has the power to appoint or dismiss his ministers. However, within the framework of this principle, a precedent can be established that can permit formation of a party Cabinet. It is true that in the final analysis, the Emperor possesses the power to appoint his ministers. But in practice, the Emperor has never appointed his ministers by solely relying on his own judgment. The Emperor normally acts on the recommendations of several persons. If consultation is to be made with a certain group, then a precedent can also be established to make the political parties perform that function. . . .

The second objection to democracy stems from a notion that participation in the political process by ignorant people is too dangerous a step to take. . . . Some people maintain that participation in the political process requires understanding of the nature of that participation and adequate knowledge of politics. There is no doubt that democracy can grow only among the people who are sufficiently advanced. However, democracy in the final analysis does not require advance in political knowledge as the necessary prerequisite. Politics is often incomprehensible not only to the common people but also to those who have received higher education. . . . For example, lately we have been debating the desirability of abolishing the business tax, or the desirability of reducing the land tax. We must judge these issues from the perspectives of our overall national interest, but I wonder how many college students or even representatives will not be baffled by the complexity of these issues. If we insist on allowing participation in politics only to those people who can determine the pros and cons of these technical questions, we have to subscribe to the idealism of Plato in which only philosophers can govern.

Under a democratic form of government, people select as their representatives those persons in whose qualifications they have confidence. The candidates for office state their views and appeal to the people for their support. . . . It does not follow that people can always pass judgment on the views expressed by the candidates. . . . The minimum requirement that democracy makes of the people is to pass judgment on the personality of the candidates, determining which one of the candidates is a better person, more dependable, or can be entrusted with the affairs of state. . . . The ability to discern the personality of the candidates does not require special training in politics, law, or economics. I am sure this is not an excessive requirement.

. . . Often those people who are closer to certain basic issues are not necessarily the best judges of the problems involved. They may not be able to transcend immediate issues and render impartial judgment. Thus occasionally it may be better to have educated guesses of outsiders. For example, many strategic decisions are made by staff officers far removed from the battle scene and not by those who are in actual command. The analogy permits us to stress from a different perspective the importance of having a representative government. . . .

The third objection to the democratic form of government comes from those people who insist that democracy brings forth many incidences of corruption and other ills. What are they referring to? Lately in Japan, some people say that the United States is suffering from mob rule and presents a sorry example of the ills of democracy. This type of argument either stems from an emotional outburst against the United States because of her recent Japanese exclusion act or from a complete ignorance of the political development of the United States in recent years. It is true that the United States shows all the ills of democracy in their extremes. But on the other hand, she is also an outstanding showcase of democracy. Oftentimes, the good points are replaced by bad ones, and vice versa. But in general the ills are few and the country benefits from the advantages given by a democratic form of government. One can look at the condition of the federal government with envy. Not a single one of its Cabinet secretaries has been under suspicion of corruption.

In short, democracy is not something to be disdained, as some people fretfully insist, but it must be welcomed. Setting aside the question of advantages and disadvantages, we must not forget that democracy is one of the rising forces in the world today. Whatever constitutional lawyers or defenders of the clan oligarchy may say, the power of the people is on the rise day after day. There is nothing one can do except to help nurture it. Assuming that democracy is not desirable, still one cannot suppress it totally. We must recognize this fact in planning the future of our nation.

There are, however, some phenomena that give us great concern. Democratic movement is a great asset to politics when it is conducted spontaneously and positively. It is not desirable if the masses congregate and indulge in demonstrations without having any concrete proposals. The demonstration against the conclusion of the Treaty of Portsmouth in September 1905 cannot be considered fully spontaneous. However, there was a definite demand among the people. There were many instances of deplorable violence, but they had certain meanings. However, most of the recent demonstrations cannot be considered positive or spontaneous. I suspect some men who witnessed the strength of the people who were united for a cause in 1905 are now organizing demonstrations to utilize that strength for other self-serving purposes. These recent demonstrations appear to have agitators behind them. . . .

If we are committed to democracy as our ultimate goal [and eliminate causes for the recurrence of demonstrations], we must remove existing inequities and work toward betterment of our constitutional government. . . .

Among the two major approaches, the first is to institute certain reforms in the implementation of our constitutional government. Disturbances occur when the constitutional government is not smoothly functioning. . . . There are several ways in which we can bring about that smooth functioning of our government. The first is expansion of the right to vote to a larger segment of our population and equitable redistribution of electoral districts. . . . The second is the establishment of party government. . . which in turn may require rivalry by two major political parties. Only future events can determine if political parties can be organized into two groups. It cannot be legislated as in the case of suffrage. What we must do at the present time is to eliminate those existing conditions that are detrimental to the development of party government. . . .

The second approach concerns the development of people themselves. This can again be divided into two main topics. The first is, of course, economic development. If life is difficult, people tend to give in to agitation and can be taken advantage of by demagogues. In the olden days we spoke of "those who have permanent treasure have steady hearts." To stabilize the strength of our people in a healthy manner, we must enact certain social legislations in order to secure livelihood for the lower class of people. . . .

Another point we must consider is the nurturing of people's intellectual and spiritual development. The first thing that comes to mind is encouragement of political education which is not done at all today. In the Western world, political parties are organized in such a way that they must continuously appeal to the people for their support. They do not neglect to reach the people by all available means. They may not make political education one of their major goals, but they conduct speeches, publish newspapers, and issue tracts and pamphlets on current problems. How poorly our political parties compare with them.

Another aspect deals with moral education of the people. We must enlighten the people, make them understand the voice of justice, and make their minds receptive to justice. Without this, democracy may not be able to rise above the abyss of corruption. On this point I am most impressed with an example set by the United States. In New York, there is a political organization called Tammany Hall, making a mockery of the municipal government. Abuses were rampant, but when some reformers began decrying against such evils, people responded by showing their determination to eradicate once for all the atmosphere of corruption. Indeed, the voice of justice should find a harmonious chord in the moral fiber of the nation. A young man in his early thirties was elected mayor after he hoisted the banner of reform.[2] His reforms are unorthodox but heartwarming. When I hear that he is succeeding in eradicating many existing ills, my heart is filled with envy. We must guide our people to attain this level of understanding. True, this can influence politics only indirectly, but I think it is the most essential condition in the development of democracy. On this point, I beseech the help and collaboration of educators and religious leaders with great expectation.

THE TWENTY-ONE DEMANDS

In 1915, England, France, Germany, and Russia were fighting in Europe and the United States was being drawn closer to the conflict. China remained neutral, but during the preceding year, Japanese troops moved freely across Chinese soil to occupy the German-leased territory of Jiaozhou. Internally, Yuan Shikai's government was being challenged by the revolutionary movement of Sun Yat-sen, and Yuan's aspiration to establish a monarchy further weakened his position. This was the setting under which the Japanese attempted to extend their influence in China.

The twenty-one demands were presented to Yuan Shikai on January 18, 1915, by the Japanese minister to Beijing. These demands were divided into five groups: three concerned with the extension of Japanese rights in Shandong, Manchuria, Fujian and one with the control of Han-yeh-ping Company, which was the chief supplier of iron ore in China. The fifth group, if accepted, would have made China virtually a protectorate of Japan.

Japan's military threat, combined with the inability of the Western powers to intervene on behalf of China, finally resulted in the acceptance of the first four groups by Yuan's government on May 9. The public, including leading intellectuals, strongly supported this unequivocal expression of continental expansion. Yoshino Sakuzō published a book, Nisshi Kōshō Ron *(On Negotiations between Japan and China), the same year to render his expert opinion and support. This*

---

[2]The thirty-four-year-old Fusion candidate, John Purroy Mitchell, was elected mayor of New York in November 1913.

political scientist and advocate of democracy was also a student of Chinese affairs with a number of books on China to his credit. In this book Yoshino claimed that the demands represented Japan's minimum conditions, and he "deeply regretted the elimination of Group V." He, however, urged the Japanese government to explain to the Chinese that Japan was forced to take this stand because of international competition and suggested that in future dealings with China empathy and respect should become part of Japan's posture. He had a foreboding that the cycle of revolution in China was not over and that the younger generation would turn that into an even uglier struggle. As Yoshino feared, the twenty-one demands became the symbol of foreign aggression for the Chinese and provided a rallying point for student nationalism which later culminated in the May Fourth Movement of 1919.

Document 2 below contains the English version of the twenty-one demands as subsequently published by the Japanese government. (The English version published by the Chinese government differed in some minor points.) To grasp the extent of Japanese demands, please consult a map of China. Place names are given first in the manner they appeared in the official version and then in pinyin *in brackets.*

2 The Twenty-one Demands Presented by Japan to China, January 18, 1915[3]

GROUP I

The Japanese Government and the Chinese Government, being desirous to maintain the general peace in the Far East and to strengthen the relations of amity and good neighborhood existing between the two countries, agree to the following articles:

ARTICLE I. The Chinese Government engage to give full assent to all matters that the Japanese Government may hereafter agree with the German Government respecting the disposition of all the rights, interests, and concessions, which, in virtue of treaties or otherwise, Germany possesses vis-à-vis China in relation to the Province of Shantung [Shandong].

ARTICLE II. The Chinese Government engage that, within the Province of Shantung or along its coast, no territory or island will be ceded or leased to any other Power, under any pretext whatever.

ARTICLE III. The Chinese Government agree to Japan's building a railway connecting Chefoo or Lungkow [Longkou] with the Kiaochou-Tsinfu [i.e., Qingdao-Jinan] Railway.

ARTICLE IV. The Chinese Government engage to open of their own accord,

---

[3]From John V.A. MacMurray, *Treaties and Agreements with and Concerning China, 1894–1919* (New York: Oxford University Press, 1921), vol. 2, pp. 1231–33.

as soon as possible, certain important cities and towns in the Province of Shantung for the residence and commerce of foreigners. The places to be so opened shall be decided upon in a separate agreement.

GROUP II

The Japanese Government and the Chinese Government, in view of the fact that the Chinese Government has always recognized the predominant position of Japan in South Manchuria and Eastern Inner Mongolia, agree to the following articles:

ARTICLE I. The two Contracting Parties mutually agree that the term of the lease of Port Arthur [Lushun] and Dairen [Dalian] and the term respecting the South Manchuria Railway and the Antung-Mukden [i.e., Dandong-Shenyang] Railway shall be extended to a further period of 99 years respectively.

ARTICLE II. The Japanese subjects shall be permitted in South Manchuria and Eastern Inner Mongolia to lease or own land required either for erecting buildings for various commercial and industrial uses or for farming.

ARTICLE III. The Japanese subjects shall have liberty to enter, reside, and travel in South Manchuria and Eastern Inner Mongolia, and to carry on business of various kinds—commercial, industrial, and otherwise.

ARTICLE IV. The Chinese Government grant to the Japanese subjects the right of mining in South Manchuria and Eastern Inner Mongolia. As regards the mines to be worked, they shall be decided upon in a separate agreement.

ARTICLE V. The Chinese Government agree that the consent of the Japanese Government shall be obtained in advance, (1) whenever it is proposed to grant to other nationals the right of constructing a railway or to obtain from other nationals the supply of funds for constructing a railway in South Manchuria and Eastern Inner Mongolia, and (2) whenever a loan is to be made with any other Power, under security of the taxes of South Manchuria and Eastern Inner Mongolia.

ARTICLE VI. The Chinese Government engage that whenever the Chinese Government need the service of political, financial, or military advisers or instructors in South Manchuria or in Eastern Inner Mongolia, Japan shall first be consulted.

ARTICLE VII. The Chinese Government agree that the control and management of the Kirin-Changchun [Jilin-Changchun] Railway shall be handed over to Japan for a term of 99 years dating from the signing of this Treaty.

GROUP III

The Japanese Government and the Chinese Government, having regard to the close relations existing between Japanese capitalists and the Han-Yeh-Ping Company and desiring to promote the common interests of the two nations, agree to the following articles:

ARTICLE I. The two Contracting Parties mutually agree that when the opportune moment arrives the Han-Yeh-Ping Company shall be made a joint concern of the two nations, and that, without the consent of the Japanese Government, the Chinese Government shall not dispose or permit the Company to dispose of any right or property of the Company.

ARTICLE II. The Chinese Government engage that, as a necessary measure for protection of the invested interests of Japanese capitalists, no mines in the neighborhood of those owned by the Han-Yeh-Ping Company shall be permitted, without the consent of the said Company, to be worked by anyone other than the said Company; and further that whenever it is proposed to take any other measure which may likely affect the interests of the said Company directly or indirectly, the consent of the said Company shall first be obtained.

GROUP IV

The Japanese Government and the Chinese Government, with the object of effectively preserving the territorial integrity of China, agree to the following article:

The Chinese Government engage not to cede or lease to any other Power any harbor or bay on or any island along the coast of China.

GROUP V

1. The Chinese Central Government to engage influential Japanese as political, financial, and military advisers;

2. The Chinese Government to grant the Japanese hospitals, temples, and schools in the interior of China the right to own land;

3. In the face of many police disputes which have hitherto arisen between Japan and China, causing no little annoyance, the police in localities (in China), where such arrangements are necessary, to be placed under joint Japanese and Chinese administration, or Japanese to be employed in police offices in such localities, so as to help at the same time the improvement of the Chinese Police Service;

4. China to obtain from Japan supply of a certain quantity of arms, or to establish an arsenal in China under joint Japanese and Chinese management and to be supplied with experts and materials from Japan;

5. In order to help the development of the Nanchang-Kiukiang [Nanchang-Jiujiang] Railway, with which Japanese capitalists are so closely identified, and with due regard to the negotiations which have for years been pending between Japan and China in relation to the railway question in South China, China to agree to give to Japan the right of constructing a railway to connect Wuchang and the Kiukiang-Nanchang line, and also the railways between Nanchang and Hangchou [Hangzhou] and between Nanchang and Chaochou [Chaozhou];

6. In view of the relations between the Province of Fukien and Formosa [Taiwan] and of the agreement respecting the non-alienation of that province, Japan to be consulted first whenever foreign capital is needed in connection with

the railways, mines, and harbor works (including dockyards) in the Province of Fukien;

7. China to grant to Japanese subjects the right of preaching in China.

RICE RIOTS AND EMERGENCE OF HARA CABINET

Rice riots began on July 23, 1918, at a fishing village in Toyama prefecture and spread quickly to the rest of the nation. The riots were not well organized, and their participants did not espouse any particular political ideology. If anything, they showed no political sophistication. Yet it still required the dispatch of troops to stop the spread of riots. This gave a sense of uneasiness to the Genrō (elder statesmen), and to Yamagata Aritomo in particular. It was translated into a distrust for the Terauchi Cabinet, and when it resigned, Yamagata agreed to the formation of a Cabinet headed by Hara Takashi (or Kei, 1856–1921) who was president of the Seiyūkai. With the exception of foreign, army, and navy ministers, the Hara Cabinet consisted of members of the Seiyyūkai, and as such became the first party Cabinet in Japan.

The following two documents are from the diary of Hara Takashi which contained eighty-two original volumes covering the period from April 14, 1875, through October 25, 1921, or from the author's twentieth year to ten days before his assassination. It is one of the most outstanding inside histories of the Meiji-Taishō periods.

3   **Rice Riots as Seen by Hara Takashi, 1918**[4] *August 15.* There has been a number of riots in different parts of the country resulting from a sharp rise in the price of rice, and some of them have required the sending of troops. In view of this, I sent a telegram [from my home in Morioka] to the Seiyūkai's branch office in Sapporo indicating my desire to proceed with the Northeast regional meeting of the Seiyūkai scheduled to be held in Sapporo on the 18th, but also suggesting that festivities and banquets must be canceled. A telegram of similar content was also sent to the party headquarters. However, a telegram from Mr. Yokota [Sennosuke, 1870–1925], the party secretary general, requested that I reconsider the matter, citing that disturbances in the Kyoto-Kobe area were getting worse. There were also other telegrams. Martial law was declared in Osaka, and Tokyo did not escape riots, which were followed by the dispatch of troops. In other areas there were major and minor disturbances. The Imperial Household graciously donated three million yen, and Mitsui and Mitsubishi each donated one million yen. The national treasury also appropriated ten million yen

---

[4]Hara Keiichirō, ed., *Hara Kei Nikki (Diary of Hara Takashi)* (Tokyo: Fukumura Shuppansha, 1965), vol. 4, p. 430.

for the relief effort. People were restive, and last night the government suppressed all news publications relating to riots. With these in mind, I became convinced that it was not appropriate to hold the projected regional meeting even though its site, Hokkaido, remained calm. Thus I sent another telegram to the Sapporo branch office canceling my previous telegram. I noted that the riots related to the rising rice price were getting much worse and troops were being dispatched to guard against further disturbances. It would not be appropriate at this time to hold the projected meeting, and it ought to be postponed. I also sent telegrams to the same effect to Secretary General Yokota and other parties.

Since last year, the agriculture minister worked diligently to adjust the price of rice, but every step he took failed and instead stimulated further rise in the price of rice. Finally, the great riot occurred. However, the government seems intent on finding a scapegoat without admitting its own mistake. At present, we do not have a shortage of rice in local areas. Yet we have riots reminiscent of the times of poor harvest. This is caused by the misrule of the government who has erroneously believed in the power of laws and regulations through which it has sought to lower the price of rice. . . .

August 19. Riots in various areas seem to have subsided somewhat. However, there are some riots in entirely new areas, and it does not mean that everything is under control. The mayor of Morioka, Mr. Kitada, came to see me saying that he heard rumors that riots might spread to Morioka. He succeeded in lowering the price of rice to 30 sen a quart (*shō*) and was continuing to look for other means of lowering the price. The city received a little over 5,000 yen as its share of the imperial donation. I immediately gave him 300 yen. The mayor said he was confident of receiving 20,000 yen. . . .

4 Emergence of the Hara Cabinet, 1918[5] *September 25.* Saionji [Kimmochi, *Genrō,* 1849–1940] called me on the phone, asking me to meet him at the Tokyo Station Hotel at 1 P.M. As I visited him there, he told me what has transpired since yesterday, which is as follows:

Yesterday morning Saionji visited Yamagata [Aritomo, *Genrō,* 1838–1922] as promised. . . . When they came to the question who should become the next prime minister, Saionji wanted Yamagata to open the discussion. Yamagata said that Itō [Miyoji, 1857–1934] was quite unsatisfactory, and neither Hirata [Tōsuke, 1849–1925] nor Kiyoura [Keigo, 1850–1942] was acceptable. In this vein he only raised negative aspects without showing any willingness to name a single candidate. Saionji felt that it was useless to hesitate any longer, and if Yamagata so disliked any of the major candidates, he might just as well make his own nomination. He then suggested the name of Hara, saying that he felt Hara seemed the right man for the present occasion. Yamagata said that it was one of

---

[5]*Ibid.,* vol. 5, pp. 12–14.

the possible solutions and asked Saionji if Hara would accept. Saionji said he had not spoken to Hara about this and could not be certain. He did hint that, unlike Saionji himself, Hara was president of a political party, and in order to accommodate the desires of his party members, Hara would have to accept if an offer were made. Yamagata then asked if the Seiyūkai would form a government in cooperation with the Kenseikai. Saionji answered that it would not happen unless the process of cabinet formation would be a prolonged one. However, if the government could not be formed quickly, some of the lower-echelon party members might collaborate with each other and influence their superiors to form a coalition government with the Kenseikai. In any event, there was no present danger of such an occurrence. Yamagata then asked how Hara felt toward him. Saionji replied that Hara would be able to talk to Yamagata frankly and would seek Yamagata's advice once he became the prime minister. He also suggested to Yamagata that the latter should feel free to call to Hara's attention what ought to be done from time to time. In agreeing to this proposition, Yamagata said that he and Hara did not differ on any of the major issues. He did say that Hara was intent on making his political party a majority party and on improving political parties as such (Hara had said this to Yamagata three years ago in Odawara) and with this he would take issue. Aside from this particular issue, Yamagata had no fundamental disagreement with Hara and agreed to have Hara form a new government. However, as to the matter of advising the throne of Hara's selection, Yamagata wanted Saionji to carry out the task. (In Saionji's view, Yamagata somehow wanted to skirt the issue [of naming a party politician] even though it was within his power to endorse it formally. A number of years ago, Yamagata had told the Kenseikai that one political party or group would not be sufficient to cope with difficult problems facing the country. Perhaps he did not want to show inconsistency in his public act.) He asked Saionji to consult with Matsukata [Masayoshi, *Genrō*, 1835–1924]. When Saionji said that he was going to see Matsukata right away, Yamagata stated that he would speak to Matsukata directly. . . .

During the Saionji-Yamagata conversation, the discussion extended to the question of bureaucracy. Saionji felt that Yamagata disliked political parties because he was interested in restoring power to the bureaucrats. Saionji explained to Yamagata that the Kenseikai formed a government with Ōkuma [Shigenobu, 1838–1922] and failed.[6] If Hara would now form a Cabinet as the leader of the Seiyūkai and fail, another nonparty Cabinet could be formed afterward. However, if the political parties were not allowed to form a government

---

[6]Ōkuma Shigenobu (1838–1922) was prime minister in 1898 and again in 1914–16. His second Cabinet was formed in cooperation with the Kenseikai. At the time of Hara's appointment, the question of consulting with Ōkuma was raised. However, Yamagata, Saionji, and Matsukata agreed that the grand chamberlain be sent to Ōkuma to inform him of Hara's selection. By utilizing the authority of the throne in this manner, any possible objection from his quarters could be forestalled.

now and became disillusioned, they might collaborate closely with each other to gain the upper hand. In that event, there would never again be another chance for forming a nonparty Cabinet. Instead, after Hara, Katō [Takaaki, 1860–1926, President of the Kenseikai] would become the prime minister, and after Katō someone else [from one of the parties]. And in this manner, the country would continuously be governed by political parties. Yamagata seemed satisfied with Saionji's reasoning.

Saionji cautioned me that Yamagata would like me to keep in close touch with him, and after the formation of the Cabinet listen to his advice.... I thanked Saionji for his kindness....

LABOR MOVEMENT

On August 1, 1912, Suzuki Bunji (1885–1946) and fourteen others, mostly electrical and machine workers, assembled at the library of a Unitarian building in Mita, Tokyo to organize a labor group called the Yūaikai (Friendship Association). It was dedicated to collaboration between capital and labor and was mainly interested in a friendly exchange of ideas and mutual aid (Documents 5 and 6).

The rice riots, Russian Revolution and other developments had a stimulating effect on labor movements in Japan, which gradually transformed the Yūaikai into a genuine labor union. In 1919 it was renamed the Dai Nippon Rōdō Sōdōmei Yūaikai (Greater Japan General Federation of Labor Friendship Association) and advocated freedom for labor unions, adoption of a minimum wage law, and universal suffrage as some of its major goals. In 1921, the term Yūaikai was dropped from its official name. At the 1924 convention of the Sōdōmei, left-wing members attacked the leadership's reliance on parliamentarianism and forced the Sōdōmei to transform itself into a more militant organization based on mass movement. The 1924 Sōdōmei declaration is reproduced as Document 7. The increased militancy of the workers would become one of the targets of the peace preservation law enacted the following year (Document 11).

Organizers of the Yūaikai and subsequent unions were the elite among workers, coming as they did from the ranks of skilled workers. Below them there was a distinct underclass of less skilled workers who manned textile and other industries. They were forced to work in factories whose squalid working conditions could almost have come from the pages of Charles Dickens. Women workers suffered most, as they were forced to complete their three year terms of service like indentured servants, with severe restrictions placed on their personal freedom. Hosoi Wakizō (1897–1925), a textile worker, wrote a book entitled Jokō Aishi *(Lamentations of Female Factory Workers). It was based on his personal observations as well as those of his wife, who was a textile worker. Document 8 contains excerpts from this book. It was against the wretched conditions like the ones Hosoi described that socialists agitated and utopian thinkers attempted to redress. They are in sharp contrast to the almost antiseptic cleanliness of Japanese factories today and the benevolent paternalism that goes with it. Japanese management as we know it today and the practices of the Taishō period remain poles apart.*

5 Basic Principles Governing the Yūaikai (Friendship Association), 1912[7]

1. We shall maintain friendly relations with each other and assist each other with a unity of spirit, in order to fulfill our basic objectives of benevolence and mutual help.

2. We shall follow the ideals commonly held by humanity and endeavor to develop knowledge, nurture virtue, and advance technology.

3. Through the power of cooperation, we shall find a practical and steady means of improving our positions.

6 The Position of the Yūaikai, 1912[8]

Some capitalists seem to entertain a false notion concerning the purpose of our organization and have spread to police officers rumors that we are an organization established to incite workers. We are surprised by this. In certain extreme cases, employers threatened some of their blue-collar workers when they were joining our association by saying that "the association is a socialist organization." . . .

How are commodities produced? Can they be produced without cooperation between capital and labor? Some scholars even suggest that capital is the end result of labor, and therefore production is acquired by labor alone. Some people maintain that in production labor is the main factor and capital is merely a subsidiary factor. We are not advocating these doctrines. We simply believe that only through the union of capital and labor can there be production. Herein lies the principle of friendly cooperation between capital and labor, and the two must not alienate each other.

The age of workers being the slaves of capitalists has passed. We may be called workers, but we are independent people and like others are beloved subjects of his majesty, the emperor. When our health is not good, education poor, and skills do not progress, can patriotic people remain silent on these shortcomings? . . .

We workers are "sons of men" and in that respect we are not different from capitalists. Is there anything wrong in our attempt to extend a bridge of under-

---

[7]Asahi Shimbunsha, ed., *Shiryō Meiji Hyakunen (A Documentary History of the Meiji Centennial)* (Tokyo: Asahi Shimbunsha, 1966), p. 460.

[8]*Ibid.*, pp. 469–70.

standing between "sons of men" to promote kindness, friendship, communication, and harmony? How can one say that our action is against humanitarian principles?

7   Sōdōmei's Declaration at the 1924 Convention[9] The labor movement in our country is now facing its most critical crossroads. . . .Before capitalism in our country has had a chance to develop smoothly, it has taken the form of imperialism because of the pressure exerted by the fierce worldwide imperialistic competition. Imperialism is the last stage of capitalism. This means that capitalism in our country, without passing through the stage of liberalism, is becoming militaristic and is endowed with the flavor of autocracy. For example, it creates many hurdles to suppress the freedom of the proletariat. We must be aware of the fact that the European war has given our proletariat a sense of self-awareness and the current hightide of worldwide class struggle has raised the intellectual standards of a minority of our proletariat. However, this minority has not been able to perceive clearly the roles and functions they must play. As a result, democratization of our proletariat movement has been difficult. In order to be true to their ideals, these minority members have tended to insist on purity, which has resulted in inflexibility. We can declare unequivocally that, in the past, the labor movement in our country developed in accordance with changes in the capitalistic development. However, if we are to persist in this same old course, we shall be committing a serious mistake for our future. This is so because more than ever we are forced to formulate policies, that are more realistic and positive. We are now able to observe accurately both the tendencies inherent in the development of capitalism in this country and the advance in the power of the working class. We are now at the threshold of turning the labor union movement of a small number of people into a movement for the masses. Frankly, we cannot expect full liberation of the working class by a Diet dominated by the bourgeoisie. We must plan for the development of labor unions in our country by the following means: after the implementation of universal suffrage, we must use our right to vote effectively and gain partial political advantages; we must promote political awareness among the proletariat; and we must find ways and means of promoting our goals through participation in international labor conferences. We must fulfill the true spirit of the labor union movement by effecting mergers of separate unions and organizing nonunion members, both of which are to be based on the community of interest among the working class. We must work toward our ultimate goals, and at the same time acquire present benefits as well. The militant labor union members of today possess a clear ability for judgment and are strongly class conscious. They may take advantage of modified policies given by the ruling class in an attempt to dull the revolutionary spirit of the working class,

---

[9]*Ibid.*, p. 471.

but they will never be corrupted by such policies. The movement to liberate the proletariat must change its tactics from time to time, taking into account the conditions of the enemy as well as the power of our friends. We hereby pledge that, regardless of whatever tactics we may take in accordance with practical considerations, we do not deviate from the basic principle of liberation of the proletariat.

Basic Principles

1. We shall endeavor to improve our economic well-being and increase our knowledge through the power of organization and through the groups established to promote mutual aid.

2. With resolute courage and effective tactics, we shall engage in an all-out war against the oppression of the capitalist class.

3. We firmly believe that the working class and capitalist class cannot exist side by side. Through the power of labor unions, we shall endeavor to build a new society in which the working class is completely liberated and where freedom and equality prevail.

8   Excerpts from Lamentations of Female Factory Workers, 1925[10] Hiring of textile workers is divided into two categories of "enlisted workers" and "recruited workers." Eighty percent of female workers are recruited workers. In contrast, 80 percent of male workers are enlisted workers. . . .There is not a company that has ever recruited male workers. At the same time, there is not a case in which female workers have not been recruited. It is clear that there is not much room for men [to work in textile mills] as machines are fast replacing men.

For more than a decade, textile mills have experienced difficulty in recruiting female workers. . . . Recruitment of female workers is just as important a task for a textile mill as actually operating the machines. If textile companies are forbidden to recruit female workers, their machines will have to be shut down within a month.

[Recruitment of female factory workers can be divided into three phases. In the first phase, or before 1894, things went smoothly as girls looked for opportunities to go to big cities. The second phase, the interwar years of 1895 through 1904, became a difficult phase. More factories were built, and demands for female workers intensified; at the same time, horror stories of factory conditions became known in the areas frequently recruited. The third phase saw companies raiding each other's factories for experienced female workers.]

One of the characteristics of the second phase is the literal observation of "forced remittance of money home," and "serving a specific term." . . . There is also established a system of ransom if the full term is not served.

---

[10]Hosoi Wakizō, *Jokō Aishi (Lamentations of Female Factory Workers)* (Tokyo: Iwanami Shoten, reissue, 1954), pp. 54, 105, 112, 165, 168, 172–73, 216–17.

Regardless of whether one has received an advance, at the time first hired, an employee must sign a contract to work for a set period of time. The term usually runs for three years, sometimes two, and in other instances three years and three months. . . .

At the first textile mill of the Naigai Cotton Co. Ltd., regardless of reason, anyone who leaves the company's employ before completing the three-year term of employment contract is denied payment from an escrow account set up in her name. The factory in question withholds from each employee's monthly pay a sum equal to one day's wages and places it in an escrow account without interest. Anyone who leaves the company, even only one month short of the full term, is denied payment from it. . . . That factory has about five hundred workers. Each year 15 percent of its workforce leave the company after working an average of eighteen months. The company has been in existence for thirty years. Assuming that an average worker receives 50 sen a day, the company has effectively stolen 20,250 yen from its employees.

. . . One cannot separate labor from the body of the laborer. However, when a worker enters into a contract with a capitalist to offer his labor in return for pay, he is bound to his employer for a specific number of hours. After these hours are completed, he is freed from his obligations. If he has sold his labor for twelve hours to a certain factory, the remaining twelve hours are his to enjoy. The purchaser of his labor cannot invade these twelve hours.

All workers, men and women alike, whether they are in steel, chemical industry, or in outdoor employment enjoy free hours after work. However, female workers who live in company dormitories do not enjoy the same freedom. . . . Once they return to their dormitories, they are subjected to a host of cumbersome regulations. . . .

First there is a restriction on going out. . . . If a worker is certified a good worker, she can receive a pass once a month, which must bear the signatures of the dormitory warden, counselor, and room supervisor. . . . The curfew is set at 10 P.M. If she is late for more than five minutes, she forfeits her next month's pass.

If she stays overnight away from her dormitory for whatever reason, all her roommates will be denied next month's pass. . . .

When there are festivals and shops are set up nearby, or when special events are held inside the dormitory, the entire dormitory is denied the privilege of going out. . . .

If she buys food from an outside source, the guard opens the package and inspects each item. . . . If her parents include any food item in a package sent from home, the package is confiscated.

Tokyo Muslin's Kameido factory had a man named Matsunaga, serving as its education director. When he found out that one of the workers was reading women's magazines, such as *Josei Kaizō* and *Fujin Kōron,* he forced her to cancel her subscription. . . . Most factories do not like their workers to read publications other than their own. . . .

Now a few words about facilities and working conditions. . . . Exits and other emergency evacuation facilities are extremely inadequate. There may be only two or three fire escapes in a factory with five to six hundred workers. And these exits are not only bolted but also padlocked.

Adding moisture to cotton fiber adds strength to it. It makes work on the fiber easier and contributes to the efficiency of the work process. So it is normal for a cotton spinning mill to maintain a high degree of moisture without considering the health of its workers. This practice is even worse in a textile mill where one's vision is hindered by the mist created because of moisture.

A sprayer is installed at ten feet above the floor for each thirty-two square yards of floor space. From its nozzle, called the ball duct, water comes through openings, which are either one thirty-second or one-sixteenth inch, at the high-water pressure of one hundred pounds. The water is sprayed constantly and becomes like mist saturating the air. It creates an insufferable condition for workers.

Female workers in textile-weaving divisions whose work stations are placed under a sprayer get the worst from the excessive moisture. If the machine is operating constantly, the situation can be tolerable. But if it stops even for an hour, it begins to rust. Their hair and clothing are constantly wet as rusty water drips on them.

Female workers have a saying: "Winter is heaven and summer is hell." This exaggerates the warmth of winter months in their factory just a bit. Whichever factory one visits, one will find an average winter temperature of over sixty five degrees, and even on the coldest day, the temperature seldom goes under fifty degrees. When one works hard it is still easy to sweat. So a single layer of work clothing will suffice. Of course, when one steps outside, the cold is difficult to bear.

They can work during the winter months without experiencing cold thanks to the heat maintained. But in the summer months, temperatures rise to an extreme level. There is body heat from the people who are working in close quarters. There is heat from the machines, to which heat from the sun is added. It is literally hell with heat. Cotton fibers like goose feathers fly around and stick to workers' faces. It is terribly uncomfortable. At starch stations steam heat is applied, and at gas drying stations, open flame gas is used. There is no word adequate enough to describe the suffering of these workers. At the starch stations, temperatures rise above one hundred and ten degrees. It is so hot [and dehydrating] that hardly anyone has to use the bathroom. . . .

UNIVERSAL SUFFRAGE AND PEACE PRESERVATION LAWS

Universal male suffrage without property qualifications passed the fiftieth Diet in March 1925 (Document 9). However, at the same Diet a stringent Peace Preservation Law was also passed (Document 11). There was obviously an attempt to make the universal suffrage law a safety valve against the tide of social protests. Yet it was against these social protests—especially those with revolutionary fervor—that the Peace Preservation Law was directed. Its reach, incidentally, went beyond Japan's borders to offenses committed by Japanese nationals overseas.

Even at the time of the enactment of the universal suffrage law, skepticism about its effectiveness remained, as shown in an editorial from the Asahi Shimbun *(Document 10).*

9 Law Governing Election to the House of Representatives, as Amended, Extending Suffrage, May 5, 1925[11]

Chapter II. The Right to Vote and Eligibility for Election

ARTICLE 5. A Japanese male citizen, twenty-five years of age or older, shall have the right to vote.

A Japanese male citizen, thirty years of age or older, shall be eligible for election to the House of Representatives.

ARTICLE 6. Those who come under one of the following categories shall not have the right to vote or be eligible for election:

1. A person adjudged incompetent or a quasi-incompetent person.

2. A bankrupt person who is not rehabilitated.

3. A person, on account of poverty, who requires relief or assistance from public or private sources.

4. A person who does not have a place of residence.

5. A person who has been sentenced to penalties heavier than six years of penal servitude or imprisonment.

[6 and 7 omitted.]

10 Editorial from Asahi Shimbun in Support of Universal Suffrage, March 30, 1925[12] We are gratified to see the passage of the compromise suffrage bill that emerged from the conference committee of the two houses after the term of this session was extended three times. It was approved by an overwhelming majority of each of the houses. However, as Prime Minister Katō [Takaaki, 1860–1926] remarked, the question of universal suffrage has not been answered or solved by this action. The major accomplishment of the fiftieth Diet session in Japan's constitutional history centered on one fact. At the final important moment when the babe, that is, the long-sought-after universal suffrage, was about to be born, a malicious midwife injured the baby. . . . As the parents of this

---

[11]*Asahi Shimbunsha, Shiryō Meiji Kyakunen,* p. 466. The date given is the date of its promulgation.

[12]*Ibid.,* pp. 467–68.

beloved baby, the universal suffrage, we as a nation must eradicate this injury before it finally grows up. We must make every effort to reform those public organs that inflicted this injury. In this sense, the fiftieth Diet session has only started the process and has not been able to complete it.

It is clear that the compromise measure that finally passed was almost a verbatim replica of the House of Peers version. . . . Take, for example, the phrase "on account of poverty" in the law. We need not have members of the Seiyū Hontō tell us how ambiguous these words are. The phrase is obviously based on the notion that property is the prerequisite to enfranchisement, which is diametrically opposed to the basic principle of universal suffrage. It does cast an unpleasant shadow over the passage of this nationally significant law. It happened this way. The three political groups [the Kenseikai, Seiyūkai and Kakushintō] and their [coalition] Cabinet, which supported universal suffrage, approved an amendment presented by the Privy Council that anyone who received public or private relief ought to be disenfranchised. Then the House of Peers claimed that the meaning was not clear enough and expanded the phrase to read: "A person, who in order to make a living, requires relief or assistance from public or private sources." But this phrase created difficulties. If a person was to be disqualified on account of receiving assistance from private sources, how could that fact be determined? Would it not infringe on the privacy of many of the citizens, and even create some uneasy feelings? Thus a clause, "on account of poverty," was inserted in place of the clause "in order to make a living." Yet this change does not alter the basic unsoundness of this provision.

Then there is another provision which imposes a one-year residence requirement. This is a digression from the present law. As a result of this provision, those mine workers and those who move from place to place to engage in seasonal employment will lose their right to vote and eligibility for election. The government claimed in the Diet deliberations that about 200,000 people would be affected by this provision. Our guess is that the number will go up much higher. . . .

In this way, on all major issues relating to the basic principles of universal suffrage, the compromise bill accepted amendments proposed by the House of Peers. . . . We suspect that the House of Representatives conferees did not expend as much effort on behalf of the basic rights of the people as they would normally do in electioneering for their own parties. The nation will forebear this inadequate law for the time being. What we have feared has been the disapproval of the universal suffrage bill, disruption in the collaborative arrangement between the three political groups before its passage, and the resulting corrosive influence of intrigues and political poison that can darken our political landscape and endanger our concept of society. Unsatisfactory as it is, we hope that once franchise is extended, there will be a change for the better, with the status quo symbolized by the established political parties and privileged politicians changing to become more responsive to the wishes of the people. We believe people will show a renewed hope in new politics, for example, politics in which the people can participate. We know that the people can anticipate another Diet session that will grant to the people the rights taken away by the amendments insisted upon by the House of Peers.

With the emergence of the compromise measure, the Seiyū Hontō could have stated that the three political groups supporting universal suffrage have acquiesced to its original view, and it could now vote for the final compromise version. This would have been a wise thing to do, but for the sake of opposition, it lost the chance to change its course. It foolishly conveyed to the nation an impression that it was a political party determined to oppose universal suffrage.

However, the worse villain to emerge from the past session of the Diet was not the Seiyū Hontō but the House of Peers. In the past election, the three groups supporting universal suffrage won overwhelmingly against the Seiyū Hontō, which was willing to serve as the mouthpiece for the House of Peers. The meaning of that election was completely negated by the House of Peers' insistence on reviving a minority view that was already rejected by the House of Representatives. The House of Peers disregarded the will of the people as shown in the general election and challenged it. We now realize that unless we can reform the House of Peers and destroy the practice of government by the privileged, our national politics can never reflect the will of the people even with this universal suffrage. The battle has not ended. We must raise anew our banners to attain true universal suffrage and to reform the House of Peers. With these new banners, those of us who are interested in participating in national politics must continue our fight through the next session of the Diet and then onto the next general election.

11 Peace Preservation Law, April 22, 1925[13]

ARTICLE 1. Anyone who organizes a group for the purpose of changing the national polity (*kōkutai*) or of denying the private property system, or anyone who knowingly participates in said group, shall be sentenced to penal servitude or imprisonment not exceeding ten years. An offense not actually carried out shall also be subject to punishment.

ARTICLE 2. Anyone who consults with another person on matters relating to the implementation of these objectives described in clause 1 of the preceding article shall be sentenced to penal servitude or imprisonment not exceeding seven years.

ARTICLE 3. Anyone who instigates others for the purpose of implementing those objectives described in clause 1, article 1, shall be sentenced to penal servitude or imprisonment not exceeding seven years.

ARTICLE 4. Anyone who instigates others to engage in rioting or assault or

---

[13]*Ibid.*, pp. 466–67.

other crimes inflicting harm on life, person, or property for the purpose of attaining the objectives of clause 1, article 1, shall be sentenced to penal servitude or imprisonment not exceeding ten years.

ARTICLE 5. Anyone who, for the purpose of committing those crimes described in clause 1, article 1, and in the preceding three articles, provides money and goods or other financial advantages for others, or makes an offer or commitment for same, shall be sentenced to penal servitude or imprisonment not exceeding five years. Anyone who knowingly receives such considerations, or makes demand or commitment for same, shall be punished in a similar manner.

ARTICLE 6. Anyone who has committed the crimes described in the three preceding articles and has surrendered himself voluntarily to authorities shall have his sentence reduced or be granted immunity from prosecution.

ARTICLE 7. This law shall be made applicable to anyone who commits crimes described in this law outside of the jurisdiction in which this law is in effect.

LIBERATION OF WOMEN

In 1911, Hiratsuka Raichō (1886–1971) founded a new literary journal, Seitō *(Blue Stockings), to promote women's causes. She was joined in this endeavor by other famed female writers including Yosano Akiko (1878–1942). Hiratsuka was inward looking, and when speaking of liberation, she often equated it with discovery of self and of one's own talent. Her work marked the beginning of women's liberation movement in Japan. The following document is her proclamation at the time of the founding of her Seitō Society.*

12 **Restoring Women's Talents, 1911**[14] In the beginning, woman was the sun and a true being. Now woman is the moon. She lives through others and shines through the light of others. Her countenance is pale, like a patient.

We must now restore the sun, which has been hidden from us.

"Let the hidden talent, our hidden sun, reemerge!" This has been our continuous outcry directed inwardly to ourselves. It represents our insatiable longings, our final instinctive feelings encompassing our total beings, unifying all our different sentiments. . . .

Freedom and Liberation! Oftentimes we have heard the term "liberation of women." But what does it mean? Are we not seriously misunderstanding the term freedom or liberation? Even if we call the problem liberation of women, are there not many other issues involved? Assuming that women are freed from

---

[14]Hiratsuka Raichō, *"Genshi, Josei wa Taiyō de Atta"* (In the Beginning Woman Was the Sun), in *Seitō,* first issue, September 1911, reproduced in the *Chūō Koron,* November 1965, pp. 354–57.

external oppression, liberated from constraint, given the so-called higher education, employed in various occupations, given the right to vote, and provided an opportunity to be independent from the protection of their parents and husbands, and to be freed from the little confinement of their homes, can all of these be called liberation of women? They may provide proper surroundings and opportunities to let us fulfill the true goal of liberation. Yet they remain merely the means and do not represent our goals or ideals.

However, I am unlike many intellectuals in Japan who suggest that higher education is not necessary for women. Men and women are endowed by nature to have equal faculties. Therefore, it is odd to assume that one of the sexes requires education while the other does not. This may be tolerated in a given country and in a given age, but it is fundamentally a very unsound proposition.

I bemoan the fact that there is only one private college for women in Japan and that there is no tolerance on man's part to permit entrance of women into many universities maintained for men. However, what benefit is there when the intellectual level of women becomes similar to that of men? Men seek knowledge to escape from their lack of wisdom and lack of enlightenment. They want to free themselves. . . . Yet multifarious thoughts can darken true wisdom and lead men away from nature. Men who live by playing with knowledge may be called scholars, but they can never be men of wisdom. Nay, on the contrary, they are almost like blind men, who lack the perception to see the things in front of their eyes as what they are. . . .

Now what is the true liberation that I am seeking? It is none other than to provide an opportunity for women to develop fully their hidden talents and hidden abilities. We must remove all barriers that stand in the way of women's development, whether they be external oppression or lack of knowledge. And above and beyond these factors, we must realize that we are the masters in possession of great talents, for we are the bodies that enshrine the great talents. . . .

ELITE AND SOCIAL CONSCIOUSNESS

In April 1910, Mushanokōji Saneatsu (1885–1976), Shiga Naoya (1883–1970), Arishima Takeo (1878–1923), and others joined together to form a group called Shirakaba-*ha, and adopted as their literary organ a journal named* Shirakaba *(White Birch). Most of the writers of this group graduated from Peers School and represented the aristocratic society and upper class of Japan. The group advocated fulfillment of human will through realization of individual talents. They were variously influenced by Christianity, humanism, naturalism, and the notion of art for art's sake. Among their heroes were Uchimura Kanzō, Leo Tolstoy, Auguste Rodin, Walt Whitman, and Romain Rolland.*

Mushanokōji envisioned an ideal society in a farm commune where everyone could work together and engage in communal sharing. Such a commune, named a new village (atarashiki mura), was established in Miyazaki Prefecture in 1918 (Document 13) only to fail not long after its founding.

Arishima established his cooperative farm in Hokkaido and leased his land to sixty-nine farm households without charge in 1922. However, his love suicide with a female journalist the following year effectively sealed the fate of this noble but poorly executed experiment. His one declaration (Document 14) was an attempt to redefine the position of intellectuals in the face of the rise of the fourth class, as he termed it, or the working class, especially the urban poor. His suicide, like that of the writer Akutagawa Ryūnosuke in 1927, gave Japanese intellectuals a sense of futility and of defeat.

13 On the New Village, 1918[15]

I am hoping that I can live in a village somewhere (preferably within one day's traveling distance from Tokyo) to live with my friends to engage in a life of mutual cooperation. . . .

Even if our endeavor fails, we can still show gains through our failure. In the final analysis, there can be no failure, as long as one is motivated to do the right thing. Superficially, our work may look as though it has failed, but it can still have a permanent impact in the sphere of the unseen.

The true victor is the one who loves people while failing, rather than one who detests people while succeeding. It cannot be called a failure if through that experience we learn to love our fellow men more.

I cannot look down on people as useless creatures and assume a nonchalant air. There is something in their seeming unworthiness. I believe in them, and I do not think my belief is misplaced. Nor do I think that I lose by believing in them.

I want to prove the worthiness of my conviction throughout my life. I am confident that I am the type of man who can gain the ultimate in happiness in this world. Or at least, I know I can gain many friends in this world.

Ideology cannot give life to people, but people can give life to ideology. When men of truth dedicate their entire lives to actuate an ideology, that cannot be the same with an ideology advocated by men of falsehood whose only commitments to the cause are their voices and expressions. It is self-evident that the two are not the same, even though they may bear the same name.

Whatever dried seeds they [i.e., men of falsehood] try to sow, no matter how hard they try, they cannot produce decent buds. But the seeds we sow are endowed with life. If they are planted on fertile soil, they cannot but sprout and grow.

We want to show to the world that by planting seeds of "a new village," we can harvest many "new villages." There will come a time when we will grow so fast that no matter how people try to stamp out our budding movement, they

---

[15]Mushanokōji Saneatsu, *"Atrashiki Mura ni Tsuite"* (On the New Village), in *Shirakaba,* June 1918, reprinted in the *Chūō Kōron,* November 1965, pp. 382–83.

cannot keep us from growing. What we have to do is simply to sow the seeds endowed with life.

When a new village is established, let us live together a life of comfort. Let us do our best in our own work, and work for our loved ones and for our comrades. Let us share our joys and sorrows. I know before success comes to us, we can all live together with friendliness, pleasant dispositions, and sincerity. When success knocks at our door, let us guard ourselves against excesses. Whether success comes or not, there is a sense of joy within us, our path is not wrong.

14 One Declaration, 1922[16] One of the most noteworthy events today in Japan is the gradual shift in the complexion of leadership of our social movement. It is leaving the hands of the scholars and philosophers and now rests in the hands of the workers themselves. When I speak of workers I mean the so-called fourth class, those people who have been the objects of labor problems, which constitute the most important of our social problems. I refer especially to those members of the fourth class who are living in the cities.

If I am not mistaken, heretofore, the workers have given the right of governance to the scholars and philosophers. They have erroneously assumed that the learned opinions of the scholars and philosophers would improve their destiny. This was understandable in that prior to the implementation of some basic social policies, debates were necessary. The workers, being deficient in the art of discussion, had to depend on someone else who could represent them. . . . As to the scholars and philosophers, they prided themselves with the thought that they were the pathfinders and leaders of the workers. Gradually they were awakened to the fact that they were mere spokesmen for the workers. Yet even with that realization, they still maintained that the basic solution to labor problems resided in their hands. . . .

. . . Sometime ago Professor Kawakami Hajime[17] spoke the following words: "There are some people who pride themselves on being philosophers or artists. For them I can only have contempt. They do not know the age in which they live. . . . They are dropouts from our contemporary society, incompetent persons belonging to the past. If they can say: 'We cannot do anything else, and that is the reason we are absorbed in philosophy and art. Please do not disturb us and leave us alone,' I can still tolerate them. However, if they insist that they are aware of what they are doing and engage in the pursuit of philosophy or art with confidence, they simply do not understand where they stand." At that time, I could not accept those words as they were. . . . If Professor Kawakami were speaking these words to me today, I would agree with him. Or I might agree with

---

[16]Arishima Takeo, "*Sengen Hitotsu*" (One Declaration), in *Kaizō,* January 1922, reprinted in the *Chūō Kōron,* November 1965, pp. 402–5.

[17]See Document 15 for Kawakami's own writing.

him in a different sense. Today, I would interpret his words in the following manner: "Professor Kawakami and I belong to the same group, though there may be a difference in degree, as we both live apart from the circles of the fourth class. Like Professor Kawakami, I do not have any point of contact with the fourth class. If I assume that I can give some revelation to the fourth class, that is my own erroneous view. If the people in the fourth class feel that they are being influenced by my words, that is their misunderstanding. We were born and raised in a surrounding alien to the lives and thought patterns of the fourth class. We are just sitting around the stove (where the only intelligent conversation that can be conducted is about the cold weather). We are in no position to discuss anything else."

I myself am not worthy to be counted. But the same reasoning will apply to the opinions of such luminous persons as [Prince Peter A.] Kropotkin (1842–1921). No matter how strong an impact Kropotkin might have had over the awakening of the workers and of the rise in the position of the fourth class, as long as Kropotkin remained a non-worker he could not live as a worker, think as a worker, or toil as a worker. What he thought he gave to the fourth class was actually not given to them but what they already possessed. The fourth class should have found it themselves. . . . Indeed workers do not need thinkers like Kropotkin or [Karl] Marx (1818–1883). Without Kropotkin and Marx, they still could have displayed their originality and instinctive approach.

Where can one find the contributions of Kropotkin and Marx? In my view, they were able to convey to those classes other than the fourth class certain ideas about them. They even imparted to them a sense of resignation to the inevitability of the rise of the fourth class. Let us take up the case of Marx's *The Capital*. What common bond do *The Capital* and the workers have? As a thinker Marx contributed most to the self-understanding of those people in the social classes who can afford to graduate from college, an institution that is a product of the capitalist society. To those college-educated, of which Marx was one, Marx gave a chance to investigate and then shut their thoughtful eyes from their own positions. The fourth class certainly could attain whatever they were going to gain without the intervention of men like Marx.

Sometime in the future, the benefit of the capitalist society may spill over, and workers may begin to understand those complex principles enunciated by Kropotkin, Marx, and others. And it may even be possible that a revolution will be successfully completed. In that event though, I would have to doubt the very nature of that revolution. The French Revolution began for the sake of the people, but in the process it became influenced by the thoughts of Rousseau and Voltaire. As a result, the people in the fourth class remained in the same condition even to this day. The present-day Russia also seems to show a similar difficulty. They claim that they engaged in the last of the great revolutions based on the power of the people. But the great majority of people in Russia, namely the peasantry, is clearly excluded from the benefit of the revolution. It is said that the peasantry is either unconcerned with the state or is openly hostile to it. Any reform movement that does not begin with the thoughts and motivations of the fourth class is bound to stop at a place that is not originally contemplated. Similarly, if a movement begins, being inspired by the opinions of philosophers and scholars of today, it is destined to fail. Those instigators may claim that they also belong to the fourth class. But in the final analysis the movement they head will become a half-caste breed born of the mismatch of the fourth class and the ruling class.

I was born outside the fourth class and received my education accordingly. I am not in any manner associated with the fourth class. . . .I cannot engage in the falsehood of apologizing, advocating or working for the fourth class. Whatever change may occur in my life, I cannot change the fact that I have been the product of the ruling class. It is just like the black people who cannot change the pigmentation of their skin by using soap to wash it. Therefore, my task must be defined as one of appealing to those people who do not belong to the fourth class. Nowadays, we hear of workers' literature. There are some critics who defend and advocate it. They write about the lives of workers in a nonchalant fashion, using letters, ideas and the means of expression invented by people outside the fourth class. They determine which work belongs to workers' literature and which one does not by using the manner of investigation, logic and thought concocted by people outside the fourth class. I cannot subscribe to that attitude.

If one can agree that class struggle is the nucleus and alpha and omega of the present-day world, one can readily justify the stand I have just taken. No matter how great a scholar, thinker, activist, or boss one may be, unless he is a worker born of the fourth class, he must not expect to contribute anything to the fourth class. To think otherwise is pure blasphemy. The fourth class in the end will only be brought to a greater degree of confusion by their futile activities.

EARLY MARXIST MOVEMENT

Kawakami Hajime (1879–1946) became professor of economics at Kyoto University in 1916, after completing a period of study in the war-torn countries of Germany, France and England that followed his graduation from Tokyo University. In the same year, he started a series in the Osaka Asahi Shimbun *entitled* Bimbō Monogatari *or the* Tale of Poverty. *He attacked the rich for their luxurious mode of living and for their profit-seeking motives. In his view, poverty was not the fault of the poor and was curable, if industries could be nationalized to eliminate profiteering, and if social legislation could be enacted to rectify existing inequities. Gradually his study shifted to Marxism, and he became the most ardent academic advocate of that doctrine.*

"I deliberately utilized my position as a university professor," he wrote in his autobiography. "In those days professors enjoyed freedom of speech that could

not be envisioned by normal socialists." Later he became a member of the Japan
Communist Party and was subsequently imprisoned. The following is his prison
letter first published in the Asahi newspapers in 1933.

15   Soliloquy in My Prison Cell, 1933[18]   As a person arrested for being a
Communist, I spend my life in prison. Nothing else is left for me if I insist on
remaining a Communist. If I wish to regain my freedom, sooner or later I must
abandon my claim to being a Communist.

I have known this all the time, and have understood what position I must take
as a Communist. I have been prepared to spend the rest of my life in prison. . . .
It is said that life ends at fifty. I am already fifty-five and there are not too many
remaining years. I am sure everyone else thinks that I shall be happy dying as a
Communist. However, once I have experienced this prison life, I have begun to
understand the feelings of an old monk, who enters a mountain in search of
medicine. True, he transcends the problem of life and death, and no longer fears
death which is inevitable. But he still wishes to avoid pain in meeting death; this
must be one of the instincts that governs people until the very end. Perhaps the
working of this instinct becomes stronger as a person ages and loses some of his
vitality.

When I was at the age of twenty-six, I once experienced facing the prospect
of spiritual death. But my own mental state is now quite different. The loss of
vitality and the weakening of my resolve that accompanies it are inevitable. I
cannot understand that there are many types of work that only youth can perform. . . . For me to abandon my claim of being a Communist is similar to
committing suicide. That is something not tolerated of Communists, but in order
to regain my freedom, I am committing that cardinal offense. I bow before my
comrades and await their judgment.

I shall henceforth renounce participation in any activities—whether they be
legal or illegal—and retire to my study. This is what I have decided for myself.
By making this public and giving it a certain social meaning, I am burying
myself as a Communist.

Political activities have never been congenial to me. In spite of this, I became
more and more involved in them after 1928 when I resigned as a professor at
Kyoto University. My faith in Marxism became so strong it no longer permitted
me to remain in my study. I participated in such activities out of a sense of duty.
But after entering this practical arena, I have suffered greatly for the past five
years. To some people, declaring their own candidacies and engaging in political
campaigns must be a joyous experience. I simply abhorred them. After working
so hard for a certain cause, I also had to leave my mother, my wife and my

---

[18]Kawakami Hajime, "*Gokuchū Dokugo*" (Soliloquy in My Prison Cell), reprinted in
the *Chūō Kōron,* November 1965, pp. 458–59.

children and enter the secluded life of a prison. When that realization came, I expressed my real sentiment in a *waka*:

> Reaching my destination
> Looking back at the rivers and mountains
> How far have I come
> Indeed how far!

I was led by my conviction to reach a certain stage, and that was most satisfying as a scholar. But at the same time I could not overlook all the sacrifices I had to make. I was born in a samurai family during the second decade of the Meiji era and received Meiji education. To reach that status under the circumstances, I could only remember hard struggles. That was only yesterday. Today I am about to bury myself as a Communist. Looking back at the fate I suffered, and sitting alone in my prison cell, I am almost speechless.

In order to avoid any misunderstanding, I want to make certain that my belief in the basic principles of Marxism remains unchanged. Unqualified as I am, I spent thirty years studying those principles against all odds, and the conviction thus acquired cannot be changed by a six-month imprisonment. Even after retiring to my study, I shall remain a convinced Marxist scholar. However, just by being a believer in Marxism does not make me either a Marxist or a Communist.

Anyone who remains aloof from political activities cannot be a scholar truly representing the advance guard of Marxism, providing direction for the development of its ideology. No matter how hard he may try, an aloof person cannot be in the company of Marxist scholars. It is possible that scholars can remain in research institutes or private studies and still be Communists or Marxists in the strict sense of the word, but it all depends on the need of society and on the ability of the individual concerned. However, they will never be divorced from political activities, and that is the difference which separates them from those pedants who merely claim their adherence to Marxism. This is the reason why only the former can contribute to the development of Marxism. After all, Marxism is not a doctrine that is coagulated and inflexible but is one that continuously and endlessly evolves. Retreating from the scene of class struggle, as a disabled soldier I can no longer make a scholarly contribution in the same manner. I know man must remain ambitious to the very end, but I am now becoming reconciled to the fate of engaging in the secondary and tertiary endeavors, even in the sphere of scholarly pursuit.

Having withdrawn from political activities, it is axiomatic that I refrain from speaking out on political issues that are directly concocted with the activities of our comrades. I am convinced that political opinions of those who have retired to their studies are only harmful, and thus for the remainder of my life I shall not write any more political opinions.

Somehow, I do wish to complete a translation of *The Capital* before I die. This has been the hope that I have not been able to eradicate from my mind. As one who covets the easy existence of a disabled soldier in my study for the rest of my life, I shall like to complete this work as soon as possible once freed from this imprisonment. This is the way I wish to redeem myself for the sin of spending my remaining days in indolence.

NISHIDA PHILOSOPHY

From the time he became a professor of philosophy in Kyoto University in 1910 to the time of his death near the end of World War II, Nishida Kitarō (1870– 1945) remained the leading intellectual of Japan. His first philosophical treatise, Zen no Kenkyū, 1911 (A Study of Good, *1960) was an all-time best seller among scholarly works, influencing several generations of students. In 1947 when his complete works were issued, lines started to form in front of the publisher three days before their publication. His Zen training and the influence of the neo-Kantian school and Henri Bergson combined to mold his philosophical speculation. His was the first genuine philosophy worthy of its name in Japan. The selection below deals with the question of Japan's cultural uniqueness, which both troubled and fascinated Japanese intellectuals in 1917. That issue resurfaced frequently throughout the twentieth century, and in the height of Japan's economic prowess in the 1980s became known as* Nihonjin Tokushuron (The Japanese Are a District People) *with a ring of ethnocentrism. Nishida's views can be read as a contemporary critique rendered today, or as part of the Taishō intellectual heritage.*

16   **On the Phenomenon of Japaneseness, 1917**[19] The conventional wisdom has it that both mental and natural phenomena follow general rules and that cultures of different nations all follow and are judged by the same rules. In our intellectual circles, however, there is a view emerging that each nation has its own culture, and that just as much as the Japanese people cannot understand cultures of the West, foreigners are incapable of comprehending Japan's unique moral perceptions and various arts. I applaud our people's self-awareness as shown in these latest tendencies. At the same time, we must retain the ability to be critical of this thought process.

We may all say "general rules." In them we still have to differentiate the law of cause and effect and the law of value judgment. The law of cause and effect is the law that "it will become thus." For example, it is the law that when oxygen is mixed with hydrogen, the mixture will turn into water. The law of value judg-

---

[19]Nishida Kitarō *"Nihonteki to Yūkoto ni Tsuite"* (On the Phenomenon of Japanese-ness), reprinted in Kamiyama Shumpei, ed., *Nishida Kitarō,* in a series on *Nihon no Meicho (Great Books of Japan),* vol. 47 (Tokyo: Chūō Kōron Sha, 1970), pp. 441–44.

ment is the law of "it must be made thus" or "it ought to be thus." When we use the term "general," we must still differentiate between the meaning that "it is general because wherever it takes place, it still turns out the same way" and "it is general because everyone must judge it the same way." For example, the mixture of oxygen and hydrogen will always turn into water is general in the sense of the former, and a certain art work is beautiful or a certain act is good is general in the sense of the latter. The law of natural science tells us that things will always turn into a certain fashion, and that must be accepted by all. With the law of value judgment everyone knows that it must be accepted by all, but it is not certain if everyone will follow it. When some of our people assert that the culture of a nation is unique to that country and does not follow general rules, they are actually saying two different things. One group may be saying that the cultural development of different nations cannot always move toward the same direction, while another may be saying that the value one attaches to a culture does not always follow general standards and the value judgment over art or morality is always unique to a nation, making it impossible for foreigners to understand.

. . . Is there a common value judgment for the cultures of different nations? We must probe into this problem further. Tastes differ among different peoples. The taste that one nation espouses in its culture cannot be tasted by people from other nations. That is a fairly well established fact. But if we allow this proposition to run its course to its logical conclusion, it will mean that we must deny the possibility of having a generally accepted value judgment and that no debate can be advanced on the issue of "taste." I do not accept this. For a certain taste to have a certain value, even if that cannot be readily understood by others at the present time, there is a requirement that others must understand this or others must feel this. This is similar to a situation where a mathematician solves one of the most difficult problems and is convinced that he has been correct in what he has done. On the matter of taste, if it is défined as "a certain individual or nation feels this way or that way," it is not different from pinpointing the idiosyncrasy of an individual or of a nation. There must be a requirement for others that "everyone must feel in this manner." Only then can there be a value judgment. When we recognize an artistic value or a moral value in a certain thing, that in itself is an act to leave the self behind. One must be attracted to something that is infinitely greater than the self. A man traveling upward on a steep hill may want to stop but cannot stop; a feeling similar to this experience must actuate that desire. There are people today who speak of "Japaneseness" without paying much attention to this very important issue just raised.

For the taste of an individual Japanese to become truly Japanese, it must become a public possession without reference to the idiosyncrasy of that individual. For a Japanese taste to become truly artistic, it must also become public, not the private possession of the Japanese people. It must become part of the public mores that are correct from the ancient times to the present and upright when applied at home and overseas. Just as a profound mathematical principle defies understanding by many, understanding of a certain taste may be confined to a select few. I fully recognize that art and morality are based on personal elements and, unlike mathematical principles, are extremely particularistic. But if they completely deny understanding by others, we cannot call them beautiful or good. Herein lies the difference between mere idiosyncrasy and artistic taste. We do not know for sure if today's Westerners can understand Japanese taste or the Japanese people the taste of foreign countries. Chances are neither party can. In spite of this observation, I believe that each nation must on the basis of its history develop its own art and morality and contribute toward world civilization from its own unique perspective. To have a unique culture does not mean it is idiosyncratic. It must be endowed with a common value. When I say "common," it does not mean that everyone must make the same thing and have the same taste. It simply means that we must recognize the value that is intrinsic in all people. We must separate sameness from unity. All parts of a human body are not the same, but each part has a unique value, which becomes an indispensable part of a human body. Misunderstanding arises when this meaning is not made clear. If artistic and moral values can require understanding by all, we must still not forget that there is a degree of understanding that can be great, small, deep, or shallow. At the same time, we must realize that in everyone's mind, at the basis there is an unifying consciousness. In academic parlance it is called a normative consciousness.

There is confusion today among those people who advocate "Japaneseness." One group believes that each nation and each individual must accept the same art and same taste, and another group believes that everyone must recognize art if it has a certain intrinsic value. I am for advocating Japaneseness and reject that which is common in the sense of the former. If we reject that which is common in the sense of the latter, we may lose precious artistic values. Let us develop our unique culture, which is endowed with even more Japaneseness. Let us make our culture into one of the indispensable elements in world civilization. Let us discard our conventional dogma and critique and study our culture with no stone unturned. With the artistic conscience born from the bottom of our heart, let us have the self-confidence that the Chinese and Koreans of old [from whom Japan imported their civilizations] can also partake of our [age-old] Japanese spirit. In this way, we can create a true Japanese culture. Our history is not merely a history. It is also endowed with might. Let our forefathers relive in our bodies and in our blood. Japanese culture need not be forced into one of isolation, but must be respected as part of the world civilization. Let us seek a great spirit that is behind the Japanese culture. In our love for cherry blossoms, let us taste a philosophy of creative will, as [Friedrich W.] Nietzsche (1844–1900) remarked: "I love those who try to exceed themselves and die in the process." (*Ich liebe den, der über sich selber hinaus schaffen will und so zu Grunde gehe.*)

CHAPTER **XIV**

Rise of Ultranationalism and the Pacific War

Like many other great issues in history, Japan's path to Pearl Harbor poses many problems but no definite answers. The conspiracy theory of Japan's foreign relations first popularized by the Far Eastern Military Tribunal has been replaced by serious reexaminations conducted by the scholarly communities both in Japan and in the United States. In viewing the tragedy of the Pacific War, in place of guilt, attention has gravitated toward the motivation of the Japanese; in place of plot, toward the unique process of decision making; and in place of hastily sketched denunciation of Japanese character, toward the historical roots of Japanese attitude.[1]

The task of reexamination and reinterpretation has been greatly facilitated by the opening of archives, not only of Japan and Germany, but also of the United States and Great Britain, and by the publication of a large number of private papers and other documents around the world. The interpretive works both in this country and in Japan have also brought to light multifarious factors that contributed to the coming of war.

In looking at these factors retrospectively, the conspiracy theory still has a predominant place in interpreting the outbreak of the Manchurian Incident of 1931 which destroyed the carefully laid balance of power in the Pacific created by the Washington Conference of 1922. However, conspiracy played practically no part in the Marco Polo bridge incident of 1937 or in the attack on Pearl Harbor. Whatever we may emphasize as causes of the Pacific War, one factor we

---

[1]Remarks of Ardath Burks and Hillary Conroy et al., in Akira Iriye, "Japanese Imperialism and Aggression: Reconsiderations, I and II," *Journal of Asian Studies,* August 1963, pp. 469–72, and November 1963, pp. 103–13.

must not overlook is that of miscalculation. In spite of almost a century of close cultural and economic contacts between the United States and Japan, there was a conspicuous lack of perceptive understanding of each other, which was accompanied by deep-seated distrust on both sides. Neither side thought seriously that the other side would ever resort to arms. Then there were the preconceived and inaccurate notions of each other. In a sense, the American imposition of economic sanctions and the stationing of Japanese troops in China were the results and not the causes of this series of misunderstandings.

The purpose of this chapter is to identify some important thought patterns and events in Japan before and during the war as a means of providing some clues, inadequate as they may be, in the understanding of the Pacific War. It thus begins with Kita advocating military fascism as a panacea for Japan's social and economic ills (Document 1), followed by Japan's continental expansion policy, which eventually led to the creation of the Greater East Asia Co-prosperity Sphere (Documents 2–4). Japan's attempt to extricate herself from diplomatic isolation by aligning with Germany and Italy is treated next (Document 5). But difficulties with the United States followed, and the impasse the two countries reached, as seen from the Japanese perspective, is given in Document 6. The doctrinal basis in support of war as articulated in the *Way of Subjects* is reproduced in Document 7. The Taiseiyokusankai, or the Imperial Rule Assistance Association, is treated in Documents 8 and 9. The war meant cancelation of draft deferment for many students (Document 10), and some of them went on to volunteer for suicide missions (Document 11). The effect of bombing and other wartime-imposed difficulties on daily life is recaptured in the diary of a housewife (Document 12).

As the fortunes of war turned against Japan, surrender became inevitable, and the remaining portion of this chapter is devoted to Japan's decision to surrender (Documents 13–16).

While the scholarly communities both in Japan and in the West have avoided assessing Japan's "war guilt," that issue has remained a politically charged issue throughout the postwar years. Unlike the United States, which has since experienced the Korean, Vietnam, and Gulf wars, the Pacific War has remained "the war" in the Japanese consciousness. To the members of the Socialist Party, Japan was a guilty party that waged an aggressive war against its neighbors. Many in the Liberal Democratic Party and those of conservative persuasion felt that Japan fought for a righteous cause. The issue is further complicated by demands from the People's Republic of China, North Korea, and lately from South Korea for an apology from Japan. "I . . . express here once again my feelings of deep remorse and state my heartfelt apology," so said Murayama Tomiichi (b. 1924), prime minister of Japan in 1995, on the occasion of the fiftieth anniversary of the end of the war. Even under normal circumstances, the statement would incite a lively debate. In this instance it was made worse by the fact that Murayama was a Socialist heading a shaky coalition government with the Liberal Democratic Party. As this incident suggests, near the end of the twentieth century, contemporary Japan is still beholden to the Japan that fought the Pacific War. In reading the documents that follow, it may be well to keep that fact in mind.

AGITATION FOR MILITARY FASCISM

Of all the extreme nationalists, none equaled Kita Ikki (1883–1937) in influence. Kita was a dreamer in his youth, attaching himself to the revolutionary activities of the Chinese nationalists. When its leader, Sun Yat-sen, "failed to live up" to his promise of building an anti-imperialist, socialist state, the disillusioned man withdrew to Shanghai and wrote pamphlets advocating reforms of Japan. His General Outline of Measures for the Reconstruction of Japan *(Document 1) first appeared in mimeographed form in 1923. Even though it was banned, Kita was able to gain adherents among young military officers. He urged that the Emperor suspend the constitution and place the country under martial law. These measures, he argued, were intended to give the Emperor complete freedom to suppress reactionary movement by the wealthy and by the peers. Destruction of the status quo would be accompanied by establishment of a socialist state that would control the national economy in the interest of the entire nation.*

The appeal of Kita lay in his relentless attack, perhaps not unjustifiably, on the status quo symbolized by the oligarchy and private wealth. Since the beginning of modernization, the Japanese government consistently aided industry by imposing an undue tax burden on peasants and urban workers. While the rich became richer, many peasants and urban workers maintained living standards not much better than those of preindustrial days. Young officers who came from poverty-stricken areas saw in Kita's outcry for reform a panacea for all ills. A close affinity was discernible between Kita's doctrine and several assassination attempts and military coups staged by young officers during the 1930s. Kita was implicated in the February 26 incident of 1936 and was executed along with other conspirators. However, his idea of internal reform and external expansion lived on. The February 26 incident helped create a climate under which the Japanese government was forced to accept the policies advocated by the army as its own. Thus was begun Japan's path toward ultranationalism.

1 General Outline of Measures for the Reconstruction of Japan, 1923[2]

Section 1. The Emperor of the People

Suspension of the constitution: In order to establish a firm base for national reconstruction, the Emperor, with the aid of the entire Japanese nation and by

---

[2]Kita Ikki, *Kokka Kaizōan Genri Taikō,* in *Kita Ikki Chosakushū (Works of Kita Ikki),* vol. 2 (Tokyo: Misuzu Shobō, 1959), pp. 219–81. Preface, epilogue, and notes are omitted from this translation.

invoking his imperial prerogatives, shall suspend the constitution for a period of three years, dissolve the two houses of the Diet, and place the entire country under martial law.

The true significance of the Emperor: We must make clear the fundamental principle that the Emperor is the sole representative of the people and the pillar of the state.

To clarify this doctrine, there shall be instituted a sweeping reform in the imperial court, consistent with the spirit shown by Emperor Jimmu in the founding of the nation and by Emperor Meiji in the Restoration. The incumbent privy councilors and other officials shall be replaced by men of ability, sought throughout the realm, capable of assisting the Emperor.

An Advisory Council shall be established to assist the Emperor. Its members, fifty in number, shall be appointed by the Emperor.

Whenever the Cabinet Council so decides or the Diet places a vote of nonconfidence against him, an Advisory Council member shall submit his resignation to the Emperor. However, this procedure shall not be interpreted to mean that council members are responsible to the Cabinet or to the Diet.

Abolition of the peerage system: By abolishing the peerage system, we shall be able to remove feudal aristocracy, which constitutes a barrier between the Emperor and the people. In this way the spirit of the Meiji Restoration can be newly proclaimed.

The House of Peers shall be replaced by a deliberative council that shall review decisions made by the House of Representatives. The Deliberative Council may reject for a single time only any decisions of the House of Representatives.

Members of the Deliberative Council shall consist of men distinguished in various fields of activities, elected by each other or appointed by the Emperor.

Popular election: All men twenty-five years of age and above shall have the right to elect and be elected to the House of Representatives, exercising their rights with full equality as citizens of Great Japan. Similar provisions shall apply to all local self-governing bodies. Women shall not be permitted to participate in politics.

Restoration of people's freedom: Existing laws that restrict people's freedom and circumvent the spirit of the constitution shall be abolished. These laws include the civil service appointment ordinance, peace preservation law, press act, and publication law.

National reconstruction Cabinet: A national reconstruction Cabinet shall be formed during the time martial law is in effect. In addition to the existing ministries, the Cabinet shall establish such ministries of industries as described below and add a number of ministers without portfolio. Members of the reconstruction Cabinet shall be selected from outstanding individuals throughout the country, avoiding those who are at present connected with military, bureaucratic, financial, or party cliques.

All present prefectural governors shall be replaced by national reconstruction governors, selected in accordance with a policy similar to the one above.

National reconstruction Diet: A popularly elected national reconstruction Diet shall convene to discuss matters pertaining to reconstruction during the time martial law is in effect. However, this Diet shall not have the power to debate those basic national reconstruction policies proclaimed by the Emperor.

Granting of imperial estate: The Emperor shall set a personal example by granting to the state, the land, forests, shares and similar properties held by the Imperial Household. The expenses of the Imperial Household shall be limited to 30 million yen per annum appropriated from the national treasury. However, the Diet may authorize additional expenditures if the need arises.

Section 2: Limitation on Private Property

Limitation on private property: No Japanese family shall possess property in excess of one million yen. A similar limitation shall apply to Japanese citizens holding property overseas. No one shall be permitted to make a gift of property to those related by blood or to others, or to transfer his property by other means with the intent of circumventing this limitation.

Nationalization of excess amount over limitation on private property: Any amount that exceeds the limitation on private property shall revert to the state without compensation. No one shall be permitted to resort to the protection of present laws in order to avoid remitting such excess amount. Anyone who violates these provisions shall be deemed a person thinking lightly of the example set by the Emperor and endangering the basis of national reconstruction. As such, during the time martial law is in effect, he shall be charged with the crimes of endangering the person of the Emperor and engaging in internal revolt and shall be put to death.[3]

Section 3: Three Principles for Disposition of Land

Limitation on private landholding: No Japanese family shall hold land in excess of 100,000 yen in current market value. . . .

. . . Land held in excess of the limitation on private landholding shall revert to the state. . . .

Popular ownership of land reverted to state: The state shall divide the land granted by the Imperial Household and the land reverted to it from those whose holdings exceed the limitation and distribute such land to farmers who do not possess their own lands. These farmers shall gain title to their respective lands by making annual installment payments to the state. . . .

Land to be owned by the state: Large forests, virgin land that requires large capital investment, and land that can best be cultivated in large lots shall be owned and operated by the state.

---

[3]Kita then advocates the establishment of a Council of Veterans Association as a permanent agency directly responsible to the reconstruction cabinet charged with the tasks of: (1) maintaining order, (2) investigating excess property held by families and individuals, and (3) collecting excess amounts.

Section 4: Control of Large Capital

Limitation on private property: No private industry shall exceed the limit of ten million yen in assets. A similar limitation shall apply to private industries owned by Japanese citizens overseas.

Nationalization of industries exceeding the limitation: Any industry whose assets exceed the limitation imposed on private industry shall be collectivized and operated under state control. . . .

Industrial Organization of the State

No. 1. Ministry of Banking: The assets of this ministry shall come from the money expropriated from large banks whose assets exceed the limitation on private industry and from individuals whose net worth exceeds the limitation on private property.

[The functions of this ministry shall include] overseas investment by utilizing its abundant assets and unified operation, making loans to other industrial ministries and to private banks, equitable adjustment of prices and currency in circulation, and guaranteeing the absolute safety of people's deposits.

No. 2. Ministry of Navigation: Ships and other assets expropriated from private lines in excess of the limitation on private property shall be utilized mainly for transoceanic voyages in order to attain supremacy over the [seven] seas. [The ministry shall also] engage in shipbuilding (naval and commercial) and other activities.

No. 3. Ministry of Mines: Large mines whose assets or market values exceed the limitation on private industry shall be expropriated and operated by this ministry. It shall also operate overseas mining industries financed by the Ministry of Banking and engage actively in developing national mines in newly acquired colonies concurrently with the development of private mining industries.

No. 4. Ministry of Agriculture: Management of nationally owned land; management of Taiwan sugar industry and forestry; development of Taiwan, Hokkaido, Karafuto (Southern Sakhalin), and Chōsen (Korea); development of South and North Manchuria and colonies to be acquired in the future; and management of large farms when acquired by the state.

No. 5. Ministry of Industries: Various large industries expropriated by the state shall be reorganized, unified, and expanded to form a truly large industrial combine through which all types of industries may acquire competitive advantages now possessed by comparable foreign industries. The ministry shall also operate industries urgently needed by the nation but not undertaken by the private sector. Naval Steel Works and Military Ordnance Factories shall be placed under this ministry's jurisdiction and be operated by it.

No. 6. Ministry of Commerce: This ministry shall distribute all agricultural and industrial commodities produced by the state and private parties, adjust domestic commodity prices, and engage actively in overseas commerce. For this purpose, the ministry shall calculate the rates of customs duties for submission to the Cabinet.

No. 7. Ministry of Railways: This ministry shall replace the present Board of Railways and place under its unified operation the Chōsen and South Manchurian Railways. It shall acquire title to railways in future colonies and engage actively in the construction of new railways.

Railways whose assets do not exceed the limitation on private industry shall be open to private operation.

Vast income of the national treasury: The vast income realized by the industrial ministries shall be sufficient for the expenditures of various service ministries and guarantee adequate living standards for the people as described below. Therefore, with the exception of basic income taxes, all other inequitable taxes shall be abolished. Without exception, all industrial ministries shall be taxed in a manner similar to all private industries.

Monopoly of salt and tobacco shall be abolished. Based on the principle that state-owned industries and privately owned industries can coexist, their production shall be open to private enterprise. . . . There shall be uniform taxes on both forms of production. . . .

Section 5: Rights of Workers

Functions of the Ministry of Labor: A Ministry of Labor shall be established within the Cabinet to protect the rights of all workers employed by state-owned and privately owned industries. Industrial disputes shall be submitted to the Ministry of Labor for arbitration in accordance with a law to be enacted independently. This arbitration shall be uniformly binding on all industrial ministries, private industries, and workers.

Wages: Wages shall be in principle determined by free contract. Disputes over wages shall be resolved by the Ministry of Labor in accordance with the law described above.

Working hours: Working hours shall be set uniformly at eight hours a day. Wages shall be paid for Sundays and holidays when no work is performed. Farm workers shall receive additional wages for the overtime work performed during the busy farming seasons.

Distribution of profits to workers: One half of the net profits of private industries shall be distributed to workers employed in such industries. All workers, mental and physical, shall participate in the profit distribution proportionate to their salaries or wages. Workers shall elect their own representatives to participate in the industry's management planning and bookkeeping. Similar provisions shall apply to farm workers and landlords.

Workers employed in state-owned industries shall receive semiannual bonuses in lieu of the profit distribution. Instead of participating in management planning and bookkeeping, such workers shall exercise their influence over the total industrial structure of the state through the House of Representatives.

Establishment of employee-shareholder system: Every private corporation shall set up a provision under which physical and mental workers in their employment shall have the right to become stockholders of the corporation.

Protection of tenant farmers: The state shall enact a separate law, based on the basic human rights, to protect tenant farmers tilling the land owned by small landlords whose holdings do not exceed the limitation on private land.

Women's labor: Women's labor shall be free and equal to that of men. However, after the reconstruction, the state shall make it a matter of national policy that the burden of labor shall not rest on the shoulders of women. In order to prepare women to replace men in providing needed labor in a national emergency, women shall receive education equal to that of men.

Section 6: People's Right to Live

Children's right to live: Children under fifteen years of age without both parents or father, having rights as children of the state, shall be uniformly supported and educated by the state. . . .

Support of the aged and disabled: The state shall assume the responsibility of supporting those men and women sixty years of age or over who are poor and do not have natural-born or adopted sons. Similar support shall be given to those disabled and crippled persons who are poor, unable to work, and without fathers and sons.

Rights to education: National (compulsory) education shall last for a period of ten years from ages six to sixteen. Similar education shall be given to both male and female. There shall be instituted a fundamental reform in the educational system, with the aim of building a foundation for the furtherance of individual talents by imparting knowledge of worldwide scope based on the spirit of Japan and developing each individual's mind and body consistently throughout the ten-year period.

English shall be abolished and Esperanto shall become the second language.[4]

Section 8: Rights of the State[5]

Continuation of the conscript system: The state, having rights to existence and development among the nations of the world, shall maintain the present conscript system in perpetuity. . . .Soldiers in active service shall receive stipends from the state. In army bases and in warships, there shall be no difference in the enjoyment of provisions among officers, soldiers and seamen, except the emblems signifying their respective ranks.

With regard to alien races residing in present and future colonies, a voluntary enlistment system may be adopted.

---

[4]In the remaining paragraphs, Kita discusses protection of women's rights, freedom from interference by governmental officials, and rights to private property not in excess of the limitations previously imposed.

[5]Section 7, which is omitted, outlines gradual incorporation of Korea into the political and administrative system of Japan proper, and application of the reconstruction principles to Korea, Taiwan, and other present and future colonies.

Positive right to start war: In addition to the right of self-defense, the state shall have the right to start a war on behalf of other nations and races unjustly oppressed by a third power. (As a matter of real concern today, the state shall have the right to start a war to aid the independence of India and preservation of China's territorial integrity.)

As a result of its own development, the state shall also have the right to start a war against those nations that occupy large colonies illegally and ignore the heavenly way of coexistence of all humanity. (As a matter of real concern today, the state shall have the right to start a war against those nations that occupy Australia and Far Eastern Siberia for the purpose of acquiring them.)

CHINA AND GREATER EAST ASIA

Among the policies advocated by young military officers were vindication of Japan's national polity, strengthening of national defense, departure from the traditional pro-Western foreign policy, and the assertion of Japan's place in the sun. Their influence became evident in the "Fundamental Principles of National Policy" (Document 2) adopted by the Hirota Cabinet on August 11, 1936. It was an attempt to put an end to the rivalry between the army and navy by dividing the military budget evenly. To justify this, it supplemented the army's traditional northward expansion policy with the navy's new southward expansion policy. Just what the Cabinet meant by bringing about "close collaboration between Japan, Manchukuo, and China" was made clear in the "Basic Administrative Policy toward North China" adopted the same day. The latter called for setting up an anticommunist, pro-Japanese area, securing necessary materials for Japan's national defense, and improving transportation facilities to guard against possible attack by the Soviet Union.

Japan's invasion of North China began on July 7, 1937. From the beginning, the conflict showed every sign of becoming a protracted war. Forced by popular pressure, the Nationalist regime headed by Chiang Kai-shek repeatedly rejected Japan's "peace" overtures. The Imperial Army occupied cities, railway lines and major coastal areas, but its sway never extended to the villages. Frustrated in its attempt to end the war, the Japanese Army created and sought collaboration from puppet regimes.

The basic treaty between the puppet Wang Jingwei regime and Japan was signed in Nanking on November 30, 1940 (Document 3). It gave Japan a "legal" basis for its "warlike operations" in China, as long as there was "a threat to the peace and well-being of the two nations" by the destructive activities of communism. Under the treaty, Wang was forced to allow stationing of Japanese troops in China indefinitely; to establish "high priority anti-Comintern areas" in North China; to set up "special areas" in the Yangzi delta region, Hainan Island, and Xiamen and its vicinity; to pledge that China would conduct no foreign policy

*contrary to the spirit of this treaty; to allow joint management of the maritime
customs and other tax collecting agencies; and to promise the hiring of Japanese
political advisers and technical experts.*

*The basic treaty, together with accompanying documents, makes fascinating
reading. The conditions enumerated in them were also the ones Japan wanted to
secure from Chiang Kai-shek in the event of a total peace, which would make
China's subjugation complete. They also anticipated the formulation of Japan's
Greater East Asia policy yet to come. The economic provisions of the basic
treaty and the accompanying documents were repeated in Japan's treaties with
French Indochina and reappeared in the demands to the Dutch East Indies.*

*After the initial success in the Pacific War, Japan granted "independence" to
Burma and the Philippines. Along with Manchukuo, China (Wang Jingwei's),
and Thailand, they were called to Tokyo for an Assembly of the Greater East
Asiatic Nations. The joint declaration of that assembly adopted on November 6,
1943, is reproduced as Document 4. It condemned the "aggression and exploitation" of the United States and Great Britain and pledged mutual respect for
one another's sovereignty and independence, racial equality, and cultural tradition. It also spoke of economic and cultural cooperation. In practice, however,
economic cooperation became nothing but a means to exploit natural resources
for Japan's war effort (compare Document 6 for the statements of Suzuki and
Kaya). As to cultural cooperation, it took the form of Japanization, including
construction of Shintō shrines in the occupied areas.*

2   Fundamental Principles of National Policy, 1936[6]

A. The basic national policy consists of solidifying the foundation of the
country internally and extending national prestige externally, which must be
executed with fairness and justice. Japan must become the stabilizing force in
East Asia both in name and in fact so as to contribute to the peace and welfare of
mankind and at the same time manifest the ideals of the founding of the nation.
The fundamental national policies that Japan must adopt, in view of the existing
domestic and international conditions, are to ensure Japan's position in the continent of East Asia diplomatically and militarily and to advance to the South Seas.
The fundamental principles are described below:

(1) Japan must strive to eradicate the aggressive policies of the great powers
and share with East Asia the joy that is based on the true principle of coexistence
and coprosperity. This is the realization of the spirit of the Imperial Way, which
must be accepted as the consistent guiding principle in Japan's policy of foreign
expansion.

(2) Japan must complete her national defense and armament to protect her

---

[6]Asahi Shimbunsha, ed., *Shiryō Meiji Hyakunen (Documents for the Meiji Centennial)*
(Tokyo: Asahi Shimbunsha, 1966), pp. 495–96.

national security and development. In this way, the position of the Empire as the stabilizing force in East Asia can be secured both in name and in fact.

(3) The policy toward the continent must be based on the following factors: in order to promote Manchukuo's healthy development and to stabilize Japan-Manchukuo national defense, the threat from the north, the Soviet Union, must be eliminated; in order to promote our economic development, we must prepare against Great Britain and the United States and bring about close collaboration between Japan, Manchukuo, and China. In the execution of this policy, Japan must pay due attention to friendly relations with other powers.

(4) Japan plans to promote her racial and economic development in the South Seas, especially in the outlying South Seas area. She plans to extend her strength by moderate and peaceful means without arousing other powers. In this way, concurrently with the firm establishment of Manchukuo, Japan may expect full development and strengthening of her national power.

B. Utilizing the above fundamental principles as the axis, we must unify and coordinate our foreign and domestic policies and reform our administration thoroughly to reflect the current conditions. The following are the basic outlines:

(1) Japan's national defense and armament must be completed in the following manner:

a. The army's arms preparations must have as their goal the ability to withstand the forces that can be deployed by the Soviet Union in the Far East. The army must expand its Kwantung and Chōsen (Korean) forces to the extent that they can deliver the first decisive blow against the Soviet Far Eastern Army at the outbreak of war.

b. The navy's arms preparations must have as their goal creation of forces sufficient to withstand an attack from the U.S. Navy to secure the control of the Western Pacific for Japan.

(2) Our foreign policy must be based on the principle of the smooth execution of the fundamental national policies. It must therefore be coordinated and reformed. In order to facilitate the smooth functioning of activities of diplomatic bureaus, the military must endeavor to give behind-the-scenes assistance and must avoid overt activities.

(3) In order to conform to the above basic national policies, in effecting reform and improvement in political and administrative organizations, in establishing financial and economic policies, and in administering other agencies, appropriate actions must be taken on the following matters:

a. The domestic public opinion must be led and unified, so as to strengthen the nation's resolve in coping with the present national emergency.

b. Appropriate reforms in administrative agencies and economic organizations must be effected to bring about improvement in industries and important foreign trade necessary for executing national policies.

c. Appropriate measures must be taken to ensure stabilization of national life, strengthening of physical fitness, and development of sound national thought.

d. Appropriate plans must be undertaken to promote rapid growth in aviation and maritime transportation industries.

e. We must promote the establishment of a policy of self-sufficiency with regard to important natural resources and materials required for national defense and industries.

f. Concurrently with the reform of diplomatic bureaus, information and propaganda organizations must be well established to enhance vigorously diplomatic functions and cultural activities overseas.

3   Treaty Concerning Basic Relations between Japan and China, 1940[7]

The Imperial Government of Japan and

The National Government of the Republic of China:

Being desirous that these two countries should respect their inherent characteristics and closely cooperate with each other as good neighbors under their common ideal of establishing a new order in East Asia on an ethical basis, establishing thereby a permanent peace in East Asia, and with this as a nucleus contributing toward the peace of the world in general, and

Desiring for this purpose to establish fundamental principles to regulate the relations between the two countries, have agreed as follows:

ARTICLE 1. The Governments of the two countries shall, in order to maintain permanently good neighborly and amicable relations between the two countries, mutually respect their sovereignty and territories and at the same time take mutually helpful and friendly measures, political, economic, cultural and otherwise.

The Governments of the two countries agree to eliminate, and to prohibit in the future, such measures and causes as are destructive of amity between the two countries in politics, diplomacy, education, propaganda, trade and commerce, and other spheres.

ARTICLE 2. The Governments of the two countries shall closely cooperate for cultural harmony, creation, and development.

ARTICLE 3. The Governments of the two countries agree to engage in joint defense against all destructive operations of communistic nature that jeopardize the peace and welfare of their countries.

The Governments of the two countries shall, in order to accomplish the purpose mentioned in the preceding paragraph, eliminate communistic elements and organizations in their respective territories and at the same time cooperate closely concerning information and propaganda with reference to the defense against communistic activities.

---

[7]S. Shepard Jones et al., eds., *Documents of American Foreign Relations,* vol. 3, *1940–1941* (Boston: World Peace Foundation, 1941), pp. 282–87. Articles 8 and 9 and the witness clause are omitted.

Japan shall, in order to carry out the defense against communistic activities through collaboration of the two countries, station required forces in specified areas of the Mongolian Federation and of North China for the necessary duration, in accordance with the terms to be agreed upon separately.

ARTICLE 4. The Governments of the two countries undertake to cooperate closely for the maintenance of common peace and order until the Japanese forces sent to China complete their evacuation in accordance with the terms as provided for separately.

The areas for stationing Japanese forces for the period requiring the maintenance of common peace and order and other matters pertaining thereto shall be determined as agreed separately between the two countries.

ARTICLE 5. The Government of the Republic of China shall recognize that Japan may, in accordance with previous practices or in order to preserve the common interests of the two countries, station for a required duration its naval units and vessels in specified areas within the territory of the Republic of China, in accordance with the terms to be agreed upon separately between the two countries.

ARTICLE 6. The Governments of the two countries shall effect close economic cooperation between the two countries in conformance with the spirit of complementing each other and ministering to each other's needs, as well as in accordance with the principles of equality and reciprocity.

With reference to special resources in North China and the Mongolian Federation, especially mineral resources required for national defense, the Government of the Republic of China shall undertake that they shall be developed through close cooperation of the two countries. With reference to the development of specific resources in other areas that are required for national defense, the Government of the Republic of China shall afford necessary facilities to Japan and Japanese subjects.

The Governments of the two countries shall take all the necessary measures to promote trade in general and to facilitate and rationalize the demand and supply of goods between the two countries. The Governments of the two countries shall extend specially close cooperation with respect to the promotion of trade and commerce in the lower basin of the Yangzi River and the rationalization of the demand and supply of goods between Japan on the one hand and North China and the Mongolian Federation on the other.

The Government of Japan shall, with respect to the rehabilitation and development of industries, finance, transportation, and communication in China, extend necessary assistance and cooperation to China through consultation between the two countries.

ARTICLE 7. According to the development of the new relations between Japan and China under the present Treaty, the Government of Japan shall abolish extraterritorial rights possessed by Japan in China and render to the latter its concessions; and the Government of China shall open its territory for domicile and business of Japanese subjects.

Excerpts from the Annexed Protocol

ARTICLE 1. The Government of the Republic of China, understanding that during the period in which Japan continues the warlike operations it is at present carrying on in the territory of China, there exists a special state of affairs attendant upon such warlike operations, and that Japan must take such measures as are required for the attainment of the object of such operations, shall accordingly take the necessary measures.

Even during the continuation of the said warlike operations, the special state of affairs referred to in the preceding paragraph shall, insofar as there is no obstacle to the attainment of the object of the operations, be adjusted in accordance with the changing circumstances and in conformity with the Treaty and its annexed documents.

ARTICLE 3. When general peace is restored between the two countries and the state of war ceases to exist, the Japanese forces shall commence evacuation with the exception of those that are stationed in accordance with the Treaty Concerning the Basic Relations between Japan and China signed today and the existing agreements between the two countries, and shall complete it within two years with the firm establishment of peace and order; and the Government of the Republic of China shall guarantee the firm establishment of peace and order during this period.

ARTICLE 4. The Government of the Republic of China shall compensate the damages to rights and interests suffered by Japanese subjects in China on account of the China Affair since its outbreak.

The Government of Japan shall, with respect to the relief of the Chinese rendered destitute by the China Affair, cooperate with the Government of the Republic of China.

Agreed Terms of Understanding between the Plenipotentiaries of Japan and China Concerning the Annexed Protocol (Excerpts)

1. With regard to those various organs for collecting taxes in China that are at present in a special condition owing to military necessity, an adjustment shall be made promptly in accordance with the spirit of respecting the financial independence of China.

2. With regard to those industrial, mining and commercial establishments under governmental or private management that are at present controlled by Japanese forces, the necessary measures shall be taken for their prompt transfer to Chinese management in a rational manner, with the exception of those that are of enemy character or under special circumstances of unavoidable character including military necessity.

3. In case any Sino-Japanese joint enterprise requires modification in the evaluation of original assets, the proportion of capital investments and other matters, measures for their rectification shall be taken in accordance with the terms to be

agreed upon separately through consultation between the two countries.

4. The Government of the Republic of China shall, in case they find it necessary to institute control on foreign trade, effect such control autonomously. They may not, however, infringe upon the principle of Sino-Japanese economic cooperation mentioned in Article 6 of the Treaty; and they shall consult with Japan with regard to such control during the continuation of the China Affair.

5. With regard to matters pertaining to transportation and communication in China that require adjustment, they shall be adjusted, as promptly as circumstances permit, in accordance with the terms to be agreed upon separately through consultation between the two countries.

4   Joint Declaration of the Assembly of Greater East Asiatic Nations, 1943[8]

It is the basic principle for the establishment of world peace that the nations of the world have each its proper place and enjoy prosperity in common through mutual aid and assistance. The United States of America and the British Empire have in seeking their own prosperity oppressed other nations and peoples. Especially in East Asia they indulged in insatiable aggression and exploitation and sought to satisfy their inordinate ambition of enslaving the entire region, and finally they came to menace seriously the stability of East Asia. Herein lies the cause of the present war.

The countries of Greater East Asia, with a view to contributing to the cause of world peace, undertake to cooperate toward prosecuting the War of Greater East Asia to a successful conclusion, liberating their region from the yoke of British-American domination and assuring their self-existence and self-defense and in constructing a Greater East Asia in accordance with the following principles:

I.   The countries of Greater East Asia, through mutual cooperation will ensure the stability of their region and construct an order of common prosperity and well-being based upon justice.

II.   The countries of Greater East Asia will ensure the fraternity of nations in their region, by respecting one another's sovereignty and independence and practicing mutual assistance and amity.

III.   The countries of Greater East Asia, by respecting one another's traditions and developing the creative faculties of each race, will enhance the culture and civilization of Greater East Asia.

IV.   The countries of Greater East Asia will endeavor to accelerate their economic development through close cooperation upon a basis of reciprocity and to promote thereby the general reciprocity of their region.

---

[8]Japanese Ministry of Greater East Asia, *Addresses before the Assembly of Greater East Asiatic Nations* (Tokyo, 1943), pp. 63–65. Its signatories were Tōjō Hideki (Japan), Zhang Jinghui (Manchukuo), Wang Jingwei (China), Prince Wan Wai Thayakon (Thailand), Ba Maw (Burma), and Laurel (Philippines).

V. The countries of Greater East Asia will cultivate friendly relations with all the countries of the world and work for the abolition of racial discrimination, the promotion of cultural intercourse, and the opening of resources throughout the world and contribute thereby to the progress of mankind.

THE AXIS ALLIANCE

The war in China brought Japan into conflict with the Western powers and caused Japan's diplomatic isolation. The Tripartite Pact (Document 5) concluded between Japan, Germany and Italy on September 27, 1940, was an attempt to secure for Japan a new international standing; to permit Japan to advance southward before Germany also claimed these territories for herself, to facilitate Japan's rapprochement with the Soviet Union and to negotiate with the United States from a "position of strength." The notion of the so-called bloc policy was also very much in evidence. Designed by Foreign Minister Matsuoka Yōsuke (1880–1946), it divided the world into four major blocs, each placed under the leadership of Japan, Germany and Italy, the Soviet Union, and the United States, respectively. The preamble and the first and second articles of the pact were expressions of this grand design, which was consistent with Nazi Germany's notion of Lebensraum.

5 The Tripartite Pact between Japan, Germany, and Italy, 1940[9]

The Governments of Japan, Germany, and Italy consider it the prerequisite of a lasting peace that every nation in the world shall receive the space to which it is entitled. They have, therefore, decided to stand by and cooperate with one another in their efforts in the regions of Europe and Greater East Asia respectively. In doing this it is their prime purpose to establish and maintain a new order of things, calculated to promote the mutual prosperity and welfare of the peoples concerned.

It is, furthermore, the desire of the three Governments to extend cooperation to nations in other spheres of the world that are inclined to direct their efforts along lines similar to their own for the purpose of realizing their ultimate object, world peace.

Accordingly, the Governments of Japan, Germany and Italy have agreed as follows:

ARTICLE 1. Japan recognizes and respects the leadership of Germany and Italy in the establishment of a new order in Europe.

ARTICLE 2. Germany and Italy recognize and respect the leadership of Japan in the establishment of a new order in Greater East Asia.

---

[9]Jones, et al., *Documents of American Foreign Relations,* pp. 304–5. Order of the names of the countries changed to conform to the Japanese version. The witness clause is omitted.

ARTICLE 3. Japan, Germany, and Italy agree to cooperate in their efforts on aforesaid lines. They further undertake to assist one another with all political, economic and military means if one of the three Contracting Powers is attacked by a Power at present not involved in the European War or in the Japanese-Chinese conflict.

ARTICLE 4. With a view to implementing the present pact, joint technical commissions, to be appointed by the respective Governments of Japan, Germany and Italy, will meet without delay.

ARTICLE 5. Japan, Germany and Italy affirm that the above agreement affects in no way the political status existing at present between each of the three Contracting Parties and Soviet Russia.

ARTICLE 6. The present pact shall become valid immediately upon signature and shall remain in force ten years from the date on which it becomes effective.

In due time, before the expiration of said term, the High Contracting Parties shall, at the request of any one of them, enter into negotiations for its renewal.

DECISION FOR WAR

Throughout most of 1941, policy disputes between the United States and Japan widened, which eventually led to Pearl Harbor. The Imperial Conference held on September 6 agreed to put a time limit on the decision for war or peace but also agreed on placing the emphasis on diplomatic negotiations. Another Imperial Conference was called on November 5 to reexamine the basic premises of the September 6 decision. This time with General Tōjō (1884–1948) replacing Konoye as prime minister. With the probability of success in diplomacy diminishing, the die was cast in favor of war. Yet the prospect for victory was not certain. Document 6 below reproduces the main part of the proceedings.

6 Imperial Conference, November 5, 1941[10]

Agenda: "Essentials for Carrying Out the Empire's Policies"

I. Our Empire, in order to resolve the present critical situation, assure its self-preservation and self-defense, and establish a New Order in Greater East

---

[10]Reprinted from *Japan's Decision for War: Records of the 1941 Policy Conferences*, edited and translated by Nobutaka Ike with the permission of the publishers, Stanford University Press © 1967 by the Board of Trustees of the Leland Stanford Junior University, pp. 209, 211–27. In addition to those officials whose statements are excerpted, the following also attended: Hara Yoshimichi, president of the Privy Council; Shimada Shigetarō, navy minister; and Itō Seiichi, navy vice chief of staff. The secretaries were Hoshino Naoki, Chief Cabinet Secretary; Mutō Akira, chief of the Military Affairs Bureau, Army Ministry; and Oka Takasumi, chief of the Naval Affairs Bureau, Navy Ministry. The document "Essentials, etc." on the agenda was not identical with the September 6 version.

Asia, decides on this occasion to go to war against the United States and Great Britain and takes the following measures:

1. The time for resorting to force is set at the beginning of December, and the army and navy will complete preparations for operations.

2. Negotiations with the United States will be carried out in accordance with the attached document. [omitted]

3. Cooperation with Germany and Italy will be strengthened.

4. Close military relations with Thailand will be established just prior to the use of force.

II. If negotiations with the United States are successful by midnight of December 1, the use of force will be suspended.

Statement by Prime Minister Tōjō Hideki:

At the Imperial Conference of September 6 "Essentials for Carrying Out the Empire's Policies" was discussed, and the following was decided by His Majesty: our Empire, determined not to avoid war with the United States, Great Britain, and the Netherlands in the course of assuring her self-preservation and self-defense, was to complete preparations for war by late October. At the same time it was decided that we would endeavor to attain our demands by using all possible diplomatic measures vis-à-vis the United States and Great Britain; and that in case there was no prospect of our demands being attained through diplomacy by early October, we would decide immediately on war with the United States, Great Britain, and the Netherlands.

Since then, while maintaining close coordination between political and military considerations, we have made a special effort to achieve success in our diplomatic negotiations with the United States. . . . During the negotiations, there has been a change in the Cabinet.

The Government and the army and navy sections of Imperial Headquarters have held eight Liaison Conferences in order to study matters more extensively and deeply on the basis of the "Essentials for Carrying Out the Empire's Policies" adopted on September 6. As a result of this, we have come to the conclusion that we must now decide to go to war, set the time for military action at the beginning of December, concentrate all of our efforts on completing preparations for war, and at the same time try to break the impasse by means of diplomacy. Accordingly, I ask you to deliberate on the document "Essentials for Carrying Out the Empire's Policies."

Statement by Foreign Minister Tōgō Shigenori:

The successful conclusion of the China Incident and the establishment of the Greater East Asia Co-prosperity Sphere would assure the existence of our Empire and lay the foundations for stability in East Asia. To achieve these objectives, our Empire must be prepared to sweep away any and all obstacles. . . .

Since the outbreak of the China Incident, both the British and American

Governments have obstructed our advance on the continent. On the one hand, they have aided Chiang; on the other hand, they have checked our activities in China or have stepped up their economic measures against us. Needless to say, Great Britain, which has acquired more interests than anyone else in East Asia, took all kinds of measures to obstruct us from the beginning. The United States, cooperating with her, abrogated the Japanese-American Trade Agreement, limited or banned imports and exports, and took other measures to increase her pressure on Japan. Particularly since our Empire concluded the Tripartite Pact, the United States has taken steps to encircle Japan by persuading Great Britain and the Netherlands to join her and by cooperating with the Chiang regime. Since the start of the German-Soviet war, she has taken unfriendly action against us by supplying oil and other war materials to the Soviet Union through the Far East, despite warnings from our Government. As soon as our Empire sent troops into French Indochina after concluding a treaty on the basis of friendly negotiations with the French Government for the purpose of defending ourselves and bringing the China Incident to a conclusion, America's actions became increasingly undisguised. Not only did she cut off economic relations between Japan and the United States, with Central and South America going along with her, under the guise of freezing our assets; but also, in cooperation with Great Britain, China, and the Netherlands, she threatened the existence of our Empire and tried harder to prevent us from carrying out our national policies. Accordingly, our Empire, which is the stabilizing force in East Asia, was compelled to try to overcome the impasse by showing firmness and determination. . . .

As I see it, the situation is becoming more and more critical every day, and negotiations with the United States are very much restricted by the time element; consequently, to our regret, there is little room left for diplomatic maneuvering. Moreover, the conclusion of a Japanese-American understanding would necessitate great speed in negotiations, partly because of the time required for domestic procedures on the American side. For this reason we have been required to carry on negotiations under extremely difficult circumstances. The prospects of achieving an amicable settlement in the negotiations are, to our deepest regret, dim. However, the Imperial Government will endeavor on this occasion to make every effort to arrive at a quick settlement in our negotiations. We would like to negotiate on the basis of the two proposals in the attached document, which assure the honor and self-defense of our Empire. The first proposal is one that has considered and acceded to as much as possible American wishes concerning stationing and withdrawal of troops in China, interpretation and execution of the Tripartite Pact among Japan, Germany, and Italy, and nondiscrimination in international trade, all of which were unsettled questions in the proposal of September 25. The second proposal, on the whole, is an agreement not to undertake a military advance in the Southwest Pacific areas, to promise each other cooperation in the procurement of materials in that area, to agree that the United States will not obstruct the establishment of peace between Japan and China, and to

428 JAPAN: A DOCUMENTARY HISTORY

mutually abrogate the freezing of assets. Finally, I should like to add that we are going to negotiate on the basis of an understanding that in the event our present negotiations lead to a settlement, all emergency measures that have been taken by the Imperial Government will be rescinded.

In case the present negotiations should unfortunately fail to lead to an agreement, we intend to strengthen our cooperative arrangements with Germany and Italy, and to take a variety of measures so as to be prepared for any situation.

Statement by President of the Planning Board Suzuki Teiichi:

I am going to give a summary of the outlook with regard to our national strength, particularly in vital materials, in case we go to war against Great Britain, the United States, and the Netherlands.

First, if we can constantly maintain a minimum of 3 million tons of shipping for civilian use, it will be possible to secure supplies in the amount called for by the Materials Mobilization Plan for the fiscal year of 1941, except for certain materials.

That is, with the exception of some materials, at least 3 million tons of shipping are needed in order to secure materials from the Zone of Self-support and the First Supplementary Zone in the amount specified in the Materials Mobilization Plan of 1941. We judge that on the average it will be possible to transport 4.8 to 5 million tons per month, using 3 million tons of shipping and assuming a 15 to 20 percent decline in shipping during wartime.

Second, if the yearly loss in shipping is estimated to be between 800,000 and 1 million tons, the maintenance of the 3 million tons of shipping mentioned above should be possible if we can obtain an average of about 600,000 gross tons of new construction each year. In other words, I think we can constantly maintain 3 million tons of shipping if we build 1.8 million gross tons of shipping in three years, or an average of 600,000 tons a year, provided we lose [no more than] 800,000 to 1 million tons of shipping a year. Building the foregoing 600,000 tons of shipping is considered possible if we rationally utilize the present civilian shipbuilding capacity of 700,000 gross tons and the engineering and forging capacity of about 600,000 gross tons and if we take such measures as standardizing and lowering the quality of the ships to be built, giving overall control of shipbuilding operations to the navy, and securing a labor force, as well as allocating 300,000 tons of steel, copper, and other necessary materials.

Third, in order to build 600,000 gross tons of new ships, more than 300,000 tons of ordinary steel will be needed. This can be secured if steel available for civilian use can be maintained at 2.61 million tons and this is allocated on a priority basis, with the allotment being kept to a minimum. . . .

Fourth, in order to maintain the shipping needed for production, it will be necessary to follow the plan agreed upon between the army, navy, and the Planning Board when it comes to determining the amount of shipping and the length of time such shipping will be needed for the Southern Operation. . . .

In the second half of 1941, particularly in the fourth quarter, transportation capacity will decline because of operations in the South; so we plan to hold the decrease in production to 150,000 tons by mobilizing sailing ships with auxiliary engines, utilizing iron foundries that can use coal shipped by rail, increasing the use of stored iron ore, collecting more scrap iron, and so on. Thus we estimate that actual production will be about 4.5 million tons, as against the 4.76 million tons called for in the plan.

Fifth, concerning rice, I think it will be necessary to consider substitute food, such as soybeans, minor cereals, and sweet potatoes, and to exercise some control over food in case the expected imports of rice from Thailand and French Indochina called for in the Food Supply Plan for the 1942 rice year (from October 1941 to September 1942) are reduced owing to operations in the South. That is, if the expected imports from Thailand and Indochina are reduced by 50 percent, the food supply will be down to 93 percent of the amount called for in the plan; and if the imports decrease by 75 percent, the supply will go down to 91 percent. However, if imports from Thailand and French Indochina can be increased by using more ships after the completion of the first phase of military operations, it may be possible to prevent the reduction from becoming too large.

As a rough estimate we plan to supply food by producing about 3.1 million *koku*[11] of rice in Formosa, about 6.28 million *koku* in Korea, and 59.13 million *koku* in the home islands; and also by importing about 3 million *koku* from Thailand and about 7 million *koku* from Indochina.

Sixth, if we can occupy important points in the Netherlands East Indies in a short period of time, we can expect to obtain the following major items in these amounts (I will discuss petroleum later under liquid fuel):

MAJOR ITEMS OBTAINABLE FROM NETHERLANDS EAST INDIES EXCLUDING PETROLEUM

[Percentages are percentages of monthly average of Materials Mobilization Plan of 1941]

Item	Tons	
Nickel ore (purity 3.5%)	6,000	(62%)
Tin (for antifriction alloy and gilding)	1,200	(144%)
Bauxite (raw ore for aluminum)	17,000	(42%)
Crude rubber	17,000	(400%)
Cassava root, theriac (for industrial alcohol)	15,000[a]	
Copra, palm oil (glycerin, substitute machine oil)	13,000[a]	
Sisal (substitute for Manila hemp)	3,000[a]	
Corn (animal feed and foodstuff)	20,000	(26%)
Industrial salt	7,000	(8%)
Sugar	20,000	(25%)

[a] A very small amount of import is expected in 1941.

---

[11] One *koku* is approximately 5.13 bushels.

Among the items listed, crude rubber, tin, and bauxite would most seriously affect the United States if their supply is cut off.

Seventh, the total supply of petroleum, in case of operations in the South, will be 850,000 kiloliters in the first year, 2.6 million kiloliters in the second year, and 5.3 million kiloliters in the third year. If an estimate is made of the future supply and demand of petroleum, including 8.4 million kiloliters in our domestic stockpile, I believe we will just be able to remain self-supporting, with a surplus of 2.55 million kiloliters in the first year, 150,000 kiloliters in the second year, and 700,000 kiloliters in the third year. Concerning aviation fuel: it is expected that, depending on consumption, we might reach a critical stage in the second or third year.

That is, according to a study of the supply and demand of petroleum resulting from the occupation of the Netherlands East Indies, which was made jointly by the army and the navy at Liaison Conferences, the quantity expected to be obtained from the Netherlands East Indies is 300,000 kiloliters in the first year, 2 million kiloliters in the second year, and 4.5 million kiloliters in the third year. . . .

Expected production of aviation gasoline is 75,000 kiloliters in the first year, 330,000 kiloliters in the second year, and 540,000 kiloliters in the third year, the breakdown being as follows:

	First Year	Second Year	Third Year
Netherlands East Indies	—	140,000 kl.	290,000 kl.
Iso-octane (in Japan)	15,000 kl.	40,000	60,000
Hydrogenolysis and cracking (in Japan)	60,000	150,000	190,000
Total	75,000	330,000	540,000

The total of oil stockpiled by army, navy, and civilian authorities as of December 1, 1941, will be 1.11 million kiloliters. . . .

In brief, it is by no means an easy task to carry on a war against Great Britain, the United States, and the Netherlands—a war that will be a protracted one—while still fighting in China, and at the same time maintain and augment the national strength needed to prosecute a war over a long period of time. It is apparent that the difficulty would be all the greater if such unexpected happenings as natural disasters should occur. However, since the probability of victory in the initial stages of the war is sufficiently high, I am convinced we should take advantage of this assured victory and turn the heightened morale of the people, who are determined to overcome the national crisis even at the cost of their lives, toward production as well as toward [reduced] consumption and other aspects of national life. In terms of maintaining and augmenting our national strength, this would be better than just sitting tight and waiting for the enemy to put pressure on us.

Next I will speak briefly on the outlook, both domestic and foreign, and on the situation with respect to vital materials in the event that we avoid war, maintain our present domestic and foreign posture, and suffer unspeakable hardships and privations.

First, materials in the Zone of Self-support will be in good supply, since the Government will guide the social situation in the proper direction. That is, maritime shipping capacity will necessarily be increased. . . . Like steel, other materials will also be in good supply.

Second, the probability that we will experience increased difficulties in obtaining materials from the First Supplementary Zone owing to pressure from the Anglo-American bloc is high. Nonetheless, it will be necessary to obtain the expected materials in the anticipated amounts from this area. Here, I believe, lurks a danger that we will enter into a war even though we wish to avoid it. That is, in order to meet our domestic needs we must obtain a supply of such materials as tungsten ore, tin ore, crude rubber, rice, corn, phosphate rock, pine resin, raw Japanese lacquer, oxhide, vegetable oil, and fat; but there is a danger that it will become difficult to obtain them because of pressure from Great Britain and the United States.

Third, serious shortages might develop in our domestic stockpiles, especially in liquid fuels. The kinds and quantities of liquid fuels necessary to ensure our national security cannot possibly be supplied solely by the synthetic petroleum industry. . . .

If we estimate that civilian demand will be 1.8 million kiloliters, and that shortages will be met by disbursements from military supplies, it will be barely possible to meet civilian needs. It is anticipated that in that event the military will also have difficulty in meeting its own needs at the end of the third year.

The foregoing is a view of the crude petroleum situation in terms of the overall quantity; but when we examine the picture with respect to specific items we note an imbalance. There will be difficulties in meeting the demand for kerosene for civilian use (in agriculture and forestry), ordinary machine oil (all industries), high-quality machine oil (railroads), and diesel oil (ships, fishing boats).

It is extremely difficult to overcome these shortages by means of the synthetic petroleum industry, in view of the present status of hydrogenolysis, cracking, iso-octane (aviation gasoline), synthetic fuel (diesel oil), and polymerization (machine oil). We fear that by the fourth year there will be nothing we can do. . . .

Fourth, there will be an imbalance in vital strategic materials, and shortcoming in our military preparedness and industrial production will be aggravated.

Fifth, in order to secure production necessary for maintaining and strengthening our defensive power, extraordinary effort will be necessary because of the need to unify the minds of the people. We fear that there is a danger that one misstep might divide public opinion.

Sixth, it is evident that as a result of permitting the United States to freely obtain materials necessary to build up her defense, there will develop differences in defensive power between the United States and Japan.

In conclusion, it would appear that if we go forward maintaining the present state of affairs, it would be very disadvantageous from the point of view of strengthening the material aspects of our national defense, if nothing else.

Statement by Finance Minister Kaya Okinori:

Although the budget of our country has constantly increased since the beginning of the China Incident and has reached more than 7.99 billion yen in the general account and 5.88 billion yen in extraordinary military expenditures (agreed upon by the 76th Diet Session), or a total of over 13.2 billion yen, we have been able to secure large amounts in taxes and assure large savings, thanks to the efforts of various institutions and of the people. On the whole, we have been able to carry on operations smoothly. However, it is clear that when we begin military operations in the South, additional large expenditures of government funds will be needed to cover them. Can our national economy bear the burden of such large military expenditures? Especially, are they feasible when the probability is high that the war will be protracted? Will there not be unfavorable effects on finance? Isn't there danger of a vicious inflation as a result of these expenditures?

However, war expenditures are mostly used to obtain vital materials, utilize facilities, and employ technology and labor. Therefore, the first question to be asked is whether there is a sufficient supply of materials to meet the need, and whether a minimum standard of living for the people can be maintained. So long as the material needs can be met, money and finance can go on for many years if that portion of national income designated for [civilian] consumption does not exceed the supply of consumer goods; surpluses are siphoned off by taxes and national savings, with the result that military expenditures put into circulation will end up as financial resources for military expenditures and production activities. . . .

The areas in the South that are to become the object of military operations have been importing materials of all kinds in large quantities. If these areas are occupied by our forces, their imports will cease. Accordingly, to make their economies run smoothly, we will have to supply them with materials. However, since our country does not have sufficient surpluses for that purpose, it will not be possible for some time for us to give much consideration to the living conditions of the people in these areas, and for a while we will have to pursue a so-called policy of exploitation. Hence even though we might issue military scrip and other items that have the character of currency in order to obtain materials and labor in these areas, it would be difficult to maintain the value of such currency. Therefore, we must adopt a policy of self-sufficiency in the South, keep the shipment of materials from Japan to that area to the minimum amount necessary to maintain order and to utilize labor forces there, ignore for the time being the decline in the value of currency and the economic dislocations that will ensue from this, and in this way push forward. Of course it is to be recognized that the maintenance of the people's livelihood there is easy compared to the same task in China because the culture of the inhabitants is low, and because the area is rich in natural products.

Statement by Navy Chief of Staff Nagano Osami:

Hereafter we will go forward steadily with our war preparations, expecting the opening of hostilities in the early part of December. As soon as the time for commencing hostilities is decided, we are prepared for war.

We are planning and getting ready with great care because success or failure in the initial phases of our operations will greatly affect success or failure in the entire war. It is very important that we carry out our initial operations ahead of the enemy and with courageous decisiveness. Consequently, the concealment of our war plans has an important bearing on the outcome of the war; and so, in putting our whole nation on a war footing in the future, we would like to maintain even closer relations with the Government and attain our desired goal.

Statement by Army Chief of Staff Sugiyama Gen:

I will comment on the following matters: (1) timing of the commencement of war; (2) prospects of the operations in the South; (3) situation in the North resulting from operations in the South; (4) relationship between operations and diplomacy.

1. On the timing of the commencement of war:

From the standpoint of operations, if the time for commencing war is delayed, the ratio of armament between Japan and the United States will become more and more unfavorable to us as time passes; and particularly the gap in air armament will enlarge rapidly. Moreover, defensive preparations in the Philippines, and other American war preparations, will make rapid progress. Also, the common defense arrangements between the United States, Great Britain, the Netherlands, and China will become all the more close, and their joint defensive capability will be rapidly increased. Finally, if we delay until after next spring, . . . there will be a higher probability that our Empire will have to face simultaneous war in the South and in the North. Thus it would be very disadvantageous for us to delay; and it is to be feared that it might become impossible for us to undertake offensive operations.

In addition, weather conditions in the area where important operations are going to take place are such that no delay is possible. Accordingly, in order to resort to force as soon as preparations for the operations we contemplate are completed, we would like to set the target date in the early part of December.

2. On the prospects of the operations:

Since the principal army operations in the initial stages in the South will be landing operations against fortified enemy bases, conducted after a long ocean voyage in the intense heat of the sun while repelling attacks from enemy submarines and aircraft, we expect to face considerable difficulties. However, if we take a broad view of the situation, the enemy forces are scattered over a wide area and moreover separated by stretches of water, making coordinated action difficult. We, on the other hand, can concentrate our forces, undertake sudden raids, and destroy the enemy piecemeal. Therefore, we are fully confident of success, given close cooperation between the army and the navy. As for operations after we land, we have complete confidence in our victory when we consider the organization, equipment, quality, and strength of the enemy forces.

After the initial stage in our operations has been completed, we will endeavor to shorten greatly the duration of the war, using both political and military strategies, particularly the favorable results from our naval operations. Nevertheless, we must be prepared for the probability that the war will be a protracted one. But since we will seize and hold enemy military and air bases and be able to establish a strategically impregnable position, we think we can frustrate the enemy's plans by one means or another.

We will firmly maintain in general our present posture with respect to defense against the Soviet Union and operations in China while we engage in operations in the South. In this way we will be able to strengthen our invincible position vis-à-vis the North, and there will be no problem in carrying on in China as we have been doing. With regard to China, the favorable results of the operations in the South should particularly contribute to the settlement of the China Incident.

3. On the situation in the North resulting from operations in the South:

The Red Army has suffered massive losses at the hands of the German Army; and there has been a marked decline in the productivity of the Soviet armament industry. In addition, the Red Army in the Far East has sent westward to European Russia forces equal to thirteen infantry divisions, about 1,300 tanks, and at least 1,300 airplanes since last spring. Its war potential, both materially and spiritually, is declining. Consequently, the probability of the Soviet Union taking the offensive, so long as the Guandong Army is firmly entrenched, is very low.

However, it is possible that the United States may put pressure on the Soviet Union to permit America to utilize a part of the Soviet territory in the Far East for air and submarine bases for use in attacking us; and the Soviet Union would not be in a position to reject these American demands. Hence we must anticipate the possibility that we might see some submarines and aircraft in action against us from the North. Consequently, it cannot be assumed that there is no danger of war breaking out between Japan and the Soviet Union as a result of such causes and charges in the situation. Thus our Empire must conclude its operations in the South as quickly as possible, and be prepared to cope with this situation.

4. On the relationship between operations and diplomacy:

Up to now, in accordance with the decision of the Imperial Conference of September 6, we have limited our preparations for operations so that they would not impede diplomatic negotiations. But from now on, given the decision for war, we will take all possible measures to be ready to use force at the beginning of December. This will have the effect of goading the United States and Great Britain; but we believe that diplomacy, taking advantage of progress in war preparations, should be stepped up. Needless to say, if diplomatic negotiations succeed by midnight of November 30, we will call off the use of force. If they do not succeed by that time, however, we would like to receive the Imperial Assent to start a war in order not to miss our opportunity and thereby to achieve fully he objectives of our operations.

DOCTRINAL BASIS FOR THE WAR

On August 1, 1941, four months before the attack on Pearl Harbor, the Japanese Ministry of Education issued a booklet entitled The Way of Subjects (Shimmin no Michi) *(Document 7), which was assigned as required reading in most universities and secondary schools. Unlike other nationalistic writings, the booklet was systematic and showed Japanese jingoism at its best. It claimed that the traditional character of the country was much impaired by the "influx of European and American culture," which brought the evils of "individualism, liberalism, utilitarianism and materialism." The way of subjects was to return to the Japanese spirit, to guard and maintain the Imperial Throne and to perform services for the state selflessly. To this end the Japanese people were called upon to make sacrifices for the Emperor and to create a national defense state in time of peace as well as in war.*

Expansionism was much in evidence. The China Affair was regarded not as a conquest, but as an attempt to rescue China from the control of the West which reduced that country to a state of "quasi colony." And Japan's new order in East Asia was viewed as the manifestation of the Shintō doctrine of Hakkō Ichiu, or of extending the benevolent rule of the emperor.

7 The Way of Subjects (Excerpts), 1941[12]

Preamble

The way of subjects of the Emperor issues from the polity of the Emperor, and is to guard and maintain the Imperial Throne coexistent with the Heavens and the Earth. This is not the sphere of the abstract, but a way of daily practice based on history. The life and activities of the nation are all attuned to the task of giving great firmness to the foundation of the Empire.

In retrospect, this country has been widely seeking knowledge in the world since the Meiji Restoration, thereby fostering and maintaining the prosperity of

[12]Japanese Ministry of Education, *Shimmin no Michi*, translated into English under the title *The Way of Subjects* and published in the *Japan Times Advertiser*, August, 1941.

the state. With the influx of European and American culture into this country, however, individualism, liberalism, utilitarianism, and materialism began to assert themselves, with the result that the traditional character of the country was much impaired and the various habits and customs bequeathed by our ancestors were affected unfavorably.

With the outbreak of the Manchurian Affair and further occurrence of the China Affair, the national spirit started to be elevated gradually, but there is still more or less to be desired in point of understanding the fundamental principle of polity by the people as a whole and their consciousness as subjects of the Emperor. It is to be deeply regretted that, well knowing the dignity of the polity of the Empire, people are likely to be satisfied with making it a mere conception, and fail to let it be manifest in their daily lives.

If this situation is left unremedied, it will be difficult to eradicate the evils of European and American thought that are deeply penetrating various strata of the national life of Japan, and to achieve the unprecedentedly great tasks by establishing a structure of national solidarity of guarding and maintaining the prosperity of the Imperial Throne. Herein lies an urgent need of discarding the self-centered and utilitarian ideas and of elevating and practicing the way of the subjects of the Emperor based on state services as the primary requisite.

Part I

An old order that has been placing world humanity under individualism, liberalism, and materialism for several hundred years since the early period of the modern epoch of history is now crumbling. A new order is now in the making amid unprecedented world changes. An outline of the modern history of the world must be looked over to give clearness to the significance of the new world order.

Modern history, in a nutshell, has been marked by the formation of unified nations in Europe and their contests for supremacy in the acquisition of colonies. Early in the modern period of history, the American continent was discovered and, stimulated by this, Europeans vigorously found their way to India and China by sounding the furrows of the oceans. Their march into all parts of the world paved the way for their subsequent world domination politically, economically, and culturally and led them to act freely as they pleased, facing them to believe that they alone were justified in their outrageous behavior. . . .

The industrial development propelled by invention of machines demanded a considerably large amount of materials and the consequent overseas markets for the disposal of manufactured goods. The result was that a severe contest for colonial acquisition and trade competition ensued naturally and that wars of the strong preying on the weak were repeated. The history of wars waged among Spain, Portugal, Holland, Britain, France, and other countries in the modern age, and the rise and fall of their influence, have close connections with their overseas aggression. . . .

. . . The self-destruction in the shape of the World War finally followed. It was only natural that cries were raised even among men of those countries after the war that the Occidental civilization was crumbling. A vigorous movement was started by Britain, France, and the United States to maintain the status quo by all means. Simultaneously, a movement aiming at social revolution through class conflict on the basis of thoroughgoing materialism like communism also was developed with unremitting vigor. On the other hand, Nazism and Fascism arose with great force. The basic theories of these new racial principles and the totalitarianism in Germany and Italy are to remove and improve the evils of individualism and liberalism.

That these principles show great concern for Oriental culture and spirit is a noteworthy fact that suggests the future of the Occidental civilization and the creation of a new culture. Thus the orientation of world history has made the collapse of the world of the old order an assured conclusion. Japan has hereby opened the start for the construction of a new world order based on moral principles.

The Manchurian Affair was a violent outburst of Japanese national life long suppressed. Taking advantage of this, Japan in the glare of all the Powers stepped out for the creation of a world based on moral principles and the construction of a new order. This was a manifestation of the spirit, profound and lofty, embodied in the Empire-founding, and an unavoidable action for its national life and world mission. . . .

Part III

Viewed from the standpoint of world history, the China Affair is a step toward the construction of a world of moral principles by Japan. The building up of a new order for securing lasting peace of the world will be attained by the disposal of the China Affair as a steppingstone. In this regard the China Affair would not and should not end with the mere downfall of the Chiang Kai-shek regime. Until the elimination of the veils of European and American influences in East Asia that have led China astray is realized, until Japan's cooperation with New China as one of the links in the chain of the Greater East Asia Co-prosperity Sphere yields satisfactory results, and East Asia and the rest of the world are united as one on the basis of moral principles, Japan's indefatigable efforts are sorely needed. The objective of the conclusion of the Tripartite Treaty is none other than the restoration of world peace. In this sense, Japan doubly and trebly owed an obligation to the world.

Japan has a political mission to help various regions in the Greater East Asia Co-prosperity Sphere, which are reduced to a state of quasi colony by Europe and America, so as to rescue them from their control. Economically, this country will have to eradicate the evils of their exploitation and then set up an economic structure for coexistence and co-prosperity. Culturally, Japan must strive to fashion East Asiatic nations to change their following of European and American culture and to develop Oriental culture for the purpose of contributing to the creation of a right world. The Orient has been left to destruction for the past several hundred years. Its rehabilitation is not an easy task. It is natural that unusual difficulties attend the establishment of a new order and the creation of a new culture. The conquest of these difficulties alone will do much to help in establishing a morally controlled world, in which all nations can cooperate and all people can secure their prosper position. The spirit of the founding of the Empire, which has penetrated Japanese history, has served greatly for the orientation of world history since the outbreak of the Manchurian Affair, amply aided by the China Affair. . . .

The development of the situation has made clear the importance of Japan's mission, and this has induced the nation to see that this country is facing an unprecedentedly serious situation, which calls for national solidarity permitting no temporizing mind. . . .

It is an urgent matter for Japan to realize the establishment of a structure of national unanimity in politics, economy, culture, education, and all other realms of national life. Defense is absolutely necessary for national existence. A nation without defense is one that belongs to a visionary world. Whether defense is perfect or not is the scale that measures the nation's existence or ruin. National growth and development can hardly be expected without the perfection of defense.

A concrete objective of the establishment of a new structure is the perfecting of a highly geared and centralized defense state and the strengthening of a total national war framework. . . .

With the change of war from a simple military to a complicated total affair, distinction between wartime and peacetime has not been made clear. When the world was singing peace, a furious warfare was staged behind the scenes in economy, thought, and so on, among nations. Unless a country is systematized even in time of peace, so that the total war of the state and the people is constantly concentrated on the objective of the country, and the highest capacity is displayed, the country is predestined to be defeated before taking to arms. If the state structure is disjointed, and political factions bicker, and economics is left to the ideas of individuals and to free competition, and cultural enterprises, including science, art and others, do not contribute to the state interest, and thought runs against polity and demoralizes the popular spirit, such a state will be a state only in name. . . .

Part IV

The cardinal objective of strengthening the total war organism is solely to help the Imperial Throne, and this can be attained by all the people fulfilling their duty as subjects through their respective standpoints. The Soviet Union has world domination through communism as its objective, and for this that country follows the policy of using compulsory rights through class dictatorship.

Standing on the national principle of blood and soil, Germany aims at de-

stroying the world domination of the Anglo-Saxon race and the prevailing condition of pressure brought to bear upon Germany. She rests on the gravity of her
voice for the right of national existence, and for this she has succeeded in
achieving thoroughgoing popular confidence in, and obedience to, the dictatorship of the Nazis, and is adopting totalitarianism. Italy's ideals are the restoration
of the great Roman Empire, and her policy for realizing them is not different
from that of Germany. The country stands on the dictatorial totalitarianism of the
Fascists.

In contrast to these, Japan, since the founding of the Empire, has been basking
under a benign rule of a line of Emperors unbroken for ages eternal, and has been
growing and developing in an atmosphere of great harmony as a nation, consisting
of one large family. However diverse the Empire's structures in politics, economy,
culture, military affairs, and others may be, all finally are unified under the Emperor,
the center. The country has lived under the Imperial rule and glory.

The ideals of Japan are to manifest to the entire world the spirit of her
Empire-founding represented by the principle that "the benevolent rule of the
Emperor may be extended so as to embrace the whole world" (*Hakkō Ichiu*).
There is virtually no country in the world other than Japan having such a superb
and lofty mission bearing world significance. So it can be said that the construction of a new structure and a defense state is all in order that Japan may revive
her proper national structure and come back to her original status of national
strength and leaving no stone unturned in displaying her total power to the fullest
extent. . . .

Part V

The Imperial Family is the fountain source of the Japanese nation, and national and private lives issue from this. . . .

The way of the subjects is to be loyal to the Emperor in disregard of self,
thereby supporting the Imperial Throne coexistensive with the Heaven and with
the Earth. . . .

The way of the Japanese subjects is made clear from the precepts bequeathed
by the Imperial ancestors and the brilliant achievements that have embellished
the annals of this country. In the course of the Imperial Rescript of Emperor
Meiji on Education it is said:

"Our subjects, ever united in loyalty and filial piety, have from generation to
generation illustrated the beauty hereof. This is the glory of the fundamental
character of Our Empire, and herein also lies the source of Our education. . . ."

In Japan, filial piety cannot exist singly without its absolute counterpart. It is
loyalty. Loyalty is the principle. Filial piety at home must be loyalty. Both are
one and inseparable. This is the Japanese characteristic unexcelled by other
countries. In Japan, husband and wife do not form the standard of home, as in the
Occident, but the relations of parents and sons are its center. It is natural that
filial piety is given great prominence. The first prerequisite of filial piety is to

fulfill the duty of subjects of guarding and maintaining the Imperial Throne in observance of the bequeathed will of their ancestors. This is the essence of filial piety. . . .

The great duty of the Japanese people to guard and maintain the Imperial Throne has lasted to the present since the Empire founding and will last forever and ever. To serve the Emperor is its key point. Our lives will become sincere and true when they are offered to the Emperor and the state. Our own private life is fulfillment of the way of the subjects; in other words, it is not private, but public, insofar as it is held by the subjects supporting the Throne. . . .

The China Affair is a bold task for Japan to propagate the ideals of the Empire founding throughout East Asia and the world over. . . . In order that Japan may be able to obtain her mission and establish a new order, it is natural that the country must be prepared to meet with many difficulties and obstructions in the future. This is the very moment that the Japanese nation should thoroughly understand the fundamental character of the Empire, eliminate selfish and utilitarian ideas, enhance national morals of service to the state as prior to all, have keen insight into the international situation, and fulfill the duty of the people with indomitable and unflinching determination, thereby diffusing the glorious and great principle of the Japanese Empire to the world.

Japan is the fountain source of the Yamato race, Manchukuo is its reservoir, and East Asia is its paddy field.

IMPERIAL RULE ASSISTANCE ASSOCIATION

The Taiseiyokusankai, or the Imperial Rule Assistance Association, came into being on October 12, 1940. By then all political parties had voluntarily disbanded, but the Association never took their place. Symbolically, the Association chose the name of an association (kai) to differentiate itself from political parties (tō). The Association covered people from all walks of life, including civil servants, schoolteachers, university professors, monks, clergymen, women, and veterans, making it an incohesive entity. It received its funding through governmental appropriation and the prime minister was the ex-officio president of the Association. Yet in Japanese domestic politics it never attained the status enjoyed by the Nazi Party in Germany or the Fascist Party in Italy.

Its chief contribution to Japan's war effort was propaganda. Its main purpose, as articulated in Document 8 (issued December 14, 1940), was to disseminate the ideals of Japan's new order to her people. And in this task the Taiseiyokusankai was remarkably successful. It controlled all channels of communication. It was divided into prefectural, city, township and village units. Each unit was further subdivided into groups of ten or so households, which were called neighborhood groups (tonarigumi). These groups were required to circulate papers sent from the Taiseiyokusankai headquarters, and to hold monthly meetings to read and discuss the contents of directives sent from Tokyo. In this way a directive sent from Tokyo reached every adult citizen, residing in urban centers as well as in the remotest corners of the country. A sample of the Association's organizational setup is given in Document 9, which was issued on September 11, 1940 (a month before the formal organization of the Association but in preparation for it).

8 Basic Outline for Implementing the Imperial Rule Assistance Association, 1940[13]

At a turning point in the world history today our Imperial country, which advocates the realization of the principle of extending the benevolent rule of the Emperor (*Hakkō Ichiu*), is destined to become the glorious moral leader of the world. Toward this end, we, the nation of 100 million, must with singleness of mind dedicate our all to the Emperor and establish a national system with unity of spiritual and material things. This Association, being an assemblage of His Majesty's subjects, shall promote mutual assistance and mutual encouragement and become the vanguard of our nation. We shall maintain a relationship of close cooperation with the government at all times and endeavor to let the will of those who are above be transmitted to those who are below, and to let the desires of those who are below be known to those who are above. In this way we shall work toward the realization of a nation highly organized for national defense.

We hereby advocate the following outline for implementation.

1. We shall fully devote our energies to the implementation of the *Way of Subjects* (Document 7). We shall believe in our national polity, which is a manifestation of the incomparable, absolute, and universal truth. We shall hold as sacred the rescripts issued by generations of Emperors, and shall make manifest the great way of restoration.

2. We shall cooperate in the building of the Greater East Asia Co-prosperity Sphere. We shall complete the system of co-prosperity in Greater East Asia and plan for its growth. At the same time, we shall work actively toward the goal of establishing a new order in the world.

3. We shall cooperate in the establishment of a political system that assists the Imperial rule. We shall endeavor to establish a strong and comprehensive political system that will unify our economic and cultural life under the spirit of assisting the Imperial rule.

4. We shall cooperate in the establishment of an economic system that assists the Imperial rule. We shall endeavor to establish a comprehensively planned economic system through the maximum utilization of our imagination, ability, and scientific knowledge. We shall endeavor to bring about a sharp rise in our productivity and thus work toward the completion of a self-sufficient economy in Greater East Asia.

---

[13]Asahi Shimbunsha, ed., *Shiryō Meiji Hyakunen*, p. 511.

5. We shall cooperate in the establishment of a new cultural order. We shall nurture a new Japanese civilization based on the spirit of our national polity and endowed with majestic, elegant, brilliant, and scientific qualities. Internally we shall promote our racial and national spirit and externally we shall encourage the formation of a Greater East Asian civilization.

6. We shall cooperate in the establishment of a new life system. We shall endeavor to establish a lifestyle that is consistent with our national ideals. We shall inculcate in the minds of all our people the ideals and desires of bringing about a new era, through spreading the public good and opening up public services. We, the people, shall all act in the spirit of belonging to one great family.

9   Outline for Organizing Village and Township Associations, 1940[14]

I. Purpose.

1. Based on the spirit of neighborhood solidarity, residents of cities, townships, and villages shall be organized into groups, so as to enable them to perform their common regional tasks consistent with the spirit of everyone supporting the Imperial rule.

2. These groups shall become the basic organizations in promoting moral training and spiritual solidarity for the nation.

3. These groups shall be utilized to disseminate information concerning our national policies to the nation and otherwise to assist in the smooth functioning of all phases of our national administration.

4. These groups shall serve as the basic regional control units in the national economy and perform such functions as deemed necessary in administering the controlled economy and in stabilizing living conditions.

II. Organization.

1. Village or township association: Cities, townships, and villages shall be divided into certain districts, and in villages, there shall be established village associations; and in urban areas, township associations. . . .

2. Neighborhood groups: Under a village association or township association, neighborhood groups shall be established, each consisting of about ten households.

In establishing a neighborhood group, the useful features of the old group office, or group of ten, shall be as much as possible preserved. . . .

3. City, township, or village general assembly: A city, township, or village general assembly shall be established in each of the cities, townships, or villages (in the case of six major cities, in each of the wards). . . .

The city, township, or village general assembly shall plan to coordinate and manage various administrative matters relating to the city, township or village. It shall also deliberate all matters that may promote the objectives described in I. above.

---

[14]*Ibid.*, pp. 510–11.

STUDENTS IN WAR

This section contains two selections on topics of greatest concern to students during the war. Document 10 contains reminiscences of a Higher School[15] day when draft deferment for liberal arts students was canceled. Document 11 contains excerpts from the diary of a young naval officer who volunteered for a suicide mission.

Shimizu Sachiyoshi (b. 1925), the author of Document 10, is a high school teacher who is also a fiction writer. This selection is excerpted from his Gakuto Shutsujin *(Students Sent to the Front) which was first published in 1964. The Higher School referred to in this selection is Osaka Kōtō Gakkō.*

Sub-Lieutenant Wada Minoru (1922–1945), author of the diary in Document 11, graduated from the First Higher School and was a student of the Law Faculty of Tokyo Imperial University when he volunteered for naval duty. His school training was considered an elite course, which under normal circumstances would have assured him a good position in the government or in the private sector. He volunteered for an assignment in a human torpedo squadron and perished in July 1945 at the age of twenty-three.

10 Cancellation of Draft Deferment for Liberal Arts Students, 1943[16]

The cancellation of draft deferment for all liberal arts students was announced on September 23, 1943. Before that time we all felt that those who had to be sent to the front before graduation were those lazy ones who did not do well in school. At least that was the way we all secretly felt. This feeling was shared by middle school students. I remember when I was studying for the entrance examination for Higher School, one comic character made lots for us to draw. The best prizes were entrance to the First or Third Higher School. And the worst ones were reserved for being drafted into the army or into factories. If one failed his entrance examination and remained a *rōnin*[17] for a long period of time, he was usually drafted to work in a factory, and when he reached the draft age he would enter the military barracks. Many of my classmates were forced to take this route. So as far as students were concerned, to enter military barracks meant to meet a dishonorable fate. This perception persisted, even though the country was

---

[15]Until 1946, Higher School (*Kōtō Gakkō*) was the institution that university-bound students had to pass through after their graduation from middle schools. Its prestige was higher than the present-day high school, and its academic contents closer to the first two years of American colleges.

[16]Okuno Takeo et al., eds., *Senjika no Haitiin (Late Teens During the War)* (Tokyo, Shūeisha, 1965), pp. 335, 339–42, 344–45.

[17]A student who aspires to higher education without being admitted to the next level of school after graduation from his middle or higher school. The term originally referred to a masterless samurai.

already at war in the Pacific theater, and middle schools were supposed to be the bastion of support for Japan's militarism.

However, things began to change in 1943. It was probably going on that way for some time, but our people were not aware of it. On February 9, the Imperial Headquarters announced that Japanese troops were pulling out of Guadalcanal, and this came as the first realization. We were not worried about losing an island in the South Pacific, but we were shocked by the tens of thousands of dead and wounded. On February 2, the German Army perished in Stalingrad. On April 18, the commander in chief of the Combined Fleet, Admiral Yamamoto Isoroku, was killed in action. On May 29, the defending troops at Attus island all perished rather than suffer the dishonor of surrender. On July 25, Mussolini lost his position, and on September 8 Italy surrendered to the Allies unconditionally.

The term "intensified fighting" began to appear in newspapers. It meant not only that our side was not winning but also that our soldiers suffered beyond description. . . .

At our schools, hours spent for foreign languages were reduced, and in their place, hours spent for military training were increased, with a minimum of one hour a day, and often three hours. Baseball was considered an American sport and was banned. One by one, other sports of foreign origin met the same fate. Increasingly, we were sent to factories and airfields to fill in for the severe shortage of labor. . . .

The sending of students to the front came around that time.

We still had an alternative course left that could save us. That was to abandon our desire of entering into the law, economics, or literature faculties of imperial universities and enter medical colleges. If we chose medical colleges, we could still get draft deferment. No one would have called us cowards if we chose that path. However, in my class of forty students, only four chose to enter medical college. A majority of us felt a longing for imperial universities. That sentiment was far stronger than the fear of uncertain death.

When the draft deferment was canceled, I was only eighteen years and seven months old. So it did not affect me immediately. There were some who could not enter higher schools or who were retained in their original classes and reached age twenty. They were the ones who became eligible for draft. A little over two months after that, on December 1 to be exact, they were to enter military barracks. . . .

There were ten people from our school who were drafted that year, and we decided to give them a big send-off party.

The send-off party was held in a private home near our school. All of us pitched in for the party. By then everything was scarce, but the proprietor of the Fukufukuya restaurant wanted to repay our past patronage by going all the way to the Kii peninsula to buy food for us. . . .

When all the food and drinks were gone, we went outside to take a stroll. . . .

We kept on singing the Nazi song called *Englandlied*.[18] We never sang Japanese military songs. Just why we chose Nazi German songs was not clear to us.

Among us, the Imperial Rule Assistance Association was held in contempt, but Nazi Germany was not. General Tōjō Hideki was never respected by us, but Hitler was, and none of us ever questioned all the atrocities committed by him. We did not choose to know the chasm that separated the Germany of Kant and Goethe from the Germany of Hitler and Goebbels. Germany purged Jews, yet it was willing to retain Heinrich Heine's "Lorelei," without giving the poet's identity. We accepted matter-of-factly the news that when all the German troops perished in Stalingrad, the German national radio sadly broadcast Beethoven's Fifth Symphony.

. . . Our elitist notions might have had some sense of affinity with the German feeling of *"Deutschland über Alles."*

Then in the song *Englandlied*, there was a sweetheart who never appeared in Japanese military songs. We wanted to be like German soldiers, who took hold of the white hand of a German maiden, wishing the best for her and then left for a march against England. . . .

11   Diary of a Student Volunteer for Suicide Mission, 1945[19]

April 18, 1945. Exactly one month from today. I feel as if I am to take my final examination.

Exactly one more month, then we will be sent to the front to face our enemy. I am going to get after our enemy, and aside from this particular feeling, I have no thought of death.

We are lucky, we need not be bothered with questions like "what is life?" or "what is death?"

I cannot talk like a sub-lieutenant by the name of N who exaggerates everything. Every word that comes out of his mouth is full of patriotism. In my placid mind now, all such thoughts are consigned to the depth of quiet reflection. Some people may say that this type of inner reflection is unwarranted at a time like this. However, we have discovered the meaning of thinking, and this is a burden we have to bear. I believe that only in bearing the burden of thinking will I be able to account for the meaning of my own life.

---

[18]The song was: *Heute wollen wir ein Liedlein singen. Trinken wollen wir den külen Wein. Und die Gläser sollen dazu klingen, Denn es muss, es muss geschieden sein. Gib mir deine Hand, deine weisse Hand. Leb' wohl mein Schatz, leb' wohl lebe wohl. Denn wir fahren, denn wir fahren, denn wir fahren gegen Engelland. Engelland.* (Today we want to sing a song, we want to drink cool wine. When glasses clink to make a sound, then it must, it must be the time to part. Give me your hand, your white hand. Keep well my sweetheart, keep well my sweetheart, keep well, keep well. Then we go, then we go, then we go to England. England.).

[19]Okuno Takeo et al., eds., *Seinen Shikan no Senshi (War History of Young Officers)* (Tokyo: Shūeisha, 1965), pp. 437–41, 443.

"Placid indeed is the mind of man, and the grave is my abode," said the writer Ishikawa Tatsuzō (1905–1985) through the mouth of his heroine in his *Tenraku no Shishū (Fallen Poetry Books)*. I think of my strange calmness of mind and can see that it can penetrate deeply to those who are around me.

I once rose up courageously, then why do I still have room for this type of thought? Am I a coward?

My comrades in arms have said to me that my face has betrayed my weariness for the past several days.

I know during the same period I have been trying to give meaning to my own death.

I have been absorbed in the task of making an angle-of-fire chart so that I can make my human torpedo hit the enemy for sure. I am now making much fewer errors in judging azimuth angles. . . .

I wrote the following letter home:

"In spite of the fierce fighting that is going on, we are leading a rather sedate life. Last year around this time, I was shocked, angered, and disgusted at practically everything. I am no longer fussy about trifles as I used to be. Instead, I can now look at the beautiful surrounding scenery quietly, and in that respect I am very much like the one I used to be in my higher school days.

"Last night I got terribly drunk. I was led to many different places and even went to the petty officers' quarters. I drank water from their flower vase, gave a lecture on Johann Gottlieb Fichte's *To the German Nation,* and then took a sip from a nearby ink bottle. I put ink stain all over the pants of an ensign who was accompanying me. Later some of the petty officers remarked that second sublieutenant Wada gets his braininess by drinking ink. . . .

"Now that I have become an officer, my meals and rooms are all taken care of by orderlies. We get top-grade *sake,* the 'Hakuroku' brand, but not many of us drink and there is plenty left. I wish I could send some to father. After dinner, I often go to the recreation room to play my violin. I have a number of music scores, and there is a Normal School graduate who accompanies me on the piano skillfully.

"We go to bed past ten. The other day I saw Captain Ōsono, who was amazed to see how well I looked."

May 6. Why am I now trying to find a logical conclusion to this otherwise confused life, knowing full well that I have only a month to live?

It's just like an hourglass that never gives up its function of marking time. . . .

May 15. Yesterday I was granted my furlough, and left the city of Hikari at 7:40 P.M. for home. . . . I did not send a telegram home. When I arrive tonight, how surprised all of them will be! My suitcase is full of cookies, shirts, whiskey, and cigarettes.

I am not sure of myself. When I see my parents face to face, I may not be able to hold back anything and tell them everything. What will they think and what will they say?

May 29. I came to the front only yesterday, but what I have in mind is the desire to give my life seven times over to annihilate my enemy. I have this ever growing hostility toward the enemy. . . .

June 12. At 11:40 A.M. I began making all necessary preparations. My intended target is likely to be an enemy aircraft carrier. . . .

June 20, the final entry. A person who is truly enlightened is said to be able to mediate on the question of life and death and eradicate it from his mind. Some people may not give thought to the question of life and death, living day after day in this world of illusion and falsehood. They can talk in a grandiose style, acting as if they were above life and death. No, they only convey falsehood.

One must endeavor to understand its meaning constantly. Passing through death and life, one can then gain enlightenment. This is really not a question that can be dismissed lightly. My life has been one of vanity and at the same time one that lacked moral courage. Yet to me this one month of quiet meditation has been a significant period in my life in more than one way. However, the fruition of this month is yet to come. In reading *Jinsei Gekijō (Human Theater)* by Ozaki Shirō (1898–1964), I realized how often I did put on an act in my life.

Now I am claiming that I have discovered my own answer to the question of life and death. Maybe it is another manifestation of my desire to put on an act. I know I must keep on reflecting on my own shortcomings and work hard toward finding an answer.

LIFE IN WARTIME TOKYO

This selection consists of excerpts from the dairy of a housewife who spent all the war years in Tokyo. Mrs. Takahashi Aiko (b. 1894) was born in Tokyo. After her graduation from Girls High School in Utsunomiya, she came to the United States, and remained in the States until 1932. She was married to a medical doctor in 1921. Her experience in the United States might have made her observation of the Japanese war effort somewhat more critical. Yet she poignantly recaptures the feelings of those people who lived in war-torn Tokyo.

12   Diary of a Housewife, 1943–45[20]

September 2, 1943. Our family is on duty as representative of the neighborhood group this month. I am really worried. Day after day, it is becoming more probable that enemy planes will come to attack us, and if that happens we have to be responsible for leading the neighborhood group. The mere thought of leading others is really inconceivable to us. . . .

---

[20]Hashikawa Bunzō et al., eds., *Shimin no Nikki (Common People's Diaries)* (Tokyo: Shūeisha, 1965), pp. 332–34, 336–37, 346, 349–50, 355–57.

When rationed materials are distributed, those of us on duty, in this case our family, are responsible for buying them. Afterward, we have to go to each household and divide them carefully according to the number of people in each household, or circulate a notice around asking everyone to come to our house. I am always annoyed with rationed distributions from grocers. To distribute the rationed vegetable evenly according to the number of people means that everything, including the straw that binds the vegetable and the dried part, must be carefully weighed and distributed as well. On the other hand, if I include the straw and dried part, people may criticize us for keeping the better portion for ourselves. . . . Going to the distribution center in itself is also a big task. As soon as a notice is given to us that there is something to be distributed, we must stop everything, leaving our half-cooked rice or precious hot water for washing made from the precious rationed fuel, and run to the distribution center. In spite of it, when we reach the distribution center, there is always a long line. I am always appalled to see those people working at the distribution center sitting around and smoking without making a move. They say that they will start working when everyone is finally assembled. . . .

January 4, 1944. We had an unexpected visitor from the countryside who came all the way to get treatment in Tokyo from my husband. How well off these people are. This simple incident testifies to that fact.

The farmers, who traditionally have not been blessed with good living, are suddenly enthroned in the most important position of being producers of food, the one commodity that holds the key to our existence. They sell their produce in the black market and receive a lot of money. The city folks, for the sake of living, are taking everything they have to the countryside. They prefer to have their sons marry girls from the countryside, and they also prefer to have their daughters marry boys from the countryside. City folks now feel that it is essential to maintain some connection with country folks in order to survive. . . . The possessions that were once in the chest of drawers of city folks are transferred to the storage boxes of country folks. City folks nowadays will say the most flattering things about country folks in the latter's presence, which in the past they never did. I can't judge how people feel toward each other when their positions are suddenly changed. But there is an undercurrent of hatred that I know the two groups hold against one another. I am saddened by all of these.

May 15, 1945. Children in grade schools or younger, and older people, are practically all evacuated to other parts of the country from Tokyo. Young people are drafted into the army, and technicians and scholars are also drafted to serve in various capacities or sent to the front. As to the youngsters like my children, one girl and one boy, who have graduated from schools but are not of draft age, they are often sent to different places to work under the national mobilization program. Emmy [the daughter] came back from school this afternoon and said that she was appointed to serve as a children's chaperon for those who are being evacuated and would have to leave shortly.

May 27, 1945. A truck was sent from the metropolitan government to take away those patients who were temporarily under my husband's care. From the second-floor window, fretfully I looked down. The truck had no side panels, and all the patients were put down in a manner not too different from piling up firewood. To me they could not look like living creatures. It was much worse than an imaginary picture of hell. Yet that was exactly what was taking place right in front of my eyes. . . .

No gas, no electricity, and our faucet is without water. Life in the city is miserable. However, our surroundings may look palatial to those people who are victims of bombing.

August 15, 1945. Most people thought the important broadcast given in person by the Emperor this noon was to be one of exhortation, urging the people to redouble their efforts as the war was approaching the main islands. The people seemed to be excited about the prospect, feeling that the time had finally come. After all, they had been vigorously trained in the use of bamboo spears with which they hoped to pierce through the advancing enemy on their landing, or even to overturn armored tanks. Our people were forced into this war without any knowledge of it. Now that the war was about to end, the people seemed to show no recognition of it. It was a sad spectacle.

Noon came. Without anyone giving suggestions, everyone stood up in front of a radio. With a dispassioned, heavy, and even trembling voice, His Majesty read his declaration of Japan's defeat. Each word, each phrase, penetrated through my heart. I could feel my eyes water, and finally could not restrain myself and had to hold a handkerchief against my eyes.

Sadness and joy. Joy and sadness. My feelings were so terribly mixed that I did not know how to separate or unify them. As we came to this final moment of war, there were so many things we could talk about, yet we were not in a mood to discuss anything at that time.

DECISION TO SURRENDER

The fall of Saipan and other setbacks in the war forced some of the responsible statesmen to reexamine the wisdom of continued resistance against the Allied powers. One of such examples can be found in the memorial of Konoye Fumimaro (1891–1945) submitted to the throne on February 14, 1945 (Document 13). There Prince Konoye spoke of the danger of world communism and the power struggles going on among the army cliques. To him the army cliques were the ones who unwittingly rendered support to the cause of communism and thus undermined Japan's national polity. These observations were especially pertinent, coming from the man who headed the Japanese Cabinet three times between 1937 and 1941.

Concern for preserving Japan's national polity, namely, retaining the Em-

peror as the sovereign ruler of the country, was to continue to the end of the war. The Potsdam Declaration (Document 14), which urged Japan's formal surrender, did not refer to this issue. Thus in accepting the declaration the Japanese government was able to point out that the "said Declaration does not comprise any demand which prejudices the prerogatives of His Majesty as a sovereign ruler." In response to this Japanese message, Secretary of State James Byrnes stated that after the surrender, "the ultimate form of the Government of Japan would be established by the freely expressed will of the Japanese people," which in effect gave no assurance of the preservation of Japan's national polity. There were possibilities of coups d'etat by young officers that had as their aims disruption of the surrender negotiations and waging of a last desperate battle in the hope of obtaining concessions from the Allied powers. However, in the end counsel of reason prevailed, and as Foreign Minister Tōgō Shigenori (1882–1950) described in his memoir (Document 15), an intervention by the emperor played a major role in the final decision to surrender. The last selection, the Imperial Rescript on Surrender, is self-explanatory (Document 16). In defeat, the Emperor was at his best. Without his active cooperation and the use of his prestige, the surrender and the occupation would have been far more difficult and painful. On August 30, General of the Army Douglas MacArthur landed at Atsugi airport, and on September 2 the instrument of surrender was signed aboard the U.S.S. Missouri. Thus was begun a new chapter in the history of Japan.

13 Memorial of Prince Konoye Urging Termination of War, 1945[21]

Your subject respectfully submits this memorial for your Imperial Majesty's consideration. He now believes that regretful as it may be, defeat in the war will become inevitable, and upon this premise he wishes to set forth his views:

It is true that defeat will be a blemish on our national polity. However, defeat alone will not endanger our national polity because public opinion in England and the United States has not insisted on a change in our national polity. (Of course, there are some extremist views and the future is by no means certain.) From the point of view of preserving our national polity, what concerns your subject most is not the defeat itself, but the possibility of a communist revolution accompanied by the defeat.

Both domestic and international situations are seemingly moving rapidly toward a communist revolution. In the international scene, there has been an outstanding advance in the position of the Soviet Union. Our people have never been able to grasp the true intent of the Soviet Union. Since the adoption in 1935 of the policy of a United Front—that is, the two-stage revolution tactics—and the subsequent dissolution of the Comintern, many of our people have taken lightly

---

. [21]Japanese Ministry of Foreign Affairs, *Shūsen Shiroku (Records of the Ending of the War)* (Tokyo: Shimbun Gekkansha, 1952), pp. 195–98.

the danger of bolshevization. This is a superficial and unrealistic view. The Soviet Union has never abandoned its policy of bolshevization of the world, and this is made abundantly clear by its recent overt maneuvering in European countries.

The Soviet Union is attempting to establish Soviet regimes in European countries bordering it and pro-Soviet regimes in other European countries. Their work has been steady and it has been mostly successful.

The Tito regime in Yugoslavia is a prime example. As to Poland, the Soviet Union first formed a government among the Polish refugees in the Soviet Union and then insisted that it could not deal with the Government in Exile in London. . . .[22]

While professing that it does not interfere in the domestic politics of other countries, in reality the Soviet Union has always interfered in the domestic politics of European countries, with a view to leading these countries to become pro-Soviet.

The Soviet intent is equally applicable to East Asia. In Yenan, Okano[23] came from Moscow to lead the Japan Liberation League, and made contact with the Korean Independence Alliance, Korean Volunteers' Corps, and Formosan Vanguard Corps. They are now appealing their causes to Japan proper.

Thus there is every reason to believe in the danger of an eventual interference by the Soviet Union in Japan's domestic politics (e.g., legal recognition of the Communist party, Cabinet portfolios for Communist party members, . . . abolition of the Peace Preservation Law and of the Anti-Comintern Pact). Now looking at the domestic scene, your subject finds that conditions are ripe for the success of a communist revolution. They are poverty, greater voice exercised by labor, proportionate increase in the pro-Soviet sentiment accompanied by the rise of enmity against Great Britain and the United States, reformist movements among military officers, bureaucratic officials joining such movements, and the underground activities of the leftists who are behind those movements. Of these, what worries your subject most are the reformist movements of some segments of the military.

A great majority of our younger officers seem to think that our national polity and communism are compatible, and their avid advocation of internal reform within the military stems from this belief. Most of our professional soldiers come from families of middle or lower classes, and many of them are thoroughly imbued with the ideal of our national polity through their military education. Therefore communist agitators attempt to appeal to them by suggesting the compatibility of our national polity and communism.

It is now clear that the Manchurian Incident, followed by the outbreak of the China Incident, and their subsequent extension into the Greater East Asia War were a chain of events carefully planned by the military. During the Manchurian

---

[22]Konoye goes on to describe Soviet activities in Rumania, Bulgaria, Finland, Iran, Belgium, the Netherlands, and France.

[23]Okano was the alias used by Nosaka Sanzo, leader of the Japan Communist Party exiled in Moscow.

Incident, they publicly stated that the incident was aimed at internal reform in Japan. This is a well-known fact. During the time of the China Incident also, the same conspirators in this group publicly averred that "it is better to prolong the incident. If it is solved then there will be no internal reform."

This clique in the military that advocates internal reform may not be aiming at a communist revolution. However, those bureaucrats and civilians surrounding them—call them rightists or leftists, for the rightists are those communists under the garb of our national polity—consciously attempt to bring about a communist revolution. It is fairly accurate to say that they are the ones who manipulate those unsophisticated, simple-minded soldiers.

The above is the conclusion your subject recently reached after calm reflections incorporating his extensive experiences dealing with the military, bureaucracy, rightists, leftists, and others during the past ten years. When your subject looks back to the happenings of the past ten years from this vantage point, there were many events that would support this conclusion.

Your subject received the mandate to form a Cabinet twice.[24] During his terms of office, he adopted some of those reformist doctrines in order to avoid internal friction. His eagerness to maintain national unity led him to overlook the true intent hidden behind their doctrines. All of these came from your subject's ignorance of the matter. He deeply regrets this and begs the forgiveness of Your Majesty.

Recently, as the fortunes of war turned for the worse, increasingly voices are raised exhorting that the 100 million suffer death rather than dishonor. Those who advocate such a cause are not the so-called rightists, but rather the communists who instigate from behind, hoping that through the resulting confusion, their aim of effecting a revolution may be realized.

While on the one hand they advocate complete destruction of the United States and Great Britain, on the other hand they are fostering pro-Soviet sentiment. One segment of the military even avers that Japan should align with the Soviet Union regardless of the sacrifice involved. Another school thinks of collaboration with the Chinese communist forces in Yanan.

This being the case, conditions for the success of a communist revolution are becoming better each day both internally and externally. Should the tide of war worsen even further, this situation might develop rapidly.

If there should be a ray of hope in the war, it would be different. However, viewing from the premise that defeat is inevitable, we are fighting a hopeless war. Should we continue it any further, we would be playing into the hands of the communists. From the point of view of upholding our national polity, we must conclude the war as soon as possible.

---

[24]Konoye was prime minister three times. The second Konoye Cabinet and the third Konoye cabinet were continuous, and most members of the second Cabinet retained their portfolios in the third. One notable exception was Matsuoka Yōsuke, the controversial foreign minister in the second Cabinet, who was dropped from the third.

The greatest obstacle to the termination of war is the existence of the clique in the military who brought about the current crisis from the time of the Manchurian Incident. They have lost confidence in pursuing the war to a successful end, but insist on resisting the enemies in order to save face.

In attempting to bring about an early end to the war, unless we make a clean sweep of this group, there may be great confusion caused by the collaboration of rightist and leftist civilian co-conspirators with this group to attain their goals. To end the war we must first make a clean sweep of this group.

Once we make a clean sweep of this group within the military, those opportunistic bureaucrats and rightist and leftist co-conspirators are likely to cease functioning. This is so because they do not have power of their own and must manipulate the military to effect their sinister designs. As it is said, destroy the roots and the leaves will wilt of their own.

Perhaps this is folly on your subject's part, but he wishes to speculate that once a clean sweep of this group is made and the military's complexion is changed, the attitudes of the United States, Great Britain, and Chongqing might become more lenient toward us. Originally the United States, Great Britain and Chongqing proclaimed that their war aims were to destroy Japanese military cliques. If the character of the military should change and its policy were altered, would they [the Allied powers] not reconsider the desirability of continuing the war?

Setting this aside the prerequisites to saving Japan from a communist revolution lie in the clean sweep of this group and rebuilding of the military. Your subject humbly begs of Your Majesty to take an unprecedented resolute step in this matter.

14   The Potsdam Declaration, 1945[25]

Proclamation Defining Terms for the Japanese Surrender, Signed at Potsdam and Issued by the president of the United States (Truman) and the prime minister of the United Kingdom (Attlee) and concurred in by the president of the National Government of China (Chiang), July 26, 1945.

(1) We—the president of the United States, the president of the National Government of the Republic of China, and the prime minister of Great Britain, representing the hundreds of millions of our countrymen, have conferred and agree that Japan shall be given an opportunity to end this war.

(2) The prodigious land, sea, and air forces of the United States, the British Empire and of China, many times reinforced by their armies and air fleets from the west, are poised to strike the final blows upon Japan. This military power is sustained and inspired by the determination of all the Allied Nations to prosecute the war against Japan until she ceases to resist.

---

[25]Raymond Dennett et. al., eds., *Documents on American Foreign Relations*, vol. 8, *1945–1946* (Boston: World Peace Foundation, 1948), pp. 106–7.

(3) The result of the futile and senseless German resistance to the might of the aroused free peoples of the world stands forth in awful clarity as an example to the people of Japan. The might that now converges on Japan is immeasurably greater than that which, when applied to the resisting Nazis, necessarily laid waste to the lands, the industry, and the method of life of the whole German people. The full application of our military power, backed by our resolve, *will* mean the inevitable and complete destruction of the Japanese armed forces and just as inevitably the utter devastation of the Japanese homeland.

(4) The time has come for Japan to decide whether she will continue to be controlled by those self-willed militaristic advisers whose unintelligent calculations have brought the Empire of Japan to the threshold of annihilation, or whether she will follow the path of reason.

(5) Following are our terms. We will not deviate from them. There are no alternatives. We shall brook no delay.

(6) There must be eliminated for all time the authority and influence of those who have deceived and misled the people of Japan into embarking on world conquest, for we insist that a new order of peace, security, and justice will be impossible until irresponsible militarism is driven from the world.

(7) Until such a new order is established *and* until there is convincing proof that Japan's war-making power is destroyed, points in Japanese territory to be designated by the Allies shall be occupied to secure the achievement of the basic objectives we are here setting forth.

(8) The terms of the Cairo Declaration shall be carried out, and Japanese sovereignty shall be limited to the islands of Honshu, Hokkaido, Kyushu, Shikoku, and such minor islands as we determine.

(9) The Japanese military forces, after being completely disarmed, shall be permitted to return to their homes with the opportunity to lead peaceful and productive lives.

(10) We do not intend that the Japanese shall be enslaved as a race or destroyed as a nation, but stern justice shall be meted out to all war criminals, including those who have visited cruelties upon our prisoners. The Japanese Government shall remove all obstacles to the revival and strengthening of democratic tendencies among the Japanese people. Freedom of speech, of religion, and of thought, as well as respect for the fundamental human rights, shall be established.

(11) Japan shall be permitted to maintain such industries as will sustain her economy and permit the exaction of just reparations in kind, but not those which would enable her to rearm for war. To this end, access to, as distinguished from control of, raw materials shall be permitted. Eventual Japanese participation in world trade relations shall be permitted.

(12) The occupying forces of the Allies shall be withdrawn from Japan as soon as these objectives have been accomplished and there has been established in accordance with the freely expressed will of the Japanese people a peacefully inclined and responsible government.

(13) We call upon the Government of Japan to proclaim now the unconditional surrender of all Japanese armed forces, and to provide proper and adequate assurances of their good faith in such action. The alternative for Japan is prompt and utter destruction.

15

Foreign Minister Tōgō Shigenori on Japan's Surrender, 1945[26] On the 13th [of August] the members of the Supreme Council met at 8:30 A.M. at the premier's official residence. The military members renewed their insistence that paragraphs 2 and 5 of Byrnes's communication being unacceptable, we should have them amended, and that we should also advance additional proposals relative to the occupation and disarmament. I disputed with them, . . . and added that the suggestion of the new demands was absurd, the Emperor having already signified his desire at the last Imperial Conference that those demands be dropped. The premier and the navy minister came to my support, but the discussion dragged on for many hours. When in the course of it the possibility of going on with the war again arose, War Minister Anami and Chief of Staff Umezu said merely that we could wage another battle in case of rupture of the negotiations, but that they could offer no promise of final victory. . . .

Unrest within the army seemed to be gathering momentum. Frequent reports had come in from the 12th of plans for coups d'etat—such as capturing the Emperor and separating the Cabinet ministers from him. The situation was growing very unquiet; the police guard of my house was greatly increased. I sensed that the war minister was feeling some influence of the activities of the younger officers of the army, which were responsible for these conditions; he continually declaimed at Cabinet meetings and elsewhere the necessity of further bargaining over the surrender terms, since as he maintained we could fight another battle. On each such occasion I argued with equal determination for immediate acceptance of the Potsdam Declaration. The war minister then endeavored, around the 12th and 13th, to entice Premier Suzuki, Baron Hiranuma, and Lord Keeper Kido to his viewpoint; these efforts I forestalled by keeping in contact with the premier constantly, and with Kido before and after each of my frequent audiences with the Emperor.

Many speculations concerning the sentiments of War Minister Anami around those days have been offered. From my observation at my divers meetings with him, when he often spoke of "seeking for life out of death," I saw that his mind was possessed by the desire of inflicting one more severe blow on the enemy before making peace. As things turned out, he did not in the end persist in this

---

[26]Reprinted with the permission of Simon & Schuster from Tōgō Shigenori, *The Causes of Japan,* trans. by Tōgō Fumihiko and Ben Bruce Blakeney, pp. 328–34. Copyright © 1956 by Simon & Schuster, Inc., renewed 1984 by Fumihiko Tōgō, pp. 328–34.

idea; but there was a danger that if the war minister and the other army leaders should be subjected to pressure—from whatever source—for peace before they had been psychologically prepared for it, the army's internal opposition might prevail, violence break out, and the entire movement for peace be jeopardized. . . .

[I attended an extraordinary meeting of the Cabinet held at the premier's official residence on the 14th.] Upon my arrival, the premier took me aside and told me that he wished to hold immediately, in the presence of the Emperor, a joint meeting of the Cabinet and the High Command, and by an imperial decision to put to rest once and for all the question of the surrender. . . .

The Emperor appeared, and the premier stated that after exhaustive deliberation on the Allies' reply to our communication of the 10th neither the Supreme Council members nor the Cabinet had been able to attain unanimity; and explaining the position of the foreign minister and the opposing views, he asked that the latter be stated in the presence of the Emperor. General Umezu, Admiral Toyoda, and General Anami, in that order, were called upon by the premier. The army men declared that we should negotiate further with the United States, as acceptance of the Potsdam Declaration on the basis of the American reply would endanger the national polity, and if we could not be sure of maintaining it, there was no alternative to carrying on the struggle even at the cost of 100 million lives. The navy chief of staff was milder in his opinion, saying only that as we could not bear to swallow the American reply as it stood, it was appropriate once more to put forward our views. The premier called on no others.

The Emperor then spoke. "It was not lightly, but upon mature consideration of conditions within and without the land, and especially of the development taken by the war, that I previously determined to accept the Potsdam Declaration. My determination is unaltered. I have heard the disputation over the recent reply given by the Allied powers, but I consider that in general they have confirmed our understanding. As to paragraph 5 of the declaration, I agree with the foreign minister that it is not intended to subvert the national polity of Japan; but, unless the war be brought to an end at this moment, I fear that the national polity will be destroyed, and the nation annihilated. It is therefore my wish that we bear the unbearable and accept the Allied reply, thus to preserve the state as a state and spare my subjects' further suffering. I wish you all to act in that intention. The war and navy ministers have told me that there is opposition within army and navy; I desire that the services also be made to comprehend my wishes." All the attendants wept at these reasoned and gracious words, and at conceiving the Emperor's emotions. It was an inexpressibly solemn and moving scene; as we retired down the long corridor, while returning in our cars, and at the resumed Cabinet meeting, each of us in his thoughts wept again. . . .

Late on the night of the 14th, it was communicated to the Governments of the United States, Great Britain, the USSR, and China, through the Swiss and Swedish Governments, that the Emperor had promulgated an Imperial rescript accepting the Potsdam Declaration. . . .

16 Imperial Rescript on Surrender, 1945[27]

To our good and loyal subjects:

After pondering deeply the general trends of the world and the actual conditions obtaining in our Empire today, we have decided to effect a settlement of the present situation by resorting to an extraordinary measure.

We have ordered our Government to communicate to the Governments of the United States, Great Britain, China, and the Soviet Union that our Empire accepts the provisions of their joint declaration.

To strive for the common prosperity and happiness of all nations as well as the security and well-being of our subjects is the solemn obligation that has been handed down by our Imperial Ancestors, and we lay it close to the heart.

Indeed, we declared war on America and Britain out of our sincere desire to ensure Japan's self-preservation and the stabilization of East Asia, it being far from our thought either to infringe upon the sovereignty of other nations or to embark upon territorial aggrandizement.

But now the war has lasted for nearly four years. Despite the best that has been done by everyone—the gallant fighting of the military and naval forces, the diligence and assiduity of our servants of the state and the devoted service of our 100 million people—the war situation has developed not necessarily to Japan's advantage, while the general trends of the world have all turned against her interest.

Moreover, the enemy has begun to employ a new and most cruel bomb, the power of which to do damage is, indeed, incalculable, taking the toll of many innocent lives. Should we continue to fight, it would not only result in an ultimate collapse and obliteration of the Japanese nation, but also it would lead to the total extinction of human civilization.

Such being the case, how are we to save the millions of our subjects, or to atone ourselves before the hallowed spirits of our Imperial Ancestors? This is the reason why we have ordered the acceptance of the provisions of the joint declaration of the powers.

We cannot but express the deepest sense of regret to our allied nations of East Asia, who have consistently cooperated with the Empire toward the emancipation of East Asia.

The thought of those officers and men as well as others who have fallen in the fields of battle, those who died at their posts of duty, and those who met with death and all their bereaved families, pains our heart night and day.

The welfare of the wounded and the war sufferers, and of those who have lost their homes and livelihood is the object of our profound solicitude. The hard-

---

[27]From F.C. Jones, *Japan's New Order in East Asia, 1937–45* (published by the Oxford University Press under the auspices of the Royal Institute of International Affairs, 1954), pp. 474–75. Reprinted with permission.

ships and sufferings to which our nation is to be subjected hereafter will be certainly great.

We are keenly aware of the inmost feelings of all you, our subjects. However, it is according to the dictates of time and fate that we have resolved to pave the way for a grand peace for all the generations to come by enduring the unendurable and suffering what is insufferable. Having been able to save and maintain the structure of the Imperial State, we are always with you, our good and loyal subjects, relying upon your sincerity and integrity.

Beware most strictly of any outbursts of emotion that may engender needless complications, and of any fraternal contention and strife that may create confusion, lead you astray and cause you to lose the confidence of the world.

Let the entire nation continue as one family from generation to generation, ever firm in its faith in the imperishableness of its divine land, and mindful of its heavy burden of responsibilities, and the long road before it. Unite your total strength to be devoted to the construction for the future. Cultivate the ways of rectitude, nobility of spirit, and work with resolution so that you may enhance the innate glory of the Imperial State and keep pace with the progress of the world.

All you, our subjects, we command you to act in accordance with our wishes.

Hirohito
(The Seal of the Emperor)
The 14th day of the eighth month of the twentieth year of Shōwa
(Countersignatures of the Ministers of State)

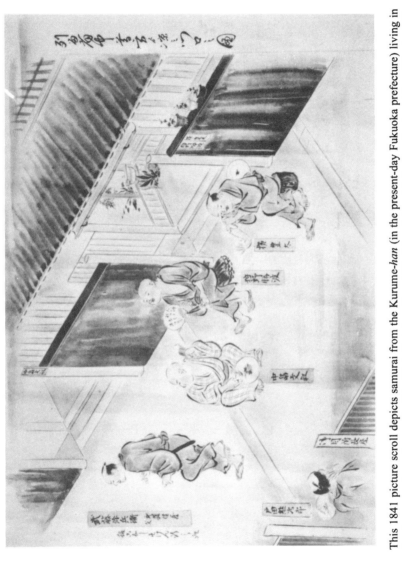

This 1841 picture scroll depicts samurai from the Kurume-*han* (in the present-day Fukuoka prefecture) living in the *han*-owned row houses in Edo. Note that the vibrant lifestyle of the *chōnin*-class is absent (see Chapter 10). (Courtesy of Edo Tokyo Museum.)

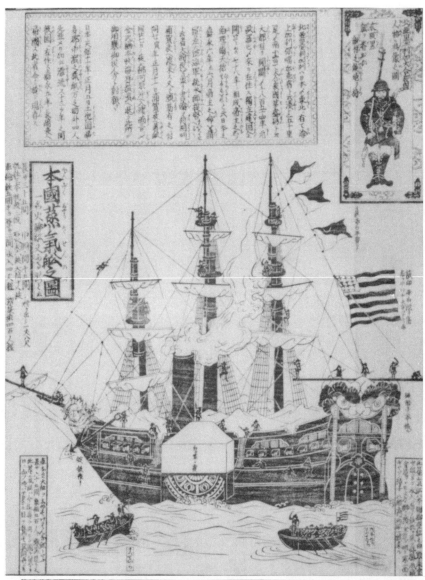

Commodore Perry's black ships anchored in Edo Bay in 1854, touching off an intense national debate (see pages 281–91). A capsule description of the history and geography of the United States is given in the upper-left-hand box, along with the story of Manjirō's sojourn in the United States and subsequent return. (Courtesy of Edo Tokyo Museum.)

Nothing symbolized modernization better than the introduction of steam-powered trains. The fascination was reflected in this September, 1872 *hanga* depicting a steam locomotive passing through Shiodome (Shimbashi) station. It was in that year that the first railway line was completed from Shinagawa to Yokohama, a span of 17.4 miles (compare pp. 321 ff.). (Courtesy of Edo Tokyo Museum.)

Even after the great earthquake, Tokyo's skyline still retained much of its traditional appearances. This *hanga* is by Yoshida Hiroshi, completed in 1926 (compare Chapter 13). (Courtesy of Edo Tokyo Museum.)

CHAPTER **XV**

Japan under Occupation

The Allied Occupation began immediately after the conclusion of the Pacific War and continued until April 28, 1952. Unlike the occupation of Germany, no separate zones were established, and it was essentially an occupation by the United States. For a period of nearly seven years, the United States exercised the most pervasive influence on Japanese politics, economy, and society, and all phases of cultural and social life were affected by it.

It was not an ordinary occupation, and was a novel experience both for the conquerors and the conquered. It was not punitive, and with almost a missionary zeal—sometimes genuinely motivated by an idealism and at other times merely reflecting a desire to see Japanese behave like Americans (which by definition was good)—a series of changes were decreed by the Supreme Commander, Allied Powers (SCAP) Headquarters (GHQ).

Among the most successful of the occupation-inspired reforms were the promulgation of a new constitution (Documents 4, 5, 6, 7 and 8) and the land reform (Documents 12 and 13). One can argue that these reforms were not necessarily innovations but rather the release of latent forces that had been suppressed by the militarist regime of the past.[1] To support this view, it can be argued that the people's rights movement of the 1870s and Taishō democracy would have provided the basis for a parliamentary democracy of the type envisioned in the new constitution. Or in the case of the land reform, like Yoshida (Document 13), one can suggest that the reform would have taken place in one form or another even without the occupation. Yet in retrospect, these two measures were so revolutionary in their implications that without the external force of the occupation to tip the scale in their favor, they could not have been implemented by the Japanese government.

---

[1]See Herbert Passin, *The Legacy of the Occupation—Japan* (New York: Occasional Papers of the East Asian Institute, Columbia University, 1968), pp. 18–19.

The Shōwa constitution was approved by the Diet in 1946 following the procedures established under the Meiji constitution. In this manner, continuity was maintained. However, it made a clear-cut departure from the past. Under the new constitution, the Emperor became "the symbol of state and of the unity of the people." Power no longer resided in him but in the Diet, which became the highest organ of state power. It renounced war and created a host of problems for constitutional scholars and politicians when dealing with the issues of creating the Self-Defense Forces, of leasing land for bases for American troops, and of participating in the UN-sponsored peacekeeping operations. With the publication of key documents in 1995 and 1996, it is now clear that the language of Article 9, the renunciation of war clause, does not deny Japan the right of self-defense. Documents 6a, 7, and 8 address the issues contained in these new disclosures.

Retrospectively, both the peace constitution and land reform became foundations on which Japan's economic growth was built. The passage of time only confirms that they remain two of the most outstanding accomplishments of the occupation.

On the other hand, the records on education reform were less than satisfactory. The SCAP's eagerness to establish a large number of universities, to decentralize control, and even to introduce the Latin alphabet as Japan's national writing system came from their lack of understanding of Japan's excellent prewar school system and of her cultural tradition. The *zaibatsu* busting was equally unsuccessful.

The occupation was an indirect one. The SCAP administrators gave directives but left the tasks of implementation in the hands of Japanese bureaucrats. This had an effect of preserving their entrenched power. Throughout the postwar period, the bureaucrats left their marks on Japan's phenomenal economic development, and the roles that the occupation played in fostering the power of the Japanese bureaucracy must now be placed under closer scrutiny.

The period of occupation brought together the Americans and Japanese in close proximity to each other, relatively free of interference by third parties. The lifestyle of American GIs and bureaucrats was closely observed by the Japanese. The changing Japanese attitudes toward America, imitation of the American youth culture, dependency on the American-inspired security arrangement, the so-called low-posture diplomacy, and the primacy that is placed on economic development are in some measure all part of the legacy of seven years of American occupation.

BASIC OCCUPATION POLICY

The following "Initial Postsurrender Policy" was transmitted to General Mac-Arthur on August 29, 1945. It defined in great detail the measures to be taken by the SCAP, which governed Japan indirectly. To attain the objective of ensuring "that Japan will not again become a menace to the peace and security of the world," Japan was to be disarmed and demilitarized, and a democratic and peaceful government expeditiously set up. Implicit in the policy were assumptions that Japanese society itself constituted a self-perpetuating instrument capable of creating destructive militarism and that the traditional framework of the society ought to be reformed before Japan could truly become a peace-loving nation. The task of disarmament and demobilization was practically completed by December 1, 1945, but the task of "reforming" the society was to consume the energy of the SCAP personnel for the next several years.

1 Initial Postsurrender Policy for Japan, 1945[2]

Part I: Ultimate Objectives

The ultimate objectives of the United States in regard to Japan, to which policies in the initial period must conform, are:

(a) To ensure that Japan will not again become a menace to the United States or to the peace and security of the world.

(b) To bring about the eventual establishment of a peaceful and responsible government that will respect the rights of other states and will support the objectives of the United States as reflected in the ideals and principles of the Charter of the United Nations. The United States desires that this government should conform as closely as may be to principles of democratic self-government but it is not the responsibility of the Allied powers to impose upon Japan any form of government not supported by the freely expressed will of the people.

These objectives will be achieved by the following principal means:

(a) Japan's sovereignty will be limited to the islands of Honshu, Hokkaido, Kyushu, Shikoku and such minor outlying islands as may be determined, in accordance with the Cairo Declaration and other agreements to which the United States is or may be a party.

(b) Japan will be completely disarmed and demilitarized. The authority of the militarists and the influence of militarism will be totally eliminated from her political, economic, and social life. Institutions expressive of the spirit of militarism and aggression will be vigorously suppressed.

(c) The Japanese people shall be encouraged to develop a desire for individual liberties and respect for fundamental human rights, particularly the freedoms of religion, assembly, speech, and the press. They shall also be encouraged to form democratic and representative organizations.

---

[2]Supreme Commander for Allied Powers, Government Section, *Political Reorientation of Japan, September 1945 to September 1948*, vol. 2 (Washington, D. C.: Government Printing Office, 1949), pp. 423–26.

(d) The Japanese people shall be afforded opportunity to develop for themselves an economy which will permit the peacetime requirements of the population to be met.

Part II: Allied Authority

1. *Military Occupation*

There will be a military occupation of the Japanese home islands to carry into effect the surrender terms and further the achievement of the ultimate objectives stated below. The occupation shall have the character of an operation in behalf of the principal Allied powers acting in the interests of the United Nations at war with Japan. For that reason, participation of the forces of other nations that have taken a leading part in the war against Japan will be welcomed and expected. The occupation forces will be under the command of a supreme commander designated by the United States.

2. *Relationship to Japanese Government*

The authority of the Emperor and the Japanese Government will be subject to the supreme commander, who will possess all powers necessary to effectuate the surrender terms and to carry out the policies established for the conduct of the occupation and the control of Japan.

In view of the present character of Japanese society and the desire of the United States to attain its objectives with a minimum commitment of its forces and resources, the supreme commander will exercise his authority through Japanese governmental machinery and agencies, including the Emperor, to the extent that this satisfactorily furthers United States objectives. The Japanese Government will be permitted, under his instructions, to exercise the normal powers of government in matters of domestic administration. This policy, however, will be subject to the right and duty of the supreme commander to require changes in governmental machinery or personnel or to act directly if the Emperor or other Japanese authority does not satisfactorily meet the requirements of the supreme commander in effectuating the surrender terms. This policy, moreover, does not commit the supreme commander to support the Emperor or any other Japanese governmental authority in opposition to evolutionary changes looking toward the attainment of United States objectives. The policy is to use the existing form of government in Japan, not to support it. Changes in the form of government initiated by the Japanese people or government in the direction of modifying its feudal and authoritarian tendencies are to be permitted and favored. In the event that the effectuation of such changes involves the use of force by the Japanese people or government against persons opposed thereto, the supreme commander should intervene only when necessary to ensure the security of his forces and the attainment of all other objectives of the occupation.

3. *Publicity as to Policies*

The Japanese people, and the world at large, shall be kept fully informed of the objectives and policies of the occupation, and of progress made in their fulfillment.

Part III: Political

1. *Disarmament and Demilitarization*
   Disarmament and demilitarization are the primary tasks of the military occupation and shall be carried out promptly and with determination. Every effort shall be made to bring home to the Japanese people the part played by the military and naval leaders, and those who collaborated with them, in bringing about the existing and future distress of the people.
   Japan is not to have an army, navy, air force, secret police organization, or any civil aviation. Japan's ground, air, and naval forces shall be disarmed and disbanded and the Japanese Imperial General Headquarters, the General Staff, and all secret police organizations shall be dissolved. . . .
   High officials of the Japanese Imperial Headquarters, and General Staff, other high military and naval officials of the Japanese Government, leaders of ultranationalist and militarist organizations, and other important exponents of militarism and aggression will be taken into custody and held for future disposition. Persons who have been active exponents of militarism and militant nationalism will be removed and excluded from public office and from any other position of public or substantial private responsibility. . . .
   Militarism and ultranationalism, in doctrine and practice, including paramilitary training, shall be eliminated from the educational system. . . .

2. *War Criminals*
   Persons charged by the supreme commander or appropriate United Nations agencies with being war criminals, including those charged with having visited cruelties upon United Nations prisoners or other nationals, shall be arrested, tried and, if convicted, punished. Those wanted by another of the United Nations for offenses against its nationals, shall, if not wanted for trial or as witnesses or otherwise by the supreme commander, be turned over to the custody of such other nation.

3. *Encouragement of Desire for Individual Liberties and Democratic Processes*
   Freedom of religious worship shall be proclaimed promptly on occupation. At the same time it should be made plain to the Japanese that ultranationalistic and militaristic organizations and movements will not be permitted to hide behind the cloak of religion.
   The Japanese people shall be afforded opportunity and encouraged to become familiar with the history, institutions, culture, and the accomplishments of the United States and the other democracies. Association of personnel of the occupation forces with the Japanese population should be controlled, only to the extent necessary, to further the policies and objectives of the occupation.
   Democratic political parties, with right of assembly and public discussion, shall be encouraged, subject to the necessity for maintaining the security of the occupying forces.

Laws, decrees, and regulations that establish discrimination on ground of race, nationality, creed, or political opinion shall be abrogated. . . . Persons unjustly confined by Japanese authority on political grounds shall be released. The judicial, legal, and police systems shall be reformed as soon as practicable to conform to the policies set forth in Articles 1 and 3 of this Part III and thereafter shall be progressively influenced, to protect individual liberties and civil rights.

Part IV: Economic

1. *Economic Demilitarization*

The existing economic basis of Japanese military strength must be destroyed and not permitted to revive.

Therefore, a program will be enforced containing the following elements, among others; the immediate cessation and future prohibition of all goods designed for the equipment, maintenance, or use of any military force or establishment; the imposition of a ban upon any specialized facilities for the production or repair of implements of war, including naval vessels and all forms of aircraft; the institution of a system of inspection and control over selected elements in a Japanese economic activity to prevent concealed or disguised military preparation; the elimination in Japan of those selected industries or branches of production whose chief value to Japan is in preparing for war; the prohibition of specialized research and instruction directed to the development of war-making power; and the limitation of the size and character of Japan's heavy industries to its future peaceful requirements, and restriction of Japanese merchant shipping to the extent required to accomplish the objectives of demilitarization. . . .

2. *Promotion of Democratic Forces*

Encouragement shall be given and favor shown to the development of organizations in labor, industry, and agriculture, organized on a democratic basis. Policies shall be favored that permit a wide distribution of income and of the ownership of the means of production and trade.

Those forms of economic activity, organization and leadership shall be favored that are deemed likely to strengthen the peaceful disposition of the Japanese people, and to make it difficult to command or direct economic activity in support of military ends.

To this end it shall be the policy of the supreme commander:

(a) To prohibit the retention in or selection for places of importance in the economic field of individuals who do not direct future Japanese economic effort solely toward peaceful ends; and

(b) To favor a program for the dissolution of the large industrial and banking combinations that have exercised control of a great part of Japan's trade and industry.

3. *Resumption of Peaceful Economic Activity*

The policies of Japan have brought down upon the people great economic destruction and confronted them with the prospect of economic difficulty and suffering. The plight of Japan is the direct outcome of its own behavior, and the Allies will not undertake the burden of repairing the damage. It can be repaired only if the Japanese people renounce all military aims and apply themselves diligently and with single purpose to the ways of peaceful living. It will be necessary for them to undertake physical reconstruction, deeply to reform the nature and direction of their economic activities and institutions, and to find useful employment for their people along lines adapted to and devoted to peace. The Allies have no intention of imposing conditions that would prevent the accomplishment of these tasks in due time.

Japan will be expected to provide goods and services to meet the needs of the occupying forces to the extent that this can be effected without causing starvation, widespread disease, and acute physical distress.

The Japanese authorities will be expected, and if necessary directed to maintain, develop and enforce programs that serve the following purposes:

(a) To avoid acute economic distress.

(b) To assure just and impartial distribution of available supplies.

(c) To meet the requirements for reparations deliveries agreed upon by the Allied Governments.

(d) To facilitate the restoration of Japanese economy so that the reasonable peaceful requirements of the population can be satisfied.

In this connection, the Japanese authorities, on their own responsibility, shall be permitted to establish and administer controls over economic activities, including essential national public services, finance, banking, and production and distribution of essential commodities, subject to the approval and review of the supreme commander in order to assure their conformity with the objectives of the occupation.

4. *Reparations and Restitution* (Omitted)

5. *Fiscal, Monetary, and Banking Policies* (Omitted)

6. *International Trade and Financial Relations*

Japan shall be permitted eventually to resume normal trade relations with the rest of the world. During occupation and under suitable controls, Japan will be permitted to purchase from foreign countries raw materials and other goods that it may need for peaceful purposes and to export goods to pay for approved imports.

Control is to be maintained over all imports and exports of goods, and foreign exchange and financial transactions. Both the policies followed in the exercise of these controls and their actual administration shall be subject to the approval and supervision of the supreme commander in order to make sure that they are not contrary to the policies of the occupying authorities, and in particular that all foreign purchasing power that Japan may acquire is utilized only for essential needs.

7. *Japanese Property Located Abroad* (Omitted)

8. *Equality of Opportunity for Foreign Enterprise within Japan*

The Japanese authorities shall not give, or permit any Japanese business organization to give, exclusive or preferential opportunity or terms to the enterprise of any foreign country, or cede to such enterprise control of any important branch of economic activity.

9. *Imperial Household Property* (Omitted)

NEW ROLES FOR THE EMPEROR

When the war ended, the Russian and British allies sought the indictment of Emperor Hirohito as a war criminal, which was strenuously opposed by General MacArthur. When Washington seemed to be veering toward the British point of view, MacArthur sent a telegram to General Dwight D. Eisenhower, then the chief of staff, advising that the Emperor's presence was vital to the success of the occupation. This telegram, reproduced as Document 3, was transmitted to the secretary of state, who in turn instructed the London Embassy to take any action "appropriate in order to forestall such development," namely, publicity on the Emperor as a war-criminal suspect.

The Emperor, who was credited by MacArthur to have "a more thorough grasp of the democratic concept than almost any Japanese," on New Year's Day, 1946, issued a rescript disavowing his own divinity (Document 2). It was a necessary step in effecting the transition of Japan into a democratic society and paved the way for making the Emperor a symbol of the state and of the unity of the people in the new constitution.

2 Emperor Hirohito's Rescript Disavowing His Own Divinity, 1946[3]

In greeting the New Year, we recall to mind that the Emperor Meiji proclaimed as the basis of our national policy the five clauses of the Charter at the beginning of the Meiji era . . . (see Chapter XI, Document 2).

The proclamation is evident in its significance and high in its ideals. We wish to make this oath anew and restore the country to stand on its own feet again. We have to reaffirm the principles embodied in the Charter and proceed unflinchingly toward elimination of misguided practices of the past; and keeping in close

---

[3]Text as reported in the *New York Times,* January 1, 1946. The rescript was drafted by Maeda Tamon (1884–1962), who was then serving as education minister. He credits the Emperor for making reference to the five clauses of the Charter Oath. See Maeda Tamon, *"Ningen sengen no uchi-soto"* (An Inside Story of the Rescript Disavowing Divinity), in the *Bungei Shunjū,* March 1962. Reprinted in *"Bungei Shunjū" ni Miru Shōwashi (A History of the Shōwa Era as Seen from the Pages of the Bungei Shunjū)* (Tokyo: Bungei Shunjûsha, 1988), pp. 18–25.

touch with the desires of the people, we will construct a new Japan through thoroughly being pacific, the officials and the people alike obtaining rich culture and advancing the standard of living of the people.

The devastation of the war inflicted upon our cities, the miseries of the destitute, the stagnation of trade, shortage of food, and the great and growing number of the unemployed are indeed heart-rending, but if the nation is firmly united in its resolve to face the present ordeal and to see civilization consistently in peace, a bright future will undoubtedly be ours, not only for our country but for the whole of humanity.

Love of the family and love of country are especially strong in this country. With more of this devotion should we now work toward love of mankind.

We feel deeply concerned to note that consequent upon the protracted war ending in our defeat our people are liable to grow restless and to fall into the slough of despond. Radical tendencies in excess are gradually spreading and the sense of morality tends to lose its hold on the people with the result that there are signs of confusion of thoughts.

We stand by the people and we wish always to share with them in their moment of joys and sorrows. The ties between us and our people have always stood upon mutual trust and affection. They do not depend upon mere legends and myths. They are not predicated on the false conception that the Emperor is divine and that the Japanese people are superior to other races and fated to rule the world.

Our Government should make every effort to alleviate their trials and tribulations. At the same time, we trust that the people will rise to the occasion and will strive courageously for the solution of their outstanding difficulties and for the development of industry and culture. Acting upon a consciousness of solidarity and of mutual aid and broad tolerance in their civic life, they will prove themselves worthy of their best tradition. By their supreme endeavors in that direction they will be able to render their substantial contribution to the welfare and advancement of mankind.

The resolution for the year should be made at the beginning of the year. We expect our people to join us in all exertions looking to accomplishment of this great undertaking with an indomitable spirit.

3 **Emperor Not Guilty of War Crimes, 1946**[4] Investigation has been conducted here under the limitation set forth with reference to possible criminal actions against the Emperor. No specific and tangible evidence has been uncov-

---

[4]MacArthur's telegram to Chief of Staff Eisenhower, dated January 25, 1946, marked "Secret, Priority." U. S. Department of State, *Foreign Relations of the United States, 1945,* vol. 8, *The Far East* (Washington, D. C.: Government Printing Office, 1971), pp. 395–97. Words in brackets were supplied by the Department of Defense.

ered with regard to his exact activities, which might connect him in varying degree with the political decisions of the Japanese Empire during the last decade. I have gained the definite impression from as complete a research as was possible to me that his connection with affairs of state up to the time of the end of the war was largely ministerial and automatically responsive to the advice of his councilors. There are those who believe that even had he positive ideas it would have been quite possible that any effort on his part to thwart the current of public opinion controlled and represented by the dominant military clique would have placed him in actual jeopardy.

If he is to be tried, great changes must be made in occupational plans and due preparation therefore should be accomplished in preparedness before actual action is initiated. His indictment will unquestionably cause a tremendous convulsion among the Japanese people, the repercussions of which cannot be overestimated. He is a symbol that unites all Japanese. Destroy him and the nation will disintegrate. Practically all Japanese venerate him as the social head of the state and believe rightly or wrongly that the Potsdam Agreements were intended to maintain him as the Emperor of Japan. They will regard Allied action [to the contrary as the greatest] . . . betrayal in their history and the hatreds and resentments engendered by this thought will unquestionably last for all measurable time. A vendetta for revenge will thereby be initiated whose cycle may well not be complete for centuries if ever.

The whole of Japan can be expected, in my opinion, to resist the action either by passive or semiactive means. They are disarmed and therefore represent no special menace to trained and equipped troops; but it is not inconceivable that all government agencies will break down, the civilized practices will largely cease, and a condition of underground chaos and disorder amounting to guerrilla warfare in the mountainous and outlying regions result. I believe all hope of introducing modern democratic methods would disappear and that when military control finally ceased some form of intense regimentation probably along communistic lines would arise from the mutilated masses. This would represent an entirely different problem of occupation from those now prevalent. It would be absolutely essential to greatly increase the occupational forces. It is quite possible that a minimum of a million troops would be required, which would have to be maintained for an indefinite number of years. In addition a complete civil service might have to be recruited and imported, possibly running into a size of several hundred thousand. An overseas supply service under such conditions would have to be set up on practically a war basis embracing an indigent civil population of many millions. Many other most drastic results, which I will not attempt to discuss, should be anticipated and complete new plans should be carefully prepared by the Allied powers along all lines to meet the new eventualities. Most careful consideration as to the national forces composing the occupation force is essential. Certainly the United States should not be called upon to bear unilaterally the terrific burden of manpower, economics, and other resultant responsibilities.

The decision as to whether the Emperor should be tried as a war criminal involves a policy determination upon such a high level that I would not feel it appropriate for me to make a recommendation; but if the decision by the heads of states is in the affirmative, I recommend the above measures as imperative.

THE SHŌWA CONSTITUTION

It was clearly recognized by SCAP that if the occupation were to bring about the strengthening of a democratic process, there had to be sweeping changes in the fundamental law of the land. In spite of the many attempts for the rewriting of the Japanese constitution by the Japanese, the final version as emerged was strongly influenced by the guidance given by SCAP. The process as seen by General Courtney Whitney, who was chief of the government section under MacArthur, is given in Document 5.

The new Japanese constitution (Document 4) came into being on November 3, 1946, and went into effect on May 3, 1947. It made the Emperor the "symbol of the State," not "sacred and inviolable" as he was under the Meiji constitution. The Diet became the highest organ of state powers, and enjoyed full budget-making power, among others. The executive branch was made responsible to the Diet, whereas previously under the Meiji constitution it was not.

In addition to the basic human rights contained in the American Bill of Rights, Chapter III of the Shōwa constitution guaranteed such rights as the right and obligation to work, the right of workers to organize and the right to maintain the minimum standards of wholesome and cultured living. The equality of women was also assured under the new constitution.

The unique feature of the new constitution, however, can be found in its Article 9, the renunciation of war clause. General MacArthur gave credit to Prime Minister Shidehara Kijurō (1872–1951) for the inspiration of incorporating this clause into the constitution (Document 6a). However, it must be noted that many Japanese authorities still claim that it was the general himself who was the author of this clause.[5]

---

[5]Among those witnesses who appeared before the Constitution Investigatory Commission (Kempō Chōsakai), which held 131 meetings between 1947 and 1964, was former Prime Minister Yoshida Shigeru, who testified that in his opinion the initiative did not come from Prime Minister Shidehara. Another witness went as far as to say that Shidehara had nothing to do with Article 9 and never discussed the matter in his Cabinet meetings. For further details, see Kempō Chōsakai, *Kempō Seitei no Keika ni kansuru Shōiinkai Hōkokusho (Subcommittee Reports on the Processes Leading to the Enactment of the Constitution)* (Tokyo: Ministry of Finance, 1967), pp. 323–38. Professor Theodore McNelly speculates that the renunciation of war provision originally stemmed from the MacArthur-Shidehara meeting in January 1946, and it was largely due to the enthusiastic support of MacArthur that the provision was incorporated in the Japanese constitution. See Theodore McNelly, "The Renunciation of War in the Japanese Constitution," *Political Science Quarterly*, 77, no. 3 (September 1962): pp. 350–78.

General MarArthur also recalled the enfranchisement of women with a flourish, and it is included as Document 6(b).

For the Japanese officials, the SCAP-initiated constitution contained two major difficulties. The most troublesome was stripping the power of governing away from the Emperor and delegating him to the position of "the symbol of the State and of the unity of the people." Document 7(a) contains excerpts from a letter of Shirasu Jirō to General Whitney explaining why it was difficult for the Japanese to accept this particular phase of the SCAP plan. Shirasu was a liaison officer between the GHQ and the Japanese Government. Document 7(b) contains General Whitney's unequivocal response. The Dr. Matsumoto referred to in Shirasu's letter as well as in Whitney's account (Document 5) was Matsumoto Jōji (1877–1954), a former law professor serving as minister of state in the Shidehara Cabinet. He was charged with the task of constitutional revision. His draft, incidentally, was rejected by SCAP on the grounds that it was mere rewording of the Meiji constitution.

Article 9, the renunciation of war clause, provided yet another challenge. It was not clear if the language permitted Japan the right of self-defense. In the summer of 1946, a subcommittee consisting of fourteen persons debated the language of the constitution article by article. It was headed by Ashida Hitoshi (1887–1959), a former diplomat, who in 1948 would become prime minister. Document 8a contains excerpts from the transcript of debates concerning Article 9. The full transcript was not made public until September 1995. The document contained herein is a selective translation from that transcript.[6]

Until the 1995 disclosure, a predominant assumption was that an amendment was made by Mr. Ashida which implied that Japan could rearm. The 1995 text suggests that it was not Mr. Ashida personally, but the Japanese Government through state minister Kanamori that made a distinction between the first and second paragraphs of Article 9. That move would make room for rearmament for defensive purposes and would allow Japan to participate in UN peacekeeping operations. The Ashida subcommittee's "amendment" was approved by the plenary session of the House of Representatives on August 24, 1946. Mr. Ashida's diary entry of that day is reproduced as Document 8b. It deals with the issues of self-defense and Japan's desire to enter the United Nations.

For many years, Japanese constitutional scholars and politicians debated whether the Ashida amendment gave Japan the right to rearm, and whether the self-defense forces were consistent with the provisions of Article 9. A document released in 1996 clearly indicates that both questions must be answered in the affirmative. A sentence "The Prime Minister and other Ministers of State must be

---

[6]In 1946, at the request of the GHQ, the Japanese Government made a translation of the transcript. However, forty-one sensitive passages, including the ones translated herein, were not contained in the version submitted to the GHQ. The existence of these passages became known only through the 1995 disclosure.

civilians" was inserted to Article 66 to become its second paragraph at the urging of the GHQ. The GHQ reasoned that with the passage of the Ashida amendment, Japan could one day rearm, and it was necessary to establish firmly the principle of civilian control.[7]

4   **Excerpts from the Shōwa Constitution, 1946**[8] We, the Japanese people, acting through our duly elected representatives in the National Diet, determined that we shall secure for ourselves and our posterity the fruits of peaceful cooperation with all nations and the blessings of liberty throughout this land, and resolved that never again shall we be visited with the horrors of war through the action of government, do proclaim that sovereign power resides with the people and do firmly establish this Constitution. Government is a sacred trust of the people, the authority for which is derived from the people, the powers of which are exercised by the representatives of the people, and the benefits of which are enjoyed by the people. This is a universal principle of mankind upon which this constitution is founded. We reject and revoke all constitutions, laws, ordinances, and rescripts in conflict herewith.

We, the Japanese people, desire peace for all time and are deeply conscious of the high ideals controlling human relationship, and we have determined to preserve our security and existence, trusting in the justice and faith of the peace-loving peoples of the world. We desire to occupy an honored place in an international society striving for the preservation of peace, and the banishment of tyranny and slavery, oppression and intolerance, for all time from the earth. We recognize that all peoples of the world have the right to live in peace, free from fear and want.

We believe that no nation is responsible to itself alone, but that laws of political morality are universal; and that obedience to such laws is incumbent upon all nations who would sustain their own sovereignty and justify their sovereign relationship with other nations.

---

[7]The January 22, 1996, issue of *Mainichi, Sankei, Tokyo* and *Yomiuri Shimbun*. The document made public is a transcript of proceedings of a House of Peers subcommittee deliberating on the constitution, meeting four times between September 28 and October 2, 1946. Its members included a number of constitutional lawyers and professors. Prime Minister Yoshida was present. According to Yoshida, General Whitney and Colonel Kades came to see him saying in essence that GHQ had no objection to accepting the Ashida amendment, which could see Japan rearm one day. In view of it, it would be necessary to establish firmly the principle of civilian control in the constitution. The language "the prime minister and other ministers of state must be civilians," was prepared by the GHQ. There was no comparable Japanese word for the English word "civilian," and the subcommittee after examining a number of alternatives finally agreed on a newly created word *"bunmin."*

[8]From the National Diet of Japan, *The Constitution of Japan, the Diet Law, Rules of the House of Representatives, Rules of the House of Councillors* (Tokyo, no date), pp. 3–24.

We, the Japanese people, pledge our national honor to accomplish these high ideals and purposes with all our resources.

CHAPTER I   THE EMPEROR

ARTICLE 1. The Emperor shall be the symbol of the State and of the unity of the people, deriving his position from the will of the people with whom resides sovereign power.

CHAPTER II   RENUNCIATION OF WAR

ARTICLE 9. Aspiring sincerely to an international peace based on justice and order, the Japanese people forever renounce war as a sovereign right of the nation and the threat or use of force as a means of settling international disputes.

In order to accomplish the aim of the preceding paragraph, land, sea, and air forces, as well as other war potential, will never be maintained. The right of belligerency of the state will not be recognized.

CHAPTER III   RIGHTS AND DUTIES OF THE PEOPLE

ARTICLE 13. All of the people shall be respected as individuals. Their right to life, liberty, and the pursuit of happiness shall, to the extent that it does not interfere with the public welfare, be the supreme consideration in legislation and in other governmental affairs.

ARTICLE 14. All of the people are equal under the law, and there shall be no discrimination in political, economic, or social relations because of race, creed, sex, social status, or family origin. . . .

ARTICLE 15. The people have the inalienable right to choose their public officials and to dismiss them.

All public officials are servants of the whole community and not any group thereof.

Universal adult suffrage is guaranteed with regard to the election of public officials. . . .

ARTICLE 19. Freedom of thought and conscience shall not be violated.

ARTICLE 20. Freedom of religion is guaranteed to all. No religious organization shall receive any privileges from the state, nor exercise any political authority. . . .

ARTICLE 21. Freedom of assembly and association, as well as speech, press, and all other forms of expression, are guaranteed.

No censorship shall be maintained, nor shall the secrecy of any means of communication be violated.

ARTICLE 22. Every person shall have freedom to choose and change his residence and to choose his occupation to the extent that it does not interfere with the public welfare.

Freedom of all persons to move to a foreign country and to divest themselves of their nationality shall be inviolate.

ARTICLE 23. Academic freedom is guaranteed.

ARTICLE 24. Marriage shall be based only on the mutual consent of both sexes, and it shall be maintained through mutual cooperation with the equal rights of husband and wife as a basis.

With regard to the choice of spouse, property rights, inheritance, choice of domicile, divorce, and other matters pertaining to marriage and the family, laws shall be enacted from the standpoint of individual dignity and the essential equality of the sexes.

ARTICLE 25. All people shall have the right to maintain the minimum standards of wholesome and cultured living.

In all spheres of life, the state shall use its endeavors for the promotion and extension of social welfare and security, and of public health.

ARTICLE 26. All people shall have the right to receive an equal education correspondent to their ability, as provided by law. . . .

ARTICLE 27. All people shall have the right and obligation to work.

Standards for wages, hours, rest and other working conditions shall be fixed by law.

Children shall not be exploited.

ARTICLE 28. The right of workers to organize and to bargain and act collectively is guaranteed.

ARTICLE 29. The right to own or to hold property is inviolable. Property rights shall be defined by law, in conformity with the public welfare. . . .

Private property may be taken for public use upon just compensation therefor.

ARTICLE 31. No person shall be deprived of life or liberty, nor shall any other criminal penalty be imposed, except according to procedure established by law.

CHAPTER IV   THE DIET

ARTICLE 41. The Diet shall be the highest organ of state power, and shall be the sole lawmaking organ of the state.

ARTICLE 42. The Diet shall consist of two Houses, namely, the House of Representatives and the House of Councillors.

ARTICLE 43. Both Houses shall consist of elected members, representatives of all the people. . . .

ARTICLE 45. The term of office of members of the House of Representatives shall be four years. However, the term shall be terminated before the full term is up in case the House of Representatives is dissolved.

ARTICLE 46. The term of office of members of the House of Councillors shall be six years, and election for half the members shall take place every three years.

ARTICLE 47. Electoral districts, method of voting and other matters pertaining to the method of election of members of both Houses shall be fixed by law.

ARTICLE 54. When the House of Representatives is dissolved, there must be a general election of members of the House of Representatives within forty (40) days from the date of dissolution, and the Diet must be convoked within thirty (30) days from the date of election.

When the House of Representatives is dissolved, the House of Councillors is closed at the same time. However, the Cabinet may in time of national emergency convoke the House of Councillors in emergency session. . . .

ARTICLE 59. A bill becomes a law on passage by both Houses, except as otherwise provided by the constitution.

A bill which is passed by the House of Representatives, and upon which the House of Councillors makes a decision different from that of the House of Representatives, becomes a law when passed a second time by the House of Representatives by a majority of two-thirds or more of the members present.

The provision of the preceding paragraph does not preclude the House of Representatives from calling for the meeting of a joint committee of both Houses, provided for by law. . . .

ARTICLE 60. The budget must first be submitted to the House of Representatives. . . .

CHAPTER V THE CABINET

ARTICLE 65. Executive power shall be vested in the Cabinet.

ARTICLE 66. The Cabinet shall consist of the Prime Minister, who shall be its head, and other Ministers of State, as provided for by law.

The Prime Minister and other Ministers of State must be civilians.

The Cabinet, in the exercise of executive power, shall be collectively responsible to the Diet.

ARTICLE 67. The Prime Minister shall be designated from among the members of the Diet by a resolution of the Diet. This designation shall precede all other business.

If the House of Representatives and the House of Councillors disagree, and if no agreement can be reached even through a joint committee of both Houses, provided for by law, or the House of Councilors fails to make designation within ten (10) days, exclusive of the period of recess, after the House of Representatives has made designation, the decision of the House of Representatives shall be the decision of the Diet.

ARTICLE 68. The Prime Minister shall appoint the Ministers of State. However, a majority of their number must be chosen from among the members of the Diet.

The Prime Minister may remove the Ministers of State as he chooses.

ARTICLE 72. The Prime Minister, representing the Cabinet, submits bills, reports on general national affairs and foreign relations to the Diet, and exercises control and supervision over various administrative branches.

CHAPTER VI   JUDICIARY

ARTICLE 76. The whole judicial power is vested in a Supreme Court and in such inferior courts as are established by law.

No extraordinary tribunal shall be established, nor shall any organ or agency of the executive be given final judicial power.

All judges shall be independent in the exercise of their conscience and shall be bound only by this Constitution and the laws.

CHAPTER VII   FINANCE

ARTICLE 83. The power to administer national finances shall be exercised as the Diet shall determine.

ARTICLE 84. No new taxes shall be imposed or existing ones modified except by law or under such conditions as law may prescribe.

ARTICLE 85. No money shall be expended, nor shall the state obligate itself, except as authorized by the Diet.

ARTICLE 86. The Cabinet shall prepare and submit to the Diet for its consideration and decision a budget for each fiscal year.

CHAPTER VIII   LOCAL SELF-GOVERNMENT

ARTICLE 93. The local public entities shall establish assemblies as their deliberative organs, in accordance with law.

The chief executive officers of all local public entities, the members of their assemblies, and such other local officials as may be determined by law shall be elected by direct popular vote within their several communities.

CHAPTER IX   AMENDMENTS

ARTICLE 96. Amendments to this Constitution shall be initiated by the Diet, through a concurring vote of two-thirds or more of all the members of each House, and shall thereupon be submitted to the people for ratification, which shall require the affirmative vote of a majority of all votes cast thereon, at a special referendum or at such election as the Diet shall specify. . . .

CHAPTER X   SUPREME LAW

ARTICLE 97. The fundamental human rights by this Constitution guaranteed to the people of Japan are fruits of the age-old struggle of man to be free; they have survived the many exacting tests for durability and are conferred upon this and future generations in trust, to be held for all time inviolate.

5   **SCAP Political Section and the Drafting of the Constitution, 1945–46**[9]
From the first meetings between MacArthur and successive Japanese prime ministers following the surrender, the supreme commander made it clear that the antiquated, restrictive, and feudalistic constitution left over from the Meiji reign would have to be completely revised. He pointed out that only thereby might be built a firm foundation upon which a democratic society might safely rest. Always the Japanese prime minister would smile and agree politely; but always, upon later questioning, MacArthur would find that nothing had been done about it.

There were innumerable reasons for the delay, a favorite one being that there must have been some misunderstanding because Minister So-and-So had received an entirely different impression from some other SCAP member. But the most popular excuse was the one of a "difference in interpretation." MacArthur was determined that we would not force an American-written constitution down Japanese throats, so he continued, quietly but firmly, to prod the Japanese into positive action.

In October 1945, a committee of Japanese political leaders was formed to draft the proposed revisions. It was established by Prime Minister Shidehara, given the title of the Constitutional Problem Investigation Committee and placed under the chairmanship of Dr. Matsumoto Jōji, a state minister without portfolio. When its members sat down to work, they were bombarded with advice by Japanese people. With no censorship, and in fact at MacArthur's urging, the constitution was debated at great length in the press of Japan, and every political party, including the Communist Party, advanced its own suggested revisions.

For three months, while SCAP staff members and MacArthur himself continued to remind Matsumoto and his colleagues of the need for speed, the Constitutional Problem Investigation Committee worked on its draft of recommendations.

There evidently was a schism in the committee between the advocates of a conservative and those of a more liberalized constitution, but the committee in general was dominated by the wishes of Dr. Matsumoto, who was an extreme conservative. Finally, by the end of January, the committee unofficially presented SCAP headquarters with two documents, one entitled "Gist of the Revision of the Constitution" and the other "General Explanation of the Constitutional Revision Drafted by the Government"; no formal submission of recommendations was ever made.

I had at that time recently taken on the duties of chief of the government section, charged with the staff responsibility for the reorganization of the Japanese government and necessary revision of Japanese law. I of course passed both the "Gist" and the "Explanation" on to the members of my staff for their study,

---

[9]From *MacArthur: His Rendevous with History* by Courtney Whitney, pp. 247–51. Copyright © 1955 by Time Inc. Reprinted by permission of Alfred A. Knopf, Inc.

and it did not take them long to discover that the two documents recommended little more than word changing of the old Meiji Constitution. For example, the Emperor system was retained intact; the Emperor would by the proposed changes become "supreme and inviolable" rather than "sacred and inviolable," and his power to rule the country as he had before was virtually unchanged. As for the "Bill of Rights" chapter of the constitution, the Matsumoto draft, far from increasing the rights of the people, seemed to reduce them. All were made subordinate to ordinary statutory law, for every constitutional grant was followed by the limitation "except as otherwise provided by law." Almost all of the other proposals for revision of the Matsumoto committee were so weak as to be of no importance, and in general would leave the constitution as flexible and open to repressive interpretation by the ruling classes as the Meiji constitution had been. We could see at a glance that the proposed revisions amounted to no revision at all.

Meanwhile, an appointment had been made by Foreign Minister Yoshida and me to discuss the Matsumoto draft on February 5. On February 2 a representative of the Foreign Office asked for a postponement of the conference. I suggested a postponement for one week. And this week was put to good use, for on February 3 MacArthur decided that the Japanese shilly-shallying had gone on long enough. The first general elections were only two months away, and he was determined that a presentable draft of revisions would be finished so that those elections would also constitute an unofficial plebiscite. If the Japanese continued to hedge and delay as they had for almost four months, the people would have no choice but to vote for or against what was nearly a carbon copy of the old Meiji constitution.

Apparently the only way to make unmistakably clear to the Matsumoto committee that their recommendations were unacceptably reactionary was to prepare a draft of our own that could be used as the basis for future negotiations. When MacArthur came to his Dai-ichi Building office on the morning of February 3, he instructed me to have this done. I was to have full latitude in the initiation of the work except for the following prescriptions: (a) the Emperor system would be preserved, though modified to bring it within constitutional limitations and subject to the ultimate will of the people; (b) war and war-making would be forsworn—a concept that had been proposed to MacArthur by Prime Minister Shidehara; and (c) all forms of feudalism would be abolished.

With these instructions the government section set out to prepare a draft for consideration by the Japanese. I immediately appointed a steering committee led by my deputy, a brilliant officer, Colonel Charles L. Kades, and composed of two other members, Lieutenant Colonel Milo E. Rowell and Commander Alfred R. Hussey. All three were lawyers of distinction. With a willing, hard-working staff of assistants, they embarked on the momentous project.

Whereas the governments of nearly all the countries in the world had been built on years of tradition, articles, amendments, repeals, and the trial-and-error of experience, we were free to use the best of all these constitutions and discard the worst—and without the slightest necessity for playing partisan politics. While our final draft would consist of principles for a revised constitution and be so labeled, the only practical method of drawing up these principles was to do it in the form of an actual constitution.

For six days all other business of the section gave way to this project. The assistants to the members of the steering committee were split into groups of experts on various subjects with which the constitution would concern itself. Lieutenant Colonel Frank Hays, for example, an able lawyer of long practice, worked out the section on the Diet; Commander Guy Swope, an accountant and government student and formerly a member of Congress and governor of Puerto Rico, specialized on the Cabinet section; the budget section was drafted by Major Frank Rizzo, an extraordinarily able engineer-turned-economist who became my successor after my departure from Japan. These specialists and others, with their assistants, drew up their proposals for a revised constitution and presented them to the steering committee members, who, article by article, prepared the final recommendations for constitutional reform.[10]

Our spirits were high. We worked with the enthusiasm natural to the challenge of our task, but also with a kind of dedication which came from the experience we had all so recently been through as combat officers. Everywhere we had seen the destruction and bloody death of war. Here was an opportunity to help an entire nation throw off the virus of militarism that had led to war.

We had arbitrarily set February 12, Lincoln's Birthday, for our deadline, and we made it. The draft had been approved by MacArthur with only one significant change, and mimeographed copies had been prepared for us to present to the Japanese committee members. Our meeting was to be at the home of Foreign Minister Yoshida, and we were met at his residence with low bows and smiles of apprehension. We were polite, but not cordial, businesslike but not brusque. We asked if our hosts could understand our English if we spoke slowly and clearly; and when they replied that they could, we requested that no interpreters be used, thereby reducing the opportunities for "misunderstanding."

While observing the amenities, I minced no words in informing the Japanese representatives that the supreme commander had found their proposals unacceptable. The Matsumoto draft, I said, fell far short of the broad and liberal reorganization of the Japanese governmental structure along democratic lines that the Allied powers could regard as significant evidence that Japan had learned the lessons of war and defeat and was prepared to act as a responsible member of a

---

[10]The major proposals and the discussions concerning them appear in Section III, Chapter V of SCAP, Government Section, *Political Reorientation of Japan, September 1945 to September 1948*, vol. 1 (Washington, D.C.: Government Printing Office, 1949), pp. 101–5.

peaceful community. I told them that the supreme commander had caused to be prepared a detailed statement of the principles he deemed basic and that we were presenting the statement to the Japanese government in the form of a draft constitution. I advised the committee to give this statement the fullest consideration and proposed that it be used as the guide in renewed efforts to prepare a revised constitution.

Then I took a chance. With no prior authorization from MacArthur, I told the Japanese that while there was no compulsion upon them to take further action; the supreme commander was determined that the constitutional issue should be brought before the people well in advance of the general election. He felt, I explained, that they should have full opportunity to discuss and freely express their will on constitutional reform. Therefore, I said, if the Cabinet were unable to prepare a suitable and acceptable draft before the elections, General MacArthur was prepared to lay this statement of principle directly before the people.

The effect of this statement upon the Japanese representatives was immediately visible. Mr. Shirasu straightened up as if he had sat on something. Dr. Matsumoto sucked in his breath. Mr. Yoshida's face was a black cloud. I broke the ensuing silence by suggesting that the Japanese read our statement of principles here and now, adding that we would be glad to wait while they did so.

Mr. Shirasu, who lived with Mr. Yoshida, already appeared quite distraught as he ushered us to another section of the beautifully landscaped grounds that are part of the Foreign Minister's residence. . . . At the end of about an hour, I decided that we should rejoin our hosts, and we were rising as Mr. Shirasu reappeared.

He seemed flustered by the drastic changes in our draft, and it occurred to me that this was an opportune moment to employ one more psychological shaft. I did not know the impressive support that I was about to receive from an unexpected quarter.

As he mumbled apologies for keeping us waiting, I replied with a smile: "Not at all, Mr. Shirasu. We have been enjoying your atomic sunshine."

And at that moment, with what could not have been better timing, a big B-29 came roaring over us. The reaction upon Mr. Shirasu was indescribable, but profound.

When we seated ourselves across the patio from the committee members again, I could see that Mr. Shirasu's colleagues were as upset by our proposals as he was. I realized that, accustomed as they had been all their lives to ordering the affairs of their country pretty much their own way, they were finding it extremely difficult to be elastic, even though they must have known by now that they were impeding the progress of their country toward democracy.

By the time we had left Mr. Yoshida's residence shortly thereafter, we were fairly convinced that our proposed draft would be accepted as the basis for the revised constitution. . . .

6   MacArthur on the Japanese Constitution, 1946[11]

(a) The Origin of Article 9

It has frequently been charged, even by those who should be better informed, that the "no war" clause was forced upon the government by my personal fiat. This is not true, as the following facts will show: Long before work was completed on the new document by Dr. Matsumoto, I had an appointment with Prime Minister Shidehara, who wished to thank me for making what was then a new drug in Japan, penicillin, available in aiding in his recovery from severe illness. He arrived at my office at noon on January 24 and thanked me for the penicillin, but I noticed he then seemed somewhat embarrassed and hesitant. I asked him what was troubling him, that as prime minister he could speak with the greatest frankness, either by way of complaint or suggestion. He replied that he hesitated to do so because of my profession as a soldier. I assured him soldiers were not as unresponsive or inflexible as they are sometimes pictured—that at bottom most of them were quite human.

He then proposed that when the new constitution became final that it include the so-called no-war clause. He also wanted it to prohibit any military establishment for Japan—any military establishment whatsoever. Two things would thus be accomplished. The old military party would be deprived of any instrument through which they could someday seize power, and the rest of the world would know that Japan never intended to wage war again. He added that Japan was a poor country and could not really afford to pour money into armaments anyway. Whatever resources the nation had left should go to bolstering the economy.

I had thought that my long years of experience had rendered me practically immune to surprise or unusual excitement, but this took my breath away. I could not have agreed more. For years I have believed that war should be abolished as an outmoded means of resolving disputes between nations. Probably no living man has seen as much of war and its destruction as I had. A participant or observer in six wars, a veteran of twenty campaigns, the survivor of hundreds of battlefields, I have fought with or against the soldiers of practically every country in the world, and my abhorrence reached its height with the perfection of the atom bomb.

When I spoke in this vein, it was Shidehara's turn to be surprised. His amazement was so great that he seemed overwhelmed as he left the office. Tears ran down his face, and he turned back to me and said, "The world will laugh and mock us as impracticable visionaries, but a hundred years from now we will be called prophets. . . ."

There were attacks made on this article of the constitution, especially by the

---

[11]*Reminiscences* by General of the Army Douglas MacArthur, McGraw-Hill Book Co., (1964), pp. 302–5. Reprinted with permission of the General Douglas MacArthur Foundation.

cynics who said that it was against the basic nature of man. I defended it, and advocated that it be adopted. Not only was I convinced that it was the most moral of ideas, but I knew that it was exactly what the Allies wanted at that time for Japan. They had said so at Potsdam and they had said so afterward. Indeed, my directive read, "Japan is not to have an Army, Navy, Air Force, Secret Police organization, or civil aviation." And now this had been accomplished by the Japanese themselves, not by the conquering powers.

Nothing in Article 9, however, prevents any and all necessary steps for the preservation of the safety of the nation. Japan cannot be expected to resist the overwhelming law of self-preservation. If attacked, she will defend herself. Article 9 was aimed entirely at eliminating Japanese aggression. I stated this at the time of the adoption of the constitution, and later recommended that in case of necessity a defense force be established consisting of ten divisions with corresponding sea and air elements.

I stated unequivocally:

"Should the course of world events require that all mankind stand at arms in defense of human liberty and Japan comes within the orbit of immediately threatened attack, then the Japanese, too, should mount the maximum defensive power which their resources will permit. Article 9 is based upon the highest of moral ideals, but by no sophistry of reasoning can it be interpreted as complete negation of the inalienable right of self-defense against unprovoked attack. It is a ringing affirmation by a people laid prostrate by the sword, of faith in the ultimate triumph of international morality and justice without resort to the sword.

"It must be understood, however, that so long as predatory international banditry is permitted to roam the earth to crush human freedom under its avarice and violence, its high concept will be slow in finding universal acceptance. But it is axiomatic that there must be always a first in all things. The great immediate purpose Japan can serve in the confusion which overrides all of strife-torn Asia is to stand out with striking and unruffled calmness and tranquillity as the exemplification of peaceful progress, under conditions of alloyed personal freedom. It can thus wield a profound moral influence upon the destiny of the Asian race."

(b) The Status of Women

In the general election of April 10, 1946, the centuries of custom and tradition in Japan were upset by the first completely free election ever held in that country. Seventy-five percent of those eligible to vote helped to elect 466 members of the Diet. More than 13 million women registered their choices for the first time, and those 13 million votes changed the whole complexion of Japanese political life. Even in modern times it had been the custom of the prime minister in power to choose the majority of the Diet members who were voted on, and all of these holdovers were now voted out of office. An analysis of election returns revealed that only six of the old-line professional politicians had been sent to the legislature. Farmers, teachers, doctors, and laboring men now sat in the house once dominated by lawyers and industrialists. These were, by and large, much younger people. Best of all, they included thirty-eight women.

The election was not without its amusing aspects. The day after the results were announced, I received a call from an extremely dignified but obviously distraught Japanese legislative leader requesting an appointment with me. The caller, who was one of a numerous group of Harvard Law School graduates in Japan, immediately launched into the subject that was troubling him so deeply. "I regret to say that something terrible has happened. A prostitute, Your Excellency, has been elected to the House of Representatives."

I asked him, "How many votes did she receive?"

The Japanese legislator sighed, and said, "256,000."

I said, as solemnly as I could, "Then I should say there must have been more than her dubious occupation involved."

He burst into a gale of laughter. "You soldiers!" he exclaimed, and dropped the subject. He probably thought I was a lunatic.

The Japanese women were quick to take advantage of their new status under the constitution. They found jobs in professions where they had never been seen before. In the next five years, some two thousand of them even became policewomen. They took an active part in the various labor unions, a million and a half of them joining workmen's organizations. For the first time in Japanese history they fought for and secured laws giving them the same pay and same hours as men. They even asked for and received maternity leave. Until the occupation there had never been coeducation in Japan except in the lower grades. This was now changed and the women received exactly the same quality of education as men. Laws concerning marriage, divorce, and adultery were revised as part of the program for equality. The old custom of contract marriages was forbidden, and concubinage was abolished.

Of all the reforms accomplished by the occupation in Japan, none was more heartwarming to me than this change in the status of women.

7   Exchange between Shirasu and Whitney on Emperor's Position, 1946[12]

(a) Letter of Shirasu to Whitney

. . . I must say your draft [of the Japanese constitution] was more than a little shock to them [Dr. Matsumoto and his colleagues in the cabinet]. Dr. Matsumoto was quite a socialist in his young days and still is a wholehearted liberal. Notwithstanding the doctor's qualifications . . . your draft came as a great surprise.

---

[12]Shrasu's letter to Whitney was written in English and dated February 15, 1946. Whitney's response was given the following day. From Etō Jun, ed., *Senryō Shiroku (Records of American Occupation of Japan)*, vol. 3, *Kempō Seitei Keika (Events Leading to the Promulgation of the Constitution)* (Tokyo: Kōdansha, 1989), pp. 213–23.

He realizes that the object of your draft and his "revision" is one and the same in spirit. He is as anxious as you are, if not more as after all this is his country, that this country should be placed on a constitutional and democratic basis once for all as he has always deplored the unconstitutionality of the nation. He and his colleagues feel that yours and theirs aim at the same destination but there is this great difference in the routes chosen. Your way is so American in the way that is straight and direct. Their way must be Japanese in the way that it is roundabout, twisted and narrow. Your way may be called an Airway and their way a Jeep way over bumpy roads (I know the roads are bumpy!). . . .

I think I appreciate your standpoint well. . . . At the same time, I see their viewpoint too. Theirs is not a party government. They have no means of knowing how much they can count on the support of the people. They see the papers every day and read about extreme leftish outbursts. But on the other hand, they know only too well a great majority of the people are enthusiastically opposed to communism and devotedly for the Emperor. They are afraid that any revision presented in a "drastic" form will only be jeered out of the House, thereby accomplishing nothing. They feel that they must approach it carefully and slowly. They still vividly remember the days of party politics in this country. Granted the parties were often short-sighted and corrupt but what they then considered "democratic principle" prevailed everywhere. All over the country, the soldiers were very much looked down on and the fever attained such a height finally that no officer ever dared to ride a street car with his saber dangling on. The budgets were cut down left and right on armaments. Sure enough, the acute reactions set in, and the militarism you know so much about appeared on the scene. They fear that too complete a reform all at once would only invite too extreme a reaction and they are most anxious to avoid it.

I think they are all unanimous in the feeling that once the right to initiate revisions is invested in the House, and not in the Emperor, the battle is nearly won and succeeding governments could revise it as much as they wished according to the will of the people. . . .

(b) Whitney's Response to Shirasu

I quite understand the graphic portrayal of the distinction in the manner in which your countrymen and mine traditionally approach a common objective—possibly more than to all else, to that distinction may be charged Japan's present plight—but Dr. Matsumoto and his colleagues appear completely to lose sight of the fact that in the attainment of that common objective sought by constitutional reform, those who sponsor the principles as stated by the supreme commander in his referenced document do so with his firm support, which in turn elevates the sponsorship well above party or other local political considerations. With that support they can be assured that the objectives may be reached promptly and directly, and without either adverse effect upon the orderly processes of civil government nor dislocation in the lives of the people. That the Diet would receive the instrument in the manner you suggest if it bear the stamp of joint approval both by the Government and the supreme commander is unthinkable.

The supreme commander, in full appreciation of the traditional place that the Emperor occupies in the hearts of the people, has precisely sought by the instrument to leave both himself and his dynasty in a position of dignity, honor, and respect, and at the same time place the ultimate political power in the hands of the people where we all agree it inevitably must rest. It is to ensure that these objectives are understood by the people that the supreme commander is determined that they be fully informed of the political reforms that they of right may expect, prior to the next general elections—that the new Diet may assume its responsibilities with their full opportunity of expression thereon.

The document in reference is by its terms clear and succinct and susceptible to no misunderstanding. While the supreme commander is not dogmatically opposed to minor changes in the language used or procédure provided, the better to bring it within the understanding of and application by the Japanese people, he will not compromise it—either in principle or basic form. He will not yield to unnecessary delay. . . .

8a   Ashida Subcommittee on Self-Defense and Article 9, 1946[13]

Fourth Session (July 29, 1946)

Chairman Ashida Hitoshi: We have here before us a draft proposal to amend Article 9. Let us discuss it. Will you be agreeable to changing the wording of the said Article to:

"Aspiring sincerely to an international peace based on justice and order, the Japanese people declare that they will not maintain land, sea, and air forces, as well as other war potential, and will not recognize the right of belligerency of the state.

"In order to accomplish the aim of the preceding paragraph, the Japanese people forever renounce war as a sovereign right of the nation and the threat or use of force as a means of settling international disputes."

Yoshida Yasushi (Progressive Party): The Progressive Party has no objection to the chairman's proposal. We agree.

Takahashi Yasuo (Liberal Party): I agree to the amendment just proposed.

Chairman Ashida: One of the reasons for proposing this amendment is the language. The original draft states that "maintaining of land, sea, and air forces, as well as other war potential shall not be permitted." It does not sound like Japanese. In Japanese we do say "I do not lie" but we do not say, "I am forbid-

---

[13]From the texts published in the *Sankei Shimbun* and *Mainichi Shimbun*, September 30, 1995.

den to tell a lie." I thought of zooming in on this wording, but that is not a judicious approach. However, if we say from the outset that the Japanese people sincerely aspire to international peace based on justice and order, and then go on to say that we do not maintain land, sea, and air forces and other war potential, the flow will be more natural.

Suzuki Yoshio (Socialist Party): I question the wisdom of placing the right of belligerency and maintenance of war potential first and putting renunciation of war last. Will you reconsider?

Fifth Session (July 30, 1946)

Mr. Suzuki: This is a technical question concerning legislation. Is it possible to speak of the right of belligerency before dealing with the issue of renunciation of war?

Kanamori Tokujirō (state minister on constitution): This is a very delicate subject that cannot be taken lightly. [In the original government version,] we used the words "forever renounce" in the first paragraph. The intent [of renouncing war] is strongly stated. In the second paragraph we did not use the word "forever." My guess is that maintenance of war potential contains a number of important issues, such as relations with the United Nations which will develop in the future. We separated our goals into the first and second paragraphs, and put those principles which are permanent in nature in the first paragraph. That is our view. In any event, the original draft was written with that in mind.

Seventh Session (August 1, 1946)

Mr. Suzuki: I am still disturbed [by the chairman's proposed amendment]. . . . A certain scholar of international law explains that by placing the issue of the right of belligerency first, it assures that the right of self-defense will not be abandoned. If this represents your view, and you have given careful consideration to the issue, I may withdraw my objection.

Inukai Takeshi (Progressive Party): Minister Kanamori spoke the other day making an inference (*fukumi*) that the principle stated in the first paragraph of Article 9 is permanent and cannot be changed, but the second paragraph allows a certain maneuverability (*hendō*). Can that inference be made?

Satō Tatsuo (deputy director, Cabinet legislation bureau): I do not think I can say outright that such an inference was made. Minister Kanamori chose those words to convey his views in an easy-to-understand manner.

Mr. Inukai: But still the order in which the two issues are placed in the government draft is rather significant. . . .

Mr. Sato: Yes, in order to convey that significance, Mr. Kanamori used that particular expression.

Eto Natsuo (Liberal Party): I think I prefer the order as appears in the original draft.

Chairman Asida: The majority obviously favors the original draft. I accept it.

Mr. Inukai: Will there be an objection to inserting the words "In order to accomplish the aim of the preceding paragraph," to the second paragraph as the chairman suggests, and retain the order as it appears in the original draft? We then insert the words "Aspiring sincerely to an international peace based on justice and order.". . .[This version became known as the Ashida amendment.]

8b   Ashida's Diary on Self-Defense and the United Nations, 1946[14]

Article 9, with my amendment, was approved by the plenary session of the House of Representatives today. On the matter of renunciation of war, I made the following report to the plenary session in my capacity as chairman [of the Constitution Revision Special Committee].

The special committee engaged in lively debates on the issues of (1) "do the provisions of Article 9 in effect deny Japan the right of self-defense?" and (2) "does a disarmed Japan have an ability to defend herself, assuming that she does not renounce her right of self-defense but without having any international guarantee for her security?"

The government's view was that while the first paragraph of Article 9 does not renounce war for self-defense, the second paragraph denies Japan's right to belligerency even for that purpose.

One of the committee members questioned as follows: "Article 51 of the Charter of the United Nations clearly recognizes the right of self-defense. Are we contemplating becoming a member of the United Nations? As a member, Japan's security will be assured since the UN Charter obligates the Security Council to take measures against a war of aggression or a threat to peace."

The government responded that it concurred with the view expressed.

SOCIAL AND EDUCATION REFORMS

State Shintō was regarded by SCAP Headquarters as one of the major culprits in the propagation and dissemination of militaristic and ultranationalist ideology, and as such its disestablishment was ordered early in the occupation (Document 9).

A similar zeal on the part of the Allied powers to transform Japanese society was reflected in its profound conviction that the system of education prevailing in Japan had to be completely revamped. An education mission consisting of twenty-seven educators from the United States was sent to Japan in March 1946. This mission, headed by Dr. George D. Stoddard, recommended decentralization of education, rewriting textbooks in history and geography, and insti-

---

[14]*Ashida Diary,* entry of August 24, 1946. First published in the *Tokyo Shimbun,* March 12, 1979, reproduced in Etō, *Senryō Shiroku,* pp. 365–66.

*tuting coeducation. It also recommended that the Latin alphabet (*rōmaji*) be adopted as Japan's national writing system in place of the traditional one. This part, incidentally, was never seriously carried out by the Japanese. The Education Mission members, in their eagerness to remake the Japanese educational system, showed a fundamental lack of understanding of Japan and of its civilization (Document 10).*

The general aim of education as envisioned by SCAP, however, was incorporated in the Fundamental Law of Education, enacted by the Japanese Diet on March 31, 1947 (Document 11).

*In spite of the many flaws and justifiable criticisms they received, a number of these reform measures survived to the end of the twentieth century. Separation of Shintō from the state remains an established fact. When some prime ministers visit the Yasukuni shrine (for Japan's war dead), they do so as private citizens, and in defiance of the ban on official visits. As violence in schools becomes a national issue, some conservative thinkers advocate reintroduction of the morals (*shūshin*) curriculum, but resistance to it remains strong. The power of making education policy has become increasingly concentrated in the Ministry of Education, contrary to what was envisioned by American reformers. But coeducation, providing equal access to education for both sexes, and many other features outlined in the Fundamental Law are now a firmly entrenched part of Japanese education.*

9 Abolition of State Shintō, 1945[15]

1. In order to free the Japanese people from direct or indirect compulsion to believe or profess to believe in a religion or cult officially designated by the state, and . . .

In order to prevent a recurrence of the perversion of Shintō theory and beliefs into militaristic and ultranationalistic propaganda designed to delude the Japanese people and lead them into wars of aggression, and

In order to assist the Japanese people in a rededication of their national life to building a new Japan based upon ideals of perpetual peace and democracy,

It is hereby directed that:

(a) The sponsorship, support, perpetuation, control, and dissemination of Shintō by the Japanese national, prefectural, and local governments, or by public officials, subordinates, and employees acting in their official capacity, are prohibited and will cease immediately.

(b) All financial support from public funds and all official affiliation with Shintō and Shintō shrines are prohibited and will cease immediately. . . .

---

[15]GHQ, SCAP, Civil Information and Education Section, Education Division, *Education in the New Japan* (Tokyo: SCAP, 1948), pp. 31–35. This SCAP directive was dated December 15, 1945.

(h) The dissemination of Shintō doctrines in any form and by any means in any educational institution supported wholly or in part by public funds is prohibited and will cease immediately. . . .

(m) No official of the national, prefectural, or local government, acting in his public capacity, will visit any shrine to report his assumption of office, to report on conditions of government, or to participate as a representative of government in any ceremony or observance.

2. (a) The purpose of this directive is to separate religion from the state, to prevent misuse of religion for political ends, and to put all religions, faiths, and creeds upon exactly the same legal basis, entitled to precisely the same opportunities and protection. It forbids affiliation with the government and the propagation and dissemination of militaristic and ultranationalistic ideology not only to Shintō but to the followers of all religions, faiths, sects, creeds, or philosophies. . . .

10 Summary of a Report of the U.S. Education Mission, 1946[16]

(a) The Aims and Content of Japanese Education

A highly centralized educational system, even if it is not caught in the net of ultranationalism and militarism, is endangered by the evils that accompany an entrenched bureaucracy. Decentralization is necessary in order that teachers may be freed to develop professionally under guidance, without regimentation. They in turn, may then do their part in the development of free Japanese citizens.

To this end, knowledge must be acquired that is broader than any available in a single prescribed textbook or manual, and deeper than can be tested by stereotyped examinations. A curriculum consists not merely of an accepted body of knowledge but of the pupil's physical and mental activities; it takes into account their differing backgrounds and abilities. It should therefore be set up through cooperative action involving teachers, calling on their experiences and releasing their creative talents.

Morals (*Shūshin*), which in Japanese education occupy a separate place, and have tended to promote submissiveness, should be differently construed and should interpenetrate all phases of a free people's life. Manners that encourage equality, the give-and-take of democratic government, the ideal of good workmanship in daily life—all these are morals in the wider sense. They should be developed and practiced in the varied program and activities of the democratic school.

Books in the fields of geography and history will have to be rewritten to recognize mythology for what it is and to embody a more objective viewpoint in textbooks and reference materials. On the lower levels, more use should be made of the community and local resources; at the higher levels, competent scholar-

---

[16]*Ibid.*, pp. 51–53. The report was dated March 1946.

ship and research should be encouraged in various ways.

The program in health instruction and physical education is basic to the educational program as a whole. Medical examinations, instruction in nutrition and public health, the extension of the physical education and recreation program to the university level, and the replacement of equipment as rapidly as possible are recommended.

At all levels, vocational education should be emphasized. A variety of vocational experiences is needed under well-trained staff members, with an emphasis on technology and its supporting arts and sciences. The contributions of artisans and workers should find a place in the social studies program and opportunities for originality and creativity should be provided.

(b) Language Reform

The problem of the written language is fundamental to all modifications in educational practice. While any change in the form of a language must come from within the nation, the stimulus for such change may come from any source. Encouragement may be given to those who recognize the value of language reform, not only to the educational program, but also to the development of the Japanese people throughout future generations.

It is recommended that some form of *Rōmaji* (Latin alphabet) be brought into common use. It is proposed that a language commission made up of Japanese scholars, educational leaders, and statesmen be formed promptly in order that a comprehensive program may be announced within a reasonable period. In addition to deciding the form of *Rōmaji* to be chosen, this commission would have the following functions: (1) to assume the responsibility for coordinating the program of language reform during the transitional stages; (2) to formulate a plan for introducing *Rōmaji* into the schools and into the life of the community and nation through newspapers, periodicals, books, and other writings; and (3) to study the means of bringing about a more democratic form of the spoken language. The commission might, in time, grow into a national language institute.

The need for a simple and efficient medium of written communication is well recognized, and the time for taking this momentous step is perhaps more favorable now than it will be for many years to come. Language should be a highway and not a barrier. Within Japan itself, and across national borders, this highway should be open for the transmission of knowledge and ideas in the interest of a better world understanding.[17]

---

[17]This is an aside from the compiler of this volume. In 1995, the use of personal computers in Japan was roughly one-third of that in the United States proportionate to their respective population. The difficulty in transcribing the Japanese language and the relative lack of good softwares were cited as reasons. The Stoddard commission could not have foreseen the coming of the PCs, but their recommendation could now be judged with this new insight.

11 **Fundamental Law of Education, 1947**[18] Having established the constitution of Japan, we have shown our resolution to contribute to the peace of the world and welfare of humanity by building a democratic and cultural state. The realization of this ideal shall depend fundamentally on the power of education.

We shall esteem individual dignity and endeavor to bring up the people who love truth and peace, while education which aims at the creation of culture, general and rich in individuality, shall be spread far and wide.

We hereby enact this law, in accordance with the spirit of the Constitution of Japan, with a view to clarifying the aim of education and establishing the foundation of education for new Japan.

ARTICLE 1. *Aim of Education.* Education shall aim at the full development of personality, striving for the rearing of the people, sound in mind and body, who shall love truth and justice, esteem individual value, respect labor and have a deep sense of responsibility, and be imbued with the independent spirit, as builders of the peaceful state and society.

ARTICLE 2. *Educational Principle.* The aim of education shall be realized on all occasions and in all places. In order to achieve the aim, we shall endeavor to contribute to the creation and development of culture by mutual esteem and cooperation, respecting academic freedom, having a regard for actual life, and cultivating a spontaneous spirit.

ARTICLE 3. *Equal Opportunity in Education.* The people shall all be given equal opportunities of receiving education according to their ability, and they shall not be subject to educational discrimination on account of race, creed, sex, social status, economic position, or family origin. The state and local public corporations shall take measures to give financial assistance to those who have, in spite of their ability, difficulty in receiving education for economic reasons.

ARTICLE 4. *Compulsory Education.* The people shall be obligated to have boys and girls under their protection receive nine years' general education. No tuition fee shall be charged for compulsory education in schools established by the state and local public corporations.

ARTICLE 5. *Coeducation.* Men and women shall esteem and cooperate with each other. Coeducation, therefore, shall be recognized in education.

ARTICLE 7. *Social Education.* The state and local public corporation shall endeavor to attain the aim of education by the establishment of such institutions as libraries, museums, civic halls, etc., by the utilization of school institutions, and by other appropriate methods.

---

[18]GHQ, SCAP, Civil Information and Education Section, *Education in the New Japan,* pp. 109–10. The law passed the Diet on March 31, 1947.

ARTICLE 8. *Political Education.* The political knowledge necessary for intelligent citizenship shall be valued in education. The schools prescribed by law shall refrain from political education or other political activities for or against any specific political party.

ARTICLE 9. *Religious Education.* The attitude of religious tolerance and the position of religion in social life shall be valued in education. The schools established by the state and local public corporations shall refrain from religious education or other activities for a specified religion.

LAND REFORM

To free the Japanese peasant "from the bondage of the feudal absentee landowners, the mountain of debt, discriminatory taxation and other economic ills that have oppressed him for centuries," SCAP on December 9, 1945, ordered the Japanese government to submit to the GHQ before March 15, 1946, a plan of land reform (Document 12). It thus began the most successful reform program to be undertaken by the occupation authorities. Its success can be measured by the fact that by 1960 only 2.9 percent of the farmers were under pure tenancy. Landlordism indeed had been wiped out of Japan.

The land-reform program was successful not merely because of SCAP's foresight, but also because of the farmer participation, and of the benefit that even the conservative politicians could see in the reform measures. Document 13 gives the reminiscences of Yoshida Shigeru (1878–1967), who served as prime minister in 1946–47 and 1948–55. The principles of the reform were incorporated in Japan's national law even after Japan regained her independence. There was a rich political dividend for Yoshida and his conservative allies in being identified with this successful reform. The farmers remained one of the major sources of support for the conservative Liberal-Democratic Party, which enjoyed a period of uninterrupted political supremacy from 1955 through 1993.

12 Excerpts from SCAP Directive on Rural Land Reform, 1945[19]

1. In order that the Imperial Japanese Government shall remove economic obstacles to the revival and strengthening of democratic tendencies, establish respect for the dignity of man, and destroy the economic bondage that has enslaved the Japanese farmer to centuries of feudal oppressions, the Japanese Imperial Government is directed to take measures to ensure that those who till the soil of Japan shall have a more equal opportunity to enjoy the fruits of their labor.

---

[19]SCAP, Government Section, *Political Reorientation of Japan,* vol. 2, pp. 575–76.

2. The purpose of this order is to exterminate those pernicious ills that have long blighted the agrarian structure of a land where almost half the total population is engaged in husbandry. The more malevolent of these ills include:

a. *Intense overcrowding of land.* Almost half the farm households in Japan till less than one and one-half acres each.

b. *Widespread tenancy under conditions highly unfavorable to tenants.* More than three-fourths of the farmers in Japan are either partially or totally tenants, paying rentals amounting to half or more of their annual crops.

c. *A heavy burden of farm indebtedness combined with high rates of interest on farm loans.* Farm indebtedness persists so that less than half the total farm households are able to support themselves on their agriculture income.

d. *Government fiscal policies that discriminate against agriculture in favor of industry and trade.* Interest rates and direct taxes on agriculture are more oppressive than those in commerce and industry.

e. *Authoritarian government control over farmers and farm organizations without regard for farmer interests.* Arbitrary crop quotas established by disinterested control associations often restrict the farmer in the cultivation of crops for his own needs or economic advancement. Emancipation of the Japanese farmer cannot begin until such basic farm evils are uprooted and destroyed.

3. The Japanese Imperial Government is therefore ordered to submit to this Headquarters on or before 15 March 1946 a program of rural land reform. This program shall contain plans for:

a. Transfer of land from absentee landowners to land operators.

b. Provisions for purchase of farm lands from non-operating owners at equitable rates.

c. Provisions for tenant purchase of land at annual installments commensurate with tenant income.

d. Provisions for reasonable protection of former tenants against reversion to their tenancy status. Such necessary safeguards should include:

(1) Access to long- and short-term credit at reasonable interest rates.

(2) Measures to protect the farmer against exploitation by processors and distributors.

(3) Measures to stabilize prices of agricultural produce.

(4) Plans for the diffusion of technical and other information of assistance to the agrarian population.

(5) A program to foster and encourage an agricultural cooperative movement free of domination by nonagricultural interests and dedicated to the economic and cultural advancement of the Japanese farmer.

e. The Japanese Imperial Government is requested to submit, in addition to the above, such other proposals it deems necessary to guarantee to agriculture a share of the national income commensurate with its contribution.

13 **Prime Minister Yoshida on Agricultural Reform, 1945–52**[20] The reform of agriculture was another major objective of occupation policy. Viewed from the standpoint of the Allied powers, the Japanese land system was not only feudalistic but weakened the national economy while providing the militarists with one of their firmest bases of support. The agrarian half of the nation represented a reservoir of soldiers and cheap labor. Rural landlords impeded the democratization of Japan equally with the militarists, the financiers, and the bureaucracy. To end this state of affairs by liberating the agricultural classes and raising their living standards was, therefore, regarded by the occupation authorities as a vital step in bringing about the demilitarization and democratization of Japan. . . .

We had, indeed, anticipated that would be the case. The agricultural problem had been a major issue confronting successive Japanese Cabinets since the early years of the century. Furthermore, agricultural controls enforced during the Pacific War had the effect of placing small farmers in a specially favored position in the country, so that by 1945 the existing state of affairs, whatever the outward form might suggest, differed to a marked degree from what was widely imagined abroad from available textbooks on the subject. It was true that the change had been occasioned by the need to maintain the food supply during the period of hostilities. But the objective became even more pressing with the end of the war, so that Japan's agricultural system would in any event have had to be reconsidered in order to bring it closer in line with the actual situation.

That circumstance led to the passing of the first agricultural reforms at the time of the Shidehara Cabinet, when Mr. Matsumura Kenzō was minister of agriculture, and before any SCAP directive had been issued on the subject. The plan then prepared had been drawn up by Mr. Wada Hiroo, at that time director of agricultural administration and later minister of agriculture in my first Cabinet, and its two main points were the substitution of payment of farm rent in money, instead of in kind as previously, and the restriction of individual ownership of agricultural land to three *chō* (one *chō* being approximately 2.45 acres), beyond which amount the plan made it compulsory for landowners to turn over the land to the tenants, a revolutionary step at the time. . . .The plan was endorsed by the Cabinet after the limit of individual holdings had been raised from three to five *chō*. . . .

The bill embodying the Matsumura plan was introduced in the lower House

---

of the Diet on December 6, 1945, and, as was to be expected, met with stiff resistance. On December 11 a GHQ directive concerning agricultural land reform, dated December 9, was read to the House Committee to which the bill had been referred. This did not differ materially in content from the bill proposed by the government, but its wording—including a demand for the raising of the living standards of the Japanese farmers who had been "enslaved . . . for centuries of feudal oppression"—left no doubt as to the real intentions of GHQ. This document transformed the atmosphere in the Diet toward the government measure, and the bill passed both Houses with only slight modifications. . . .

The law based upon the Matsumura plan was promulgated before the end of 1945 and became effective from February 1946. That part of the measure dealing with the compulsory transfer of land was not enforced because General MacArthur's headquarters thought the provisions of the law on that point could be improved upon; wherefore landownership remained unchanged until the implementation of the second agricultural land reform.

Officially, GHQ was waiting for the Japanese government's reply to be submitted by March 15, 1946, but, unofficially, the occupation authorities had early indicated to the Ministry of Agriculture flaws which they had detected in the details of the first agricultural reform. These were made public for the first time at a press conference held by William J. Gilmartin and Wolf I. Ladjinsky, the experts within GHQ in charge of the reform, on March 12, 1946, just before the deadline fixed for the government's repay to SCAP, and consisted of two points: that the maximum holding of five *chō* was too large and would leave too many tenant farmers in the same position as before, and that, in order to ensure that land transfers were carried out and to shorten the period for this to be accomplished, the government itself should act as agent instead of transfers being direct between landlords and tenants. However, a general election had already been ordered at that time by a directive from GHQ, and Mr. Matsumura had in the meantime been purged from public office. . . .

General MacArthur next referred the question to the Allied Council for Japan. As a result of the deliberations of this body, agreement was for once reached between the American, British, Soviet, and Chinese representatives and their conclusions were submitted to General MacArthur on June 17. It seems that during the meetings both Mr. W. Macmahon Ball, the British Commonwealth's representative, and General Kuzma Derevyanko, representing the Soviet Union, presented individual plans, and the one finally adopted broadly followed the lines suggested by the British representative. . . .

The general election was held on April 10, 1946, as a result of which the Shidehara Cabinet resigned on April 22. By that time the food shortage had become acute and social unrest had grown. What was called "Food May Day" was held on May 19, following the usual May Day observance on May 1, and the political scene at the time appeared mainly composed of masses of red flags and demonstrations. In such an atmosphere, I found it a difficult matter to form my first Cabinet, but the appointment of Mr. Wada Hiroo as minister of agriculture finally completed the list of members, and the first Yoshida Cabinet came into being on May 22, with agricultural land reform now a matter of pressing importance.

The population in the rural districts had in the meantime remained relatively calm in the face of the mounting unrest in the cities and gave the impression of eyeing the burgeoning agitation in the urban areas with distrust and disapproval. One does not care to think what would have happened had events taken another course and if the farmers had made common cause with the city crowds. Again, if at that time the government had failed to carry out a thorough agricultural land reform, and aroused discontent in the rural areas, the result would have been incalculable. Fortunately Mr. Wada, the new minister of agriculture, had not only planned the first reform, but had been in charge of all subsequent negotiations with GHQ. . . .

The major points of the reform as finally agreed upon were that all agricultural land belonging to landowners who did not reside in the districts where the land was located, and which was being tilled solely by tenants, was to be transferred to the tenants; and that individual ownership of tenant land was to be limited to the average of one *chō* (four *chō* in Hokkaido); that the total amount of agricultural land to be owned individually, including tenant land, was to be limited to three *chō* (twelve *chō* in Hokkaido); that it was to be made compulsory for land beyond that limit to be sold to the government for resale to tenant farmers; and that payment to landowners for their requisitioned land was to be made in government bonds. A bill embodying these provisions was introduced into the Lower House of the Diet on September 7, 1946 and passed both Houses without amendment on October 11, 1946.

As a result of the outcome of the general election of April 1947, my first Cabinet resigned and power passed to the Socialists. The date for the completion of the transfer of farm land had been set for the end of 1948, and so when, after the terms in office of the Katayama and Ashida Cabinets, I came to form my second Cabinet in October 1948, the transfer operation was still incomplete. And as it was realized by all concerned that the redistribution of land was a permanent measure, and one to be conducted smoothly and efficiently, the completion date was postponed until July 1950.

The final result was that two million *chō* of agricultural land was requisitioned from some 1.5 million landowners and turned over to those who had previously been tenant farmers, numbering around four million persons. In addition to which operation, 450,000 *chō* of pasturage and 1,320,000 *chō* of uncultivated land were also disposed of in the same manner. Tenant-tilled land, which until that time had accounted for 46 percent of Japan's agricultural land, diminished to 10 percent. The tenant farmer practically ceased to exist, while the great landowners of the old days and absentee landlords passed into history.

The effects of such sweeping changes on Japan's agriculture as a whole are, of course, incalculable. The agricultural land reform was, in fact, a revolutionary measure, and to have carried it out without any major friction, and certainly without anything in the nature of serious disturbance or bloodshed, was an achievement that cannot be dismissed lightly, particularly when one remembers the unsettled state of the country at that time. The possible outbreak of such troubles had been feared by some during the deliberations on the reform bill in the Diet, but the event showed our apprehension to have been groundless.

There occurred, of course, a certain amount of confusion in some districts; there were bound to be details in the reform plans that were open to criticism. But no one can deny that the reform contributed immeasurably toward raising the standards of living of the agricultural classes, or that the effects this stabilization and improvement of life in the rural areas had on the social unrest in Japan as a whole were profound. This was one of the immediate benefits of the land reform. And when we think of what that fact saved us from, we should also remember at the same time the sacrifice paid by the landowners and their uncomplaining attitude throughout. . . .

Following the signing of the San Francisco Peace Treaty, there were those who demanded, and others who vaguely expected, that as the agricultural land reform had been enacted with the strong support and encouragement of the occupation authorities, some of its measures should be repealed. We decided, on the contrary, to incorporate the principles of the reform into the body of our national laws by combining them in one law, for which purpose a bill was introduced during the thirteenth session of the Diet held in 1952, while my third Cabinet was in office, under the title of the Agricultural Land Bill. This was passed by both Houses by an overwhelming majority, including the Socialists, and became law on July 15, 1952.

TOWARD ECONOMIC RECOVERY

Japan's economic recovery during the first three years of occupation was not insignificant, but the country was still plagued by rising prices and labor disputes. In July 1948, General MacArthur urged the Japanese government to commence an austerity program that was not well received by the minority coalition Cabinet headed by Ashida. The government changed hands on October 19 when Yoshida Shigeru formed his second Cabinet, but it proved to be equally recalcitrant. To strengthen General MacArthur's hand, on December 18 of the same year, the State and Army Departments issued a joint statement saying that General MacArthur would direct the Japanese government to carry out a program of economic stabilization (Document 14). Known to the Japanese as the "Nine Basic Economic Principles," it spearheaded some drastic economic reforms that were to follow, including the "Dodge budget" or "Dodge line" for the following fiscal year. It took its name from the Detroit banker who came to help implement the anti-inflationary economic measures. Government subsidies for key products, such as steel, coal, nonferrous metals, and fertilizer, were gradually and steadily reduced.

In 1948, the occupation of Japan was costing the United States about $450 million a year, not counting the actual expenditures for maintaining the occupation troops. By stabilizing the Japanese economy and boosting its production of export goods, it was hoped that the order would improve Japan's recovery and eventually reduce the cost to the United States of occupying Japan.

Domestically, the austerity budget forced a massive firing of government workers, including a large number of railway workers. Three incidents involving the Japanese National Railways, in which murder and sabotage were suspected, underscored the seriousness of these austerity measures.

One of the major features of the stabilization efforts was fixing the yen's exchange rate against the U.S. dollar at 360 yen to a dollar. This rate remained in effect until 1972.

14   SCAP Program for Economic Stabilization, 1948[21] The Departments of State and Army announced on December 18 that the supreme commander for the Allied powers will direct the Japanese Government to carry out an effective economic stabilization program calculated to achieve fiscal, monetary, price, and wage stability in Japan as rapidly as possible, as well as to maximize production for export. . . .

Economic stability is a most urgent requirement for assuring the continuation of Japan's economic recovery and ensuring the maximum effect from use of United States-appropriated funds. General MacArthur and responsible officials in Washington have been encouraged by the marked general recovery in Japanese industrial production through 1948 (with November at 62 percent of the 1930–34 average and 47 percent above a year ago) and by the anticipated increase in exports this year to about $260 million, 48 percent above 1947. General price and monetary inflation have continued, however, with the consumer price level and note issue increasing 60 percent over the period between November 1947 and November 1948. The retarding effects of this general and continuing inflation, together with the dangers to the gains already achieved, have made apparent the necessity for more resolute and intensive action by the Japanese.

Improvements in the Japanese general standard of living will be contingent on the degree to which the Japanese give wholehearted support to the achievement of economic stabilization and recovery. Their performance in carrying out their program will be weighed in connection with future requests for appropriated funds for Japan.

---

[21]*Department of State Bulletin* 20, no. 497 (January 9, 1949): p. 60.

Countries that are recipients of United States assistance under the Economic Cooperation Act of 1948 have also undertaken certain measures similar to those specified in this program. These include financial and monetary measures necessary to stabilize their currencies, to establish or maintain valid rates of exchange, to balance their budgets as soon as practicable, and generally to maintain confidence in their monetary system. The action in Japan is in line with the efforts of the United States in other parts of the world to contribute to general economic recovery.

The necessity for such a program was recognized by General MacArthur in July 1948 when he urged upon the Japanese Government a program that was substantially that which he has now directed they carry out. The specific objectives of the program are:

A. Achieving a true balance in the consolidated budget at the earliest possible date by stringent curtailing of expenditures and maximum expansion in total governmental revenues, including such new revenues as may be necessary and appropriate.

B. Accelerating and strengthening the program of tax collection and ensuring prompt, widespread, and vigorous criminal prosecution of tax evaders.

C. Assuring that credit extension is rigorously limited to those projects contributing to the economic recovery of Japan.

D. Establishing an effective program to achieve wage stability.

E. Strengthening and, if necessary, expanding the coverage of existing price-control programs.

F. Improving the operation of foreign trade controls and tightening existing foreign exchange controls, to the extent that such measures can appropriately be delegated to Japanese agencies.

G. Improving the effectiveness of the present allocation and rationing system, particularly to the end of maximizing exports.

H. Increasing production of all essential indigenous raw material and manufactured products.

I. Improving efficiency of the food-collection program.

[The above program must be implemented before steps can be taken toward an early establishment of a unified exchange rate for the Japanese currency.][22]

END OF THE AMERICAN OCCUPATION

The occupation of Japan officially came to an end when the Treaty of San Francisco (Document 15) took effect on April 28, 1952. The treaty, which was

---

[22]This provision is found in the version published in Japanese newspapers on December 19, 1948, but is missing from the version in the *Department of State Bulletin*. It is retranslated from the Japanese version.

signed on September 8, 1951, however, was not joined in by the Soviet Union, nor was either of the Chinas invited to the conference.[23]

A separate Security Treaty between the United States and Japan was signed, also on September 8, 1951, which granted to the United States the right to station its land, sea, and air forces in and about Japan, to be utilized for the maintenance of peace and security in East Asia (Document 16).

The treaties reflected the existing climate of the Cold War and left a long-lasting impact on the future conduct of Japan's domestic and foreign affairs.

Within less than two weeks after the coming into effect of the peace treaty, the Asahi newspapers conducted a public opinion survey to determine the reaction of the Japanese public. The survey was conducted on May 9, 10, and 11, and was published on May 17. It is reproduced as Document 17

15 Treaty of Peace, San Francisco, September 8, 1951[24]

Chapter I   PEACE

ARTICLE 6. (a) All occupation forces of the Allied powers shall be withdrawn from Japan as soon as possible after the coming into force of the present Treaty, and in any case not later than 90 days thereafter. Nothing in this provision shall, however, prevent the stationing or retention of foreign armed forces in Japanese territory under or in consequence of any bilateral or multilateral agreements which have been or may be made between one or more of the Allied powers, on the one hand, and Japan on the other. . . .

16 Security Treaty between the United States of America and Japan, 1951[25] Japan has signed a treaty of peace with the Allied powers. On the coming into force of that treaty, Japan will not have the effective means to exercise its inherent right of self-defense because it has been disarmed.

There is danger to Japan in this situation because irresponsible militarism has not yet been driven from the world. Therefore, Japan desires a security treaty

---

[23]Japan subsequently concluded a peace treaty with the National Government of China at Taipei on April 28, 1952. A joint "peace declaration" was signed in Moscow on October 19, 1956, but there has been no official peace treaty between Japan and the USSR or its successor, Russia. [As of September 1996 as this book goes to press.] On September 29, 1972 Japan signed a joint communiqué with the People's Republic of China that declared that the legal "state of war" was terminated. At that time, Japan's 1952 treaty with Taipei was nullified. A formal treaty between Beijing and Japan, "A Treaty of Peace and Friendship," was signed on August 12, 1978.

[24]Full text in Raymond Dennett and Katherine D. Durance, eds., *Documents on American Foreign Relations*, vol. IX, *1951* (Boston: World Peace Foundation, 1953), pp. 470–79.

[25]*Ibid.*, pp. 266–67.

with the United States of America to come into force simultaneously with the treaty of peace between Japan and the United States of America.

The treaty of peace recognizes that Japan as a sovereign nation has the right to enter into collective security arrangements, and further, the Charter of the United Nations recognizes that all nations possess an inherent right of individual and collective self-defense.

In exercise of the rights, Japan desires, as a provisional arrangement for its defense, that the United States of America should maintain armed forces of its own in and about Japan so as to deter armed attack upon Japan.

The United States of America, in the interest of peace and security, is at present willing to maintain certain of its armed forces in and about Japan, in the expectation, however, that Japan will itself increasingly assume responsibility for its own defense against direct and indirect aggression, always avoiding any armament which could be an offensive threat or serve other than to promote peace and security in accordance with the purposes and principles of the United Nations Charter.

Accordingly, the two countries have agreed as follows:

ARTICLE 1. Japan grants, and the United States of America accepts the right, upon the coming into force of the treaty of peace and of this treaty, to dispose United States land, air, and sea forces in and about Japan. Such forces may be utilized to contribute to the maintenance of international peace and security in the Far East and to the security of Japan against armed attack from without, including assistance given at the express request of the Japanese Government to put down large-scale internal riots and disturbances in Japan, caused through instigation or intervention by an outside power or powers.

ARTICLE 2. During the exercise of the right referred to in Article 1, Japan will not grant, without the prior consent of the United States of America, any bases or any rights, powers, or authority whatsoever, in or relating to bases or the right of garrison or of maneuver, or transit of ground, air, or naval forces to any third power.

ARTICLE 3. The conditions that shall govern the disposition of armed forces of the United States of America in and about Japan shall be determined by administrative agreements between the two Governments.

[Articles 4 and 5, and witness clauses omitted.]

17 Asahi Public Opinion Survey on Coming into Effect of Peace Treaty, 1952[26]

a. *Interest in the Peace Treaty.*

To determine how much interest people are showing to the coming into effect of the peace treaty, the following three questions were asked: "What day was

---

[26]Shimizu Kitarō, ed., *Shiryō Sengo Nijūnenshi*, vol. 5, *Shakai (Society)*, pp. 113–15.

April 28?" "Which one was the main country with whom the treaty was signed?" and "Which one was the major country with whom no peace treaty was signed?" Sixty-two percent of the respondents correctly answered that April 28 was the day when the peace treaty went into effect; 74 percent identified the United States as the main country with whom the treaty was signed, and 65 percent identified the Soviet Union as a major power with whom no peace treaty was signed.

b. *Reaction to the Coming into Effect of the Peace Treaty.*

Q. Do you think that as a result of the coming into effect of the peace treaty, Japan is now independent? or do you think that Japan is not independent?

Became independent	41%
Independent in name	32%
Not independent	8%
No opinion	19%

The number of people who thought that Japan regained her independence was slightly over 40 percent. At the same time, however, the number of those who felt that there was no independence or in name only reached 40 percent. When they were asked why they felt that way, they answered that "it was not concluded with all the powers," "Japan could not be economically autonomous," "Japanese politics could not exercise independence," and "there would remain on the Japanese soil foreign troops." These views comprised about one-half of the responses to this question.

The views toward "Japan's independence" showed no difference among sex or age groups. People of different educational levels did not show any noticeable difference in their views.

c. *Attitudes towards the Soviet Union and Communist China.*

Q 1: Do you think Japan should conclude a peace treaty with the Soviet Union, or in your opinion such a treaty need not be concluded?[27]

In favor of a peace treaty	54%
Not in favor of a peace treaty	20%
No opinion	26%

Q 2: Do you think the relations between Japan and Communist China can remain as they are or cannot remain the way they are?

---

[27]See footnote 28. A whopping 42 percent of the respondents came from the fishery and forestry group. Fishermen would stand to benefit from a treaty with the Soviet Union who presumably would be persuaded to allow Japanese fishing in its territorial waters. This distortion should be kept in mind in reading the survey results. Some pundits argue that major papers deliberately choose respondents in such a way that survey results would become consistent with their editorial policies. On the issue of press bias, see Chapter XVI, Document 6.

Can remain the way they are	11%
Cannot remain the way they are	57%
No opinion	32%

More than 70 percent of those who favored concluding a peace treaty cited the following as their reasons: to promote world peace; to avoid war against the Soviet Union; to achieve total, not partial peace; to end the state of war; and to enter into friendly relations with a neighboring country. On the other hand, there was a sizable number who, for the purpose of economic intercourse, wanted to conclude a peace treaty with the Soviet Union, citing that "quite aside from ideology, there ought to be the establishment of trade relations," or "reopen the fishing privileges for Japanese fishermen."

Among those who said that the relations should not remain as they are with regard to Communist China, a significant number actively expressed their desires to see restoration of trade relations with Communist China or to recognize its government. On the other hand, those who were satisfied with the status quo came to only about 10 percent. The most important single reason cited by this group was their anticommunism.

More men than women showed preference for a peace treaty with the Soviet Union. This was especially noticeable among those who were highly educated. A similar spread was found among those who favored changing the existing relations with China. . . .

d. *On the Occupation Policy.*

Q 1: During the period when Japan was under occupation, was there anything which SCAP or the Japanese government did, which in your opinion is good?

Yes	47%
No	14%
No opinion	39%

Q2: Was there anything they did, which you consider to be undesirable?

Yes	28%
No	26%
No opinion	46%

A far larger number of people gave positive evaluation of the occupation policies than those who gave negative evaluation. However, close to 40 percent of the people expressed no opinion. Those who held positive opinions were asked to give concrete examples. The result was the thorough manner in which democracy was promoted, 13 percent; land reform, 9 percent; imports of foodstuff, 7 percent; improvement of women's position, 6 percent; economic assistance, 4 percent; extension of compulsory education, 3 percent; and others, 13 percent. Discrepancy in the total percentage occurred because of the inclusion of more than one reply from the same respondent.

The sex and age breakdowns for those who responded positively are as follows: About 60 percent of all men cited some positive accomplishments of the occupation, and there was no significant spread between the old and young. Among the female respondents, only about 30 percent cited some positive accomplishments. About 40 percent of those in their twenties responded favorably, and the older they got, the rate of favorable response decreased. In the age sixty or older group, less than 20 percent responded favorably.

. . . Almost one-half of the people expressed no opinion on the occupation policies. About 30 percent of men and 60 percent of women belonged to this category. Among those who engaged in forestry, fishing, and industrial labor, about one-half responded with no opinion. Among the salaried workers, the ratio was 36 percent.

More concretely, those who felt the occupation was not desirable cited the following reasons: education reform, 4 percent; too much stress on freedom, 4 percent; land reform, 2 percent; high taxes, 25 percent; and miscellaneous, 17 percent. (More than one response from the same individual included in the compilation.) There was not a single issue that was considered by a large number of people to be undesirable.

e. *On the Continued Stationing of U.S. Troops.*

Q 1: U.S. troops are stationed in Japan even after the conclusion of the occupation. Why are they in Japan?

To protect Japan	21%
To guard against the USSR, Beijing, and other communist forces	18%
To maintain Japan's internal security	13%
Due to Japan's lack of defense power	11%
For the protection of the U.S. herself	4%
To place Japan under surveillance	3%
No opinion	30%

Q 2: Has the stationing of U.S. troops been requested by the Japanese government or by the American side?

By both parties, Japan and America	29%
By the American side	24%
By the Japanese government	21%
No opinion	26%

Q 3: Do you wish to see U.S. troops remain in Japan?

Yes, hope they remain	48%
No, hope they do not	20%
We have no choice, either way is fine	16%
No opinion	16%

By far the largest number of respondents cited "to protect Japan" as the reason for the stationing of U.S. troops. Those other reasons cited, such as "to guard against communist aggression," and "due to Japan's lack of defense power" were restatements of "to protect Japan."

The stationing of U.S. troops is inseparable from the issue of Japan's independence. Among those who felt that the troops were stationed for the protection of Japan, a little over half thought that Japan's independence was in name only. About 70 percent of those who replied that the troops were remaining in Japan "for the protection of the U.S. herself" thought that Japan was not independent. About 60 percent of men and slightly less than 40 percent of women thought the purpose of the stationing of troops was to "guard against aggression."

. . . About 40 percent of those who thought that the stationing of troops came about at the request of the Americans preferred that the troops did not remain in Japan. On the other hand, about 70 percent of those who thought that the stationing was effected at the request of the Japanese government expressed their desire for the continued stationing of the troops.[28]

Among the supporters of the Liberal Party and Progressive Party, 60 to 70 percent thought that the stationing was effected either at the request of the Japanese government or by the expressed desire of both the Japanese and American governments. Among the supporters of the Socialist Party, not too many respondents thought that the stationing was effected at the request of the Japanese government. About 70 percent of those who preferred continued stationing of troops in Japan recognized the lack of a peace treaty with the Soviet Union as one of the factors influencing them to take that view. About one-half of men and 40 percent of women preferred continued stationing of American troops. Those who did not prefer constituted about 20 percent of both men and women.

---

[28]As to the method of investigation, a random sample selection method was used throughout the country. From 365 areas across Japan, 3,000 people were selected for personal interview. Due to death, moving away, traveling, absence, or illness, 15.9 percent (477 people) were not interviewed. The rate of response was 84.1 percent (or 2,523 people). The sex, age, occupation, and educational level breakdowns are as follows: Sex: 1,236 men (49 percent); 1,287 women (51 percent). Age: in their 20s, 620 persons (25 percent); in their 30s, 579 persons (23 percent); in their 40s, 552 persons (22 percent); in their 50s, 405 persons (16 percent); 60 and over, 367 persons (14 percent). Occupation: in salaried positions, 402 (16 percent); industrial workers 496 (20 percent); commerce and industry, 489 (19 percent); forestry and fishing, 1,056 (42 percent); others, 80 (3 percent). Educational level: university, college of Higher School graduates, 133 (5 percent); middle school graduates, 517 (21 percent); grammar school graduates, 1,873 (74 percent). On possible bias in this survey, see footnote 27.

CHAPTER XVI

Politics and Problems of Security

Shortly after he retired as Japan's prime minister in 1972, Satō Eisaku (1901–1975) was asked what constituted his basic approach to foreign affairs. His response was simple and direct: "Historically whenever Japan took a path counter to the United States, the country suffered; and whenever the two countries worked together closely, Japan prospered. My policy therefore was to cooperate fully with the United States to ensure peace in the world." He also spoke of his admiration for John Foster Dulles (1889–1959), the late U.S. secretary of state, for concluding a nonpunitive peace treaty with Japan.[1]

The desire to work closely with the United States—based in part on enlightened self-interest for Japan and in part on the residue of goodwill toward the United States—characterized the basic foreign policy approach of the ruling Liberal Democratic party (LDP) at least for its first two decades. Before this policy could take hold, however, it had to meet several serious challenges. They came from the left and from "progressive" intellectuals who contended that Japan's close alignment with the United States would mean Japan's siding against the Soviet Union and the People's Republic of China in the Cold War.

The main focus of this chapter is the security treaty crisis of 1960, which was the culmination of a series of confrontations between the government composed of the LDP and its oppositions, with the Japan Socialist Party (JSP) taking the lead. Both the LDP and the JSP came into being through mergers in 1955, creating the so-called 1955 system, which lasted into 1993. This chapter begins

---

[1]Interview with this writer, August 17, 1972.

with a brief look at the formation of these two parties, followed by an examination of a conservative viewpoint articulated by Yoshida Shigeru, before entering into a full discussion of the security treaty crisis.

THE 1955 SYSTEM

In 1951, over the issue of whether or not Japan should conclude a partial peace treaty, the Socialist Party became divided into the right and left wings, each maintaining its separate existence and political agenda. They were, however, united in their opposition to the revision to the constitution proposed by the Hatoyama Cabinet. In the general election of February 1955, the left-wing Socialists gained eighty-nine seats and the right-wing Socialists, sixty-seven. A movement to reunite the party, to give it a voting bloc of 156 votes, gained momentum, and on October 13 the Japan Socialist Party was reunited. When the party was first formed in 1945, its leadership came primarily from the party's right wing. In the reunified party of 1955, the left wing was in the leadership position. The declaration for reunification (Document 1) reflects this changing posture of the JSP, as it became an ideologically charged and more combative party.

The same 1955 general election gave the Democratic Party 185 seats and the Liberal Party 112. Neither party commanded an absolute majority in the House of 467 members. Three years earlier, the four economic groups[2] had urged the two political parties to "discard petty differences for the greater common good, and act responsibly to establish a stable government." The implication of that message was not lost on the politicians. The two conservative parties were merged on November 15, 1955, to become the Liberal Democratic Party (Document 2). Its reign was uninterrupted until August 9, 1993, when an anti-LDP coalition government headed by Hosokawa Morihiro took office.

1   A Declaration on the Reunification of the Japan Socialist Party, 1955[3]

Workers across the nation, and comrades:

We have just accomplished the extraordinary task of reunifying the Japan Socialist Party amid attentions and expectations cast upon us both at home and from abroad. The Japan Socialist Party holds as its historical roles the attainment of peace and independence for Japan and the completion of a socialistic revolution. Today we are reborn with a new strength.

---

[2]They were: Keidanren (Federation of Economic Organizations), Keizai Dōyūkai (Japan Association of Corporate Executives), Nikkeiren (Japan Federation of Employers' Associations) and Nisshō (Japan Chamber of Commerce and Industry).

[3]Nakamura Naomi et. al., eds., *Shiryō Nihon Kin-Gendaishi (Documents on Modern and Contemporary Japanese History)*, vol. 3, *Sengo Nihon no Dōtei (Path of Postwar Japan)* (Tokyo: Sanseidō, 1985), pp. 136–37.

For a little over four years, the unfortunate split in our ranks allowed the conservative government to prevail. We were unable to do an adequate job of preventing the progress toward rearmament. Today we have succeeded in creating a system with which we can make a counterattack and an advance.

We deeply regret our past split. At the same time, we rejoice with all of you workers over the strengthening of our camp.

The world is changing. We are not blind to the dangers of war lurking behind, but the direction toward peace is firmly established. The voices of people wanting to be freed from the capitalistic oppression and enslavement are heard loud and clear from Asia and from Africa. These people are standing tall with a vigorous fighting spirit to protect their country's independence and peace and to fight for their own livelihood.

The reunification of the Japan Socialist Party is a catalyst to realize these national and international desires. The advances in the power of the progressive elements centered in the Japan Socialist Party are the very lights that will shine upon the future of Japan and of the world.

To respond to these desires, we must oppose any and all policies to promote war. We must do our utmost to obtain peace and preserve it. Today a war using hydrogen bombs will mean an end to all humanity. We must therefore prohibit the use of hydrogen bombs. We must decisively implement disarmament. We must fight to eradicate war from the face of this earth. This fight must begin with our strong opposition against our country's rearmament policy.

We also fight to protect the livelihood of the working masses. Our responsibilities are to protect the livelihood of all classes, including industrial workers, farmers, fishers, small and medium-size entrepreneurs and intellectuals, provide social security and secure jobs, health, and cultured life for all of them. Therefore we must oppose all reactionary policies and fight against any system that will enslave people under the capitalists.

We also know that the working people's ardent desire is to see Japan recover her complete independence. The Japanese people have traditionally relied on themselves to secure their independence. There is no reason whatsoever that we cannot obtain a complete independence through our own will and our own efforts. The reunified Japan Socialist Party shall become the vanguard for these working masses and work toward the recovery of our independence. . . .

Long live workers of Japan! Long live the Japan Socialist Party! . . .

2   Character of the Liberal Democratic Party, 1955[4]

1. *Our party is a national political party.*

Our party is not a class-based party that represents special interests of specific

---

[4]*Ibid.*, p. 132.

classes or strata whose actions may be divisive in the country. We are a political party that serves the interest and happiness of the entire nation. We work together with the people of this country to bring about prosperity for our people.

2. *Our party is a peace-loving party.*

Following the Charter of the United Nations, our party strives to secure peace and justice for the world and to bring about progress and advancement for mankind. These are the ardent goals expressed by our nation.

3. *Our party is a true democratic party.*

Our party respects and protects individual freedom, dignity of an individual and basic human rights, recognizing that securing of these rights is the motivating force in the advancement of mankind. We reject forces of communism and class-based socialism, which through the dictatorship of a certain class rob people's freedom and suppress human rights.

4. *Our party is a parliamentary party.*

Inasmuch as the parliamentary form of government represents the freely expressed will of the people in whom sovereignty resides, our party does its utmost to uphold it and work toward its further development. We are committed in our opposition to the totalitarianism of either the extreme right or extreme left, which rejects the existence of an opposition party and attempts to perpetuate a one-nation one-party rule.

5. *Our party is a progressive party.*

Our party rejects political goals that are accompanied by struggles and destructions. We uphold the spirit of cooperation and construction and move forward consistent with the requirements of our times while preserving the right tradition and order. We are a progressive party that actively engages in reforming the present and eliminating existing evil conditions.

6. *Our party is a party committed to the realization of a welfare state.*

Our party rejects the socialist economy based on nationalization of land and means of production accompanied by a bureaucratic control. At the same time, we also reject monopolistic capitalism. Our fundamental commitment is to free enterprise. We respect individual initiatives and responsibilities. We endow it with characteristics of a comprehensive planning to enhance production and vigorously implement social security policies. We work toward the realization of full employment and a welfare state.

A CONSERVATIVE VIEWPOINT

Yoshida Shigeru (1878–1967), as prime minister during and after the occupation, was one of the principal architects of Japan's postwar recovery. His political success was one of the key factors in the predominance of the conservative forces in Japanese politics.

In 1955, Yoshida retired to his villa in Ōiso to lead the life of an elder statesman. The following article (Document 3) was written in 1957 outlining his views on the U.S.–Japanese relations and on domestic politics. Except for his tirade against Hatoyama Ichirō (1883–1959), his former political mentor and benefactor, and later a rival who ousted him, the article generally describes the conservative philosophy adhered to by him and by his followers.

3 **Yoshida's Reflections on Japanese Politics, 1957**[5] British Prime Minister Macmillan said after the Bermuda conference in March 1957 that Britain and the United States had conducted their discussions "with the freedom and frankness permitted to old friends." One would hope that Japan and the United States could talk frankly and with such friendliness as well.

The United States policy toward Japan tends to be indecisive, a fact that I always regret. This irresolution gives rise to the so-called anti-American sentiment. For instance, the United States concluded a security pact with Japan presumably not only out of her fondness for Japan but also in consideration of her own national policy and her strategic needs in the Pacific. Japan also accepted the pact for her own protection as well as in the interests of her national policy. In these circumstances, would it not be sensible for the two nations to discuss various issues in a more straightforward manner? . . .

During the period immediately after the war, America sent a considerable amount of relief materials to Japan, such as food and clothing, and the Japanese were grateful because, thanks to that aid, they were able to ward off starvation. The Japanese are still grateful, but anti-American impulses are encouraged because of this feeling that the United States aid policy is half-hearted.

Hasn't the United States been irresolute and indecisive in her policy toward Japan? Was she ever quite sure of what she was doing? There is little doubt about America's good intentions, but on occasions when she should have taken a definite attitude, she tended to vacillate. For instance, if America judged that the foreign policy of the Hatoyama Cabinet was wrong, she should have said so firmly and uncompromisingly from her feeling of friendship for Japan as well as from the standpoint of her own policy.

---

[5]Yoshida Shigeru, *Random Thoughts from Ōiso* (Tokyo: Sekkasha, 1962), pp. 9–16. First appeared in *This Is Japan,* No. 5, 1958, copyright 1957 by the Asahi Shimbun Publishing Company.

Irresolution seems to pervade United States foreign aid policy as a whole. Many of the actions taken by the United States give the impression that she is wanting in knowledge and assurance. Take, for instance, her aid policy toward the Southeast Asian countries. Unless she has a thorough knowledge of the conditions in that part of the world, the costly aid she gives may mean no more than "throwing a piece of gold to a cat." That cat does not know how to make use of the gold. What it needs is fish. Now, it appears sometimes that Washington is trying to force a guinea piece on the cat for the reason that gold has more value than fish. If America earnestly desires to bring prosperity and higher living standards to that area and to protect it from communist infiltration, she should above all consult with Japan, who is most familiar with conditions in that region, use Japan's profound knowledge, and work out an aid policy in cooperation with Japan. The development of Southeast Asia is a vital issue to Japan. Since the door to China is now virtually closed, Japan is seeking to obtain her food and raw materials from Southeast Asia. America should make use of Japan's needs because, in doing so, she could carry out her own plans more economically, and the recipients of the aid would be getting what they need.

According to the Marxist theorists, the capitalist world is supposed to collapse because of its own inherent defects. But, in my opinion, it is the communist countries themselves that must disintegrate. There are examples before our eyes. The living standard is still low in countries like Poland and Hungary, and this was the real cause of the uprisings. The communist system is one that can exist only in impoverished countries. When the shortage in the necessities of life goes beyond a certain limit, the system loses its power. It is said that the number of communist party members in West Germany is already decreasing. In any event, communism finds its existence only at a certain degree of poverty. Poverty beyond that degree provokes rebellions against communism to its natural death. Aren't these phenomena actually now taking place? The nations of the free world should raise their voices louder in pointing out these facts.

Communist China looms as a major problem in Japan's foreign policy of the future because the Chinese continent must be opened to Japan for trade. Japan must import raw materials from that continent, which will be, at the same time, an important market for middle and small enterprises of this country. When the door to China is opened, Japan's rehabilitation will be further enhanced. I think that the United States should adopt a policy that will eventually bring trade and prosperity to China, and, instead of just trying to block her trade, help the Chinese people to understand that free trade is more profitable than communism. The Chinese have an instinctive understanding of a philosophy which teaches that free trade is a paying proposition.

Communist China and the Soviet Union form the axis of the communist countries. Free countries should think more seriously about finding means to separate these two. Britain seems to understand this. The United States and other free countries should also give thought to concrete steps in the same direction. . . .

Now, let us turn our eyes to the political situation within Japan. At present, there is political stability of a sort, with the Liberal Democratic Party, headed by Prime Minister Kishi, enjoying an absolute majority in the national Diet. It must be remembered, however, that Mr. Kishi is still new in his dual position of prime minister and president of the party. Under these circumstances, party leaders should join their efforts in his support. Any action within the party that, in effect, hampers or discourages his activities should be regarded as most undemocratic. He will gain in self-confidence and decision if he is enabled to carry out important work in domestic and foreign policies by loyal and disinterested cooperation of all party members. With the liquidation of intraparty strife, the ability of those who help will also develop.

It is not desirable for a well-ordered conservative party to appoint its president by vote. A decision as to who will be president should come about naturally, logically, even automatically. In the Liberal Democratic Party, one can expect that the status of each of the members will be gradually established in the course of their cooperation with the party chief, and the appointment of a successor will thus come about of its own accord.

A few words about the Japan Socialists' talk about setting up a welfare state, and in their platform planks vigorously upholding social reform. So far, so good. But noting the strong influence of the Sōhyō (General Council of Trade Unions of Japan) and its constant involvement in strikes and wage-raising campaigns, and recalling the party's irrelevant call for the opening of diplomatic relations between Japan and Communist China despite its condemnation of communism, the detached observer gains the impression that the Socialist Party's only aim is to gain power by any means, and without any real concern for the nation's interest. As long as the Socialists are preoccupied with these motivations, the possibility of their gaining political power in the near future is slight. nor does such a party deserve to gain office.

The Japanese nation does not comprise only the working class. A responsible government must think in terms of the Japanese people as a whole. A class party is not worthy of government powers. I earnestly hope that the Socialists become more prudent and farsighted and responsible.

Japan's economic revival during recent years has been phenomenal. What other country in the world with less than ten years of independence after the end of the war has shown such rehabilitation?

Some time ago, I happened to be passing through a main thoroughfare running from Ueno to Shimbashi in Tokyo. I noticed that all those areas along the road that were in ruins at the end of the war were now lined with handsome new buildings, and there was not a trace of war to be seen. Goods displayed in the shops, ranging from those in daily use to very highly priced ones, were rich in variety, quantity, and quality. Motor traffic exceeded that of London and Paris. The crowd in the street was still larger.

I cannot help feeling happy in the thought that this prosperity was brought

about by the ability and industry of the Japanese people. They should be confident of their inborn qualities and be determined to continue their efforts for the
further prosperity of their own country and the peace of the whole world.

SECURITY TREATY CRISIS OF 1960

*The revised security treaty of 1960 between Japan and the United States con-
tained a provision pledging mutual consultation (Article 4) and an exchange of
notes that obligated the parties to prior consultation with regard to major
changes in the U.S. military deployment (Document 4b). Its terms were more
favorable toward Japan than the one it was to replace (Chapter XV, Document
16). Confident that he could count on public support, Prime Minister Kishi
Nobusuke (1896–1987) vigorously pursued its ratification.[6] However, a series of
protest demonstrations broke out in Tokyo that resulted in the cancellation of
President Eisenhower's state visit, which would have been the first by a sitting
American president. An assassination attempt on Kishi was followed by his
resignation as prime minister.*

*A variety of factors contributed to the crisis. Among them were internal
factional struggles within the ruling Liberal Democratic Party, and uncompro-
mising delaying tactics employed by the opposition Socialist Party. The latter
saw in the security treaty a viable political issue. They were supported in their
opposition by a People's Council for Preventing Revision of the Security Treaty.
Organized on March 28, 1959, the council included among its thirteen original
sponsors the Japan Socialist Party, Sōhyō, and a number of pro-Communist
"peace groups" (see Document 5). Eventually the Japan Communist Party
joined these thirteen as an observer on the board of directors of the council and
exercised an all-pervasive influence over the activities of the council along with
the Japan Socialist Party and Sōhyō. The council was committed to a policy of
absolute opposition to the treaty, and left no room for compromise, thus setting
the stage for the 1960 confrontation.*

*The press was critical of the government and of the treaty. The Asahi,
Japan's leading daily, for example, implored the government to limit the purpose
of U.S. bases in Article 4 to the maintenance of Japan's security only, and*

---

[6]The revised treaty was signed in Washington on January 18, 1960. Prior to that, on
October 9, the government conducted a public opinion survey on the treaty revision. The
results were: 15 percent for, 10 percent against, 25 percent no opinion, and 50 percent did
not know what it was all about. This 50 percent was a "silent majority," which Mr. Kishi
felt he could persuade. At the time this public opinion survey was taken, most protest
movements hardly had any impact on public opinion. See Kishi Nobusuke et. al, *Kishi
Nobusuke no Kaisō (Reminiscences of Kishi Nobusuke)* (Tokyo: Bungei Shunjū sha,
1981), p. 237.

*charged the government for its "insincerity" and the "dictatorship of the major-
ity." When the foreign press became critical of the Japanese press on their
biased handling of the matter, the* Asahi *found it necessary to issue a reply,
which is reproduced as Document 6.*

*Among the "moderates" who spoke out against the treaty was one Nishi
Haruhiko, a retired career diplomat who was vice minister of foreign affairs at
the time of the Pearl Harbor attack, and in postwar years served as ambassador
to Great Britain. Drawing on his experience while serving in the Moscow Embassy, Nishi argued that Japan should not voluntarily enter into a treaty that
would hamper a successful peace treaty negotiation with the Societ Union. He
would have preferred continuation of the old treaty to which Japan did not enter
of her own free will. Nishi's opinion, reproduced as Document 7, must be read in
light of the frequent Soviet missile test firings into the Pacific in 1960, which
crossed the airspace of Japan before reaching their targets.*

*Excerpts from the treaty and the first exchange of notes are reproduced as
Document 4.*

4   Treaty of Mutual Cooperation and Security, 1960[7]

(a) Excerpts from the Treaty

ARTICLE 2. The Parties will contribute toward the further development of
peaceful and friendly international relations by strengthening their free institutions, by bringing about a better understanding of the principles upon which
these institutions are founded, and by promoting conditions of stability and well-
being. They will seek to eliminate conflict in their international economic policies and will encourage collaboration between them.

ARTICLE 3. The Parties, individually and in cooperation with each other, by
means of continuous and effective self-help and mutual aid, will maintain and
develop, subject to their constitutional provisions, their capacities to resist armed
attack.

ARTICLE 4. The Parties will consult together from time to time regarding
the implementation of this Treaty, and, at the request of either Party, whenever
the security of Japan or international peace and security in the Far East is threatened.

ARTICLE 5 Each Party recognizes that an armed attack against either Party
in the territories under the administration of Japan would be dangerous to its own
peace and safety and declares that it would act to meet the common danger in
accordance with its constitutional provisions and processes.

Any such armed attack and all measures taken as a result thereof shall be

[7]U.S. Department of State, *United States Treaties and Other International Agreements,*
vol. 2., pt. 2 (Washington: Government Printing Office, 1961), pp. 1633–35.

immediately reported to the Security Council of the United Nations in accordance with the provisions of Article 51 of the Charter. Such measures shall be terminated when the Security Council has taken the measures necessary to restore and maintain international peace and security.

ARTICLE 6. For the purposes of contributing to the security of Japan and the maintenance of international peace and security in the Far East, the United States of America is granted the use by its land, air and naval forces of facilities and areas in Japan. . . .

(b) Exchanges of Notes between Prime Minister Kishi Nobusuke
and Secretary of State Christian Herter (January 19, 1960)

. . . the following is the understanding of the Government of Japan concerning the implementation of Article VI thereof:

Major changes in the deployment into Japan of United States forces, major changes in their equipment, and the use of facilities and areas in Japan as bases for military combat operations to be undertaken from Japan other than those conducted under Article V of the said Treaty, shall be the subjects of prior consultation with the Government of Japan.

5 Formation of the People's Council for Preventing Revision of the Security Treaty, 1959[8] Through the Japan–U.S. security treaty and accompanying administrative and mutual security agreements, Japan has allowed American troops to be stationed on Japanese soil and provided military bases for them.

During this period, the Korean War and conflicts over the Taiwan strait occurred. These bases have thus become American outposts, and Japan has become a participant in these conflicts.

We are heavily burdened with fear when we see these bases, which were once maintained for the purpose of protecting us, being transformed into military outposts for attack.

When we protested against Sunakawa and other military bases, the Japanese government mobilized its police forces and let their sticks rain over farmers, workers, and students who were guarding their own land. The government willingly sacrificed the demands and interests of the Japanese people in order to follow faithfully the policy of the United States.

Through these variegated experiences, we have learned that the Japan–U.S. security treaty has obligated Japan to "restrict her independence and become a participant in conflicts without the knowledge of her people." Realization of that cold reality has been the motivating force in our continuing fight for its repeal.

Now the government is attempting to revise this treaty. The revision is not for

---

[8]Tsuji Kiyoaki, *Shiryō Sengo Nijūnenshi (Sources on the History of the Two Decades after the War)*, vol. 1, *Seiji (Politics)* (Tokyo: Nihon Hyōronsha, 1966), pp. 144–45.

the purpose of its repeal, but for the purpose of strengthening its provisions. With this revision, Japan will be obligated to engage in joint defense and will be asked to expand and strengthen the Self-Defense Forces and to begin her own nuclear armament. Japan may become an ally of South Korea and Taiwan and willingly supply military bases for attacking China and the Soviet Union. It means denial of our constitution and destruction of the bases of peace and democracy. These are serious matters, which will impact adversely on the destiny and future of Japan and of her people.

Let us not forget that irresponsible militarism and military alliances once led us into a path of war against China and other nations of Asia. It was done against the will of our people and forced us to suffer great miseries.

The path that the Kishi Cabinet is about to take is too similar to the path that we once trod.

We unequivocally oppose the revision of the security treaty, which will only endanger peace and democracy in Japan and destroy the lives of her people.

We believe that Japan's security can be obtained by not joining any military bloc, by holding fast to the position of independence, and by steadfastly maintaining a positive foreign policy of neutralism.

These can be implemented by adhering strictly to the peace constitution without making any deviation.

People of Japan!

To realize these goals, we have formed "The People's Council for Preventing Revision of the Security Treaty" to serve as an organ for our common struggle.

We hope all types of organizations all over the country will join this People's Council. Let us utilize the power of the people, which defeated the regressive revision of the Police Duties Performance Law. Let us stand up to be counted and work for "the abrogation of the security treaty and prevention of its revision."

Hark, peace-loving organizations all over the country!

The Central People's Council will hold its organization meeting on March 28.

Organize similar regional meetings in all localities with all political parties and organizations that demand abrogation of the security treaty and are against its revision. Let us work together to alert the people and develop this into a people's movement.

Let us work closely with scholars and intellectuals. Let us move our struggles constantly forward.

All the workers!

You may maintain an illusion that the security treaty and your workplace have nothing to do with each other.

However, you must be well aware that the policies of the government and monopoly capital—which suppress unions' organization activities, which insist on evaluation of teachers' work, and which fire workers in the name of rationalization—are manifestations of the same policies that are at work in trying to restore militarism.

If the working class does not rise up to prevent these policies, the Kishi Cabinet will be able to implement those warlike policies without resistance. Please hold study group meetings at once at your workplace. Make the general assembly of workers to be held on April 15 as the starting point and obtain a clear-cut consensus of our determination and resolve.

Stand up in the same manner as we once stood up against the regressive revision of the Police Duties Performance Law. Let us use our power to prevent the signing of the revised treaty.

The struggles that the working class wages with confidence will sustain the hearts of the people.

> The Japan Socialist Party; National Federation of Farmers' Unions; National Federation for Safeguarding the Constitution; Japan Peace Committee; Japan Council against Atomic and Hydrogen Bombs (Gensuikyō); Japan-China Friendship Association; People's Council for Restoration of Diplomatic Relations between Japan and China; Women's Council for Safeguarding Human Rights; National Liaison Council against Military Bases; Joint Struggle Council of Youths and Students: General Council of Trade Unions of Japan (Sōhyō); Tokyo Joint Struggle Council for Safeguarding Peace and Democracy; and National Liaison Council of Neutral Labor Union.

6 **"Free Press Gone Wrong?"—Time vs. Asahi, 1960**[9] the two-month upheaval in Japan over the approval by the Diet of the new U.S.-Japan Security Treaty was not easy to analyze correctly, even for those observers who watched it close at hand. The onlooker who dismisses it as an antigovernment campaign—perhaps the fiercest since the war—due to the activities of international communism does not, of course, need to analyze at all.

The background to the movement, however, was too complex for any such simple view of the matter. In discussing the confused situation at the time, many foreign newspapers tended to focus only on the physical skirmishes—the "Battle of Tokyo," as they were referred to. While recognizing a certain inevitability in this, we in Japan could not help feeling a deep concern at the impression the sensational reporting of this kind might create abroad.

At the same time, it became clear after a certain period had elapsed that, as might be expected, there were also some foreign journalists who, with excellent insight, saw what underlay the chaos. The *Christian Science Monitor,* for one, declared that the disturbances that led to the cancellation of President Eisenhower's visit to Japan were "no more than the surface manifestation of

---

[9]Shimada Tatsumi, "Free Press Gone Wrong?" *Japan Quarterly* 7, no. 4 (October–December 1960): 417–21. The *Japan Quarterly* is a publication of the Asahi Newspaper Company. On the role played by the mass media, see George R. Packard III, *Protest in Tokyo: The Security Treaty Crisis of 1960* (Princeton: Princeton University Press, 1966), pp. 278ff.

deep-rooted problems." The heart of the question, it suggested, "is the passivity, not to say the pacifism, of the Japanese people."[10] And it proceeds to examine Japanese pacifism from many different angles.

Walter Lippman, on the other hand, issues a stern warning concerning America's policies in the Far East: "The cancellation of President Eisenhower's visit to Japan, and his embarrassing experience in Okinawa, stem from the refusal in Washington to look squarely at the U-2 affair and its significance." Here is the kind of observation one might expect from an expert. Mr. Lippmann also has this to say on the subject:

"There is no use deluding ourselves, as Hagerty does, that the opposition to the President's visit was confined to a small minority of Communists incited and paid for by Peking (Beijing) and Moscow. The preponderant opinion of any Asian country within the military reach of Russia and China is bound to be neutralist. When we urge them to be anti-neutralist, they respond by being anti-American, and it is a great error to act as if an anti-neutralist policy can rally popular support."[11]

Here is an appropriate comeback to those shortsighted people, including former Prime Minister Kishi himself, who facilely attributed everything to "the plotting of international Communism."

We are not, of course, so simple that we gratefully swallow whole the "tributes" that the confusion in Japan evoked from the communist countries. We are quite well aware also that the nature of the upheaval was not such as to permit facile criticism from outside countries. It was, perhaps, those countries of the West, which, unlike the United States, had no direct interest in the affair that made the fairest comments; those made in Britain were particularly worthy of attention.

However, the most intolerable of all the criticisms, made in foreign countries, particularly to those of us in the newspaper world, was the utterly wrong-headed argument that put the blame for the chaos on the Japanese press. The worst offender here was the magazine *Time*. In its column on press affairs, it singled out three newspapers—the *Asahi,* the *Mainichi* and the *Yomiuri*—for a startling and utterly unfounded attack.[12] The *Time* column was reprinted by certain minor newspapers in the United States, one of which makes the following sweeping misinterpretation:

"The Japanese press was responsible to a large degree for the violence which blocked President Eisenhower's visit."[13]

The sudden proposal from Japan's side that President Eisenhower's visit

---

[10]*Christian Science Monitor,* June 23, 1960.
[11]"Trouble in Japan," *New York Herald Tribune,* June 22, 1960. Mr. Hagerty was President Eisenhower's press secretary.
[12]*Time,* June 27, 1960.
[13]*Burlington Free Press,* June 24, 1960.

should be canceled was, one can well imagine, exasperating to public opinion in the United States. Even so, it is quite impossible to fall in with the view that all the responsibility for bringing things to such a pass lay on Japan's side. This view is, to begin with, completely at variance with the facts. To prove this it is necessary here to put forward our own standpoint on the various arguments advanced against the Japanese press by *Time* and other sources. Since the present writer is a lead writer for the *Asahi Shimbun,* he will perhaps be forgiven for drawing on that paper's pages for most of his evidence.

(1) Under the heading "Free Press Gone Wrong" *Time* deals with the joint declaration made on June 17 by seven Tokyo newspapers, in which they appealed for the rejection of violence and the safeguarding of parliamentarism. According to *Time*:

"Such sentiments were admirable—except for one thing. As much as any other agency, the Japanese press was responsible for the very violence that it now, all so suddenly, came to condemn."

In other words, the Japanese press stirred up trouble for all it was worth, then got frightened and switched to trying to calm it down again. A few quotes from the *Asahi* alone will be sufficient to show the foolishness of the idea that the press instigated violence. As early as May 22—immediately after the trouble in the Diet on the night of May 19–20 and before any violence on a large scale had erupted—the *Asahi Shimbun* issued an editorial warning against excesses in demonstrations. Again, on May 26, it called for "Self-Restraint" and "Moderation in Demonstrations."

"Demonstrations are an expression of the will of the people. But they should be carried out without excessive emotion and in decent, orderly fashion; the slightest suspicion of violence is impermissible. What good can it do to break into the prime minister's official residence? Such behavior, it must be realized, may well have the reverse effect of that intended."

It should also be noted that the *Asahi*, in its editorial of May 28, calls on the Socialist Party also to exercise self-restraint:

"The immediate problem, in short, is to rescue parliamentary democracy from the peril in which it now stands. It would be deplorable if the masses, by the excesses of their own actions, provided a pretext for others to oppress them. For this reason, the Socialist Party, as the opposition party, is wrong to exult over the size of the demonstrations without doing anything to restrain them. It ought, rather, to feel responsible for those very excesses just mentioned."

Yet again, in an editorial on the morning of June 10—the day that Mr. Hagerty arrived in Tokyo—the *Asahi Shimbun* warned against excesses in any demonstration directed at him. Despite this, an unfortunate incident occurred, and the next morning its editorial criticized the violent discourtesy done Mr. Hagerty as "an incident harmful to the national reputation."

The foregoing examples are surely sufficient to disprove the criticism that the Japanese press fanned the flames of violence.

(2) *Time* further criticizes the *Asahi* for allegedly describing as "a dictatorship of the majority" the Liberal Democratic Party's action in forcing the revised Security Treaty through the Lower House during May 19–21, when the vote was, in fact, a majority vote by the government party. According to *Time*:

"*Asahi* called the action 'a dictatorship of the majority' [and] provocatively suggested that violence was the only appropriate response."

This complete perversion of the facts deserves a particularly strong protest. Dealing editorially on May 21 with the situation in the Diet during the period May 19–21, the *Asahi* stated quite plainly that the Socialist Party's Diet tactics "had included what it calls a "resort to force.' This is not parliamentary government." It went on to stress that "the Diet is not an arena for scoring victories over the other side. Even less is it a battlefield." The most careful debate, it stressed, must be given the revising of the Security Treaty, and to make this possible the Diet session must be extended. The phrase "dictatorship of the majority"—paradoxical in a supposed parliamentary democracy—was not used by the *Asahi* itself. The *Asahi*, in fact, was critical of the phrase, and the facts are, rather, the reverse of what *Time* claimed.

"Rule by the majority," the *Asahi* says in the same editorial, "is a natural part of parliamentary government. The majority, however, must be that majority that decides for or against an issue after every possible argument has been put forward on both sides. Provided it is agreed that discussion will go on till the last possible moment, there can be no such thing as a 'dictatorship of the majority.' It is because the government party tries to cut short deliberation and debate and to decide things according to a proportion of votes fixed from the beginning that the odd phrase 'dictatorship of the majority,' a phrase peculiar to Japan, had put in an appearance."

This quotation, I believe, should immediately make it plain that the *Asahi* did not, as *Time* claims, label the actions of the Liberal Democratic Party as "violence," or "provocatively suggest" that violence could only be met with violence. At the end of its article, in fact, the *Asahi* takes, rather, the opposite stand. "Any unwise action by Prime Minister Kishi," it points out, "might cause fresh outbreaks of violence in the vicinity of the Diet, which could only serve to aggravate the situation still further. The life and death of parliamentary democracy in Japan is, we believe, at stake."

It is worth mentioning here that the *Asahi* editorial that was put in print on the afternoon of May 19—before any trouble had started—and that was specially shifted from its normal position to a conspicuous place on the front page, made an appeal to those concerned "to save parliamentary government." The forced vote on the Security Treaty had not yet taken place, and the prospects were that there would be a clash between the government and opposition parties in the Diet around the twenty-fourth of that month. The article, the main aim of which was to prevent such a clash, appealed to the Liberal Democratic Party not to rely on its majority to cut debate short and force a vote, and to the Socialist Party to give up any idea of resorting to force in the Diet. Contrary to expectation, however, the Diet was thrown into confusion without warning on the night of that same day. This was the very thing the editorial had tried to prevent, but since the next morning's paper would carry stories on the confusion in the Diet and the forced vote, its warnings had become meaningless, and the *Asahi* had reluctantly decided to remove it from the city edition that appeared the next morning. What happened here should in itself be enough to make the *Asahi*'s intentions evident.

(3) Again, *Time* declares that Japan's newspapers are constantly attacking the government and quotes a "leading Tokyo editor" as saying: "We would similarly attack any government, including a Socialist one; it is the duty of the press to be antigovernment."

People from countries where political party newspapers have a strong influence, or whose newspapers have grown up out of the advertising business, seem to find the position of Japan's newspapers difficult to comprehend. Most of Japan's newspapers today proclaim themselves to be completely independent. Besides criticizing the actions of the government, they also reserve the right to criticize the opposition party at any time. It is inevitable that, since a conservative government is at present in power, it should, as the body chiefly responsible for governing the country, be subject to more criticism from the newspapers than the opposition party. Even so, the newspapers are constantly making complaints to the Socialist Party also—not only concerning its political views but also its relationship with Sōhyō and other labor unions supporting it. Nor should it be forgotten that, in the matter of revising the U.S.–Japan Security Treaty as in other cases, the newspapers have constantly strongly criticized the intransigence of the Socialist Party in opposing from the outset all ideas of revision.

Time also claims that the owners of Japan's leading newspapers, while in fact supporting the conservative forces, "are journalistic eunuchs, interested mainly in profit, who have literally surrendered their papers to the hundreds of young liberal 'intellectuals' in Japanese newsrooms." That this piece of excessive discourtesy is false is well known to all foreign journalists who have spent any length of time in Japan.

Perhaps an excessive amount of space has been devoted here to the views of *Time.* However, it is impossible for anyone concerned in the Japanese press to let such mistaken ideas pass uncorrected. That a magazine like *Time,* which since the end of the war has had an office in Tokyo and a capable staff presumably well versed in Japanese affairs, should still report in this fashion, influencing untold numbers of foreign readers, brings home to one with peculiar force the difficulties and importance of international reporting.

7   On the Revision of the Japan–U.S. Security Treaty, 1960[14] It seems
clear that the ruling Liberal Democratic Party is ready to reach a decision on the

---

[14]An opinion submitted to Prime Minister Kishi and Foreign Minister Fujiyama by Nishi Haruhiko, as contained in his *Kaisō no Nihongaikō (Reminiscences on Japanese Diplomacy)* (Tokyo: Iwanami Shoten, 1965), pp. 183–89.

policy with regard to the revision of the Japan–U.S. Security Treaty. There has been a great deal of discussion from different viewpoints on the Security Treaty revision in the Diet and elsewhere. However, the government has not elaborated on what should be the major points requiring revision, nor has it indicated how the revision will be effected. The debates in the Diet fail to give any further clarification. If the demands of the two nations can be met even in a small degree through this revision, it is to be welcomed. However, we must further investigate one problem, namely, whether or not the international situations surrounding Japan today can permit her to effect a treaty revision without hindrance.

From this standpoint, I wish to treat the problem of our relations with the Soviet Union and Communist China. This is the problem often neglected. I wish to deal with it from the perspectives obtained through my personal experience. I hope not only the Japanese government but also the U.S. government, the other party to the negotiation, will take heed to what I shall discuss here.

If I may be permitted to give my conclusion first, I consider the proposed Security Treaty revision to contain enormous danger for our country when viewed from the perspective of our relations with the Soviet Union and China. Why is this so?

The Soviet Union has steadfastly maintained that the Security Treaty was imposed on powerless Japan by the United States at the time of the conclusion of the peace treaty. She has not condemned Japan on this account. However, the proposed revision of the pact will be carried out by the free will of Japan. Even if the revised treaty would contain the result of negotiations conducted in the spirit of give and take between Japan and the United States, it would be Japan who would be signing and ratifying the treaty. We must be prepared to face a protest coming from the Soviet Union and Communist China. Unless we are prepared to face this, we cannot begin negotiating for the treaty revision. It goes without saying that the Soviet Union and Communist China will hold Japan responsible for all the provisions of the treaty, not just those articles that are being revised.

Setting aside the question of whether or not Okinawa and the Bonin islands should be placed under the application of the treaty, the problem that concerns me most is the fact that U.S. soldiers can embark from bases located within Japan. As it has been reported, after the treaty revision, consultation with or consent of the Japanese government will be required in this matter, and thus the American military's freedom of action will be somewhat more restricted than before. However, within the limitation thus set on the action of the American military, Japan will become equally responsible in that she is party to the American action. In this sense there is potentially a great danger. For example, if the crisis over Quemoy and Matsu[15] of last year is revived, or the situation governing North and South Korea becomes worsened, it is conceivable that the Ameri-

---

[15]Quemoy and Matsu are islands off the shores of the Fujian province of China still held by Taiwan.

can military will adopt a far stronger military measure to cope with the situation. And in this connection if American soldiers must take off from bases in Japan, we must be prepared to face a charge of joint responsibility in the military action that can be levied against us from the Soviet Union and Communist China. I need not go into detail in describing the gravity of the possible consequences. It is said that after the revision of the Security Treaty, all actions will be in principle taken in accordance with the Charter of the United Nations or with its resolutions, and thus we need not be unduly concerned about such a problem. But in reality the experience of the Korean War teaches us that the Soviet Union consistently supported the positions of North Korea and Communist China in defiance of UN resolutions.

I cannot forget the bitter experience of having to serve in the Moscow Embassy immediately after the conclusion of the Japan-Germany Anti-Comintern Pact. Ironically, Ambassador Shigemitsu [Mamoru, 1887–1957] arrived in Moscow on the very day the pact was concluded in Berlin, namely, November 25, 1936. With the conclusion of this pact, the Soviet Union treated Japan and Germany as hypothetical enemies and placed restrictions on our interests in a manner similar to a country that had broken off diplomatic relations.

As a first step, the Soviet government refused to sign a revised Russo-Japanese fishery agreement that was ready for signature. Thereafter we had to negotiate and conclude a temporary fishery agreement each year in order to make the best out of the difficult situation. . . . Many Japanese employees working for oil and coal concessions in northern Sakhalin were jailed under the pretexts of either violating minor provisions of the concessions agreement or having engaged in espionage. Whenever equipment was needed for maintaining the work of the concessions, the Soviet government delayed and delayed the issuance of import license, and in this manner the Japanese enterprises had to curtail their activities, resulting in a serious loss of profit.

International relations have changed very drastically since that time, but the conflict between the East and West has not been dissolved. The Soviet Union warns its neighboring nations each time the latter enter into military and political agreements with the United States and Great Britain. On this matter of our Security Treaty revision, the Soviet Union has already issued a very serious warning. However, some people argue that the Soviet Union issues such warnings to other nations as well, and thus we need not be overly concerned with it. Well is it not too much of a self-deception?

To treat a warning by the Soviet Union as a mere bluff is to ignore the lessons of history. The Soviet Union has not forgotten that during the Second World War, Japan aligned herself with Germany and that the Soviet Union suffered under that alliance. She is now insisting on maintaining her influence over East Germany. Meanwhile, regardless of the substance of the proposed revision in the Security Treaty, she will regard the revision as the strengthening of military cooperation between the United States and Japan and will deal with it accordingly. This is the attitude of the Soviet Union, which cannot forget the Axis alliance between Japan and Germany of the past. I can well understand the delight expressed by some of our citizens that the proposed revision will clarify American responsibilities for the defense of Japan. But we must question whether or not this is something that should make us unconditionally happy.

We must always bear in mind that once the United States accepts defense of Japan as an obligation under a treaty, the Soviet Union and Communist China will regard the treaty revision as merely a means to strengthen military cooperation between the United States and Japan, and they may begin putting pressure on Japan.

Assuming another war becomes a reality, as long as Japan is considered one of the major bulwarks against communism in the Western Pacific, it is conceivable that the United States will protect us with all her might without any treaty obligations. On the other hand, if the worst comes to the United States, for example, if the mainland of the United States is destroyed by the nuclear arms of the Soviet Union, can the United States continue to defend Japan in accordance with the obligations she assumed under the treaty? That, or course, cannot be expected. In an emergency, would it not be more likely that the Security Treaty will give an excuse for the Soviet Union and Communist China to invade Japan by terming us as a common enemy along with the United States?

In the conduct of foreign affairs, one cannot simply consider the self-interest of one's own nation. It is necessary to think of the positions of other nations, and consider all the possible implications. Otherwise we may regret a century later the actions we are taking today. In the Diet debates over the Security Pact revision, no attempt has been made by the government to consider our relations with the Soviet Union and Communist China. I am very much concerned about this omission.

The Berlin crisis has given a renewed zeal to the United States in lessening the vicissitudes of the Cold War. At this particular juncture, why must we revise the Security Treaty, which will remind the Soviet Union of the Japan-Germany Axis of the past? Will this be the right step for Japan and for the United States? Will this contribute to the common concern of mankind, namely the restoration of world peace? Is the proposed move really wise? I hope the government will seriously reconsider its stand. In deliberating on the most important foreign policy issue that will affect our security, we must always take into account the worst that could happen under the new treaty. In this manner we can ensure the security of our nation. The national power of Japan, compared to the prewar era, has been reduced to such a level that if we commit one false move, we can even be completely annihilated.

The country that will be exposed to that kind of danger as a result of the Security Treaty revision is Japan and not the United States. We all know the poor relationship existing between the United States and the Soviet Union and Communist China. We can expect no radical change in these existing relations as a result of the treaty revision.

Those who are in positions of power must be circumspect in discharging their responsibilities. Any action that can be detrimental to the security of the nation must be firmly suppressed. The past relations or even the dignity of our nation are only secondary to this ultimate concern.

I have given my opinion on the question of treaty revision from the standpoint of our relations with the Soviet Union and Communist China. Unless the government can provide a convincing explanation to the contrary, I cannot change my opinion.

CHAPTER **XVII**

Emergence of an Economic Superpower

The 1956 *Economic White Paper* began with the phrase "the postwar period is over." Nothing captured the imagination of the Japanese people better than those words. It was a signal to begin the process of Japan's unfettered economic expansion that lasted well into the early 1990s. From 1955 to the end of the 1960s the annual growth rate in GNP was generally registered in the double digits. In the 1970s Japan faced head-on the challenges brought about by the two oil crises. For example, in 1974, the country faced a serious inflation. The nominal growth rate of its GDP was 19.3 percent, but in real terms, it was −1 percent. However, through rationalization and reduced use of energy, the country emerged even stronger economically. In the 1980s Japan became the world's largest creditor nation. Her multi-national industries were found in every corner of the world. She experienced trade surplus against all industrialized nations, with deficit registered only against oil-exporting nations.

Several factors contributed to Japan's remarkable success. Her well-educated and well-trained people created the best imaginable combination of management and line workers. Luck also played a part. Special procurement the United States placed for the Korean War in the early 1950s accelerated the recovery process, and continuation of the Cold War forced the United States to look upon Japan benignly in her quest for economic prosperity. Open access to the vast American market through the 1960s made it easier for Japanese companies to plan for expansion and enjoy the advantage of economy of scale in production. In spite of a series of economic disputes with the United States in later years, Japan's open access to the American market has not been hampered.

The government played its part well, becoming an indispensable part of the equation. The income-doubling plan of the Ikeda Cabinet (Documents 1 and 2) and other economic studies made by the Satō and Tanaka Cabinets outlined the course to be followed by the nation succinctly and defined the roles to be played by the public sector. Investments in infrastructure, such as the building of Shinkansen (Documents 3 and 4), were intended to maximize Japan's economic performance, which role the rail line admirably fulfilled.

No matter how well trained the people are, and no matter how dedicated the government may be, if the companies do not manage themselves well, everything will come to naught. One of the reasons for Japan's success during the period under study is the consistency with which the companies have shown their management acumen. There is indeed a so-called Japanese management style. This includes the market-driven, customer-oriented management philosophy, dedication to quality, and concern for the welfare of workers. A portion of this chapter is dedicated to this topic, with discussions of Sony's management philosophy (Document 5), practice of total quality control (Document 6) and the Toyota production method (Document 7).

Workers' attitudes toward the work in general and toward the company in particular are good indicators of whether a company will remain successful or not. A Toyota manager's personnel policy, applied effectively to line workers, is given as Document 8. It is followed by an article on the changing conditions surrounding salaried workers (Document 9).

The term "Japan, Inc." suggests a symbiosis of the government and industries, hinting that they speak with one voice. This has not always been the case. The business community has been capable of exerting pressure to bring about changes it desires. In 1955 the business community forced two contending conservative parties to merge into the Liberal Democratic Party. The threat of withholding political contribution acted as the leverage. In 1982, persuasion alone sufficed. Dokō Toshio successfully lobbied the government to undertake administrative reform (Document 10). By attempting to make the government run more efficiently, and by privatizing some government-owned key industries, the administrative reform prolonged Japan's ability to continue her economic expansion.

The Plaza accord of the group-of-five finance ministers is reproduced as Document 11. It is included because it represented the realization that without the participation of Japan, major industrial powers would be powerless attempting to make adjustment in their economies. Japan enjoyed a huge trade surplus against all of these powers. Her agreement to raise the value of the yen against other currencies narrowly averted a protectionist legislation contemplated by the U.S. Congress.

Ishihara Shintarō's *The Japan That Can Say No* provides a fitting conclusion to this chapter (Document 12). The ever-present economic friction between Japan and the United States has hardened the minds of people from both sides of the Pacific. Ishihara states Japan's position forcefully. His argument may never convince his critics, but his plea for mutual understanding through dialogue must be treated with respect. He asks if Americans and Japanese alike are too preoccupied with the occupation era. The 1956 *Economic White Paper* was correct in stating that the postwar period was over, at least in the economic sphere. In the psyche of men, however, old memories may never die. History seems to have gone full circle, restoring consciousness about the postwar period four decades after it officially ended under totally different economic circumstances.

PLAN FOR DOUBLING INDIVIDUAL INCOME

Ikeda Hayato (1899–1965) became prime minister on July 19, 1960. His name is often associated with the "doubling individual income plan." The plan, reproduced below as Document 1, is contained in a decision reached by the Ikeda Cabinet on December 27, 1960. The plan had to be revised substantially within the first two years, due to errors in basic assumptions, especially on the rates of individual consumption and on private investment, which were found to be too conservatively calculated. However, the fact remains that it was the optimistic outlook of this document that set the tone for Japan's growth-oriented economy of the 1960s. During that decade, Japan's GNP grew at an annual rate of 10.6 percent in real terms, far outpacing the 4.1 percent experienced by the United States. The share of value added by heavy and chemical industries among manufacturing industries reached 60 percent in 1970. Fully 30 percent of Japan's GNP came from the manufacturing sector in the same year, slightly above that of the United States at 29.6 percent. Japan joined the ranks of advanced industrial nations and her products were ready to be shipped to every corner of the world. Her path toward an economic superpower was thus begun.

The inspiration for the plan to double the individual's income came from the Economic Council (keizei shingikai) *which was a deliberative and consultative organ consisting of appointees of the prime minister from both the public and private sectors. Its report, submitted on November 1 of the same year, is reproduced as Document 2 to provide background information.*

1 Plan to Double Individual Income, December 27, 1960[1]

(1) *Objectives of This Plan*

The plan to double the individual income [hereafter referred to as the plan] must have as its objectives doubling of the gross national product, attainment of full employment through expansion in employment opportunities, and raising the living standard of our people. We must adjust differentials in living standard and

---

[1]Nakamura Naomi et. al, eds., *Shiryō Nihon Kin-Gendaishi (Documents on Modern and Contemporary Japanese History)*, vol. 3, *Sengo Nihon no Dōtei (Path of Postwar Japan)* (Tokyo: Sanseidō, 1985), pp. 238–39.

income existing between farming and nonfarming sectors, between large enterprises and small and medium-sized enterprises, between different regions of the country, and between different income groups. We must work toward a balanced development in our national economy and life patterns.

(2) *Targets to Be Attained*

The plan's goal is to reach 26 trillion yen in GNP (at the fiscal year [FY]1958 price) within the next ten years. To reach this goal, and in view of the fact that there are several factors highly favorable to economic growth existing during the first part of this plan, including the rapid development of technological changes and an abundant supply of skilled labor forces, we plan to attain an annual rate of growth of GNP at 9 percent for the coming three years. It is hoped that we shall be able to raise our GNP of 13.6 trillion yen (13 trillion yen in FY1958 price) in FY1960 to 17.6 trillion yen (FY 1960 price) in FY 1963 with application of appropriate policies and cooperation from the private sector.

(3) *Points to Be Considered in Implementing the Plan and Directions to Be Followed*

The plan contained in the report of the Economic Council will be respected. However, in its implementation we must act flexibly and pay due consideration to the economic growth actually occurring and other related conditions. Any action we undertake must be consistent with the objectives described above. To do so, we shall pay special attention to the implementation of the following:

(a) Promotion of Modernization in Agriculture

To secure a balanced development in our national economy, we shall enact a Fundamental Law of Agriculture as a means of promoting modernization in agriculture. The proposed law shall serve as the basis of our new agricultural policies on issues ranging from agricultural production, income and structure, to various other measures.

Concurrent with this, we shall actively secure investment for infrastructure required for agricultural production, and moneys required for promoting modernization in agriculture.

Enhancement of coastal fishing shall be undertaken in a similar manner.

(b) Modernization of Medium and Small Enterprises

To enhance productivity in medium and small enterprises, to relax the ills associated with our economy's dual structure, and to promote vigorously various measures required to attain these objectives, we shall secure an adequate and just supply of funds for modernization of medium and small enterprises.

(c) Accelerated Development of Less Developed Regions

To accelerate development of those less developed regions (including southern Kyushu, western Kyushu, Sanin region, and southern Shikoku) and to adjust difference in income levels, we shall establish without delay a plan for comprehensive multi-purpose development of the land. This will enable us to develop these regions' resources. Special consideration will be given to tax incentives, financing and rates of assistance permitted for public sector investment. We shall study legislation necessary to implement these measures. We shall see to it that industries appropriate to these regions will be located there. In this manner the welfare of the inhabitants in these regions may be advanced and the regions' less developed status may be rectified.

(d) Promotion of Appropriate Locations for Industries and Reexamination of Regional Distribution of Public Sector Projects

It is certainly important to respect the use of sound economic reasons in selecting industrial locations, if we are to maintain for a long period of time our country's high rate of growth, to strengthen international competitiveness, and to heighten the utility of our social capital investment. This must not be carried out in a manner that will promote greater differentials between regions.

While respecting rationality in making economic decisions and at the same time preventing spread of differentials between regions, we must adjust flexibly the amount of moneys invested or loaned for public works in different regions according to the special conditions existing in these regions. In this manner we shall be able to enhance the utility of public works project consistent with economic development which at the same time contribute toward minimizing differentials between regions.

(e) Active Cooperation with the Development of World Economy

Raising productivity means strengthening our export competitiveness. Bearing in mind that an important key to the success of this plan is in the expansion of our exports and an increase in revenues in foreign currencies, we must promote a viable export strategy accompanied by other measures increasing nontrade revenues such as tourism and maritime transportation. We shall actively seek cooperation with other countries in promoting economic development in less-developed countries and raise their income levels.

2   **Background for Income Doubling Plan, November 1, 1960**[2] It has been almost three years since the implementation of the "New Long Term Economic Plan," which was approved by the Cabinet at the end of 1957 and which is still in effect. During this period, the Japanese economy experienced a high degree of growth seldom matched elsewhere in the world. . . .

The growth rate during fiscal years (FY) 1947–52 was 11.5 percent per year, and during FY 1953–59, it was 8.3 percent per year. In each instance it went far above the projected growth rate of 6.5 percent per year under the "New Long Term Economic Plan." It shows that our economic growth has been far greater than previously anticipated. In this process of growth, the following five factors are worthy of note.

---

[2]Asahi Shimbunsha, ed., *Shiryō Meiji Hyakunen (A Documentary History for the Meiji Centennial)* (Tokyo: Asahi Shimbunsha, 1966), pp. 561–62.

First, according to the view heretofore held, the high rate of economic growth postwar Japan experienced was largely sustained by the postwar recovery, and with the passage of time, the growth rate would be substantially reduced. The facts prove otherwise. Today, fifteen years after the end of the war, we continue to maintain a very high rate of growth which was 17 percent in FY 1959 and is about 10 percent for the current fiscal year.

Second, in spite of this high rate of growth, we have maintained a well-balanced savings and investment profile. The price level has been relatively stable. The rate of inflation for basic commodities between FY 1956, the base year for the New Long Term Economic Plan, and FY 1959 has been at 0.6 percent per year. The fear that the economic growth might result in deficit in foreign trade has not materialized. Instead, today we have foreign currency reserves in excess of $1.6 billion.

Third, as a result of this high rate of growth, our industrial organization has advanced significantly at an unexpected high speed. With the machine industry as the vanguard, other industries are developing at a breathtaking pace. A high level of investment in plant and equipment is being carried out alongside the on-going technological revolution.

In this way, our economy is gradually phasing out the postwar stage to enter a new development stage. At the same time, there is a trend toward change in our total economic outlook. In short, it is represented by the intensified technological revolution and modernization. The significant technological revolution that has been taking place since 1956 has brought about basic changes and improvement in the nature of our economy. It has also induced a very sharp rise in our productivity. Other technological innovations to follow may spread their economic benefits from specialized industries and enterprises to a large number of related small and medium-sized enterprises. We expect that such technological innovations will also greatly affect consumers.

Fourth, there has been a change in our dynamic population. Our population, heretofore, has been abundant and has been one of the reasons for our lower wage scales. However, our population pattern is changing gradually into one of a smaller number of births and deaths, a pattern common in advanced countries. Our total population has increased slightly over that of the prewar figure. However, with respect to the fifteen years or older group who newly enter the labor market, the condition is somewhat different. In the first half of the Economic Plan, the increase in the number of young men entering the labor force is expected to reach 1.5 million to 1.8 million, which is caused by the postwar baby boom. After 1965, however, the increase will be sharply reduced. In other words, during the first half, there may be some young men who are underemployed, and the pressure of population on the job market will continue to exist. In the second half, however, there is a strong indication of an overall labor shortage especially of younger workers, which is already apparent in specialized industries and areas.

Fifth, there have been significant changes in international conditions. During the past decade (1950–59), world trade showed an exceptionally high rate of growth of 6.2 percent in real terms. This rate may decline somewhat in the coming decade, but it is safe to assume that the rate of growth can be maintained at 4.5 percent. In that same period, it is expected that the foreign trade conditions of advanced countries will become more normalized than before, and their balance of trade pictures will also stabilize. In contrast, among developing nations, in spite of their industrial growths, their foreign trade in relative terms will slow down. The advanced nations are likely to help promote liberalization of our foreign exchange market, and the developing nations are likely to show greater necessities for entering into economic cooperation. We also expect that the East-West trade will be gradually normalized, and our country will be able to maintain regular trading relations with communist nations.

As described above, basic changes are occurring in economic conditions both internally and externally. Under these circumstances, if we are to maintain our high level of growth, it is necessary to draft a new long-range economic plan. And on the basis of this plan, it is necessary to nurture actively the growth capabilities of our economy and to remove those conditions that hinder such economic growth. At the same time, it is necessary to utilize the people's desire and vitality for greater production through this income-doubling plan. In this way, in a broad sense, we must replenish the wealth of our nation. Our national economy must take into account the changes that are taking place. The implementation or success of this plan is dependent on the desire of our people, and the contents of the plan cannot be in any manner injurious to the desire of the people.

SHINKANSEN—BIRTH OF THE BULLET TRAIN

The Shinkansen, or the new trunk line for high-speed bullet trains, today covers most of the Honshu island and part of Kyushu. When it was first opened between Tokyo and Osaka in 1964, it cut the travel time from over eight hours to three hours and ten minutes. The widely available speed travel brought along with it a profound change in travel patterns, business practices, and lifestyles of common people.

Even though the Shinkansen would have answered a number of economic needs articulated in the income-doubling plan and other long-term development plans preceding it, the plan to build it was at first greeted with suspicion. Railways were considered things of the past, and existing rail lines were neither well managed nor meeting the transport requirements of the nation. Then there was the huge cost for its construction. Initially, the Shinkansen was a dream of one Sogō Shinji (1884–1981), serving as president of the National Railways between 1955 and 1963. To forestall opposition from within, he held five strategy meetings with his subordinates between 1956 and 1957. The art of nemawashi, touching base with everyone concerned, was very much in evidence. Document 3 contains excerpts from these five meetings. This document is also of interest in studying Japan's decision making process. One can observe how the participants reached the decision to abandon the use of the traditional narrow-gauge railway tracks in constructing the Shinkansen. Attainment of high speed was the major goal. There were also discussions on electrifying the trains instead of using steam locomotives, financial implications of the new project, and the number of stations which would be designated for the bullet trains' stops. These portions are omitted.

Document 4 is a short excerpt from the reminiscences of an engineer, Fujishima Shigeru, who worked on the design and construction of the Shinkansen. His observations on the state of Japanese technology are precisely on the mark. Without the pervasive spreading of modern technology across the nation, the coming of the Japanese economic miracle would not have been possible.

In economic development, the proper function of the public sector is not always easy to define. However, when it comes to the Shinkansen, a remarkable consensus has emerged. In spite of the huge outlay required, plans are underway to construct additional lines and eventually linking Hokkaido with Honshu. Tanaka Kakuei (1918–1993), who served as prime minister between July 1972 and December 1974, once spoke of making Japan into a land of "one-day commuting distance," "one-day living zone," and "one-day cultural zone." That is closer to becoming a reality because of the Shinkansen.

3 Preparing for the Shinkansen, 1956–57[3]

First Meeting (May 19, 1956)

Mr. Sogō: Ten years after the war, one thing that we have been constantly criticized for by the public is our inadequate transport capabilities. . . .

As compared to other means of transportation, railways must never be thought of as things of the past. When railways are modernized, they become the indispensable means of transportation. I hear that the Germans are intent on restoring their railways and West Germans are making a substantial investment. Some people say that railways are not doing well in America, but the president of the Pennsylvania Railways dismisses it by saying "That's preposterous. Modern railways are one of the basic industries." Great Britain is now embarking on an unprecedented reform of its railway network.

The Japanese islands are long and narrow, and the population is large. There is no better way to transport a large number of passengers and cargoes than by railways.

[3]"Tōkaidosen Zōkyō Chōsakai Secchi no Keii" (Events Leading to the Establishment of the Study Committee for Expanding the Tōkaidō Line) in *Sogō Shinji, bessatsu (Companion Volume to the Biography of Sogō Shinji)* (Tokyo: 1988), pp. 272–93.

I personally think that improvement of the Tokaido[4] line must come by changing it into a broad-gauge railroad. Widen the track gauge, and increase the speed for mass transit. In the future we may even use atomic power for railways' engines. If so can we retain the present narrow-gauge track lines? . . .

Fourth Meeting (January 23, 1957)
Deputy Chief Engineer: Concerning the speed, the maximum speed possible for narrow-gauge track lines will be 140 to 150 kilometers per hour. In our previous study we considered 140 kilometers per hour to be the maximum. Any increase beyond that requires a total change in the train design and formation. For broad-gauge lines, we can easily attain 170 kilometers per hour. Based on our past experience, attaining the speed of 200 kilometers per hour is entirely possible. In some locations we may even reach 300 kilometers per hour. . . . In determining the speed, we should not dwell on the issue of how to compete against airplanes. . . .

Chief Engineer: We are not thinking of competing against airplanes or cars, but in arriving at the number of hours needed to travel between Tokyo and Osaka, we must be concerned with the issue of how it will be judged by world standards. . . .

Chief of the Technical Institute: When express highways are completed, cars can attain a speed of 100 kilometers per hour. To compete against that, the National Railways must have a speed of 200 kilometers per hour. My alternative suggestion is that we first make up a schedule of when we want the trains to arrive. We can then start designing trains and railways to attain that scheduling.

Director B: To attain the speed that is still unknown to us, laboratory testing and actual testing must both be conducted. We are now engaged in the issue of either to maintain the narrow gauge or to adopt the broad gauge. I will be satisfied by simply knowing the percentage increase in speed if we adopt the broad-gauge system. . . .

Technical Officer: Our current thinking is that for passenger trains the upper limits are 160 kilometers per hour for the narrow-gauge system, and 200 kilometers per hour for the broad-gauge system.

Mr. Sogō: . . . You must read the study results with a grain of salt. The speed performance of the narrow-gauge system is exaggerated. Our technical staff must not be influenced by political consideration to arrive at the results.

Chief, Bureau of Electricity: Within a decade, the narrow-gauge system will become passé. There are invisible benefits in having high speed and efficiency. A broad-gauge system will permit us to introduce a number of modern facilities. Why not take the plunge?

Mr. Sogō: Most foreign countries can cover the distance between Tokyo and Osaka in four hours. It now takes us eight hours. How can we compete in the world if this condition is allowed to persist?

---

[4]The "Eastern Shore" line linking Tokyo and Osaka, via Nagoya and Kyoto.

Director B: As an engineer I love to tackle new issues and new projects. But we must take into account the national railways' finance and conditions of its facilities. I do not think it is wise to move into a new project too quickly. As for the issue of either the broad or narrow gauge, we must give each an equal chance to be heard.

Mr. Sogō: That is what I call political thinking. Here we only have to investigate technical issues, economic considerations can follow afterward. The trend of the world is toward the broad-gauge system. I cannot bear the thought of foreigners finding out that our speed is less than par.

4   When We Built the Shinkansen, 1964[5] When we started building the Shinkansen, we did not even question that it had to be an electric train. The technology of using alternate current that we introduced in 1957 became very useful.

This was to be a high-speed train. We were not worried about the motor, but brakes became a serious concern. "Anything which cannot stop itself has no business moving," and "The one who moves fast must stop fast."

The motor is used to brake a motion when we want to reduce speed. Once we are on low speed, we must use an air brake to stop the rotation of wheels. We do not put pressure on the tires. Otherwise all the wheels will soon wear out. We need a disk brake that will stop the disk which is rotating with the wheel. Fortunately we already had this type of disk brake in use in our "Kodama" series of trains.

Some observers complain: "You guys in the National Railways, all you do after the war is make new series of trains one after another." It's true and some of us feel that we are guilty as charged.

Indeed there are the "Shōnan" series, the "Tōkai" series, the commuter series, and the "Kodama" series. They all look different in color and design, and they may appear to be built so distinctly from one another that they have no bearing on today's Shinkansen. The fact is, if any of these steps were missing, today's Shinkansen would not have been born.

Each advance we make in our technological development becomes a building block for the next step. For our technology to come to its fruition, we need a clear-cut and justly determined direction. Without it, everything will be in vain.

Technicians in the railways share a common dream. That is speed. How to build a train that can be operated safely while obtaining a high speed? In this sense, the notion of the Shinkansen was not born overnight. After the war when

---

[5]Fujishima Shigeru, "Shinkansen, Jisoku 200 kiro no Misshitsu" (The Totally Sealed Room at 200 Km. per Hour—A Story of Building the Shinkansen) in *Bungei Shunjū*, September 1964. Reprinted in *"Bungei Shunjū" ni Miru Showashi (A History of the Showa Era as Seen through the Pages of the Bungei Shunjū)*, vol. 2 (Tokyo: Bungei Shunjūsha, 1988), pp. 576–77.

the National Railways restarted its operations, some of us engineers began to talk about our shared dream.

It looks almost comical now when we look back to the time when we had our test run between the two stations of Mishima and Numazu. When the speedometer registered 120 kilometers per hour, those senior members who were gazing intently at the speedometer suddenly burst into a chorus of "Banzai." In the National Railways, senior colleagues are always there to share their joys with younger technicians and give them encouragement.

As I reminisce on the horizontal relations we have had, my thought wanders to the sight of India I experienced earlier.

India was just beginning her industrialization, and it exuded a vibrant air. I visited a number of factories in different localities. One day I was at a telephone assembly line in Bangalore. The factory was a recipient of technical assistance from overseas, and their telephone receivers were well built. At the corner of one of the work stations, they were making carry-on phones. As a factory committed exclusively to the making of telephone receivers, their carry-on phones were equally well made.

Well, a carry-on phone requires a carrying case and a shoulder strap. A simple case and strap, but unfortunately they did not do their job. It was mere vinyl, but unfortunately of low quality.

Back in Japan whether we go out or stay at home, we see all sorts of commodities, from sandals and tablecloths made of vinyl to many other items. I sometimes feel that we are too wasteful. These things on the surface appear unrelated. Indeed, taken separately each of these items may not amount to much. However, by having all these seemingly unimportant industries, and having the ability to make all of them, we have the base to manufacture the things we truly need.

A group of American observers came to study the Shinkansen. They reported how impressed they were with the liberal use of transistors and diode in our automated control devices. This cannot be unrelated to the saturation of transistor radios in our towns that started a number of years ago.

In Japan, to a degree we can do almost everything with things we have within our borders. We have enough technological abilities in our related industries. If we have a problem, we can ask them for help, and they will do their best to respond. We speak of the National Railways' technology. But in the final analysis, it is the industrial capability of the country that has made it possible for us to create the Shinkansen. I think that is the reason people from overseas speak so highly of the Shinkansen.

MANAGING A COMPANY

What made Japanese companies perform better than other companies world over in the glory days of Japan's economic supremacy? The answer is decep-

tively simple. They were managed better. Reproduced below are three distinct but complementary approaches to management, all accepted as models of excellence across the country.

Sony has been the Japanese company that has always been at the cutting edge of technology. It has a corporate culture that has been conducive to innovation as well as to shrewd marketing. Its success comes from its willingness to allow employees to participate in decision making. To make that system work, the company nurtures its employees and treats them as members of the family. The most important issue in management has always been the enhancement of jinzai, human resources, which must be treasured. Document 5 comes from an autobiographical account given by Morita Akio (b. 1921), a co-founder of the company, its chairman until early 1994, and one of Japan's most articulate spokesmen for its industries.

Document 6 deals with the issue of quality control. Originally introduced to Japan by Dr. W. Edward Deming (1900–1993) of the United States, quality control has become the hallmark of Japanese industry. Everywhere one goes there is a QC circle, and there is an attempt to build quality in at every stage of manufacturing. Workers are taught to use their minds as well as their hands. Things must be done right the first time, and every team or QC circle works diligently toward that goal. The practice of quality control has been successful in Japan because of their willingness to change the entire corporate culture and because of their insistence on companywide participation. Their top executives are often found discussing quality issues alongside their line workers. It is called TQC, or total quality control. In the United States, it is better known under the term TQM, or total quality management. The selection comes from the standard work written by Ishikawa Kaoru (1915–1989), the dean of TQC in Japan.

Toyota, the giant auto maker, has invented a manufacturing system called Just-in-Time, or JIT for short. It means "to supply to each process what is needed when it is needed and in the quantity that is needed." There are more than 20,000 parts needed to manufacture a car. Under the JIT system, only the parts needed are delivered just-in-time to each process. In this way wastes are eliminated and efficient production is assured. Document 7 comes from a training manual on JIT prepared for the Japan Management Association. It is not within the scope of this volume to provide a lessen in JIT. The selection contains only its emphasis on facts, and on elimination of various categories of waste. It is hoped, however, the attitude with which the Japanese workers face their tasks can be gleaned from this selection. The "five Ws and one H" reproduced in 7(b) is a useful tool for manufacturing. It is also an efficient tool in any scientific investigation.

The Japanese management techniques have had a profound impact on the rest of the world. The resurgence in American industry experienced in the late 1980s and early 1990s could not have taken place without the adoption and application of QC and JIT in many workplaces.

5   **It's All in the Family—Sony's Management Style, 1986**[6]   There is no secret ingredient or hidden formula responsible for the success of the best Japanese companies. No theory or plan or government policy will make a business a success; that can only be done by people. The most important mission for a Japanese manager is to develop a healthy relationship with his employees, to create a family-like feeling within the corporation, a feeling that employees and managers share the same fate. Those companies that are most successful in Japan are those that have managed to create a shared sense of fate among all employees, what Americans call labor and management, and the shareholders.

. . . The emphasis on people must be genuine and sometimes very bold and daring, and it can even be quite risky. But in the long run—and I emphasize this—no matter how good or successful you are or how clever or crafty, your business and its future are in the hands of the people you hire. To put it a bit more dramatically, the fate of your business is actually in the hands of the youngest recruit on the staff.

That is why I make it a point personally to address all of our incoming college graduates each year. The Japanese school year ends in March, and companies recruit employees in their last semester, so that before the end of the school year they know where they are going. They take up their new jobs in April. I always gather these new recruits together at headquarters in Tokyo, where we have an introductory or orientation ceremony. This year I looked out at more than seven hundred young, eager faces and gave them a lecture, as I have been doing for almost forty years.

"First," I told them, "you should understand the difference between the school and a company. When you go to school, you pay tuition to the school, but now this company is paying tuition to you, and while you are learning your job you are a burden and a load on the company.

"Second, in school if you do well on an exam and score 100 percent, that is fine, but if you don't write anything at all on your examination paper, you get a zero. In the world of business, you face an examination each day, and you can gain not one hundred points but thousands of points, or only fifty points. But in business, if you make a mistake, you do not get a simple zero. If you make a mistake, it is always minus something, and there is no limit to how far down you can go, so this could be a danger to the company."

The new employees are getting their first direct and sobering view of what it will be like in the business world. I tell them what I think is important for them to know about the company and about themselves. I put it this way to the last class of entering employees:

---

[6]From *Made in Japan* by Akio Morita with Edwin M. Reingold and Mitsuko Shimomura, pp. 130–31, 143–44, 149–50. Copyright © 1986 by E.P. Dutton. Used by permission of Dutton Signet, a division of Penguin Books USA Inc.

"We did not draft you. This is not the army, so that means you have voluntarily chosen Sony. This is your responsibility, and normally if you join this company we expect that you will stay for the next twenty or thirty years."

[Mr. Morita goes on to discuss the history of lifetime employment in Japan, and discusses his relations with Sony employees.]

The reason we can maintain good relations with our employees is that they know how we feel about them. In the Japanese case, the business does not start out with the entrepreneur organizing his company using the worker as a tool. He starts a company and hires personnel to realize his idea, but once he hires employees he must regard them as colleagues or helpers, not as tools for making profits. Management must consider a good return for the investor, but he also has to consider his employees, or his colleagues, who must help him to keep the company alive, and he must reward their work. The investor and the employee are in the same position, but sometimes the employee is more important because he will be there a long time whereas an investor will often get in and out on a whim in order to make a profit. The worker's mission is to contribute to the company's welfare, and his own, every day all of his working life. He is really needed. . . .

We have a policy that wherever we are in the world we deal with our employees as members of the Sony family, as valued colleagues, and that is why even before we opened our U.K. factory, we brought management people, including engineers, to Tokyo and let them work with us and trained them and treated them just like members of our family, all of whom wear the same jackets and eat in our one-class cafeteria. This way they got to understand that people should not be treated differently; we didn't give a private office to any executive, even to the head of the factory. We urged the management staff to sit down with their office people and share the facilities. On the shop floor every foreman has a short meeting with his colleagues every morning before work and tells them what they have to do today. He gives them a report on yesterday's work, and while he is doing this he looks carefully at the faces of his team members. If someone doesn't look good, the foreman makes it a point to find out if the person is ill or has some kind of a problem or worry. I think this is important, because if an employee is ill, unhappy, or worried, he cannot function properly. . . .

A company will get nowhere if all of the thinking is left to management. Everybody in the company must contribute, and for the lower-level employees their contribution must be more than just manual labor. We insist that all of our employees contribute their minds. Today we get an average of eight suggestions a year from each of our employees, and most of the suggestions have to do with making their own jobs easier or their work more reliable or a process more efficient. Some people in the West scoff at the suggestion process, saying that it forces people to repeat the obvious, or that it indicates a lack of leadership by management. This attitude shows a lack of understanding. We don't force suggestions, and we take them seriously and implement the best ones. And since the majority of them are directly concerned with a person's work, we find them relevant and useful. After all, who could tell us better how to structure the work than the people who are doing it? . . .

In Japan, workers who spend a lot of time together develop an atmosphere of self-motivation, and it is the young employees who give the real impetus to this. Management officers, knowing that the company's ordinary business is being done by energetic and enthusiastic younger employees, can devote their time and effort to planning the future of the company. With this in mind, we think it is unwise and unnecessary to define individual responsibility too clearly, because everyone is taught to act like a family member ready to do what is necessary. If something goes wrong it is considered bad taste for management to inquire who made the mistake. That may seem dangerous, if not silly, but it makes sense to us. The important thing in my view is not to pin the blame for a mistake on somebody, but rather to find out what caused the mistake.

6   Total Quality Control—A Thought Revolution in Management, 1981[7]

(a) *Definition of QC and Thought Revolution*

Japanese quality control is a thought revolution in management. It is an approach representing a new way of thinking about management.

My definition of quality control is as follows:

"To practice quality control is to develop, design, produce and service a quality product which is most economical, most useful, and always satisfactory to the consumer."

To meet this goal, everyone in the company must participate in and promote quality control, including top executives, all divisions within the company, and all employees. . . .

As I discussed in Chapter 1 [about the origin of QC in Japan], one of the reasons I began QC was:

"The eight years that I spent in the nonacademic world after my graduation taught me that Japanese industry and society behaved very irrationally. I began to feel that by studying quality control, and by applying QC properly, the irrational behavior of industry and society could be corrected. In other words, I felt that the application of QC could accomplish revitalization of industry and effect a thought revolution in management."

To associate revitalization of industry with a thought revolution in management may sound somewhat excessive. But that expression represented the goal to which I aspired. Many companies transformed themselves after applying QC. The manner in which they were transformed may be classified in the following six categories.

1. Quality first—not short-term profit first.

---

[7]Ishikawa Kaoru, *What Is Total Quality Control? The Japanese Way,* trans. by David J. Lu (Englewood Cliffs, N.J.: Prentice Hall), pp. 44, 104–106. English translation copyright © 1985 by David J. Lu.

2. Consumer orientation—not producer orientation. Think from the standpoint of the other party.

3. The next process is your customer—breaking down the barrier of sectionalism.

4. Using facts and data to make presentations—utilization of statistical methods.

5. Respect for humanity as a management philosophy—full participatory management.

6. Cross-function management.

(b) *Quality First*

If a company follows the principle of "quality first," its profit will increase in the long run. If a company pursues the goal of attaining a short-term profit, it will lose competitiveness in the international market, and will lose profit in the long run.

Management that stresses "quality first" can gain customer confidence step by step, and the company's sales will increase gradually. In the long run, profits will be substantial, and will permit the company to have stable management. If a company follows the principle of "profit first," it may obtain a quick profit, but it cannot sustain competitiveness for a long period of time.

These things are easier said than done. In practice, many companies are still operating on the basis of profit first. They may proclaim "quality first," but at the shop they are only interested in cutting cost. Some people still fear that raising quality means raising cost, which in turn will reduce profit. It is true that cost will rise temporarily when the quality of design is upgraded. However, the immediate tradeoff can be found in the company's ability to satisfy the requirements of consumers and to meet competition in the world market.

The additional advantages are not difficult to find. If the "quality of conformance" improves, defects become fewer and fewer, and the "go-straight-percentage"[8] increases. There will be a substantial decline in the amount of scrap, in reworks, in adjustment, and in the inspection cost. This will bring about a very substantial cost saving, accompanied by higher productivity. Without this benefit, automation of the process becomes virtually impossible, and factories operated by robots become inconceivable. In fact, improvements in the quality of design is the first step toward higher sales and profits and lower cost.

This truth is made abundantly clear in Japan's competition with the United States in the markets for automobiles, color televisions, integrated circuits, and steel. Only recently have some Americans begun to realize this fact. In many areas, America is still governed by an old-fashioned capitalism. The owner, the chairman, or the directors are the ones who scout and hire a new president. The president thus chosen must show a quick profit or else may be fired. He has no

---

[8]In assembly, a good product is created when it goes straight from the first process to the final process without adjustment or modification. The rate of its becoming a good product in this fashion is called the go-straight percentage.

time to think about long-term profit. He is forced to choose a short-term profit, and in so doing loses his match with the Japanese.

In the case of automobiles, American manufacturers did produce compact cars before 1970 to compete against the Japanese. However, the profit from a large-sized car came to from five to ten times that of a compact, so American manufacturers worked on their compact cars only half-heartedly. When the need arose, American consumers bought Japanese-made compacts irrespective of price because of their reliability and fuel efficiency.

In steel, in automobiles, and in integrated circuits, American companies have not been able to make the investments in equipment that they need in order to seek long-term profit. They have lagged behind in plant modernization. In addition, the Securities and Exchange Commission requires that reports be issued every three months. This relatively recent development has further contributed to the myopic views of American managers.

Some managers in the United States are simply tired of managing, so they sell their companies to enjoy their retirement. What is lacking is their concern for their social responsibility and the welfare of their employees. Society suffers from their unconcern and the companies are also affected because they cannot be expected to attain long-term profit.

Generally speaking, the higher the manager is on the corporate ladder, the longer must be the period used for evaluating his work. In the case of the president, marketing division head, and manager of the factory, evaluation must be based on their work extending over a period of three to five years. Without this safeguard, these people may seek only short-term profit, and neglect both quality and equipment investment. It is a sure way to lose long-term profit for the company.

(c) *QC Circle*

As QC circle activities gain momentum and their number increases, many activities that bear no resemblance to QC circles start using the same name. Thus it becomes necessary to give a clear-cut definition of what a QC circle is and what its aims are. To answer these questions, the QC Circle Headquarters published *The General Principle of the QC Circle (Kōryō)* in 1970 and *How to Operate QC Circle Activities* in 1971. The following are excepts from these two volumes:

1. What is the QC circle?

The QC circle is a small group to perform quality control activities voluntarily within the same workshop.

This small group carries on continuously as a part of company-wide quality control activities, self-development and mutual development, control and improvement within the workshop, utilizing quality control techniques, with all the members participating.

2. Basic ideas behind QC circle activities

The basic ideas behind QC circle activities carried out as part of company-wide quality control activities are as follows.

(1) Contribute to the improvement and development of the enterprise.

(2) Respect humanity and build a worthwhile-to-live-in, happy, and bright workshop.

(3) Exercise human capabilities fully, and eventually draw out infinite possibilities.

7 Waste Elimination and Emphasizing Facts in Toyota Production System, 1985[9]

(a) *Waste Elimination*

What the Toyota production system seeks is a total elimination of waste.

We say that "a manufacturer's profit can be found in the way he makes things." It reflects our philosophy of attaining cost reduction through the elimination of wasteful operations. There are many types of wastes. At Toyota, in order to proceed with our man-hour reduction activities, we divide wastes into the following seven categories:

1. Waste arising from overproducing.
2. Waste arising from time on hand (waiting).
3. Waste arising from transporting.
4. Waste arising from processing itself.
5. Waste arising from unnecessary stock on hand.
6. Waste arising from unnecessary motion.
7. Waste arising from producing defective goods.

The most common sight found in many workplaces is the excessive progression of work. Everything moves too fast. Normally, it must be consigned to waiting, but workers proceed to the next stage of work. Thus the time that is supposed to be waiting time becomes hidden. When this process is repeated, materials or parts produced accumulate in between or at the end of the production line, creating unnecessary stock on hand. To transport this stock or to rearrange it for storage requires creation of another type of work. By the time this process takes its course, it becomes more and more difficult to find where the wastes are.

Under the Toyota production system, we call this phenomenon the *waste arising from overproducing*. Of the many infractions of wastefulness, this is considered by far the worst offense.

The waste arising from overproducing is different from other wastes because, unlike other wastes, it overshadows all others. Other wastes give us clues as to

---

[9]From *Kanban: Just-in-Time at Toyota: Management Begins at the Workplace*, ed. by Japan Management Association and trans. by David J. Lu, pp. 16–20, 27–28. English translation copyright © 1986 by Productivity Press, Inc., PO Box 13390, Portland, Ore. 92713–0390, (800) 395–6868. Reprinted by permission.

how to correct them. But the waste arising from overproducing provides a blanket cover and prevents us from making corrections and improvements.

Thus, the first step in any man-hour reduction activity is to eliminate the waste arising from overproducing. To do so, production lines must be reorganized, rules must be established to prevent overproduction, and restraints against overproduction must become a built-in feature of any equipment within the workplace.

Once these steps are taken, the flow of things will return to normal. The line will produce one item at a time as needed. The waste becomes clearly discernible as the waste arising from time on hand. When a production line is reorganized in this fashion, it becomes much easier to engage in the activity consisting of "elimination of waste—reassignment of work—reduction of personnel."

This waste is also created when the preceding process fails to deliver parts needed in the present process, thus preventing workers in the latter from working. . . .

The waste arising from transporting refers to waste caused by an item being moved a distance unnecessarily, being stored temporarily or being rearranged. For example, traditionally parts are transferred from a large storage pallet to a smaller one and then placed temporarily on a machine several times before they are finally processed. By improving the pallets, we have been able to dispense with these temporary placement procedures and let one worker operate two machines.

Another instance of waste arising from transporting occurs when parts are moved from a warehouse to the factory, from the factory to the machines and from the machines to the hands of workers. At each of these steps, parts have to be rearranged and moved.

The waste arising from processing itself occurs, for example, when a guide pin in the jig does not function properly and the worker has to hold the jig with his left hand. The processing does not go smoothly and time is wasted.

In addition, there are wastes arising from unnecessary stock on hand, from unnecessary motion and from producing defectives. Explanations for each of these are not necessary.

(b) *Scientific Attitude Emphasizing Facts*

At the workplace, we start from the actual phenomenon, investigate the cause and find a solution. We do not deviate from this approach. In other words, anything related to the workplace is based on facts. No matter how much information is provided through data, it is difficult to see the true picture of the workplace through data. When defects are produced, and we find out only through data, we miss the chance to take appropriate corrective actions. Thus we may not be able to discover the true cause of the defects, resulting in our inability to take effective countermeasures against recurrence. The place where we can accurately capture the true state of the workplace is the workplace itself. We can catch defects on the spot in the workplace and then find the true cause. We can immediately take countermeasures. That is why under the Toyota system, we say that data are important but we emphasize facts even more at the workplace.

When a problem occurs, if the manner of probing into the cause is insufficient, measures taken can become blurry. At Toyota, we have the so-called five Ws and one H. The five Ws are not the conventional "who, when, where, what and why," but every word is replaced by a "why," and we say "why, why, why, why and why" five times before we finally say "how?" In this way we delve into the true cause that is hidden behind the various causes. It is essential that we come face to face with the true cause.

To make this method thoroughly understood by all, we take the following steps:

(1) Make sure that everyone can understand where the problem is.

(2) Clarify the purpose behind the task of problem solving.

(3) Even if there is only one defective item, provide a corrective measure.

JAPANESE WORKERS

How do line workers and office workers feel about their working conditions? Do they respond willingly to the management's call for teamwork, quality work and exhortation for excellence? The perceived virtues of Japanese management are sometimes powerless in the face of insurmountable obstacles.

Document 8 comes from a thoughtful book by a Toyota executive, Nemoto Masao (b. 1919), who rose through the ranks to become a Toyota director and eventually reached the presidency and chairmanship of its subsidiary, Toyoda Gōsei. Coming as he does from his rich manufacturing experiences, he knows how to turn a potential battleground into a happier and livelier workplace. He does this by not scolding his subordinates. Reading between the lines, however, one can also sense the fact that many other manufacturing plants are still operated with cohesion where cacophony prevails.

Sakaiya Taichi (b. 1935), the author of Document 9, is a former official of the Ministry of International Trade and Industry (MITI). His view is that the era of salaried workers as the privileged class is over, and their position must be replaced by entrepreneurs. This script is closer to the actual conditions in the United States of 1990s than in the Japan of 1980s that he describes. The twin pillars of modern Japanese management—lifetime employment and promotion based on seniority—still persist. In the early 1990s Japan also experienced a wave of corporate restructuring. But the number of affected employees remained small. For the purpose of this chapter, Sakaiya's perceptive article can be read with benefit as a description of the privileges enjoyed by white-collar workers.

8   Practicing Improvement after Improvement, 1983, 1986[10]

(a) *There Is a Reason for Not Scolding*

After finishing college, I worked in an arsenal for a while. The facilities for which I was responsible malfunctioned one day, and it was my fault. If found out by my superior officer, all hell would break loose. I decided to remain silent and asked a fellow officer who knew about it: "Keep it quiet, will you? When you are in trouble, I will, of course, say nothing." It was a pact of mutual assistance, so to speak, and I took temporary corrective measures to cover up my mistakes.

I thought to myself then: "If only I was sure that I would not be reprimanded severely, I would have implemented basic corrective measures which would have avoided recurrence. When I have subordinates of my own, I will never scold them." More than thirty years have passed since that time, and I have overseen numerous subordinates of my own. During this entire period, I have never scolded any of my subordinates.

"What, you have never scolded your subordinates?" Some people may feel that this is proof positive of my lax manner of management and inability to teach. This is not so. I believe that "people are not gods and they are bound to make mistakes no matter how hard they try. There is no benefit in assessing responsibility for committing errors. it is better to clarify the facts and work toward prevention of recurrence." I check very carefully to see if my subordinates submit their plans for prevention of recurrence on time. My reputation among my subordinates is that I do not scold, but when it comes to work I am very demanding.

Let me share with you my experience with "not scolding when mistakes occur." When we gather to establish our annual policy, we begin by looking back at the performance of the past twelve-month period. If a person has been scolded by his superior, he is not likely to be candid, reflective or able to examine himself carefully. It is rare for anyone to have a record of implementing everything in the way he had initially planned and obtaining the results expected. Mistakes and failures are bound to occur along the way. If they are not candidly stated, then the goals that we set for the following year cannot be appropriate ones.

For example, a division manager may state in an abstract manner: "We need to do a little better in handling our meetings." It is not clear what has gone wrong and no appropriate measures can be taken. What he should have said candidly is: "The rate of attendance is good, but the rate of participation in discussion is poor."

In our day-to-day operations, I always tell my people that they must "have ears to listen to the mistakes committed by their subordinates." It is always embarrassing to admit one's own mistakes, but it is important to create an atmo-

---

[10]Masao Nemoto, *Total Quality Control for Management: Strategies and Techniques from Toyota and Toyoda Gosei,* trans. David J. Lu (Englewood Cliffs, N.J.: Prentice Hall, 1987), pp. 8–10, 109. English translation copyright ©1987 by David J. Lu.

sphere that is conducive to making a report of mistakes committed by workers. If a superior raises his voice and shouts, his subordinate will think twice before coming to him.

. . . There are a number of examples taken from Toyoda Gōsei showing how products not meeting our standards are uncovered. All of these examples are known to us, because our supervisors have been willing to report to us their own mistakes. We can compile examples of our mistakes for future reference, because we have steadfastly abided by our policy of "having ears to listen to the mistakes committed by our subordinates."

Caution must be exercised in disciplining employees. About nine years ago, a parts manufacturer delivered poor-quality parts to us. I called the president of the firm and received this response: "We are still investigating, but as soon as we know what has happened you will receive our report, we are planning to convene our disciplinary board to look into the matter." This last part of his response bothered me, and I called him back immediately. "If the mistake is committed deliberately, the person(s) responsible, or course, must be punished," I said to the president. "But most of those unexpected defectives are caused by an accidental miss. If workers are punished for an accidental miss, their tendency is to cover up any and all mistakes which may occur at the workplace. Supervisors, sympathetic to their workers, will subtly distort the facts to make sure that those workers responsible for the mistake will not face disciplinary action. You gain nothing by convening the disciplinary board."

"One punishment deters one hundred similar offenses," says a proverb. It may be valid for preventing murder or other serious crimes. But it is not an appropriate principle to follow in the workplace, where prevention of recurrence must be promoted in a different manner."

(b) *When Standards Are Not Observed.*

When you uncover incidences of noncompliance with the standards you set, how do you proceed from there?

Most supervisors will probably shout: "Why don't you do it the way you are taught?" This sentence, when written down on paper, is expressed in the form of a question, but when it is heard in the workplace, it is an inquisition. Everyone knows the supervisor is angry. And anger does not get him anywhere.

Now how would the worker feel about this? He would probably say: "Sorry, I am going to do it the way you say" on the spot. But there is no guarantee that he would abide by it afterward. More often than not, workers do not abide by the manuals because it is not always easy to do the work by following the standards set. Thus as soon as the supervisor is out of sight, they revert to their old ways.

In cases like this, a supervisor must ask the right question. "Do you see anything that's difficult to do? Let's try to change it to make it easier." If words like these are added, the question becomes a true question. But please remember, do not just mouth the words. You must truly feel that way when you speak.

In a survey we conducted, a supervisor reported that out of fifty items, forty items were caused by a difficulty in work standards. This is proof positive of the ability of the supervisor to ask the right question. If many types of work are difficult to do, that must be known immediately. If supervisors do not know the true state of affairs, then it becomes a problem for the company.

9 **The Destiny of Salaried Workers, 1984**[11] During the era of rapid economic growth, Japan was a country where salaried workers had things pretty much their way. Protected by lifetime employment and with a pay scale that gave them steady increases in income every year as they advanced in seniority, most secured a status befitting their age throughout their careers. As soon as they reached a certain level in the hierarchy, elite salaried workers were also granted one of the perquisites of the corporate scene: The authority to use "entertainment funds." This type of expense account was unknown in prewar Japan and much more lavish than expense accounts in other countries, and with it these workers would wine and dine the company's clientele.

The past few decades of Japanese history have been, in other words, a paradise for salaried workers. Not surprisingly, large numbers of youths left their home towns and family businesses to work for leading companies. But the good old days are over, or will be soon.

The age of rapid economic growth was a time when resources and energy were indiscriminately spent to fuel mass production and distribution. For businesses, big was beautiful, and consumption was a virtue. Companies made massive investments, gambling their fortunes in order to realize vast scales of production and sales volumes. The job of the top executives as they waited for a consensus on an investment to take shape within their organization was to bring the project to the attention of administrative bodies, politicians, banks, and industry associations so that these parties would be favorably disposed toward the company's investment plans. It was the hallmark of good management to have the stage set for implementation as soon as a company consensus had been reached.

The patience with which consensus was awaited was not, however, the monopoly of top management; it was shared by management at every level, from headquarters to individual sections. What evolved was a sort of waiting game style of management. The foremost requirement of any manager was bureaucratic-style administrative ability. . . .

The 1970s, though a decade of change, were in a sense the culmination of the

---

[11]From Sakaiya Taichi, "New Role Models for the Work Force," *Economic Views from Japan: Selections from Economic Eye* (Tokyo: Keizai Kōhō Center, 1986), pp. 166–73. Mr. Sakaiya's article was orginally published in the March 1984 issue of the *Chūō Kōron*.

society's bureaucratization and a dead end for the bureaucratic approach. This approach placed form over substance. Consensus was all important, and objections were ironed out while waiting for the consensus to take shape. No decision was reached in thoughtless haste, for the way the decision sounded counted more than what it accomplished. . . .

In line with the reigning trend toward formalism and bureaucratic control of society, the worth of a salaried worker was judged chiefly on the basis of personal self-sacrifice. The number of hours and the amount of effort devoted to a job were more important than how the job turned out. It was the process, not the outcome, that counted.

The era of rapid economic growth was one of abundant resources and energy, and mass consumption was a virtue. The value of resources, energy, and materials was stable; although prices might vary, value was nearly constant. A sudden rise in prices would be followed by a fall, and a sudden drop in prices would lead to a price recovery. The value of factories processing materials was therefore guaranteed. It could be assumed that any large-scale investment in a steel, petrochemical, or cement production facility would more than pay for itself through a long, productive life. The rapid growth era was accordingly a time of stability.

The same considerations held for consumer goods. The production of standard products in large quantities led to mass consumption and lower costs. The same product could be marketed nationwide and achieve uniform sales. Consumers did not bother to demand originality; they were happy to have standardized products that they could throw away after use.

But the times are changing. The two oil crisis of the 1970s led people to question the abundance of resources and energy and the wisdom of their wasteful consumption. People began seeking new types of products with original designs, new technology, and unique functions. "Clever" products came into demand.

The 1980s are turning into a decade of short production runs of a wide variety of products. The value of a product and of the knowledge it embodies is no longer stable, and may even be ephemeral. A necktie that sold for 20,000 yen last year will not even fetch 5,000 yen today if it has gone out of fashion, nor is it ever likely to be sold for 20,000 yen again. An age has come where new needs must be satisfied by cramming more functions into each of many different products that will be manufactured in relatively small quantities, nearly all of which must be sold to turn a profit. That is why I call the present era the "culture of ideas." An age of value born from knowledge and of a cultural or spiritual content is upon us. . . .

Without doubt, the privileges of salaried workers in big business will disappear with the arrival of the new age. Specifically, the systems of seniority-based wages and lifetime employment will be gradually dismantled. In the process, the social esteem enjoyed by the elite salaried workers will be undermined. The new role models will be the people who are now starting up venture-capital businesses; their names and faces will soon pervade the media as televisions and the press begin to lionize them. . . .

What will the new age mean to the salaried work force in the company organization? First, organizations will be broken into subdivisions to facilitate flexible production. Large firms will become aggregates of smaller units designed along the lines of venture-capital businesses. Seniority-based pay and promotion schedules will be replaced by schemes delegating more authority to each subdivision. Competence and performance will begin to be rewarded.

It will no longer be possible merely to wait one's turn to become a department chief. As the age factor decreases in importance, only those who steadily improve their performance on the job will rise to key positions and be rewarded accordingly. Performance will be judged by three elements of business acumen: foresight, decisiveness, and dynamism. The self-sacrifice demanded of salaried workers in the past will no longer be needed; the test will be the ability to devise new lines of business and make them profitable.

The division of organizations into smaller units will put real power into the hands of branch offices. In a change from the age of mass production and mass consumption, consumer needs will ramify. The particular needs of each local community will have to be identified and quickly satisfied. Often, as has occurred in the past, new businesses and fashions will begin in outlying areas and only later sweep into the metropolitan centers.

Branch offices should not exist merely to execute orders from headquarters: being a source of information, they should function to create ideas. As each of the units of the large organization becomes a decision-making body in its own right, the number of people involved in making decisions will grow. . . . Having such experience, some of these people will want to start their own businesses, for generally the desire to open a business is strongest in the most capable individuals. More companies will come to welcome this. . . . Eventually big businesses will foster clusters of satellite companies, and the best and the brightest of their former employees, who left to start up their own companies, will be doing their part to ensure the success of their corporate cluster—independently. . . .

What will be required of top-level corporate management in the culture of ideas? Two things already discussed will, of course, be required: decentralization of the enterprise and transfer of decision-making authority to lower levels to make the organization more responsive. Three further conditions must also be met.

The first is the creation of an atmosphere in which opinions can be freely voiced to anyone. The second is the creation of an environment in which people's opinions are listened to. The third is the creation of channels whereby opinions and ideas are swiftly transmitted to upper-level management. In other words, what is required is the creation of an atmosphere and an organization enabling the expression of views from as many people as possible and the prompt implementation of the best ideas. The waiting-game approach of Japanese management in the past, when patient preparations were made to form a consensus, will be too slow to answer needs and will mean lost opportunities.

The era of elite salaried workers is over, and with its passing, the way this elite is viewed by society will change. . . . In the community where I grew up, the people perceived to lead the stablest life were those farmers who owned and worked their own land. The life of salaried workers, however high their positions, was not considered entirely stable. The seats of honor at community functions were given to independent farmers; even company presidents and former ambassadors ranked lower in the social hierarchy.

You might even hear a farmer voice doubts about consenting to his daughter's marrying an ambassador's son. There was no guarantee that for all the ambassador's high rank, the son would succeed in the world or become a wealthy property owner. The son of an independent farmer, however, was considered likely to follow in his father's footsteps. The farmer was viewed as holding a far more stable position than the salaried worker, and in addition, many independent farmers counted among the most cultivated individuals. They were practiced in the tea ceremony and calligraphy, and they were accomplished *go* players and writers of *haiku*.

There was a time when the business world centered on men who had bet on growth and knowingly accepted insecurity, while the landed gentry, the men who sought security, constituted the foundation of society. This social scheme was neither feudal nor class-based; it was simply a social structure adapted to differences in life goals and tastes.

Now that the short era of salaried workers has ended, the time has come to reexamine different styles of life. Each person must accept the new realities and take a careful look at the future paths to choose between. Only by doing so will the individual successfully survive in the new and turbulent culture of ideas.

ADMINISTRATIVE REFORM

The Japanese economy continued to grow in the 1970s in spite of the two oil crises and other setbacks. Japan's dependence on imported oil was 99.8 percent. Only extraordinary energy-saving measures and rationalization stood between disaster and recovery. Belt-tightening was the key word, as industries sought ways of modernizing their facilities for better energy utilization. At the beginning of the new decade, Japanese industries found themselves still enjoying competitive trading advantages over the rest of the world.

The government contributed to the economic recovery through a series of stimulus packages. However, their results were at best mixed. The huge debts incurred in the process threatened to endanger the gains obtained by the private sector. The latter demanded a similar belt tightening from the public sector. It eventually took the form of a series of administrative reforms. Among its accomplishments were the privatization of the national railways, which oc-

curred in 1987, followed by the privatization of telephone and telecommunications industries.

The Keidanren[12] spearheaded the business community's demands for administrative reform. Its most articulate voice came from Dokō Toshio (1896–1988) who eventually became chairman of the council established for that purpose. A one-time president of the Keidanren, Dokō was widely respected for his business acumen and management ability as shown in his restructuring of Ishikawajima-Harima and Toshiba. His selfless devotion to the cause he believed in and his Spartan lifestyle made him a folk hero. Rich and poor alike could identify with him as he expounded on his view of how to make Japan a better place to live. His reminiscence follows.

10 **Dokō Toshio on Administrative Reform, 1982**[13] My favorite phrase is found in the Chinese classic, the *Great Learning,* chapter two: "Indeed the day is new, day after day it is new, again the day is new." This is the saying of King Tang of the Shang dynasty who carved these words on his wash basin, so every morning as he washed his face, he could remind himself of the importance of the day. This is what these words teach us: "As we face this day, this is the first day that has ever been made since the time of creation. It comes equally to kings and beggars. It is an important day. We must use it to the fullest. To do so, let us keep in mind that what we do today must be better than what we did yesterday. And as we look forward to tomorrow, we must aim to do better than today."

I try to act accordingly. I say to myself every morning "I am going to do my utmost in living my life today." Alas, being a man of no special accomplishment, there are many more days that are spent unsatisfactorily than ones with which I am pleased. At least I know I must do my level best everyday. And when I fail, I try to look back and do not let my regrets stay with me overnight. I read the Buddhist sutras for twenty to thirty minutes each morning and each night before going to bed. This is the way I have found to expiate my inadequacies. In doing so, I am assured of a good night's sleep, and I am spared bad dreams. The following day, I rise refreshed and start my work.

From the credo I have, it is meaningless to speak about the past, as I am doing now in writing my own life story. . . . Even talking of my life story, an issue that interests me most is the "present." And among those events of my "present," one

---

[12]Abbreviation of Keizai Dantai Rengōkai, or the Federation of Economic Organizations. It is the representative of big business in Japan, whose members consist of 119 industrywide groups and 916 of the largest corporations. Mr. Dokō was president of the Keidanren from 1974 through 1980.

[13]Dokō Toshio, *Watakushi no Rirekisho (My Curriculum Vitae),* contained in volume 8 of the ten-volume special edition of the *Watakushi no Rirekisho* series (Tokyo: Nippon Keizai Shimbunsha, 1992), pp. 67–74.

issue transcends everything, namely my role as the chairman of the Second Administrative Reform Council.[14]

Administrative reform is the most important issue facing Japan today which must be resolved without delay. At present, our national debt exceeds 82 trillion yen and the total of local debts comes close to 40 trillion yen. It means per capita, every Japanese (even a baby) owes one million yen, and a family of three owes three million yen. No nation in the West has incurred this much debt, and our present debt exceeds the level experienced during the Pacific War.

In his mid-term financial projection while the fiscal year 1981 budget was formulated, Finance Minister Watanabe [Michio, 1923–1995] speculated that in FY1984, there would still be a budget shortfall of 6.8 trillion yen even with the projected issuance of national bonds in the amount of nearly 6.8 trillion yen. It was only a matter of time before the outstanding national bond issues would exceed 100 trillion yen. Japan would be bankrupt in FY1984.

The Second Administrative Reform Council was formed to make sure that we would not reach that nadir of financial insolvency. It is a difficult problem. It is not just the elimination of national and local debts. We have to find the direction that Japan, nay the world, must follow. Without that, there can be no true administrative reform.

It was around 1975 that I became convinced of the need for administrative reform. That year an article, "Japan's Suicide," appeared in the February issue of the *Bungei Shunjū*. Co-authored by members of "Group 1948," it gave a chilling message: "Japanese society, while enjoying its seeming prosperity, may actually be treading on a path of its own destruction. It is secretly walking a path of suicide."

The article probed in detail the processes that led to the destruction of Greece and Rome and showed how they resembled today's Japan. Yes they were too similar for comfort. My privately held angst was made crystal clear with proofs needed. I wanted as many people as possible to read it. So with the permission of the publisher, I made several tens of thousands of copies and distributed them to interested industries.

To stop Japanese society from taking the path of self-destruction, we needed an operation called administrative reform. I spoke to that effect at the general assembly of the Keidanren held in May of 1975.

Thereafter, whenever I had a chance, I stressed the need for administrative reform to politicians and colleagues. To state my position strongly, or to stress

---

[14]This was an ad hoc committee that worked feverishly for forty-five days between May and July of 1981. Its work was continued by a formal Council for the Promotion of Administrative Reform, for which Mr. Dokō again served as chairman. Its tenure lasted five years and three months (1,980 days). It tackled about 16,000 issues and evaluated 2,446 documents prepared by the government and the private sector. Mr. Dokō personally presided over 313 meetings, some of which were held outside Tokyo.

it, sounds rather officious on my part, but the nation's future was too important for me to remain silent. Prime Minister Fukuda [Takeo 1905–1995], and Prime Minister Ōhira [Masayoshi 1910–1980], who were then in power, rendered understanding ears. But when it came to fundamental reforms, neither of them could start implementing them.

I became president of the Keidanren in 1974. Since that time, the Japanese economy has changed drastically and suffered many unforeseen setbacks, including the oil crisis, inflation, business downturn, scarcity of energy supply, problems related to raw materials, and trade friction.

Our industries were able to overcome these difficulties through their efforts in saving energy, in preserving resources, and in rationalization, all through exceptional sacrifices and cutbacks. Today, they may still face problems, but altogether they have succeeded in turning the corner.

The private sector has done well, but no comparable efforts have been undertaken by the public sector. It is fine to work toward establishing a welfare nation as a goal. But our finance has become bloated, and the government does not even attempt to reduce wastes or to rationalize its operations. It is too easy for them to say, "increase taxes, increase taxes." I got so tired hearing that and in 1974 I blurted out: "Engage in administrative reform before you ever say tax increase. As long as you do not undertake reform, we will not listen to your request for a tax increase."

Mr. Ōhira died suddenly, and Mr. Suzuki [Zenkō, b. 1911] became prime minister. Mr. Suzuki never dreamed of becoming prime minister, and in that sense, he was a selfless person to assume that position. He is that kind of a man. Mr. Suzuki said that he would undertake the task of administrative reform seriously and asked me to head the task force.

To engage in administrative reform is to engage in the task of changing the world (yonaoshi), so to speak. It would not make sense for me, a man at the age of eighty-five, to undertake the task. But as long as I could not detach myself from the concern for the nation's future, I had to accept it. . . .

Five days before I was officially appointed, or on March 11, 1981, to be exact. I was called in to meet the prime minister. I wrote my "requests" in four articles.[15] The first one stated that implementation of the proposed administrative reform depended on the determination of the prime minister. While I pledged to do my utmost, I wanted the prime minister to make a counter-pledge that he would implement recommendations rendered by the council. I had his word. In subsequent meetings he told me frequently that he would put his political life on the line for the administrative reform.

---

[15]The remaining three were (2) financial reconstruction without tax increase; (3) simultaneous administrative reform in prefectural governments and other self-governing bodies; and (4) fundamental changes in the National Railways, national health insurance, and government subsidy for rice.

Our council met for the first time on March 16, in the second floor conference room of the prime minister's official residence. There were nine council members, and twenty-one specialist members. . . .[In the fall of that year, the magazine *Gendai* carried an article consisting of a transcript of discussions held by council members.] That article describes well the essence of administrative reform and the efforts expended by council members. I am reproducing it [partially] below, in an informal conversation style, adding some comments of my own.

Mr. A: I remember Mr. Dokō saying: "With the administrative reform we propose, Japan will become a better country in the next five to ten years. It is up to all of you in the next generation. I may die in a year or two. So I will observe what you are doing from the bottom of hell." Boy, was I moved by his wanting to work for the betterment of my generation. Guess what happened? I now work more than fifty hours a week for the Council, and after that is over, I get back to my company to do its work. (*laughter*)

Mr. A: We just completed our first report. We are still at the stage of knowing administrative reform in abstract terms. I am concerned for an unspecified time in the future when the standards of governmental services will become lower. What will happen to the administrative reform at that stage? We must have a strong determination to pursue our goal and be prepared for all contingencies.

Mr. B: We must have the determination that can withstand any challenge. We may face minute problems not always easy to solve. But we have to be courageous enough to disregard little things and act for a greater common good.

Dokō: That's right. We don't have to worry, do we? Once the administrative reform is on course, nothing will go wrong. Altogether different types of wastes will be eliminated from the country, and the government will become more efficient. I don't think there will be anyone who will exploit the administrative reform for his own advantage. As for taxes, they will come down!

Dokō: We have to implement administrative reform from a much broader perspective. It's not just Japan, but the entire world will become lethargic, if we allow the present conditions to continue. Japan must start this movement because she is endowed with the best conditions (we do not have experiences as bad as other nations in unemployment and in inflation). We can contribute mightily to the world through what we are doing. This is a great turning point for the world.

Mr. A: In our first report, we selected as one of the themes "to examine the way a welfare state ought to be, with new vitality in the 1980s." The other theme concerned with the issue of Japan's responsibility among the family of nations and how to shoulder our responsibility.

Mr. B: We the Japanese people, including myself personally, must shoulder the responsibility [for bringing our country to the brink of bankruptcy]. We have accepted the policy aiming at economic growth, disregarding all other issues, with hardly any question. We have been numbed by it. We have become accustomed to thinking that the government will do anything and everything for us by simply asking for it. The supremacy of economy, pursuit of materialism and economic profits have become so pervasive that they have inundated the entire Japanese archipelago. We have forgotten how to become reflective, how to become thankful, and how to be respectful of things made for us. The acquisitive society's notion of the superiority of materialism is at the root of these ills. The government, financial circle, and public and private sectors all seek wealth and convenience. We are going bankrupt because we have no other concerns except to fulfill our present desires.

Mr. A: In talking about administrative reform, the issues of materialism and money always come to the forefront. That has to change. We must have a parallel concern about reforming the "minds" of our people.

Dokō: We have to get away from the way we think about depending on the government. We must be prepared to help ourselves and work hard at it. We must become accustomed to a little inconvenience now and then. We have to reform our thought patterns. In this sense, our administrative reform can be termed a national movement and a movement for thought revolution. . . .

THE PLAZA ACCORD

On September 22, 1985, finance ministers and central bank governors of the so-called Group of Five nations[16] met behind closed doors at the Plaza Hotel in New York. In the previous year, the United States experienced a trade deficit of $123 billion, of which $50 billion was with Japan alone. To provide relief to the United States and to prevent Congress from enacting protectionist legislation, the meeting proposed to lower the overvalued dollar and raise the undervalued yen through timely joint intervention. It was a defining moment in the U.S-Japanese relations. It made it abundantly clear that the United States could not determine its own economic policy without Japan's active participation, by then a recognized economic superpower.

The Plaza accord had only a modest initial impact. The trade gap between Japan and the United States narrowed slightly in the yen amount, but in terms of the dollar it increased by over $8 billion to a record $58 billion. With the sharp rise in the value of her currency, Japan suddenly found herself controlling 60

---

[16]In addition to Japan and the United States, the Group of Five included Great Britan, France and West Germany. This meeting was called by Secretary of Treasury James Baker. Paul Volcker, Federal Reserve chairman also represented the United States. The Japanese representatives were Finance Minister Takeshita Noboru, and Sumita Satoshi, president of the Bank of Japan. Membership in the group subsequently was raised to seven with Canada and Italy participating. Russia is invited to attend its meetings but not as formal member.

percent of the world's capital assets by the end of 1986. Eight of the ten largest banks in the world that year were Japanese.

11 Excerpts from Statement of G-5 Nations on Economic Problems, 1985[17]

Policy Intentions

The finance ministers and governors affirmed that each of their countries remains firmly committed to its international responsibilities and obligations as leading industrial nations. They also share special responsibilities to ensure the mutual consistency of their individual policies. The ministers agreed that establishing more widely strong, noninflationary domestic growth and open markets will be a key factor in ensuring that the current expansion continues in a more balanced fashion, and they committed themselves to policies toward that end. In countries where the budget deficit is too high, further measures to reduce the deficit substantially are urgently required.

Ministers recognized the importance of providing access to their markets for LDC [lesser developed country] exports as those countries continue their essential adjustment efforts, and saw this as an important additional reason to avoid protectionist policies. They welcomed the GATT preparatory meeting scheduled for late September and expressed their hope that it will reach a broad consensus on subject matter and modalities for a new GATT round.

In this context, they recalled and reaffirmed the statement in the Bonn Economic Declaration on the debt situation: sustained growth in world trade, lower interest rates, open markets and continued financing in amounts and on terms appropriate to each individual case are essential to enable developing countries to achieve sound growth and overcome their economic and financial difficulties.

The ministers agreed that they would monitor progress in achieving a sustained noninflationary expansion and intensify their individual and cooperative efforts to accomplish this objective. To that end, they affirmed the statements of policy intentions by each of their countries.

Conclusions

The ministers of finance and central bank governors agreed that recent economic developments and policy changes, when combined with the specific policy intentions described in the statements, provide a sound basis for continued

---

[17]*The New York Times,* September 23, 1985, D12

and a more balanced expansion with low inflation. They agreed on the importance of these improvements for redressing the large and growing external imbalances that have developed. In that connection, they noted that further market-opening measures will be important to resisting protectionism.

The ministers and governors agreed that exchange rates should play a role in adjusting external imbalances. In order to do this, exchange rates should better reflect fundamental economic conditions than has been the case. They believe that agreed policy actions must be implemented and reinforced to improve the fundamentals further, and that in view of the present and prospective changes in fundamentals, some further orderly appreciation of the main nondollar currencies against the dollar is desirable. They stand ready to cooperate more closely to encourage this when to do so would be helpful.

THE JAPAN THAT CAN SAY NO

To resolve the huge trade deficit annually accumulating in the U.S. trade with Japan, the two governments took a series of measures, including voluntary quotas on car exports to the United States and some market opening mechanisms. None of these measures proved satisfactory, and both sides continued to engage in the ritual of trade talks. The proceedings were often confrontational and were reported with passion in the mass media. American negotiators charged their Japanese counterparts with intransigence, and the latter in turn accused the former of using unwarranted high-pressure tactics. This was the background which greeted the publication in 1989 of a small book entitled The Japan That Can Say No.

Co-authored by Morita Akio, the Sony chairman, and Ishihara Shintarō (b. 1932), an award-winning author of literary novels turned politician, the book became an instant best seller. In his book Ishihara asserted that America's entire nuclear arsenal depended on Japanese microchips. If Japan sold them to the Soviet Union instead of the United States, the entire military balance of the world would be upset. When a pirated translation of the book appeared in the United States, this particular portion of Ishihara's view became of serious concern to American policymakers. Ishihara was at that time a serious contender for the presidency of the ruling Liberal Democratic Party.

An authorized translation of Ishihara's work, along with later additions, was published in the United States in 1991. Document 12 below comes from this American edition. To some, Ishihara's book is an unfettered expression of Japan's national hubris. To others, it is a plea for the beginning of a serious dialogue as an equal partner with the United States. His reference to Japan's position in the world, and the perception of how American actions and words affect Japan, must be read with this in mind.

12   Japan and America: The Major Players in the New Era, 1991[18]

The handshake between George Bush and Mikhail Gorbachev opening the Malta summit signaled the end of Cold War, the titanic clash between communism and democracy. Bush reacted ambivalently to the earlier East German decision to tear down the Berlin Wall. Although he praised the act, his face betrayed mixed emotions. A unified Germany will probably be a troublesome factor in U.S. plans. . . .

Bush's perplexed look . . . evinced the confusion people feel in the transition from one era to another, whether they welcome or deplore the shift. The unfamiliar is disorienting. Nevertheless, societies, like individuals, change with the passage of time; the surging tides of history transform civilizations. Nations that fail to adjust lose control of their own destinies.

Buffeted by events, ties between countries ebb and alter. There is no permanent bilateral status quo. . . . The Japan-U.S. relations will also change in the future. Although the two countries have been very close since World War II, it has not always been marked by full mutual understanding. . . .

The United States has not sufficiently appreciated Japan and even taken us all that seriously, because since 1945, we have been under Uncle Sam's thumb. Today, Americans may feel that Japan is getting out of hand. My own view is that Japan should not immediately disassociate itself from the U.S. security system. For our sake and that of the whole Pacific region, the special Tokyo-Washington relationship must be preserved. A breakup could destroy the budding new developments in that region. Japan should play an expanded role in the post-Cold War world order. Effective use of our economic power—technology, management skills, and financial resources—at our own initiative can be the key to stable progress.

The economic dimension of the next era is already unfolding. That communism, a political doctrine no longer meaningful or functional, has remained powerful until recently is an irony of history. Prolonged obsession with ideology was a cultural lag between technology and the human beings who created it. To Japanese, as a pragmatic people inclined toward craftsmanship rather than metaphysics, the end of idiology is good news.

History shows that technology creates civilization and determines the scale and level of its economic and industrial development. Eastern Europe and the Soviet Union want state-of-the-art technology and financial aid to make them productive. What country can provide them? Only Japan. But we cannot meet this challenge alone. It must be a joint undertaking with our partner, the United States.

---

[18] Reprinted with permission of Simon & Schuster from *The Japan That Can Say No: Why Japan Will Be First Among Equals* by Shintarō Ishihara, pp. 103–119. Copyright © 1989 by Shintarō Ishihara. English Language Edition, translated by Frank Baldwin. © 1991 by Shintarō Ishihara.

Japan's World Role

In its opinions about Japan, Washington is divided into the so-called Cherry Blossom Club and the Japan-bashers, with the former in the departments of State and Defense and the latter headquartered on Capitol Hill. The U.S. military and foreign service are well aware that Japan's high technology and mass-production system are indispensable in America's global strategy and consider the torrent of congressional attacks unwise. Still, the Cherry Blossoms and the Japanese-bashers agree on one thing: they do not want Japan to become more powerful than it is now.

Ronald Morse, a Japan specialist at the Library of Congress, and Alan Tonelson, former editor of *Foreign Policy,* co-authored an unusually freewheeling article in the *New York Times* entitled "Let Japan Be Japan" (October 4, 1987). They wrote: "Clearly, Japan should stand on its own two feet, strategically and politically as well as economically. By continuing to treat Japan as a subordinate, America only makes the inevitable breakup speedier and nastier." Morse and Tonelson concluded that "if Japan assumes a constructive role in regional and world affairs, both countries will benefit."

The message is clear: We must think and act for ourselves and stop being a dutiful underling who leaves all the hard decisions up to the boss. . . .

Some scholars say that in peacetime relations between nations do not change overnight. Nevertheless, in a period of great historical upheaval like the present, there are seminal events that alter our perceptions of the world. To the careful observer, history provides valid principles for a nation's course of action and approach. The echoes of the past reverberate for a while, but it is only the past, after all. Our task is to define the elusive future, to hear those faint portentous sounds of tomorrow. We look back at history to see ahead.

As the tempestuous twentieth century draws to a close, I would like to add a postscript to modernism. Caucasians deserve much credit in the creation of modern civilization, but they were not the only agents of change. Historian Arnold J. Toynbee concluded that we had simply imitated the West. Regrettably, some Japanese agree with the British scholar's interpretation and are delighted at this "high praise." This sad lot does not understand history. What to superficial observers seems like the instantaneous aping of Western ways was actually the fruition of innumerable cultural advances over the course of many centuries.

The modernization that started in Japan in the late nineteenth century was built upon the highly sophisticated culture of the Tokugawa period (1603–1847), which in turn evolved from the Azuchi-Momoyama culture of the late sixteenth century that was so admired by Spanish and Portuguese priests and merchants. Ashikaga Yoshimasa's (1436–1490) aesthetic splendor graced the fifteenth century and so on back a millennium. How preposterous to assert that somehow modern Japan sprang full-blown from Western seeds! China dates from antiquity but lacks cultural continuity and consistency because of dynastic upheaval and foreign rule. In contrast, Japan's superior cultural ethos enabled us to modernize successfully. Toynbee, whether intentionally, unconsciously, or from ignorance, said nothing about this historical heritage.

At any rate, Japanese must understand that today the nation is riding the crest of a great historic wave and, with the United States, will shape the next age. I disagree with the oft-stated view that the twenty-first century will be a pentapolar world—the United States, Japan, Europe, the Soviet Union, and China. The United States will probably pull itself together and continue to be a leader. Eastern Europe and the Soviet Union, however, will ultimately be part of the global network of Japanese technology.

The United States wants to provide massive aid to Eastern Europe, such as the Marshall Plan that stimulated Western Europe's recovery after World War II. Many Americans trace their ethnic heritage to the Old World, and to keep the upper hand with Moscow, Washington should try to establish hegemony over the former Iron Curtain countries.

Mired in debt, however, the United States lacks the financial wherewithal to be the principal aid donor and will be unable to revive its economy and mount such an initiative until early in the twenty-first century. First there must be a massive federal program to improve the school system and retrain the labor force. The investment in human resource development will not pay off for at least fifteen years.

The Japanese have shown great technological competence, especially in commercializing and mass production of quality goods. The United States is ahead in many aspects of basic research, but brilliant breakthroughs in the laboratory are useless until engineers and lathe operators turn them into products. By bridging the gap between the ivory tower and the assembly line, Japanese know-how contributes to the world economy.

Here is the probable scenario for Eastern Europe: Our funds and technology will resuscitate the region. Then the former satellites will gradually transfer know-how to the Soviet Union, bringing it within our technological sphere of influence. From Tokyo to Moscow via Warsaw and Prague will be a short journey. . . .

In the coming decades, Europe will be dominated by a reunited Germany. The Soviet Union and China will be less dynamic than at present, whereas the Pacific region and Southeast Asia will be more. The Japan-U.S. team must be a constructive influence in this new configuration.

A Partnership for the World

Japan's foreign policy is obviously inadequate for a world in flux. . . . A comment about the old war by Raymond Aron, the French educator and writer, comes to mind—that peace is unattainable but war is impossible. With the Malta thaw, that observation can be updated to peace has been obtained but war is possible. An East-West conflict would have escalated to an all-out nuclear exchange, so a major showdown was avoided. Regional clashes, however, remain a great danger. In a sense, the world is more complicated now. . . . Also with the shift from military confrontation to economic competition, Japan needs a national strategy for global trade relations.

The conflicts among nations will be increasingly economic in nature. With the Cold War over, friction on trade and investment will inevitably intensify. Over the next few years, Japan-bashing in the United States will become even more virulent. Although I see the bilateral relationship as the dominant force in the next century, before we reach that level of cooperation, U.S. policy toward Japan will approximate the stance against the Soviet Union at the height of the Cold War.

First, Americans will argue that Japan is different and therefore a threat. Next, a "collective security system" will be created to block Japan's economic expansion. Then protectionist measures and sanctions against Japanese products will follow one after the other. An alliance is already being formed against Japan. Finally, there will be a witch hunt directed at everything Japanese. We must be prepared for stormy days ahead.

If we try to bend with the wind, making concessions and patchwork compromises as usual, the tempest will abate for a while, only to recur with even greater force. We must not flinch in the face of pressure. The only way to withstand foreign demands is to hold our ground courageously. No more temporizing. When justified, we must keep saying no and be undaunted by the reaction, however furious. A prolonged standoff forces both sides to find areas of agreement. That is the best way to resolve disputes, not unilateral concessions by Japan, which leave the other party unaware of how we really feel. Our lack of assertiveness in the past has led to disparaging epithets like "the faceless people."

Our "yes, yes" style of diplomacy limits freedom of action and confuses the public. Asakai Kōichiro, former ambassador to the United States, . . . has decried our concession-prone foreign policy and continued deference to the United States. For example, suppose a Soviet foreign minister said, "We will return the four northern islands. You abrogate the Japan-U.S. security treaty. The Soviet Unions is no threat to Japan." A certain segment of the public would welcome the Soviet proposal. How would politicians respond to Moscow and approach Washington? A misstep might cause a political upheaval in Japan, according to Asakai, and he wondered whether the government had the gumption to make the first move.

A deal with the Soviet Union over semiconductors cannot be completely ruled out. As I have noted, microchips determine the accuracy of weapons systems and are the key to military power. U.S. strategists count on Japan's ability to mass-produce quality chips. Yet some Japanese businessmen believe that if Moscow returns the Northern Territories, we should terminate the security treaty and become neutral. They hope Japan would then receive exclusive rights to develop Siberia.

Quite conceivably the Soviet Union would prefer tie-ups with Japan in some areas over the United States. We have maglev technology for a high-speed rail network in Siberia which the United States does not, and are ahead in some other major high-tech fields, too. We should indicate to the Americans that Tokyo and

Moscow have this option. However, even saying this to Washington is, at present, out of the question for the Japanese establishment. . . .

Industrial Robots and the Tea Ceremony

For some time I have proposed that Japan and the United States form a Super Group of Two analogous to the Group of Seven major industrialized nations. The two leading economic powers must coordinate and cooperate in many areas, from trade to the environment. Unquestionably, the United States is the cutting-edge country in high technology. Yet as Peter Drucker says, technology must be combined with management. Granted a U.S. lead in basic research, Japan skillfully links technology and management to make products for worldwide marketing. Japanese would bring very sophisticated assets to the G-2 team, resources the United States now lacks. Congressional acquaintances admit that the U.S. manufacturing sector is losing this dynamic dimension. We agreed that Japan's strengths would complement those of the United States, and vice versa. . . .

Japan has plenty of other know-how to offer the United States, most notably corporate culture. Japanese companies are distinctive for their warm interpersonal relations. There is an emotional attachment to company, workplace, colleagues, and even the machinery. To cite an extreme case, workers affix photos of popular singers like Yamaguchi Momoe and Sakurada Junko to industrial robots and nickname the machines "Momoe" or "Junko." Silly as this may seem, it enhances productivity. Thinking of a cold piece of metal in human terms generates a kind of empathy, a personal connection. Employees regard the robots as coworkers and quickly spot and repair trouble. Less time is lost on the assembly line.

Many Japanese mistakenly think this emotional ambiance cannot be transferred abroad. Actually, it is relatively easy to do, especially compared with high culture like Noh, the tea ceremony, and flower arranging, rarefied tastes not easily acquired. Sharing our know-how in the industrial sphere is more efficient and useful. Understanding the emotional context of a Japanese-style factory provides some background for the refined aesthetics of the Way of Tea and *ikebana*. An appreciation of Japanese culture will lead to respect for Japan as a country. Despite my (undeserved) reputation as a trouble-maker, I am always looking for constructive ways to present Japan to other countries.

CHAPTER **XVIII**

Heisei: Age of Uncertainty

When the new era of Heisei was proclaimed with the accession to the throne of Emperor Akihito in January 1989, the Japanese economy was at the apogee of its power. The Cold War was over, confirmed later that year in the Malta declaration between the United States and the Soviet Union. America remained the only superpower, but was beset by financial woes. It was widely believed that *Pax Americana* was not possible without the active participation of Japan. If the major antagonists in the past conflict were to "beat their swords into ploughshares," then the path Japan had taken in the postwar years had to be proven correct. Economic prosperity under the peace constitution worked wonders. The new reign era name Heisei, or "achieving peace," seemed to signify the renewed self-confidence of the nation. To some, the coming century was Japan's to claim. There was wealth, better distributed than most. There was security, with the crime rate lowest among all advanced nations. Japan became "the country closest to heaven."[1] If anyone were worthy of inheriting the earth, they thought, it would almost have to be the Japanese.

Things changed quickly in directions totally unexpected. The Gulf War of 1991 saw Japan making a contribution of $13 billion toward the war effort, without having anything to say about the conduct of war. The country was not able to reach a consensus, even on the issue of organizing rescue missions for refugees.

The economy also suffered a setback. The manufacturing sector kept on producing quality products for exports, contributing in the process to the worsening of trade friction with other nations. However, its profit margins were cut sharply. The high value of the yen made it necessary to transfer production sites to

---

[1]This phrase comes from Sakaiya Taichi, *Nihon towa Nanika (What Is Japan?)* (Tokyo: Kōdansha, 1991), pp. 14–31.

America, Southeast Asia, China and almost everywhere in the world. The hollowing of Japanese industry created a phenomenon previously unknown in Japan, restructuring of industries. To make things worse, the discovery of illegal trading by major security companies sent shock waves throughout the country, causing the stock market to plunge (October 1, 1990).

In 1991 a recession hit Japan. Unlike the two previous slumps of 1974 and 1986, the latest recession was home-grown and refused to go away even with the application of a large stimulus package.[2] While the public's trust in the government's ability was waning, a series of irregularities was found in the banking institutions as well as among the ranks of the once incorruptible bureaucracy. For a nation accustomed to economic growth based on a relationship of mutual trust, the best of times had suddenly turned into the worst of times.

That uncertainty created a fertile background for a political change. The Liberal Democratic Party, which had held power continuously since 1955, was swept aside in 1993. From 1993 through 1996, Japan experienced four new Cabinets, two of which were headed by opposition parties, and two formed by a coalition of the Liberal Democratic Party with the Socialist Party and another minor party. Lack of political stability initially favored the bureaucracy to assume greater power. However, when they were proven inept in the aftermath of the Kobe earthquake and the poison gas attack in the Tokyo subways, both of which occurred in 1995, the public's respect and sense of trust for them diminished. It was sobering to discover that Japan did not have an adequate system of crisis management in place.

It is too soon to characterize the *élan* of the Heisei era. Ardor is strangely absent. Its first decade is likely to be known as a decade of reflection, as the people begin to restudy and question those well-established notions and institutions of the past. No longer is anything taken for granted. For want of a better term, we shall call this an age of uncertainty. Accompanied by the *fin-de-siècle* mentality, the Japanese people are searching for alternative ways. It can take the form of a demand for political reform, an inquiry into how the Japanese look at themselves (*nihonjin-rōn*), or a quest for an alternative lifestyle. The Japanese society may yet emerge stronger and better through this period of self-examination.

Most of the selections included in this chapter are samples of these self-examinations. They can take the form of a demand for political reform (Document 1),

---

[2]The 1974 slump was induced by the first oil crisis, and the 1986 slump by the sharp climb in the value of the yen after the Plaza accord. Professor Miyazaki Yoshikazu wrote a book, *Fukugō Fukyō* (*Combined Recession*) (Tokyo: Chūo Kōronsha, 1992) to explain the 1991 phenomenon. According to him, financial liberalization created a bubble economy. After the bubble burst, banks were suddenly saddled with problem loans and saw their own assets tumbling. The flows which created the gross national product were cut off at their source. A stimulus package aimed at increasing demand would not be effective in the recession that was caused by the financial institution's credit crunch.

a look at Japan's education system (Document 2), making a case for deregulation (Document 3), reflecting on the experience of the Kobe earthquake (Document 4), and examining a proposal to relocate the capital away from Tokyo (Document 5). There is one underlying common theme in these five documents. While the Japanese people are feeling uncomfortable with the intrusiveness of their government and wishing to curtail its power, they also depend on the government to provide security and other services. It is a dilemma shared with other modern societies, and the suggested Japanese solutions have a universal ring to them.

Questioning of the status quo does not end with political, economic, and organizational aspects. Document 6 gives a view of a search for a different lifestyle, in this case, harking back to Japan's older tradition for the enjoyment of a simple life. Document 7 deals with the issue of death and dying. Document 8 provides a rare insight into an architect's view of traditional beauty, and his application of that insight to the present-day economic friction. Document 9 is an essay by a prominent journalist looking into the past for lessons for the coming century.

REFORMING POLITICS AND EDUCATION

No single individual was more responsible for the collapse of the 1955 political system than Ozawa Ichirō (b. 1942). In 1992, at the age of fifty, Ozawa was already a major figure in Japanese politics, having served three terms as secretary general of the LDP. He was also the acting head of the Takeshita faction, the largest one within the LDP. He was an advocate of political reform, in the form of creating a single constituency to replace the multiseat constituency for the House of Representatives. On this and on other matters, he was at odds with his elders within the party. On December 11, a group of forty-four supporters sympathetic to him formed a new faction. The following year, in 1993, this same faction joined the opposition in a non-confidence vote against an LDP prime minister (Miyazawa) and effectively ended the LDP's monopoly of power.

A Political reform law creating a modified single-constituency system passed on January 29, 1994. Its main features were: (a) creation of 300 single-seat constituencies for the House of Representatives, and 200 additional members to be elected proportionately from eleven electoral blocs established for that purpose; and (b) institution of a limited amount of public financing for general elections to discourage corporate contributions.[3] It was the vehicle through

---

[3]Under this plan, each voter receives two ballots, one for the single-seat constituency, and the other for the electoral bloc. For the former, the voter casts his vote for a candidate, for the latter, he casts his vote for a party. Each party is allocated a number of seats in the bloc proportionate to the votes received. The amount of public subsidy for a party is limited to forty percent of the expenditures of that party for the preceding year. The amount of corporate contribution to each individual politician is limited to 500,000 yen. This provision is valid for five years.

which Ozawa hoped to establish a genuine two-party political system in Japan. He subsequently became the head of the newly formed New Frontier Party (Shinshintō, established on December 10, 1994).

The first general election under the new electoral law was held on October 20, 1996. The anticipated political realignment did not occur. The single-constituency districts favored well-known incumbents and gave an edge to the LDP. However, by denying an absolute majority to the LDP, the election forced continuation of a coalition government. As for campaign reform, political spending increased at an even faster pace than before. Substantive changes may not have occurred in the political arena, but demands for administrative reform have remained strong. And in defeat, Ozawa's stand still echoes much of the public sentiment.

Document 1 is Ozawa's political manifesto that served as the rationale for the electoral reform. In 1993 Ozawa's Nippon Kaizō Keikaku (A Plan to Reform Japan) became a best seller. In it, he spoke not only of electoral reform, but also of freedoms from Tokyo, from industries, and from long hours of work. He urged Japan to assume a greater share of responsibility in world affairs. All in all, he insisted that education had to be transformed if Japan were to change sufficient. Document 2 gives his view of Japanese education.

1   Ozawa's Plan for Political Reform, 1992[4]

(a) Electoral Reform: A Means, Not an End

The politics of what I call the conservative camp in the LDP took shape in the framework constructed after World War II. With the Cold War raging, Japan was able to get by without playing a major role on the international scene. That meant the job of Japan's politicians was simply to see to it that the fruits of people's hard work were distributed as equitably as possible. About all the ruling party had to do was decide how to allocate the money in the budget after negotiations with the opposition.

"Negotiations" sounds dignified, but actually it was just a matter of deciding how to divide the spoils. There was no need for discernment or farsighted policies. With the economy chugging along under its own power, the Japanese paid no attention to the costs of preserving the peaceful and free global setting in which their country's development was taking place. The United States and other Western countries created that setting, and Japan took free advantage of their efforts. Such was the structure of Japanese politics in the Cold War era.

A turbulent period has now begun with the Cold War's end. The Soviet Union has disintegrated, the leadership power of the United States has greatly declined, and for the first time the world is looking to Japan to shoulder various costs and responsibilities. Never having contemplated such a role, the political world does

---

[4]This is a condensed version of "My Commitment to Political Reform" by Ozawa Ichirō as it appeared in *Japan Echo* 20, no. 1 (Spring 1993): pp. 10–12. The original of this article first appeared in the December 1992 issue of the *Bungei Shunjū*.

not know what to do. Japan's body has grown to gigantic proportions, but its brain and nervous system have failed to develop accordingly. Our country lacks the maturity to get along in the international community. This is why reform is such an urgent issue. We must develop a political system capable of thinking for itself, one that can get down to work, move into action, and deal with the chores before it.

Given the severity of the gaze the world is now directing at Japan, we obviously have to act quickly. My personal feeling is that if we do not radically revamp our politics within a few years, other countries will turn their backs on us. Of course reform is essential in a number of areas, but our group's opinion is that political reform must come first. And if we expect to reform Japan's political structure, we must first put an end to the cozy Cold War era setup in which one party is perennially in power and the others are the perennial opposition.

People say that I am a champion of the plan to replace the multiseat electoral districts in the lower house with single-member constituencies, but that is not entirely accurate. This plan represents just one of a number of means that might be used to effect a reform. The point is that whatever means is selected, the end must be an altered power balance between the complacent LDP and the equally complacent opposition. A system of single-seat districts would, I believe, provide a realistic way of reaching that goal. No doubt the LDP would win crushing victories for a while. But as can be seen from the July 1989 House of Councillors election, when an angry electorate denied the Liberal Democrats a majority in the upper house, the single-seat system is capable of vaulting the opposition parties into power, provided only that they pull themselves together when a chance comes along. Thus while the configuration of the electoral system is not the real issue, single-member districts offer a convenient tool for getting started on reform. As I see it, they would enable us once again to try to build a two-party political system. In any event, we have to overhaul the political system and, in the process, secure a powerful leadership system.

(b) A Decentralization Plan

As part of the reform, we must take a scalpel to the administrative machinery. To remedy the evils of too much power in the center, we should embark on bold decentralization. Beginning in the Meiji era (1868–1912), the highly capable and thoroughly centralized bureaucracy played a key role in guiding latecomer Japan's catch-up efforts. I have no intention of belittling its accomplishments. I believe, however, that this style of administration will not do any longer. Like the economic system of mass-producing quality goods inexpensively, it has reached its limit. More than that, excessive centralization is retarding the political maturation of the public. We have entered an age when all Japanese should be thinking for themselves and making their own decisions, but few are capable of that. In politics as in business, people cannot kick the habit of letting those in power set the targets, after which everybody pulls together to reach them. We have become far too comfortable with a "consensus society" in which everybody holds the same values. That way of thinking and acting has become outdated. Though we may not need to go as far as Western societies have toward putting the individual first, we need to foster a social climate that encourages individuality and respects each human being. Progress in this direction is hampered by the concentration of power at the center.

Today's bureaucrats are still thoroughly convinced of their own importance. They see Tokyo as the brain and the regions as arms and legs. With their kind of mind-set, efforts to give birth to dynamic and creative regional communities will never make much progress, nor will ordinary Japanese gain the leeway to flower as individuals. But the times are changing. In the economic sphere, companies must come up with products that are original and have a large value-added content. And that means we must foster talented individuals with ample creative powers.

The need for a centralized bureaucratic system has come to an end. Bureaucrats must shed their lordly pretensions and turn their attention to altering the country's institutions and systems in ways that make the most of the creativity and traditional culture of the people of the regions. Administrative reform must be carried out with determination. The government's ministries and agencies must, in a sense, be dismantled. Fierce resistance from bureaucrats can be expected, but ways of placating them can be found. The main motivation for their resistance is, I would say, their perception that they will be stripped of their powers. They should be encouraged to think of the change in positive terms as something that will allow them, along with the members of the national legislature, to concentrate on the bigger job of considering the future of Japan as a whole.

(c) New Roles for Japan in the World

The Japanese have been acquiring a new attitude toward their country's international duties. Basically the public remains conservative, but it is somewhat more receptive to change than are the old-line politicians, the bureaucrats, and the leaders of the business community. When the crisis in the Persian Gulf broke out, many people failed to comprehend why Japan should get involved in this distant affair, and I, as the LDP's secretary general, was kept busy in the endeavor to see that Japan made a meaningful contribution to the conflict's resolution. Today, however, public consciousness about Japan's world role has changed considerably. While their thinking continues to be disturbingly vague, most people endorse the recent dispatch of Japanese troops to Cambodia, where they have joined the United Nations' peacekeeping operations. In this sense, I am satisfied with our efforts.

I was not equally pleased, however, with the decision-making process that enabled these peacekeepers to go overseas. Before soldiers are sent into action, political leaders must determine whether this is truly in the country's best interests, and while asking the nation's understanding of their decision, they must take responsibility for the dispatch of the troops. What is involved here is the concept of civilian control over the military. No country is more dangerous than one in which the armed forces operate in isolation from the people. This means that sometimes military personnel should be called to the Diet to answer questions from legislators. We should not be entrusting weapons to people who know nothing of the world. In Japan today, however, civilian control is being treated more as a question of protocol, of seeing to it that the civilians in the Defense Agency preserve their superiority over the agency's uniformed officials. Thus when I recommended that military personnel be asked to testify in the Diet, the opposition and my own party turned the request down, arguing that such a step would amount to a violation of civilian control. Frankly I find that line of thinking ridiculous.

By and large, the nation seems willing to let unfolding events carry it along, just as in the prewar period. We urgently need to transform the way the Japanese think. As Japan seeks a place for itself in the international community, it will be forced to make decisions on grave matters it has never given much thought to, and it is apt to make the wrong decisions if attitudes do not change quickly.

(d) The Need for Political Reform

As representatives of the electorate, politicians are by no means unblemished individuals. They do not stand head and shoulders above everybody else in terms of talents and abilities, and they may not be as dependable as one might hope. But it is the system of democracy that entrusts the reins of government to these somewhat limited representatives. Despite the risk of a democracy turning into a mobocracy, civilization has selected it as the best form of government in the light of the far greater dangers when an oligarchy run by a few people embarks on a mistaken course. If we are to safeguard the wisdom of this choice, we must now join hands to push through a comprehensive political reform.

2 **Freedom through Education Reform. 1993**[5] Why is it that we have lost so much of our freedom after the war? We have probed into its various causes, but in the final analysis, our people themselves must bear the largest share of responsibility. As it is known, democracy had its beginning in the people's wrestling the power away from their kings and sovereigns. It was the desire for self rule that created democracy. Naturally it is premised on the fact that people take responsibility to nurture democracy. Without that premise, democracy cannot survive even when politics and administrative measures all point to its realization.

Postwar Japan was supposed to have introduced American-style democracy. However, without our knowing it, freedom has been taken away from us. It is true that part of the problem came from the fact that the bureaucracy of the

---

[5]Ozawa Ichirō, *Nihon Kaizō Keikaku (A Plan to Reform Japan)* (Tokyo: Kōdansha, 1993), pp. 251–57.

prewar period survived into the postwar period. In the final analysis, however, there were not enough conditions existing among our people to sustain the healthy growth of democracy.

For example, the imperial army and navy of the prewar era were well trained and maintained a tight discipline. They were strong and the best in the world. However, with the defeat in the war and as the organization of the armed forces crumbled, the troops immediately turned into a motley crowd. What did this indicate? They were great pawns within an organization, but they were not independent individuals with their own values and judgment.

It was not possible for the defeat, an important "moment" in history, to transform the Japanese people from the very foundation of their existence. Not having adequate preconditions for democracy, Japan introduced American-style postwar democracy. To this day, it has never taken root. That is the reason why we lack freedom in our present-day society.

Postwar education was supposed to create an environment suitable for the growth of democracy. It went the opposite way from its mission. Our children are faced with the serious issues of an increase in misdeeds and crimes, an increase in the use of force at home and in school, and an increase in substance abuse and AIDS. Instead of attaining the full development of their personality, our youths are facing problems that could destroy them. We cannot totally dissociate the present state of education with these devastating issues.

If we are to secure true freedom for Japanese society, we must vigorously pursue the task of education reform. . . . First let us deal with the issue of our primary education.

At this level, Japanese education is often praised by foreign observers. International Educational Assessment places Japan at the top. In contrast, American children place near the bottom. This comparison is frequently discussed. Does it mean that the status quo in Japan's primary and secondary education must be maintained?

In reality, behind these accomplishments, Japanese children's independence and initiative are nipped in the bud. An American cultural anthropologist came to Japan to study our high schools. What he saw was the sight of high school students placed in an immovable fetter dictated by the entrance examination system. The road they had to travel was straight and narrow. They were bound to their homes and to schools. Those who failed to work diligently were punished.

They were encouraged to conform to the world instead of trying something new. They were taught to become outward-oriented instead of examining inwardly. They had to deny themselves, and were taught that maturity meant to be able to adjust to one's own surrounding, no matter how superficial it might be. They were not taught how to express their views. They were not encouraged to speak or to write, and were not educated in thinking and debating. They were not informed that on one particular issue, different interpretations were possible. Recitation, not thinking, was placed in the forefront, and in the official curriculum, humanity and artistry were either neglected or ignored.

That was the anthropologist's observation. I fully agree. Our high school students are forced to gulp down information. The same observation can apply to our grade schools and middle schools. In American and English schools, teachers at first do not challenge what the children say, but ask them the reasons and bases for making those particular statements. They may provide counterpoints, but always encourage the children to think. In contrast, in Japan it is the teacher who holds the right answers. They ask the children to guess those answers. Once a right answer is given by a child, no more is said about that question. If the first child fails, another is called to answer immediately. It is the role most suited to computers, but live teachers perform the same task.

From grade school through high school, Japanese children are force-fed right answers. Their ability or habit to think for themselves remains untested, and while still in this state, they enter college. A person of independence cannot be born this way. I am not saying that the United States and Europe are right and whatever Japan is doing is wrong. Why does democracy not take root in Japan? When I probe into its reason, I cannot ignore the difference in education between Japan and the West.

Education reform must begin with reforms in our primary and secondary education.

In concrete terms, we must stop the system of giving uniform guidance from the central government. In other words, let us not have a uniform curriculum throughout the country as we now have. I suggest that we differentiate basic abilities and applied abilities. The central government still controls matters pertaining to basic abilities. As for applied abilities, school boards established by local governments must be empowered to take charge.

By basic abilities, I mean the so-called three Rs, reading, writing, and arithmetic. The central government must establish guidelines as to the age at which children are expected to reach at certain levels. As to how to reach these levels and what curriculum must be employed to reach each level, that task can be left to the local school boards. Likewise the school boards can independently determine the contents of courses in civics [called *shakai,* or society] and sciences. In this way education will be based on the unique culture of each region, there will be nurtured more diverse Japanese as a result of this education. Once education becomes based on the unique culture of a region, the force-fed type of education will correct itself. We must demand that it must be done so. This will eradicate the uniform centralized testing, and the entrance examination system will be forced to change. . . .

DEREGULATION

One of the most frequently spoken phrases in Heisei Japan is Kisei Kanwa, *or deregulation. It is safe to say that no one disagrees with the need for loosening the grip of the government on the industries and on people's daily lives. How-*

ever, once the discussion moves on to the case-by-case examination of regulations to be suspended or amended, however, interest groups begin to bicker. Another phrase "sōron sansei, kakuron hantai (agreeing in principle, but opposing in specifics)" describes well the dilemma Japan faces. In this, Japan is not alone in her ability for equivocation.

In Document 3 below, Professor Yoshida Kazuo (b. 1948) of Kyoto University argues that deregulation must be implemented to revitalize the private sector, as a cure for Japan's long-lasting recession. He is an advocate of corporate streamlining and of the use of technology. His view is that regulations somehow get in the way of progress. Speaking against special-interest groups, the author gives a higher mark for the bureaucracy than most other pundits in their ability to effect deregulation. Incidentally, before commencing his academic career, the author was an official of the Ministry of Finance.

3 **A Case for Deregulation, 1994[6]** Japan's economic policymakers have two major tasks to tackle. One is to put an end to the recession, which is in its fortieth month and has become the longest slump since World War II, and the other is to trim the current account surplus, which has risen above $100 billion per year. The two together pose a classic question asked of economic managers: How is it possible to achieve both internal and external balance simultaneously? In what follows I shall first explain the conventional answer supplied by economists [omitted], and next I will relate how their prescriptions have not been working [partially reproduced]. Then I will explore the problems involved and discuss what should be done [reproduced].

(a) Constraints on Private-sector Vitality

The Japanese market is not a place where relations form between faceless entities; the relations within and among companies are based on face-to-face exchange, and they form a vast network tying society together. In this "network society," which resists easy elucidation using the price mechanism—the guiding force in a normal market economy—systems become extremely complicated. In order to consider these complex systems, we need a form of economic theory suited to the analysis of this society.

I have already given a few examples of the ways in which the design of Japan's society greatly influences the Japanese economy, and here I will suggest another. When we inquire into sources of power capable of lifting the economy out of recession, we find that there is basically just one: a recovery of vitality in the private sector. Only corporate efforts to streamline operations and upgrade technology can drive Japan's economy forward.

[6]Yoshida Kazuo, "A Dose of Deregulation to Buoy Business," in *Japan Echo* 21, no. 4 (Winter 1994): pp. 21, 25–28. The original of this article first appeared in the August 1994 issue of *Shokun.*

Ever since the first oil shock of 1973–74, the government has been responding to downturns by pumping money into the economy, but this spending has not had much effect. After the second oil shock of 1979–80, a period of sluggish growth set in, and it lasted until the long "Heisei boom," named after the start of the Heisei era in 1989, got under way. How are the economy's recovery and subsequent strong growth to be explained? Certainly we cannot cite a favorable exchange rate, since from the start of this phase the yen, which began appreciating in 1985, was on a rising trend. And the government's austerity program for rehabilitating public finance and balancing the budget was certainly not the driving force either. The boom was rather the fruit of the business world's rationalization efforts and technological innovations centered on the semiconductor. Having elevated productivity and developed new products, companies gained renewed vigor.

After the boom came the current recession, and the reason it has lasted so long is that companies have been slow to regain strength. One problem was that management grew sloppy when, as the boom progressed, enormous speculative bubbles engulfed the economy. Other problems can be attributed to the economic system itself.... The Japanese company is an organization whose members, when faced by a threat, do whatever is necessary to keep the firm alive; this is what got companies through the oil shocks and enabled them to withstand repeated buffeting from the climbing yen. Entities in the economic system also place great emphasis on preserving order in industries and markets, and this has held bankruptcies to the minimum. The disadvantage of such behavior is that it works against the recovery of corporate vitality.

Companies in a capitalist economy acquire vitality through competition. Their managers aim first to avoid bankruptcy and next to achieve growth with the help of innovation. Those firms that successfully innovate thrive, and those that do not fall by the wayside and close down. Through this process the overall economy becomes more efficient....

The potential power of competition is not being fully utilized in Japan, however, and this is because organizations that try to avoid rivalry as far as possible are being carefully preserved. Here the role of government must be examined, since Japan's ministries and agencies have been actively involved in building the order within each market sector. Unlike Western governments, which function as regulators of industry, the Japanese bureaucracy serves more as a facilitator, an organization dedicated to securing cooperation in keeping economic activities going smoothly. Whenever something unexpected happens, Japanese companies run to the authorities for help. And whenever the government does not step in, the media lash out at it for failing to do its job. In this setting, bureaucrats feel compelled to consult regularly with businesses and to clear away any obstructions in their path.

The government's regulations all have one objective or another, and they play a vital role in enabling the economy to function properly. For instance, because of "information dissymmetry," or the tendency for producers to know more than consumers about goods and services, rules to protect the consumer must be enforced. But some regulations devised to attain one objective turn out to cause unintended damage in other areas, and other regulations supposedly designed to help the consumer actually function to protect the producer and preserve the status quo.

Again, the passage of time can cause the effect of controls to deviate from [what was] initially intended, and if outdated controls are not removed, they will clutter up the marketplace. A case in point is the system of periodic safety inspections for autos. When this system was set up, the public welcomed it because inadequate maintenance of shoddily built Japanese cars was causing many problems. Now that cars are built not to break down, the only beneficiaries of the expensive inspections are the garages that carry them out.

Bad regulations undermine economic dynamism. At a time when industrial structure is being transformed by forces like the rise of the yen, they are apt to be used to protect sunset industries and have their ears attuned to cries for relief in industries that are reaching the end of the line, but they are likely to ignore oppressive rules affecting industries waiting to be born, since these businesses have no voice.

All in all, deregulation is the key to energizing private enterprise at the present time, when industry is in the midst of structural transformation. Thus far the ministries have been limiting new entrants in various fields on the grounds that this is necessary to preserve order. While the limits give an advantage to insiders over the short term, over the long run they deprive companies of independence of action, and this makes recovery from a recession more difficult. Both to put the current slump behind and to strengthen industry for the twenty-first century, deregulation is a must.

(b) The Forces Arrayed against Deregulation

It is now relatively widely recognized that deregulation has become a critical task, one that holds promise of breathing new life into companies and launching industry into a growth orbit. The general view is that deregulation will not give the economy an immediate boost but should provide buoyancy over the long run. When Prime Minister Hosokawa moved into office, an advisory panel popularly called the Hiraiwa group was set up to study how the economy should be restructured. Led by Hiraiwa Gaishi, then chairman of Keidanren (Japan Federation of Economic Organizations), the group concluded that economic regulations should be eliminated in principle and retained only in exceptional areas, and it advised that social regulations be reduced to the necessary minimum, with the principle of self-responsibility applied wherever possible. Deregulation became a leading item on Hosokawa's agenda, but enthusiasm for it waned when his administration collapsed.

The slow progress in deregulation to date is said to be the fault of the bureaucratic organs clustered in Tokyo's Kasumigaseki district. The thinking is that if controls were lifted, public officials would run out of things to do. Their budgets would be cut; their influence over companies would wane; and their chances of moving into plush retirement jobs in private industry would dwindle. This perception of "Kasumigaseki's obstructionism" has even triggered a round of bureaucrat bashing. Actually, however, the lack of progress cannot be explained that easily. More fundamentally, public administrators cannot function without some regulatory powers.

In any event, where attention should be focused is on the groups that have a vested interest in leaving regulations in place. In the case of the car inspection system—a hot topic in the decontrol debate—only a handful of civil servants in the Ministry of Transport are engaged in supervising procedures and revising policies, but half a million workers in the private sector are said to be making money from inspection work. By the same token, a multitude of small shops is benefiting from the limits placed on big outlets by the Large-Scale Retail Store Law, which is administered by a small group of officials in the Ministry of International Trade and Industry. Though I myself cannot say how much extra work has been created by the existence of controls in Japan's regulated sectors, the economist Nakatani Iwao has estimated that comprehensive deregulation would eliminate ten million jobs. Obviously most of the opposition to deregulation comes from the people in these jobs, and public officials are merely acting on their behalf.

Regulations generate profits in controlled industries. If a license is required before a business can open, those who hold licenses can naturally be expected to make money. When new entrants are shut out, limits on supply are apt to push up prices and fatten profits. Even if there is no official licensing system, moreover, a plethora of other regulations will have a similar effect. The insiders, who will be familiar with ways to utilize red tape, will gain an advantage, and new entrants will have trouble competing. Price controls offer another way to sweeten profits. In setting prices, officials generally use figures based on costs plus a certain profit margin measured in percentage points, and this means that profits can be boosted by allowing costs to inflate.

The presence of huge special-interest groups deters bureaucrats from easing or abolishing regulations. Because civil servants keep in close touch with the industries in their jurisdiction and frequently call on them for cooperation, they find it hard to act against their interest. They hope above all to avoid a bitter confrontation between government and industry, since that would make it hard for them to administrate smoothly. Businesses, for their part, have developed management systems predicated upon an inflow of profits derived from regulation. They adamantly refuse to go along with any rule change that might work against them, and they often enlist the help of politicians to dissuade bureaucrats from pressing forward with reform programs.

One reason why bureaucrats are reluctant to remove present controls is that they worry about future situations in which they may need them again, and reinstating a once-discarded control is not easy. Complicating the situation, once a new regulatory system is authorized, it gives birth to a set of organizations. A system of safety standards, for instance, will bring into being a screening association operating under the concerned ministry as well as industrial organizations engaged in the system's actual implementation. Eliminating a system thus means firing the people in these organizations, and in Japan's case that further means finding them new jobs. As hard as this may be for companies to accomplish, it is harder yet for a government organ. Recruitment into the bureaucracy is not an option, since staff sizes for public employees are set by law. In the end, all the authorities can do is to ask major corporations to take the surplus personnel off their hands.

Because of the strict legal limits on recruitment by ministries and agencies, there are not nearly enough civil servants to handle all the work involved in administration. The way the government circumvents this constraint whenever it needs personnel for new regulatory systems is by creating quasi-official positions. The ranks of these quasi civil servants, among whom can be found bureaucrats sent out to pasture, have grown to enormous proportions. Deregulation will require dismantling many of the organizations involved. In some cases, however, the organizations have become the tail that wags the dog. For instance, an extensive network of agricultural cooperatives was created to help implement Japan's farm policy, but now it is not clear whether the cooperatives exist to support the policy or the policy exists to keep the cooperatives intact.

The presence of the many quasi officials notwithstanding, it would be inappropriate to attribute slow progress to opposition from officialdom. Lashing out at bureaucrats will not cause reform to pick up speed. Special-interest groups will only conclude that Kasumigaseki's obstructionism deserves to be encouraged, and their estimation of the bureaucracy's value will move up a notch. The proper place to direct criticism is at the businesses that are benefiting from regulations. Were it not for the facts that these businesses are comfortable with the way they are being regulated, public officials would be unable to keep them in line in the first place. And the proper authority to get deregulation going is not the bureaucracy but the political leadership. Since any changes will have negative as well as positive effects, our elected representatives must make the final decisions.

(c) Formulating a Strategy for Deregulation

Many reasons have been advanced to explain the long duration of the latest recession. It is said that corporate investment and recruitment during the bubble years went to such excessive lengths that companies needed time to rid themselves of surplus capacity, and surely there is some truth to this argument. It is also said that damage has been caused by collapsing asset prices, and surely this is also true, even if the damage has not been as great as some people assume.

Nobody can deny, for instance, that falling stock and land prices have saddled banks with a heavy load of nonperforming loans.

Such points noted, has the most important reason not been a decline in entrepreneurial spirit? I would suggest that corporate managers were slow to put their companies back on solid footing because they had their minds on using regulations to secure profits and because, given the presence of regulatory barriers, they gave little thought to pioneering new businesses.

Recently some all-out price wars have begun, and efforts to harness the private sector's vitality are being made. What with the moves to bring out new products, it seems that a recovery cannot be far off. But developments like these require greater vigor. People need to recognize that the key precondition for a robust Japanese economy in the coming century is a business milieu in which companies have freedom of action.

What we need is a bold program to cut red tape. Calls for the establishment of a third-party organization to oversee the process make little sense, since its members would not know as much as bureaucrats do about the regulatory system. A system capable of imposing limits on the number of regulations and phasing out unnecessary ones must be built, and this is a job for politicians. Deregulation inherently means requiring businesses to take more responsibility for their own actions, and a degree of confusion will inevitably have to be tolerated. Above all, we must formulate a strategy for a meaningful deregulation drive.

KOBE EARTHQUAKE AND CRISIS MANAGEMENT

At 5:46 A.M., January 17, 1995, Kobe was struck with an earthquake in which five thousand people lost their lives. It was the worst natural disaster since the Great Kantō Earthquake of 1923. The government's response was slow and rescue missions were poorly coordinated. There was also a mounting criticism against the Self-Defense Forces. Why did they not respond on their own, and why were they not ordered to proceed with the rescue operations immediately? There were some perceived constitutional barriers, and politicians generally assumed the politically correct posture of having very little to do with the Self-Defense Forces. These restraints aside, the SDF became a favorite whipping boy of the mass media. The document reproduced below is a reminiscence of General Matsushima Yūsuke (b. 1939), since retired, who was then the commanding general of the Central Area Ground Self-Defense Force whose jurisdiction extended from Toyama and Aichi to the East to the western tip of the Honshu island, and the island of Shikoku.

The responsibility for the inability to respond must be shared by political leaders and the SDF alike, but with a greater burden placed on the civilian leaders. In the final analysis, however, it was the system that failed them. The government was hierarchically structured, which was ill suited for horizontal

coordination or delegation of power. The communications gears were inopera-
tive in an emergency, and there was no provision made for redundancy. In short,
Japan did not have an adequate system for crisis management. The vaunted
Japanese style of management notwithstanding, the Kobe earthquake became a
sobering experience for the nation.

4 **Self-Defense Forces in the Kobe Earthquake, 1995**[7] The Self-Defense
Forces have been the target of criticism for not responding quickly in the initial
phase of the Kobe earthquake. As the commanding general of the Central Area
Ground Self-Defense Force at that time, responsible for conducting rescue missions, I was determined not to say anything to defend myself, especially when
there were five thousand who died in this natural disaster.

On September 1, there was a nationwide training for natural disaster relief. I
was shocked. In the capital region of Tokyo and elsewhere, there was a sign that
the public was becoming more favorably disposed to the participation by the
Self-Defense Forces. However, the role assigned to us was nothing more than
demonstration. What happened to the lessons of the great earthquake of the
Hanshin (Osaka and Kobe) region? Not to waste the sacrifices of the many, and
to keep alive the lessons we learned, I want to make public the truth as I saw it,
and provide some suggestions for the future.

[General Matsushima was awakened at 5:46 A.M. by the quake. He was unable to make telephone contact, but staff officers reached him at 6:20. An order
was issued to assemble the troops for information gathering, and to prepare for
rescue missions. That was at 6:30. A call was placed to the Central Command
Post located in Roppongi, Tokyo, through a special defense microwave transmit-
ter, and communication with the rest of the nation was maintained through this
channel.]

When there is a typhoon, flood, or earthquake, the regiment stationed in that
district may start operations on its own. This is called by the Self-Defense Forces
"the regiment responsible for the district." The regiment is taught that in an emergency it is their duty to start moving, to engage in the rescue work even without
orders from the division headquarters or from the Central Area Command. . . .

The first report came on 6:35. "Hankyū's Itami station has collapsed. Some
are buried alive." Itami's No. 36 Regiment sent out a scouting group at 6:42. By
7:35, forty-two troops were engaged in rescue work at the sole discretion of
the regiment commander. . . . The Area Command's air unit located in Yao,
Osaka, sent a helicopter to Kobe and Awaji island at 7:14 as dawn was breaking. This was again done at his sole discretion. The pilot reported back at 8:30

---

[7]Matushima Yūsuke, "*Saikō Shikikan ga Akarasu Jieitai Shutsudō no Shinsō*" (Truth
about the Deployment of Self Defense Forces, by the Highest Commander on the Scene)
in *Bungei Shunjū*, December 1995, pp. 166–74.

confirming that there were collapsed buildings and expressways in the center of Kobe. . . .

The regiment responsible for Kobe was the regiment stationed in Himeji, the Third Special Regiment. By 8:30 they were ready to move, but did not receive request for assistance from the governor of Hyōgo until 10:00. Immediately, 250 troops were dispatched. The distance was fifty kilometers, but it took three hours for the first troops to arrive in the Nagata ward [the most damaged district] because of the serious traffic tie-ups. . . .

The dispatch of the Self-Defense Forces has as its primary goal "assistance" of the relief activities conducted by local government bodies. Himeji's Third Regiment kept on asking the Hyōgo governor's office if they needed assistance. We had a "short-wave emergency line," which was not working, and the telephone system of NTT was of no use at that time. We found out only later that the satellite transmission system of the governor's office was not operational because of the destruction of its generator. . . .

We reached the prefectural office once by phone at 8:20. All officers were unable to concentrate and could not respond well. When our staff officers asked about the conditions prevailing in Kobe resulting from the earthquake, the response received was: "We just established our Disaster Rescue Center. We do not have information on the disaster itself.". . .

[General Matsushima goes on to describe how his troops who reached Kobe started to gather information on the spot.]

Normally any of the administrative units, be it the prefecture, city, or ward, could engage in information gathering if it knew how to utilize its own administrative structure fully. But they were not used to crisis management and had no operational capabilities. The Disaster Rescue Center, established by the prefectural government, did not function well. . . . They were absorbed in solving administrative issues, such as how to request rescue funds, what regulations and systems would have to be established and the like. Issues directly connected with the rescue, such as shortage of water and food supply at what location, which road was unpassable, and what factors were preventing rescue operations, if there were adequate emergency shelters, and the like were discussed. But they could hardly arrive at any conclusion.

The meetings were lengthy, usually meeting twice a day from 9 to 11 in the morning and 2 to 4 in the afternoon. Often the meeting went on beyond those assigned time slots. Many top officials spent their time in these meetings, leaving the actual rescue operations without identifiable leaders. . . . I participated in the Disaster Rescue Center's meetings a couple of times when Prime Minister Murayama and Defense Agency Director Tamazawa came to Kobe. There was no map, and no data were provided for the visitors. We sat aimlessly around the table. . . .

The prefectural government did not know where relief supplies were to be sent. When we received donations of food, we asked them where they should be delivered. A response would come asking us to deliver to a certain ward. But they did not have hard data on which to base their decision. We delivered food supplies as requested. At some wards that were functioning smoothly, they knew what to do. At other ward offices, where nothing seemed to go right, food supplies were left there to rot. . . .

Fires started burning in various districts of Kobe, and response on the ground was too slow. The Self-Defense Forces suggested that helicopters might be used to fight fire. At that particular juncture, aftershocks were expected. We were also fearful that fires could start in the mountain forests as well. We wanted to be prepared. However, this was the response we received. "We asked the Fire Department to study the issue. They do not believe that fighting fire from the air would be effective, and there might be more harm done by the firefighting activities. Even with the anticipated aftershocks, we still do not wish to use the helicopters." We persisted. . . . The response remained the same. "No thank you."

I have two important suggestions to make based on my experience with the Kobe earthquake.

The first one concerns local government's crisis management readiness. It may be too unkind to single out the Hyōgo prefecture government for its inability. It is more important for all local government bodies to realize the limitation of their own capabilities. These bodies are administrative bodies, and their responsibilities are minutely divided vertically. Coordination takes up enormous time. And their administrative system is not suitable for rescue operations. Nor have they actually experienced rescue operations.

My plea to them is that they utilize the resources we have in the Self-Defense Forces wisely. I want them to know our capabilities as well as limitations. We possess organizational skills, implementation skills, along with information gathering capabilities. We are also used to crisis management operation. In the case of the Kobe earthquake, once we entered the area and got the feel of the situation, we were able to gather information concerning damages and placed our data on a map. By looking at it, the commander would know the overall situation instantly. He could single-handedly render judgment on what was needed and order dispatch of troops quickly, or ask the command post for the dispatch of a helicopter. Unfortunately, local self-governing bodies, including the Hyōgo prefecture, hardly knew the Self-Defense Forces as an organization or their capabilities. . . .

To redress that situation, there is no substitute for creating an enforceable plan and preparing and training towards it. If a local self-governing body is to request assistance from the Self-Defense Forces, it must know where the troops are stationed and how they are equipped. I cannot overemphasize the need for joint exercises for rescue operations by local self-governing bodies and the Self-Defense Forces. . . .

Another suggestion concerns the national government's readiness for crisis management. The National Land Agency sponsors a conference on measures to be taken in the event of an earthquake to which the Defense Agency is invited as an observer, just to sit there and watch. This has very little meaning to it. The

Self-Defense Forces have the organization and ability to engage in rescue operations. They must include us actively in future planning.

On the matter of the Defense Agency director's "order for action," the Kobe earthquake provides us many valuable lessons. Along with local self-governing bodies, the Defense Agency director has the right to issue such an order. The line of command in such an instance is from the Defense Agency director to area commanders of Ground, Maritime and Air Self-Defense Forces.

For example, if the Central Area wants to borrow helicopters or water-supply wagons from the Hokkaido Area or Kyushu Area, each area commander must make that request to the Defense Agency director through the chief of staff of the Ground Self-Defense Force. Unless the director orders the area commander of Hokkaido to lend that water-supply wagon, no action can be taken. Staff officers of the three services in Tokyo coordinate the actual transfer.

At the time of the Kobe earthquake, I made a request to the director that helicopters, water-supply wagons, kitchen wagons, and rescue equipment be sent from other area commands. The Defense Bureau within the Self-Defense Agency handled the clerical matter. They had to circulate papers around all the bureaus within the agency before they could get the approval of the Director. In each of the bureaus, several officers were responsible for approving the papers. It took time. To make matters worse, some people were not familiar with the equipment we were requesting. As for the director, he had to be at the Diet while it was in session. On the matter of water-supply wagons, it took anywhere from thirteen to fifteen hours before the necessary papers from the chief of staff reached the desk of the director. And we did not have ferries from Hokkaido contracted in advance. It took four to five days for us to borrow water-supply wagons from Hokkaido. . . .

In an emergency such as this, the director could have given a blanket order: "All area commanders are ordered to assist the central area commander. Detailed instruction will be issued by the chief of staff." With that we would not have had to go through the rigmarole of the office procedure and could have handled everything smoothly. There was the so-called civilian control, and moving of equipment from one area to another was placed under the sole jurisdiction of the director. But I was not asking to borrow a missile from Hokkaido. . . .

There is one more lesson to be learned. . . . Transportation within the affected Osaka-Kobe area was paralyzed. But the Shinkansen was open to Osaka and both Itami and Osaka airports were operating almost normally. We could have sent a massive amount of supplies to these locations and utilized helicopters of the Self-Defense Forces and fire departments to deliver supplies to affected areas. Why was this step not taken?

In undertaking an operation of that nature, the national-level leadership would be indispensable. When helicopters of the Self-Defense Forces carried emergency gears to Itami, they were not allowed to land. The reason was: "There has been no precedent in allowing an airplane of the SDF to land in Itami." At the

Kansai International Airport, our planes were likewise not allowed to land throughout the crisis. . . .

It was an emergency. Why was political leadership not exercised to offer security and to protect lives? To this day, I regret [my superiors'] inaction. . . .

RELOCATION OF THE CAPITAL

The excessive concentration of power in Tokyo has been criticized for many ills visited on Japan in recent years. And on the issue of planning for the future, Tokyo and the rest of the country are often at loggerheads. An example of it can be found in the debates surrounding the publication of the Fourth Comprehensive National Development Plan in 1987. Earlier, when the National Land Agency made an interim report, suggesting that the making of Tokyo into a true world city and regional development of other areas be concurrently undertaken, it was criticized as too pro-Tokyo. One prefectural governor even suggested that with it "the revolt of local areas" would begin. His name was Hosokawa Morihiro (b. 1938), who in 1993 became prime minister of Japan.

The debates over the viability of Tokyo as a city have been going on for a number of decades. The severe water shortage of 1963 exposed the danger of overpopulation, and created a climate conducive to the discussion of relocating the capital elsewhere. The success of the Tokyo Olympics (1964) gave this discussion a pause, but the issue never died down completely. In the late 1980s, most public officials spoke approvingly of transferring some central management functions away from Tokyo. Nothing of substance was accomplished, however, and in the meantime a government commission was given the task of studying the feasibility of relocating the capital with recommendations. This was completed in December 1995.

Document 5 reproduced below shows the enthusiasm local businessmen feel toward the proposed relocation. They see in the moving of the capital an impetus for reform and a possibility of making the government smaller. The article is written by Tejima Norio (b. 1928), head of the Sendai branch of Keizai Dōyūkai, or Japan Association of Corporate Executives.

5 **Relocation of the Capital—A View from Outside the Capital Zone, 1996**[8] The final report of the Commission to Investigate Relocation of the National Diet and Other Organizations was issued in December 1995. This report deals with the issues of relocating the Diet and major administrative and judicial

---

[8]Tejima Norio, *"Nihon ni Aratana Katsuryoku o: Chihō kara mita Shuto Kikō no Iten"* (Giving Japan a New Vitality: Moving Capital's Functions as Seen by a Local Citizen), in *Sekai to Nippon,* February 19, 1996.

functions to local areas. I would like to add my voice in support, as a concerned citizen from outside the capital zone.

Nine criteria are selected in identifying the location of a new capital. They are:

(1) The new capital must be located in such a way that imbalance will not be created in the access to it from different regions of the country.

(2) It must be located at a site not less than 60 kilometers and not more than 300 kilometers from Tokyo.

(3) It must be located within forty minutes commuting distance from an international airport.

(4) It must be possible to obtain quickly and smoothly the land needed for building a new capital.

(5) Areas that are likely to be devastated by serious earthquakes and other calamities must be avoided.

(6) Due consideration must be given to maintenance of normal urban living even in case of emergencies caused by natural calamities.

(7) Places that are mountainous or with precipitous topography must be avoided.

(8) Avoid areas where the emergence of a new urban area with a population of six hundred thousand people may cause water shortage.

(9) A proper distance must be maintained from those major urban centers designated as administratively designated cities.

Most people seem to be interested only in these nine criteria. The media generally discuss the competition that exists between the three prime candidates for the site of the new capital, namely, Northern Kantō, Tohokū, and Tōkai regions. People outside these regions may be less interested, but the matter is of concern to everyone regardless of from which region he comes. Relocation of the capital is a bold move to restructure Japanese politics and administration for the twenty-first century and beyond. It is accompanied by an attempt to redefine the respective roles of the central and local governments.

This is not an issue exclusively of concern to the 30 million people living in the Greater Capital District or of concern to those people who live near the candidate regions for the new site. The entire nation, 100 million of us, must consider this important issue carefully. As for me, I share the view expressed in the proposal to explore the new site that "in the beginning of the twenty-first century, we must transfer functions performed by the capital" away from Tokyo.

The most important reason is to provide security for the political and adminis-trative functions that are tantamount to the nervous system for our body politics. It is widely believed that the days of another great earthquake in the Kantō region are not far off, the same region that has frequently experienced great earthquakes. We need not refer back to the lessons of past earthquakes. It is the duty of the nation to protect its central command structure, a task that is more urgent than ever as Japan has emerged a great power in the world. At present a number of private industries are already planning to transfer their central command structure away from Tokyo.

The second reason is to create a "small government" through the relocation of the capital. This is the expressed desire of our people, and the relocation will accomplish that goal through the sharing of power with local government and by deregulation. Mr. Uno Osamu,[9] chairman of the commission of capital relocation, was an advocate of power sharing with local government. He called it "invisible capital relocation" that would bring out the same results as the moving of the capital. But nothing moved in the direction he anticipated. He now believes that "we can destroy the status quo only through the triune approach of capital relocation, power sharing with local government, and deregulation."

The report has a memorable passage. It likens the capital relocation with moving into a new residence. "In moving we select from among our furniture those we need to start a new life." There is the intent of shock therapy to be administered on our existing systems through this relocation. I fully concur. Without this, the benefit we realize from the relocation will be minimal. To those who do not at present live in Tokyo, this is an important concern. Let me explain further.

As an industrialist who has had experience in helping local government, I am always amazed by the number of petition drives needed to implement projects in local areas. A large number of people assemble at the first floor of the local branch offices of ministries or agencies having jurisdiction over the particular project. These branch offices are overwhelmed in the task of making appointments for local people to go to Tokyo. If the petitioners can go to Tokyo and meet top people in the ministries and agencies, bureaus and departments, that trip is considered a great success. Frequently the people they want to see are absent, so a batch of petitions and business cards (*meishi*) are left, probably just to be thrown away later in the wastepaper baskets. Once in a while we even receive prodding from the central government. "Petitioners from region A come frequently, where are petitioners from region B?" Are we supposed to thank them for this solicitude?

This is Japan, a self-proclaimed great power. I wonder how much the commission members and Tokyo people are aware that this old-style decision-making process in its terrible irrationality is still practiced as before? Ministries and agencies in Tokyo micromanage too many things. It is a truism that the main functions of the central government must be limited to basic issues such as crisis management including diplomacy and defense, establishing basic fiscal policies, and coordinating matters that transcend regional interests. These are not matters that render themselves to pressures coming from petitions. The government can obtain information from local areas and assess prevailing conditions. It can seek

---

[9]Born in 1917, Mr. Uno was chairman of Tōyō Textiles and the Kansai Federation of Economic Organizations. He is also chairman of the Organization to Promote the Establishment of an Academic and Research City in Kansai.

opinions to serve as a means of reaching judgment and creating a broadly based policy. On these matters local areas need not kowtow to the central government.

The power to implement most projects must be delegated to the branch offices of the central government located in prefectures and regions. With the exception of basic national projects, local branch offices must in principle be given the power to approve and disapprove. There are a number of projects that go beyond the borders of prefectures, such as international airports, trade ports, and expressways. It means that we need branch offices of the central government to coordinate them. In performing these functions, I hope we do not fall into the habit of relying on the hierarchical decision-making process. Why not adopt a committee formula with its horizontal coordination? Let talented bureaucrats come from ministries and agencies to the local areas. Free them from the old-style hierarchical system and let them help one another to create better approaches to regional development. I am confident that we can expect substantial and positive results.

As the precondition, we must undertake boldly the paring down of government offices, just as the private sector has been doing. I am at a loss of words when I hear that some government business entities whose tasks had been completed many years back finally were eliminated only recently. That practice is inconceivable in the private sector. Those government organizations that have completed their missions or tasks must be promptly downsized or abolished. This is a major principle that must be firmly established. We are now talking about deregulation. Let us implement first those that require our prompt attention. Another means left to us is that of contracting government businesses to the private sector. The government must learn to rely on the private sector and eliminate its overall workload.

What can we do to revitalize local areas and make them more independent? There are several steps we can take.

(1) The hierarchical order that always places Tokyo at the top must be changed. It has made local areas subservient to Tokyo and has stifled the spirit of independence. Along with this, the decision-making process that relies on the ill-conceived and inefficient petition system must be eliminated.

(2) As described earlier, there must be a new delineation of the power of the central government against that of the local government, and a new system of allocation of financial resources for them.

(3) The central government must be encouraged to send to local areas their best *jinzai,* or human resources.

(4) We can create a more rational and efficient decision-making process through the use of multimedia information and communications systems.

In speaking of returning power to the local areas, the prefecture as a unit to receive that power may be too small to be effective. When our thought process cannot depart from the small prefecture-based unit, any project we present becomes indistinguishable from the rest, and we compete against each other needlessly. I suggest that we form a local bloc that is premised on the active cultural and economic interaction within that bloc. For example, if we form a bloc with the six prefectures in the Tōhoku region, its population will be 10 million, and its GDP will be at the level of Australia. In other words, it will be a unit comparable to an independent state. Let this bloc interact directly with other blocs domestically, and internationally with blocs in foreign countries. The cultural level of the bloc and vitality of its economy will increase significantly. Kyushu, in recent years, has shown us the way. By interacting with Asia and absorbing its vitality, it has continued to progress at a rapid pace. We do not have to change the name of our bloc to a province. But we can take necessary steps to make our bloc akin to a province.[10]

Finally, I must raise the issue of the site to be selected, which must have an area of 9,000 hectares. It will be about one and one half times the size of the area encircled by the Yamanote line[11] in Tokyo with a population of about 600,000. As discussed earlier, the moving of the capital is an issue of national concern. It must be accessible to other regions of the country within two hours either by air or by the Shinkansen (bullet train). That fairness of access must be adopted as the major premise in the selection.

Whether or not a given area can fit all the nine criteria for selection, the national government must begin the process of investigation objectively and in a transparent and aboveboard manner. It must study those sites where the local people show signs of cooperation. No competitive petition drives must be allowed to enter into the selection process.

Among the criteria, the problem of water supply can pose problems. It may become necessary to create a pipeline across prefectural borders. On the matter of an international airport, a similar consideration [of crossing prefectural borders] applies.

Initially, the capital relocation was considered a good development project. As the issue reaches the selection-process stage, we begin to realize that there are sacrifices asked of the selected site also. This problem is especially keenly felt on the matter of land acquisition. It may be possible that the issue will be turned into the familiar pattern of "agreeing in principle, but opposing in specifics (*sōron sansei, kakuron hantai*)." A mere ripple effect of the development investment expected to go beyond 10 trillion yen will not be a sufficient inducement for cooperation. What we hope to accomplish is to engage in a massive reform of our political and administrative systems that have accumulated over one hundred years. The relocation of the capital is a means to inject a new perspective and

---

[10]Here the author, Mr. Tejima, is playing on the word Kyu-shū. The second character *shū* is the character used by the Chinese to denote a province, a practice that started by the Sui dynasty (581–618). Prefectures known as *ken* was placed under the jurisdiction of the *shū*. The word *shū* is also used by the Japanese today for the American state. For example, the state of Iowa becomes in Japanese, Iowa-*shū*.

[11]A round-loop Japan Railway line that cut through the central district of Tokyo.

renewed vigor into the Japan of the twenty-first century. Unless we have such a vision in undertaking this massive project with idealism and enthusiasm, we will not be able to acquire the land needed or secure the cooperation of the entire nation.

ALTERNATE LIFESTYLE

Foreigners, used to the sight of Japanese travelers flocking to fashionable stores to buy brand-name products, may be surprised to discover that there is another strain in the Japanese lifestyle. That one forsakes luxury in favor of internal contentment. It is a life governed by the love of nature and disdain for material possessions. In 1992, Nakano Kōji (b. 1925), a professor of German literature, wrote down his thoughts in a series of essays and later made them into a small book entitled Seihin no Shisō, *or* Thoughts on Enjoyment of Simple Life. *Little did he realize that it was to become one of the most talked-about books of the year. His call for a return to the tradition of a simple life touched a responsive chord among the people who were seeking a lifestyle different from the glory days of the Japanese economy. His essays consist mainly of vignettes of Japan's old masters and men of letters. Document 6 comes from his sixteenth topic, which also gives the reasons for his wanting to write this book.*

To live is also to know about death, and when people are turning inwardly in search of the meaning of life, interest in the phenomenon of death invariable arises. As in the United States, there is a more open discussion about death. In October 1994, this writer was in Kinokuniya, the largest bookstore in Osaka. In came two well-dressed couples in their early twenties. They were probably on a date. Very excitedly one of the girls found Ei Rokusuke's Daiōjō *(A Peaceful Death), and bought a copy; her three companions followed suit. It was clear that all four of them were eager to start reading. In that moment, this writer found evidence of their interest in death and dying. Document 7 is a book review on this subject that appeared in the December 1994 issue of* Publisher's Monthly.

6 **Joy of Simple Life, 1992**[12] Recently I took up a theme, "another face of Japanese civilization," and started to jot down my thoughts. "Another face" does not cover the gamut of what the Japanese civilization is all about. I use this phrase loosely as I started to collect thoughts about some important elements inherent in the Japanese civilization. Whenever I was asked to give a talk in a foreign country, I repeated this subject just like a fool with his broken record. For me these are the aspects of Japanese civilization I want my foreign friends to know.

---

[12]Nakano Kōji, *Seihin no Shisō (Thoughts on Enjoyment of Simple Life)* (Tokyo: Sōshisha, 1992), pp. 134–43.

Foreigners' interest in Japan is running high. Not everything is directed to finer things, but it is clear that they are interested in knowing more about Japan, about her people, and about her culture. The reason is obvious. Everywhere we go we encounter Japanese products. Markets are saturated with fine products from Japan. There are electric and electronic products, watches, and automobiles. At the same time, the Japanese people who make these products remain practically invisible. So there is a natural curiosity about what Japan is and who the Japanese are. . . .

I have my own reason to select this topic for my talks. Relatively speaking, I travel a lot overseas. Whenever I am in the EC or Southeast Asian countries, I hear numerous comments about Japan and the Japanese. Unfortunately most of them are not complimentary. The majority of Japanese people going to these countries are businessmen. . . . Seeing how these people behave, the indigenous people get irritated and vent their frustration on me [even though I am not a businessman].

These are the words I heard. They are unpleasant, but I do not think they are untrue, so I shall put them down below:

"Japan is so proud of being an export-driven great power. She thinks only of her own interest and keeps on devastating foreign markets. Japanese products, such as cars, household electric appliances, electronics, watches, and cameras are of high quality and yet inexpensive. We know that, but there is that transparent attitude of 'what is wrong if we sell quality products cheaply.' There is no concern for our local needs. We cannot live together this way. You are making yourselves unbearable in this world."

"The Japanese people, businessmen and tourists alike, know only one topic of conversation, 'money.' Don't they have any other interest beside money? They don't seem to know how to talk intelligently about politics, music, international affairs, philosophy, racial issues, or history. They convey to us an impression that money determines the value of man."

"Young girls bring a lot of money and buy up one brand-name product after another. They don't show a bit of interest in local history or culture. They come here but behave as if they were still at home. They are noisy and obnoxious. Have all Japanese youths become such uncaring egoists?"

"I seldom meet a Japanese who has his own philosophy, is proud of his own lifestyle, and has a considered view on every issue. There are not too many Japanese at a party who can talk to indigenous people on an equal footing on varied subjects. They do not even know their own history."

"The Japanese are so arrogant when meeting people from poorer countries. Do they think that being rich gives them license to do what they want to do?"

There is more, but it is unpleasant, so I must stop. Each time I heard such an opinion, I became unhappy but unfortunately I also had to admit that there was an element of truth in what they were saying. But I always managed to add: "You are talking about some Japanese of today. But Japanese have not always been that kind of people before. There is a totally different side to the Japanese." That was the beginning of my speaking out on "another face of Japanese civilization."

We became a nation of seekers of efficiency and productivity first only in the past half century. We sought a better life because we lost everything in the war. To a certain extent we can justify our present-day pursuit of materialism, when we know that its origin was in the lack of possession we experienced through the ruins of war. But we are beginning to realize that is not what life is about.

Japan has become an economic superpower. But it does not translate into the Japanese people having a better life or having leisure. We are a nation of workaholics, and we continue to work very hard. We live in tiny houses, commute a long distance in overcrowded trains, and work late. And as you are aware, we even have a special term, *karōshi,* for death resulting from overwork.

It is true that today we have more material possessions. Our markets are as abundant as any in the European Community countries. Yet, no matter how much the production of goods becomes abundant, it does not bring about happiness in life. We are now beginning to realize that to obtain happiness, we need a new principle or way of life that is not attached to material possessions.

Actually, we are beginning to realize also that as long as we are enslaved to material possessions, being entrapped in a cycle of buying, possessing, consuming, and throwing away, we cannot have fulfillment in our inner selves. We also know that to live together on this earth with other peoples, we cannot have unlimited production of material goods and consuming them unnecessarily. We know we have to protect our environment and resources. True richness, in other words, inner fulfillment, can come only from our willingness to limit our possessive urges and from our regaining the freedom of nonpossession. Many of us are now returning to basics and are questioning what is needed and not needed to gain happiness in our daily living.

In Japan there used to be a beautiful philosophy called *seihin,* or contentment in the simplicity of life. There was even a paradoxical thought that by restraining possessive urges to the absolute minimum, one could make a quantum jump in inner freedom. Let us now return to that subject.

The above was essentially the rationale behind my talking about "Another face of Japanese civilization." Usually, I begin my talk with the following passage from the *Essays in Idleness.*[13]

> What a foolish thing it is to be governed by a desire for fame and profit and to fret away one's whole life without a moment of peace.
> Great wealth is no guarantee of security. Wealth, in fact, tends to attract calamities and disaster. Even if, after you die, you leave enough gold to prop

---

[13]The two quoted passages come from *Essays in Idleness: The Tsurezuregusa of Kenkō,* translated by Donald Keene, pp. 34–37. Copyright © by Columbia University Press. Reprinted with permission of the publisher.

up the North Star,[14] it will only prove a nuisance to your heirs. The pleasures that delight the foolish man are likewise meaningless to the man of discrimination who considers a big carriage, sleek horses, gold, and jeweled ornaments all equally undesirable and senseless. You had best throw away your gold in the mountains and drop your jewels into a ravine. It is an exceedingly stupid man who will torment himself for the sake of worldly gain.

This passage comes from a chapter in the *Essays in Idleness,* written by Yoshida Kenkō (1283–1350) who lived in the fourteenth century. Like *The Essays of Michel de Montaigne* (1533–1592), *Essays in Idleness* was a classic widely read by Japanese and has had a profound influence on the Japanese taste and judgment. The foolishness of man is to end one's life a busybody unable to enjoy life serenely because of one's worldly desire for honor, position, or wealth. This view, the essay so aptly describes, has been transmitted through the Edo period to this day, and has had an enormous impact on the way of life in Japan.

Kenkō speaks of the foolishness of people who have no other interest except to make money. His essay can apply easily to our current situation. He is exposing our foolishness in wanting to acquire new possessions, such as homes and cars that have been created for us one after another. It hits us, and the message goes straight to our hearts.

He continued to talk about the foolishness of acquiring social positions, government positions, and reputations. He also spoke of the vanity of acquiring knowledge and learning for the sake of receiving worldly accolade. This is his conclusion:

> The truly enlightened man has no learning, no virtue, no accomplishments, no fame.[15] Who knows of him, who will report his glory? It is not that he conceals his virtue or pretends to be stupid; it is because from the outset he is above distinctions between wise and foolish, between profit and loss.

A true man gives no thought to profit or gain, name or recognition. He seeks only fulfillment of his own mind. That is the essence of Kenkō's message.

I find a similarity in his thought with that of St. Francis of Assisi (1182–1226). St. Francis sought fulfillment of his heart's desires before God. Kenkō did not address God, but to him a wise man is the one who has lived his life without shame, and thus can face the Almighty who is uncontaminated by the ills of this world. One thing we must remember is this. The thought that is expressed in the *Essays in Idleness* was not just the thought of fourteenth-century Japan. It has been accepted by many people in different forms and expressions, put into prac-

---

[14]The phrase is borrowed from a poem by Bo Zhuyi, containing the line "Even if, by the time you die, you have amassed gold enough to support the North Star, it is not as good as having a cask of wine while you are alive" (Mr. Keene's footnote).

[15]From *Zhuang zi,* the work of the Taoist philosopher.

tice in real lives, and has become a basic thought in Japanese art and literature. It has been transmitted through the ages and has influenced the lives of not just men of letters but of people who have remained unknown. It has become our way of life and part of our tradition. . . .

Living in the state of *seihin* does not mean to live in abject poverty. It is a state of simple living actively created by one's own thought and will. Hon-ami Kōetsu (1558–1637) [the great painter and calligrapher] and his mother, Myōshū, could have lived a life of luxury and splendor. They chose instead a life of minimal possessions and needs. Why? Just as St. Francis of Assisi sought to live closer to God by his consecration to poverty in place of a life his merchant father could bestow, Kōetsu came upon the same conclusion through another route.

In talking to a foreign audience, I had to explain the meaning of the term *seihin*. It is a term no longer in use in the Japanese language. Even when I say "purity in poverty," the true meaning still does not emerge. I had to rephrase it by stating that *seihin* is an expression of one's thought that chooses to delight in the simplest of lifestyle. . . .

Once possessed by a desire to possess, a man may become interested only in increasing his own possessions, becomes a slave to money, and does not worry about other people's concern. Such a man may even forget to love his own family or to be compassionate to others, those things that are most important to a man. A rich person without fail becomes a gruff Scrooge. This was the wisdom that Myōshū imparted to us. To these Kōetsu added his own thought. A man loses his spiritual freedom when his mind is preoccupied with acquiring possessions and retaining them. He even gave up his best implements for the tea ceremony, as he did not want to be distracted by the thought of "don't drop it, don't lose it."

They knew that minimal possession would set them free to engage in spiritual activities. . . . Transference of this thought in our lifestyle is the next logical step. By making our life [simple and] minimal, great masters of earlier days were able to find a principle of setting one's spirit free, and of enhancing creativity. Ike Taiga (1723–1776) was absolutely disinterested in money. The otherworldliness and elegance of his paintings were made possible because of his indifference to gain. In *haiku*, transcending this-worldliness became the first principle of creativity. Bashō (1644–1694) found nobility of spirit much easier in the minds of mendicant monks and beggars than in any other people. The grace found in the poems and calligraphy of the monk Ryōkan (1758–1831) could not be dissociated from the fact of his living in a grass hut.

If I were allowed to probe into their minds, I am certain they were thinking in this fashion: "Make this earthly life simple and minimal. We can then commune with the universal principle."

7 **On Death and Dying, 1994**[16] The rapid graying of Japanese society has been accompanied by a burgeoning interest in the subject of aging and, perhaps more conspicuously, that of aging's inevitable consequence. Death is not a subject that has received much attention in Japan over the past few decades—not, at least, until now. The December 1994 issue of *Shuppan Geppō* (Publisher's Monthly) has this to say about the phenomenon in a report on "Publishing Trends in 1994."

"With the advent of an aged society, books on the subject of death have hit the bookstores one after the other and have drawn wide attention. Among the year's most talked-about books are several dealing with views of life and death, including [Ei Rokusuke's] *Daiōjō* [*A Peaceful Death*; Iwanami Shoten], which became the year's number two bestseller, as well as Nishibe Susumu's *Shiseiron* [*On Life and Death*] (Nihon Bungeisha), Minakami Tsutomu's *Kotsutsubo no hanashi* [*A Discussion of Mortuary Urns*] (Shūeisha), *Chishikijin 99-nin no shinikata* [*99 Intellectuals' Ways of Death*], edited by Aramata Hiroshi (Kadokawa Shoten), and Yamada Taichi's *Korekara no ikikata, shinikata* [*Living and Dying in Today's World*] (Kōdansha). Two noted books by Tachibana Takashi dealt with what happens to people when they die: the two-volume *Rinshi taiken* [*Near-Death Experiences*] and *Sei, shi, shinpi taiken* [*Life, Death, and Mystical Experience*] (Shoseki Jōhōsha). Meanwhile, Tsurumi Wataru's controversial 1993 book *Kanzen jisatsu manyuaru* [*The Complete Manual of Suicide*] (Ōta Shuppan) continued to sell well this year, racking up a total of 635,000 copies."

To get a better sense of the kinds of publications that are sustaining this new trend, let us take a closer look at three of those mentioned above: Ei Rokusuke's *Peaceful Death*, Tachibana Takashi's *Near-Death Experiences*, and Tsurumi Wataru's *Complete Manual of Suicide*.

Appearing in March 1994, *Peaceful Death* had already sold over 1.45 million copies by year end. In his preface to the book, author Ei Rokusuke, a noted lyricist and writer, explains his reasons for writing such a work.

"As one who was born and raised in a temple of the Jōdo Shinshū sect and nearly became a Buddhist priest myself, I have always regarded death as something rather close to home. Because of my background, I helped with the funerals of friends. I tended my father on his deathbed, and in 1992 I lost two of my closest friends, [songwriters] Izumi Taku and Nakamura Hachidai. So it was that I ventured out to tackle the subject of death in my own way."

Peaceful Death is divided into five main chapters, "Old Age," "Sickness," "Death," "Friends," and "Father," with a final section entitled "A Eulogy for Myself." The first three of these feature comments and insights gathered from ordinary people that Ei has met during his travels around the country. Many of

[16]"Dealing with Death," a book review written by Ueda Yasuo, in *Japan Echo* 22, no. 1 (Spring 1995): pp. 88–89.

these quotations are extremely compelling. In the chapter "Old Age," a man remarks, "People are always their youngest right now. You're younger today than you'll be tomorrow." And in the chapter on "Death," someone says, "Live, live, live, live, live! You can die when you decide you want to." Another remarks, "A peaceful death would be when the person doesn't notice he's dead."

Given Ei's Buddhist background and the subject matter, the book is by no means light entertainment. But the tenor of the comments compiled in its pages is dry-eyed and basically optimistic, never mawkish, and their effect on the reader is soothing. Ei has journeyed extensively in Japan, and in this work he skillfully draws on the countless conversations and stories he has recorded during his travels.

Death is approached from a very different angle in *Near-Death Experiences,* by the journalist Tachibana Takashi. The author explains the subject of his book as follows: "Near-death experiences are strange sensory experiences related by people who recover consciousness after coming close to death in an accident or illness." Having studied numerous cases, Tachibana discusses these and elucidates the nature of near-death experiences.

A typical example is that of a man by the name of Ōhira Mitsuru from Niigata Prefecture, who fell into a coma after massive hemorrhaging from a stomach ulcer. During that time, Ōhira stopped breathing several times, and for three days he lay at death's door. He relates the following experience.

"I am lying in bed. Gradually, I leave [my body] from the head. I see my body lying in bed. Then I notice a thread running diagonally upward from my body. From above I can see the doctor, my brothers, and my parents. I call to them and try to touch them, but no one notices."

Tachibana introduces the experience of psychologist Carl Jung, who believed that near-death experiences could provide insight into the very nature of human existence. And in the final chapter, "Rehearsal for Death," we learn that those who have been through such an experience speak almost unanimously of having lost their fear of death and of their resolve to make the most of life. It seems that they come to accept the fact that they will die when their time comes and to want to make the most of their lives in the meantime. By showing us how near-death experiences open the door to this sort of understanding, Tachibana makes us aware that life and death are two sides of the same coin and brings us closer to a basic truth of human existence.

Finally, in the *Complete Manual of Suicide*, Tsurumi Wataru approaches death as a matter of choice. The promotional copy attached to the book calls it "more useful than the Bible as a written suicide aid," with advice on everything "from store-bought drugs that can kill to the most painless way to die." Tsurumi's book covers almost every conceivable method of taking one's own life. The book provoked so much controversy when it first appeared that some distributors elected to supply bookstores with copies only to fill customers' advance orders. Be that as it may, young readers in particular seem taken with the author's stance: "I am not saying anything so ridiculous as 'Everyone go out and kill yourself.' If you want to live, you should live as you please, and if you want to die, you should die as you please. There is not much more to life than that." Since its publication in July 1993, the manual has sold steadily, going through fifty press runs.

Hoping to capitalize on the book's success, the publisher, Ōta Shuppan, has since put out the *Kanzen shissō manyuaru* (*The Complete Manual of Disappearing*) by Kashimura Masanori for those who want to abscond without leaving a trail. It has also published a compilation of reactions to the suicide manual in a volume entitled *Bokutachi no "Kanzen jisatsu manyuaru"* (*Our "Complete Manual of Suicide"*). Among the letters contained therein is one addressed to the author by the father of Yamada Hanako, a comic-book writer who killed herself. "In a sense." he writes, "your book might be considered a warning to us all, cloaked in black humor." In this succinct observation, he may well have put his finger on the secret of the book's ongoing success.

KYŌSEI—LIVE AND LET LIVE

Kurokawa Kishō (b. 1934) is the representative architect of the Metabolist group formed in the 1960s. The concept of "metabolism," used in biology to express the complex of physical and chemical processes involved in the maintenance of life, is transferred to urban planning where cities and buildings alike are built in such a way that they are constantly renewing themselves and sustaining each other. It is from this notion of continuous self-renewal and dependence on others, and from some Buddhist precepts, that Kurokawa received his inspiration for the ideal of Kyōsei. Kurokawa attended Tōkai Gakuen, a secondary school maintained by the Jōdo sect. He attributes his commitment to Kyōsei to his mentor, the priest Shiio Benkyō. In Shiio's words: "We are committed to the true meaning of Kyōsei (or tomo-iki, live and let live) and aspire to the coming of the Pure Land of Kyōsei. We work together, and there is no distinction between the wise and the slow-witted, and between the strong and the weak. In this world nothing can exist without thinking of its relations to its surroundings. We are all bound by the common karma. Everything exists in relation to one another. Based on this principle, let us create an ideal world step by step."

Kurokawa applies this ideal in judging art and architecture of the past as well as trade relations. Document 8 contains samples taken from his Kyōsei no Shisō (Ideals of Symbiosis). In discussing the Katsura detached palace, long considered the most representative Japanese architecture, Kurokawa challenges the conventional wisdom. Why not accept Nikkō equally? He asks, and then calls the judgment of the German architect Bruno Taut into question. It is a new departure for Japanese aesthetics. On trade matters, Kurokawa brings out a notion of the consecrated ground (seiiki) which cannot be tampered with by foreign na-

tions. The consecrated grounds include rice cultivation in Japan and the auto industry in the United States.

Kurokawa's other works include New Tokyo Plan, 2025 *(1987). His proposal to relocate the city's center onto the reclaimed land and to create self-sustaining "villages" within the confines of the metropolitan area is widely discussed and praised. He is the recipient of the 1986 Grand Prize for Architecture from the French Academy.*

8 Ideals of Kyōsei in Art and in Economy, 1991[17]

(a) Wrong Views of the Katsura Detached Palace

When the tea master Rikyū spoke of *wabi,* or the taste for quietude, he gave it an extreme interpretation because of the stormy relations he experienced with Hideyoshi. This is the primary reason for the shallow interpretation we now give to the concept of *wabi.* There is another reason, I fear, that comes from the praises that German architects Bruno Taut (1880–1938) and Walter Gropius (1883–1969) heaped on the Katsura detached palace.

Japanese architects began paying attention to their own tradition after these modern architects proclaimed that the Katsura detached palace and the Grand Shrine of Ise were the very models for modern architecture.

So without giving much thought, Japanese architects accepted the notion propagated by these Westerners that the simple and restrained beauty that stresses silence and nothingness shall be regarded as the very essence of Japanese beauty.

I must caution here, however, that Bruno Taut and Walter Gropius gave their assessment of Katsura and Ise [not on the traditional notion of Japanese beauty, but] within the framework of modern architecture.

The beauty that modern architecture seeks is the unadorned, simple, and straight-line form that can be created through mass-produced industrial materials. Taut and Gropius found an icon, or idealized image, of modern architecture in the Katsura detached palace. They overlooked other things. Even in Katsura, considered representative of simple and unadorned beauty, there are many instances of rich ornamentations. There are the staggered shelves in the Chūshoin with their decorative metal fittings, the bold checkered patterns on the flour of Shōkintei, the shapes so refreshing to unsuspecting eyes found in the side windows near the floor of Shingoten and in the round transom window of Shōiken, or the expressiveness of velvet used to paper the lower part of wall in the same Shōiken. Elegance, at once breathtaking and abundant, is hidden in these simple spaces.

---

[17]Kurokawa Kishō, *Kyōsei no Shisō: Mirai o Ikinuku Raifusutairu (Ideals of Symbiosis: Lifestyle to Live Positively in the Future)* (Tokyo: Tokuma Shobō, 1991), pp. 44–49, 94–102. The quoted passage in the introductory paragraph comes from *ibid.,* pp. 394–95.

These examples alone show how one-sided their assessment of Katsura has been. Another proof comes from their inability to give the rightful place to the Tōshōgū shrine in Nikkō. To them the Tōshōgū represented "the poor taste" that the shōgun possessed.

To those modernists, the Tōshōgū was a heretical text difficult to quote. However, let us not forget that the Tōshōgū and Katsura were built in the same period. By putting the Tōshōgū and Katsura side by side, one can get a bird's eye view of Japanese architecture of those times. Why must they deny one completely, and cite the only part that is convenient to them in the other? Can they speak about Japanese architecture intelligently? I think they are opportunists [in the guise of modern architects].

. . . In our tradition, we have always had the coexistence of the vibrant and glittering sense of beauty and the simple and fine sense of beauty which is devoid of ornamentation. These were represented in the Jōmon culture and the Yayoi culture. It stands to reason that at the same time in the Edo period Katsura and Tōshōgū were completed. One can not deny that the Tōshōgū is part of Japanese tradition by dismissing it as the bad taste of a shōgun with a penchant for glittery showiness.

The tradition of beauty represented by the Jōmon culture was fiercely decorative. It blossomed into the unique and opulent castle architecture of the Azuchi Momoyama period, and its lineage runs through the ages to this day.

One may visit Buddhist temples in Kyoto and find the origin of Japanese civilization in those pagodas that utilize natural wood without paint. However, both the Tōdaiji and Tōshōdaiji, when they were first built, had their pillars painted in ruby red and ancones in red, gold and green. One must remember that it was a world of dazzling primary colors.

Some Zen temples were indeed built with natural wood. With those few exceptions, Japanese pagodas had the brilliance of the Tōshōgū at one time.

Once the painted colors faded, however, the Japanese people preferred to retain the sober color of the exposed natural wood instead of repainting. In this I find the full gamut of the Japanese people's susceptibility, one that is so intriguing as to provide a new meaning to the traditional sense of beauty. But that is not all.

Live and let live, allowing two divergent or even extreme elements to coexist side by side is an attitude which can transcend the world of esthetics. I have a feeling that it will not only define our post-modern present day sense of beauty but also become a way of life in the twenty-first century.

(b) Consecrated Ground and Economic Friction

There was a meeting of the International Design Conference in Aspen, Colorado, in 1979. Its main theme was "Japan and the Japanese." I served as co-director of the conference with Louis Dorsfman, a senior vice president of the CBS Broadcast Group.

I established a subtheme "rice" as an important topic of discussion. I expressed a view that rice produced in California is for food, but rice produced in Japan is not just for food but represents a culture in Japan. For more than a decade since that time, I have maintained this rice-as-a-culture view, and opposed the liberalization of rice import. The reason is simple. I want to preserve the "consecrated ground" for our people.

Time and again, I have spoken that the ideal of *kyōsei* (live and let live) will overcome dualism. It is not the same as the coexistence spoken of during the Cold War between the United States and the Soviet Union. Nor is it the same as the Western dialectic that lifts and breaks up (*aufheben*) the inherently contradictory aspects of a notion. Naturally *kyōsei* does not presuppose tangled existence of heterogeneous elements that come to terms only temporarily. The major characteristics of the ideal of *kyōsei* rest in its assertion of maintaining the "middle ground" and "consecrated ground."

. . . Let us discuss the notion of "middle ground" briefly. It is a notion that endeavors to establish tentatively a third ground that does not belong to either one of the two contending elements. To establish a "middle ground"—between two poles that are clearly in opposition, polarized and rationalized—is to pick up once again those issues that were discarded because they were considered vague or irrational during the process of polarization and rationalization.

There are many "middle grounds" in this world that are excluded from the two contending main streams. They are forgotten, discarded, ignored, and abridged. . . . In creating our middle ground, we allow the principles (*tatemae*) of being in contention or of being different to remain as they are. Each party simply submits something to the "middle ground," and even if one particular party occupies only one-tenth of the territory, we still endeavor to create a common third ground.

In this way, we avoid hegemony by a strong party that attempts to place all territories under its control. Ours is a method that is similar to an approach that seeks common concerns and common rules without eradicating all opposing elements. The notion of a "middle ground" opposes hegemonism, universalism, and revolutionarism. Basic to the ideal of *kyōsei* is that there will always be middle grounds and common areas even in different cultures, in opposing ideologies, and in polar-opposite approaches. In this sense, the ideal of *kyōsei* differs from coexistence, compromise, dualism, dialectic, or terrorism.

There is one fundamentally new idea within the ideal of *kyōsei*. That is the notion of a "consecrated ground."

As I discussed earlier, I oppose the liberalization of rice import. The reason is grounded in the notion of the "consecrated ground."

For each country, for each race, for each culture, for each industry, and for each individual, there is a "consecrated ground."

In the history of mankind, a religiously consecrated ground or a culturally and traditionally consecrated ground has sometimes been called a taboo. In India the cow is sacred, and in Islamic countries, the pig is a taboo, and one cannot eat it. One who does not abide by the taboo takes a risk that is an equivalent of a death sentence. No one has ever thought of investigating the reasoning behind it scientifically.

These taboos and consecrated grounds have been termed irrational and unscientific and taken as a sign of underdevelopment in modern days. A thoroughgoing scientific and economic investigation has resulted from this new attitude. It has become fashionable to think of the rules maintained by strong nations as universal. At the same time, the consecrated grounds existing in weaker nations have become objects of attack, as irrational or nontariff barriers.

Presently in the SII[18] talks, Japan's traditional practices such as trading among the *keiretsu* companies, *dangō,* and rice are considered contradictory to the rules of the world (i.e., rules of the stronger power), and are attacked as such by the United States.

In contrast to this, the ideal of *kyōsei* is an approach that wishes to recognize each other's consecrated ground.

It is true that a consecrated ground transmitted in a specific cultural tradition does not remain forever. It may change or disappear with the times. Thus it is incumbent on each country to declare the minimum boundary of its consecrated ground for today.

To me the following belong to Japan's consecrated ground: the imperial system, rice cultivation, *sumō* wrestling, *kabuki,* tea ceremony (and the *sukiya*-style of building for the tea ceremony).

The consecrated ground for a given nation is embedded in that country's lifestyle and pride. It provides the roots for that nation's cultural tradition and is strongly connected to its religion and language.

For example, rice produced in California is becoming tastier with the improvement of plants. There are some brands that are even tastier than the standard brand in Japan. They sell for a fraction of the price of Japanese rice. So it sounds very logical to question why Japan does not import California rice. As long as we consider both Japanese rice and California rice as foodstuff, there can be no valid argument against it.

However, I consider Japanese rice part of Japanese culture and belongs to Japan's consecrated ground. In contrast, California's rice is mere food. Let us assume that rice cultivation in California ceases to exist. It does not change the scenery of California, nor will the American people's lifestyle and pride be endangered by it.

What will happen if rice cultivation is eradicated from Japan? Trees over a country home, wooden areas near a shrine, hills in the countryside, paddy fields, and plowed fields stretching a distance—all the scenes that we associate with the Japanese countryside will forever be lost. Along with them, the artistry in the

---

[18]Abbreviation of the Structural Impediments Initiative, promoted by the Bush administration in its trade negotiations with Japan in 1989.

making of *sake,* craftwork, folk songs, and festivals will be gone. Our local cultures have been transmitted through village festivals. That will be gone also.

In the farming villages, there is a trend toward having a second job, and there are more salary-based jobs. However, farming villages remain the repository of the craft of our artisans. In the slack season, farmers help out in the forestry and participate in the making of the lacquer ware in Wajima.[19] Farmers take their children to places where they can transmit to them knowledge of traditional festivals and ceremonies. This they do while preparing for the grand festivals held in the summer or fall. The *kagura* dance, the Kurokawa *nō,* and Awaji's *ningyō-jōruri* are all transmitted in this fashion.

Unlike America, if rice cultivation is eradicated from Japan, it will be accompanied by a wide-ranging disappearance of Japan's traditional culture. I have advocated the theory of rice culture and have opposed liberalization of rice import for over a decade for this very reason.

Today, the Japanese government, the bureaucrats, and even farmers' cooperatives are arguing against the United States by saying that rice cultivation is needed for Japan's national security or that Japan is self-sufficient in rice. As long as their argument is based on the concept that rice is mere food, they are not going to win this argument.

The course Japan must adopt is to declare that rice cultivation belongs to Japan's consecrated ground and cannot be placed as an object of economic friction. At the same time Japan must declare that she respects other nations' consecrated grounds.

The way the Imperial system is handled in Japan today, that the Emperor is the "symbol of the State and of the unity of the people" is the very reflection of the Japanese culture consistent with Japanese history. I consider it the pride of Japan. It belongs to Japan's consecrated ground. I do not share the view that the Emperor must be treated exactly the same as other mere mortals. In *kabuki* and in the tea ceremony, the position of grand master is claimed by right of descent. In the *sukiya*-style of architecture, techniques are transmitted from one generation to another. *Sumō* is not really a sport. From its inception it was connected to rice cultivation and to the Imperial system. All of these are typical cultural heritages that belong in Japan's consecrated ground.

The conditions of a consecrated ground becoming a consecrated ground cannot be analyzed through scientific investigation. Nor are there international rules to determine such conditions. There are elements in which they cannot be understood fully. They may belong in the mystery's domain and serve as the bases of self-identity and cultural pride. This kind of consecrated ground is found not just in Japan but in other countries.

---

[19]Wajima is a city located in the northern part of the Ishikawa Prefecture on the Noto Peninsula. Its lacquer ware, or the *Wajima-nuri,* is known for its durability and deep-glittering gold designs

America is not an old country. So most of its consecrated ground is newly created. I can cite Hollywood, musicals, jazz music, baseball, and the automobile and aircraft industries as belonging to its consecrated ground.

After the war, through American movies, Japanese people became fascinated with the American way of life in which automobiles played a major part. Cars were always eye-catching. In musicals and in jazz, we saw the prosperity surrounding the American civilization. Baseball was the very manifestation of America.

America and Europe are champions of modernism and they are leaders of universalism, rationalism, and dualism. They will not be caught dead admitting that a consecrated ground exists in their own backyards. The very existence of such irrationality puts them to shame. However, there is no mistake about the pride that the Americans have toward their Hollywood, baseball, and automobile, aircraft, and aerospace industries.

By their sheer economic prowess, Japanese industries purchased America's Hollywood (businesses), and America's major league baseball team. Neither the Japanese government nor the industrialists are aware of how offended the American people were by those moves.

If the automobile industry is a mere industry, winning or losing in that industry must be governed by the principle of competition. However, cars happen to be the very essence of the American culture, and earlier of the European culture. Cars symbolize their aspiration for the future. The society built on cars, or a lifestyle with cars, is the pride of the American culture. Likewise, the aircraft and aerospace industries symbolize the American civilization's quest for frontiers into the future. They belong in America's consecrated ground.

The Japanese government or industries may not be aware of this. If they step in this consecrated ground like upstart millionaires from the countryside with their dirty shoes and all, they are bound to hurt the pride of Europeans and Americans.

By having a consecrated ground, it becomes possible to live in harmony in the spirit of *kyōsei*, with nations respecting one another.

I think the same can be said of man's relations with one another. . . .

LOOKING FORWARD TO THE NEW CENTURY

With the old century about to close, most pundits are in a reflective mood. It is time for soul searching and for formulating visions for the future. It is in this spirit that Kiyomiya Ryū (b. 1928) writes a New Year's message for his readers in the Sekai to Nippon *weekly. Kiyomiya is president of the Naigai News Co. and has rich experience in journalism. His tours included serving as the Moscow bureau chief for the Jiji Tsūshin, an organization similar to the AP. He has visited Great Britain and the United States fairly frequently, and occasionally represented his country in international conferences. He has written political biographies of prime ministers Fukuda Takeo (1905–95) and Miyazawa Kiichi (b. 1919) as well as works on the history of war in Okinawa and an inside history of the LDP.*

9 **Past Is Prologue, Looking into the Twenty-first Century, 1996**[20] The Naigai News Company's weekly, *Sekai to Nippon* (The World and Japan), has decided to adopt "Assessing the Past Century to Create Visions for the New Century" as its common theme for the New Year's issue. We are at the threshold of a new century. It is time for us to look back and assess the past one hundred years. By getting a good overview of the past, we shall be able to find new directions for the coming one hundred years, the directions that can infuse new vitality into our nation.

It was the thirty-third year of Meiji when Japan entered the twentieth century. The country was at the midpoint between the Sino-Japanese and Russo-Japanese wars. It was moving along the path of *fukoku kyōhei* (rich nation, strong army) vigorously. With the passage of time, after experiencing a series of ups and downs, Japan has become the richest or second-richest nation in the world. However, amid this sea of unprecedented prosperity, the state and nation have both lost sight of the direction to follow. It is like a luxury ocean liner cruising in uncharted waters. The *SS Nihon-maru*, with its 120 million passengers aboard, is aimlessly floating in the ocean.

Some say history repeats itself. There is a similarity between today's Japan, seemingly prosperous but spiritually poor, and the Japan of the final years of the Meiji era (1868–1912). At the turn of the century, Japan fought two wars in which the nation's future was at stake. She won the Sino-Japanese War of 1894–95 and the Russo-Japanese War of 1904–5, and was recognized as a truly independent and strong nation by the rest of the world. This was the major goal that the Japanese people—both those who governed and those who were governed—aimed to accomplish through thick and thin from the time of the Meiji Restoration.

However, as the nation was transformed from a weak feudal state to a modern nation, the Japanese people became intoxicated with the two successive victories. They forgot the traditional value of "finding strength in frugality" and vainly sought luxury. Morality and the beautiful mores that so characterized Japan of the past were suddenly gone. That was not all. Arrogance came into play, and the Japanese began to look down on poorer nations with contempt.

We can find similar trends in today's Japan. Fifty years ago, from the rubble

---

[20]"*Tokutakaki Sonkei-sareru Kokka: Genten ni Kaeri, Aratana Kunizukuri-o*" (Let Us Build a Morally Sound Nation: Rebuilding the Nation by Returning to Basics), *Sekai to Nippon (The World and Japan),* January 1, 1996.

of defeat, the Japanese people dreamed of becoming rich like the victorious Americans, and worked diligently to create today's prosperity. Their determination was similar to the Japanese at the time of the Meiji Restoration who were engaged in the task of building a modern nation.

However, once we began to enjoy the life of unprecedented wealth, our people and society were turned into materialistic and money-worshipping crowds. As the late prime minister Fukuda Takeo aptly remarked, "during the Showa-Genroku[21] era, overnight millionaires were created almost everywhere, and the nation engaged in merrymaking day and night. In the process, we forgot our traditional virtues of humility and of treating everything with respect (*mottainai*)." Indeed, in the bubble of economic prosperity, our people sought wealth and immersed themselves in search of finer clothing and finer food. Moderation was gone, morality was unheeded, and our souls became poorer. As for our standard of behavior, it was governed by whether or not one particular transaction would bring a profit.

Some of our industrialists, who successfully charted the course of Japan's miraculous economic development, have the temerity to express sentiments like "Japan is the greatest economic power in the world. There is nothing we can learn from America." They are intoxicated with success and are overly confident of their own ability. As a nation too, we have not shown any sense of commitment to our mission. We say "the Japan that contributes to the world," but in reality we only know how to scatter our money around. Without a sense of mission and a desire to implement it, we are still far away from receiving trust and respect from the world.

This reminds me of the Boshin imperial rescript[22] which was promulgated on October 13, 1908. Alarmed by the degeneracy of people after the Russo-Japanese War, the Katsura Cabinet urged the nation to renew themselves and showed them the basic principles of morality through this rescript. The text is relatively simple.

It began with a clear-cut exposition of Japan's diplomatic posture that insisted on friendship, coexistence, and co-prosperity with other nations:

> In view of the unceasing and rapid advancement of civilization which, actuated by the common efforts of all nations in the East and West, contribute to the common weal of the whole world, it is Our wish, while strengthening our relations of good intelligence and close friendship with other powers, to share fully in the benefits of the general amelioration and improvement. . . .

Then came a passage giving the people standards to be followed in their daily lives:

---

[21]The most luxury-laden era (1688–1704) in the Tokugawa period.
[22]Or *Boshin Shōsho*. Boshin was the designation in the sexagenary cycle for the year 1908.

We desire all classes of Our people to act in unison, to be faithful to their callings, frugal in the management of their households, submissive to the dictates of conscience and calls of duty, frank and sincere in their manners, to abide by simplicity and avoid ostentation, and to inure themselves to arduous toil without yielding to any degree of indulgence.

Opinions were divided as to how effective this rescript had been. It is my view that the government exercised good judgment and dealt with the problems well. Otherwise, Meiji Japan could have met a disaster from which it could not have recovered.

As stated earlier, today's Japan lacks goals and is simply floating. Politicians lack visions and philosophies. They know only their own personal profit and gain. The corruption of the bureaucracy is now at an extreme stage. As for industrialists, once the prosperity turned into a prolonged recession, their arrogance was quickly substituted by their loss of confidence. There is now a conspicuous lack of vitality. Opinion makers are supposed to serve as the conscience of society. But they too have turned into profit seekers. No wonder our country is aimlessly floating. We do not know how long the prosperous society that we have built will last. The future is dark indeed.

It is instructive to hear another voice, even though it may discomfort us. So let us hear what Prime Minister Mahathir Mohamad of Malaysia has to say. When asked what he held as a model of advanced nations, he answered: "I am not interested in emulating advanced nations of today who have a lot of social problems. A country may be wealthy, but if there are people among them who will spread poison gas, of if their people use drugs and bring insecurity into their society, I for one am not interested in becoming one of them." In a *Nikkei* interview he said: "When your prices are ten times as high as those of Malaysia the fact of your having ten times our GNP no longer makes much sense."

On another occasion, Mr. Mahathir states: "You have more economic friction with Western nations than with Asian countries surrounding you. Could this be that the Western nations continue to look down on Asia? There are many instances in which we can still observe such attitudes." Looking back into the past, and looking carefully into our present conditions, can we say the same thing about Japan also? Are we looking down on Asia? When we think of the future of our nation, we must be vigilant in paying attention to this issue. If we want to become a nation trusted by our Asian neighbors, we must not be arrogant because of our wealth, but work toward building a bridge of friendship based on mutual benefit and equality. That requires our constant effort.

What kind of goal can Japan set for her future?

Yoshida Shigeru presided over the period when Japan began its recovery from the ashes of defeat. In his waning years, the former prime minister stated in his book while observing a Japan that had become wealthy: "It is not easy in this day and age to recognize and implement accurately our mission. Look back to the past one hundred years, and turn your attention to the world. Gradually, we will be awakened to the tasks we must perform." To him, "the most important thing for the present-day Japan is to have a dream, and to seek widely a theater of action in the world."

Let us follow what Mr. Yoshida has said and return to our starting point in the Meiji era. Let us assume again our task of nation building. We must possess a high sense of morality and ethical behavior that can help us realize a society and nation worthy of the respect of all other nations. That is our dream for the coming century. To that end we must place the highest priority in the education of our youth.

Bridging the Past
and Present

In 1968, Kawabata Yasunari (1899–1972) was awarded the Nobel Prize in Literature. By then, Japan already had two other Nobel laureates, both in physics, but Kawabata was the first one to be so honored in literature. In a sense, it was a recognition by the world of Japan's traditional sense of beauty, which Kawabata himself also modestly suggested.

Three more prizes in physics and one peace prize later, in 1994 another prize was awarded in literature to Ōe Kenzaburo (b. 1935). This time, it was obviously in an attempt to recognize the work of Japan's postmodern writers. It was a controversial decision, as Ōe had often shown his strong affinity to postwar political writers. The heroes in Ōe's works were often disaffected youths who turn to violent behavior. His description of Japan's affluent society was far from charitable, and his investigation of the aftereffects of the atomic bomb in Hiroshima was gruesome. The chorus of praise that greeted Kawabata's selection in 1968 was absent when Ōe's selection was announced in 1994.

The works of Kawabata and Ōe show two separate strains in Japanese literature. To study them, Kawabata's Nobel lecture is followed by an article defending the awarding of the prize to Ōe in this chapter. Each in its own way shows its link to the past and creates a bridge to the future.

JAPAN THE BEAUTIFUL

Best known to the West through his subtle, psychological novels Yukiguni (Snow Country) *and* Sembazuru (A Thousand Cranes), *Kawabata was an accomplished prose writer. He received his inspiration from the style of literature of the Heian period (794–1185), and freely acknowledged his debts to the past. As Ansers Oesterling of the Swedish Academy remarked, there is something in Kawabata's works that show "the necessity of trying to save something of the former Japanese beauty and transfer it to the present." Praised for helping to bridge the East and West, Kawabata responded by saying that the prize was "a symbol of understanding and friendship between East and West, of literature moving from today into tomorrow." His Nobel lecture follows:*

1   Japan the Beautiful and Myself, 1968[1]

"In the spring, cherry blossoms, in the summer the cuckoo.
In autumn the moon, and in winter the snow, clear, cold."

"The Winter moon comes from the clouds to keep me company.
The wind is piercing, the snow is cold."

The first of these poems is by the priest Dōgen (1200–1253) and bears the title "Innate Spirit." The second is by the priest Myōe (1173–1232). When I am asked for specimens of calligraphy, it is these poems that I often choose.

The second poem bears an unusually detailed account of its origins, such as to be an explanation of the heart of its meaning: "On the night of the twelfth day of the twelfth month of the year 1224, the moon was behind clouds. I sat in Zen meditation in the Kakyū Hall. When the hour of the midnight vigil came, I ceased meditation and descended from the hall on the peak of the lower quarters, and as I did so the moon came from the clouds and set the snow to glowing. The moon was my companion, and not even the wolf howling in the valley brought fear. When, presently, I came out of the lower quarters again, the moon was again behind clouds. As the bell was signaling the late-night vigil, I made my way once more to the peak, and the moon saw me on the way. I entered the mediation hall, and the moon, chasing the clouds, was about to sink behind the peak beyond, and it seemed to me that it was keeping me secret company."

There follows the poem I have quoted, and, with the explanation that it was composed as Myōe entered the mediation hall after seeing the moon behind the mountain, there comes yet another poem:

"I shall go behind the mountain. Go there too, O moon.
Night after night we shall keep each other company."

---

[1]Delivered before the Swedish Academy on December 12, 1968. The English translation is rendered by Edward Seidensticker, the translator of his other works. Copyright © The Nobel Foundation, 1968. Reprinted by permission.

Here is the setting for another poem, after Myōe had spent the rest of the night in the mediation hall, or perhaps gone there again before dawn: "Opening my eyes from my meditation, I saw the moon in the dawn, lighting the window. In the dark place myself, I felt as if my own heart were glowing with light which seemed to be that of the moon:

"My heart shines, a pure expanse of light;
And no doubt the moon will think the light its own."

Because of such a spontaneous and innocent stringing together of mere ejaculations as the following, Myōe has been called the poet of the moon."

"Bright, bright, and bright, bright, bright, and bright, bright.
Bright and bright, bright, and bright, bright moon."

In his three poems on the winter moon, from late night into the dawn, Myōe follows entirely the bent of Saigyō, another poet-priest, who lived from 1118 to 1190: "Though I compose poetry, I do not think of it as composed poetry." The thirty-one syllables of each poem, honest and straightforward as if he were addressing the moon, are not merely to "the moon as my companion." Seeing the moon, he becomes the moon, the moon seen by him becomes him. He sinks into nature, becomes one with nature. The light of the "clear heart" of the priest, seated in the mediation hall in the darkness before the dawn, becomes for the dawn moon its own light.

As we see from the long introduction to the first of Myōe's poems quoted above, in which the winter moon becomes a companion, the heart of mountain hall is engaged in a delicate interplay and exchange with the priest, sunk in meditation upon religion and philosophy, there in the moon; and it is this of which the poet sings. My reason for choosing that first poem when asked for a specimen of my calligraphy has to do with its remarkable gentleness and compassion. Winter moon, going behind the clouds and coming forth again, making bright my footsteps as I go to the mediation hall and descend again, making me unafraid of the wolf: does not the wind sink into you, does not the snow, are you not cold? I choose the poem as a poem of warm, deep delicate compassion, a poem that has in it the deep quiet of the Japanese spirit. Dr. Yashiro Yukio, internationally known as a scholar of Botticelli, a man of great learning in the art of the past and the present, of the East and the West, has summed up one of the special characteristics of Japanese art in a single poetic sentence: "The tie of the snows, of the moon, of the blossoms—then more than ever we think of our comrades." When we see the beauty of the snow, when we see the beauty of the full moon, when we see the beauty of the cherries in bloom, when in short we brush against and are awakened by the beauty of the four seasons, it is then that we think most of those close to us, and want them to share the pleasure. The excitement of beauty calls forth strong fellow feelings, yearnings for companionship, and the word "comrade" can be taken to mean "human being."

The snow, the moon, the blossoms, words expressive of the seasons as they move one into another, include in the Japanese tradition the beauty of mountains and rivers and grasses and trees, of all the myriad manifestations of nature, of human feelings as well.

That spirit, that feeling for one's comrades in the snow, the moonlight, under the blossoms, is also basic to the tea ceremony. A tea ceremony is a coming together in feeling, a meeting of good comrades in a good season. I may say in passing, that to see my novel *Thousand Cranes* as an evocation of the formal and spiritual beauty of the tea ceremony is a misreading. It is a negative work, an expression of doubt about and warning against the vulgarity into which the tea ceremony has fallen.

> "In the spring, cherry blossoms, in the summer the cuckoo.
> In autumn the full moon, in winter the snow, clear, cold."

One can, if one chooses, see in Dōgen's poem about the beauty of the four seasons no more than a conventional, ordinary, mediocre stringing together, in a most awkward form of representative images from the four seasons. One can see it as a poem that is not really a poem at all. And yet very similar is the deathbed poem of the priest Ryōkan (1758–1831).

> "What shall be my legacy? The blossoms of spring,
> The cuckoo in the hills, the leaves of autumn."

In this poem, as in Dōgen's, the commonest of figures and the commonest of words are strung together without hesitation—not to particular effect, rather— and so they transmit the very essence of Japan. And it is Ryōkan's last poem that I have quoted.

> "A long, misty day is spring: I saw it to a close,
> playing ball with the children."

> "The breeze is fresh, the moon is clear.
> Together let us dance the night away, in what is left of old age."

> "It is not that I wish to have none of the world,
> It is that I am better at the pleasure enjoyed alone."

Ryōkan, who shook off the modern vulgarity of his day, who was immersed in the elegance of earlier centuries, and whose poetry and calligraphy are much admired in Japan today—he lived in the spirit of these poems, a wanderer down country paths, a grass hut for shelter, rags for clothes, farmers to talk to. The profundity of religion and literature was not, for him, in the abstruse. He rather pursued literature and belief in the benign spirit summarized in the Buddhist phrase "a smiling face and gentle words." In his last poem he offered nothing as a legacy. He but hoped that after his death nature would remain beautiful. That could be his bequest. One feels in the poem the emotions of old Japan, and the heart of a religious faith as well.

"I wondered and wondered when she would come.
And now we are together. What thoughts need I have?"

Ryōkan wrote love poetry too. This is an example of which I am fond. An old man of sixty-nine (I might point out that at the same age I am the recipient of the Nobel Prize), Ryōkan met a twenty-nine-year-old nun named Teishin, and was blessed with love. The poem can be seen as one of happiness at having met the ageless woman, of happiness at having met the one for whom the wait was so long. The last line is simplicity itself.

Ryōkan died at the age of seventy-three. He was born in the province of Echigo, the present Niigata Prefecture and the setting of my novel *Snow Country,* a northerly region on what is known as the reverse side of Japan, where cold winds come down across the Japan Sea from Siberia. He lived his whole life in the snow country, and to his "eyes in their last extremity," when he was old and tired and knew that death was near, and had attained enlightenment, the snow country, as we see in his last poem, was yet more beautiful, I should imagine. I have an essay with the title "Eyes in Their Last Extremity."

The title comes from the suicide note of the short story writer Akutagawa Ryūnosuke (1892–1927). It is the phrase that pulls at me with the greatest strength. Akutagawa said that he seemed to be gradually losing the animal something known as the strength to live, and continued:

> I am living in a world of morbid nerves, clear and cold as ice. . . . I do not know when I will summon up the resolve to kill myself. But nature is for me more beautiful than it has ever been before. I have no doubt that you will laugh at the contradiction, for here I love nature even when I am contemplating suicide. But nature is beautiful because it comes to my eyes in their last extremity.

Akutagawa committed suicide in 1927, at the age of thirty-five.

In my essay "Eyes in Their Last Extremity," I had to say: "However alienated one may be from the world, suicide is not a form of enlightenment. However admirable he may be, the man who commits suicide is far from the realm of the saint." I neither admire nor am in sympathy with suicide. I had another friend who died young, an avant-garde painter. He too thought of suicide over the years, and of him I wrote in this same essay: "He seems to have said over and over that there is no art superior to death, that to die is to live." I could see, however, that for him, born in a Buddhist temple and educated in a Buddhist school, the concept of death was very different from that in the West. "Among those who gave thoughts to things, is there one who does not think of suicide?" With me was the knowledge that that fellow Ikkyū (1394–1481) twice contemplated suicide.

I have said "that fellow," because the priest Ikkyū is known even to children as a most amusing person, and because anecdotes about his limitlessly eccentric behavior have come down to us in ample numbers. It is said of him that children climbed his knee to stroke his beard, that wild birds took feed from his hand. It would seem from all this that he was the ultimate in mindlessness, that he was an approachable and gentle sort of priest. As a matter of fact he was the most severe and profound of Zen priests. Said to have been the son of an emperor, he entered a temple at the age of six, and early showed his genius as a poetic prodigy. At the same time he was troubled with the deepest of doubts about religion and life. "If there is a god, let him help me. If there is none, let me throw myself to the bottom of the lake and become food for fishes." Leaving behind these words, he sought to throw himself into a lake, but was held back. On another occasion, numbers of his fellows were incriminated when a priest in his Daitokuji Temple committed suicide. Ikkyū went back to the temple, "the burden heavy on my shoulders," and sought to starve himself to death. He gave his collected poetry the title *Collection of the Roiling Clouds,* and himself used the expression "Roiling Clouds" as a pen name. In this collection and its successor are poems quite without parallel in the Chinese and especially the Zen poetry of the Japanese middle ages, erotic poems and poems about the secrets of the bedchamber that leave one in utter astonishment. He sought, by eating fish and drinking spirits and having commerce with women, to go beyond the rules and proscriptions of the Zen of his day, and to seek liberation from them, and thus, turning against established religious forms, he sought in the pursuit of Zen the revival and affirmation of the essence of life, or human existence, in a day of civil war and moral collapse.

His temple, the Daitokuji at Murasakino in Kyoto, remains a center of the tea ceremony, and specimens of his calligraphy are greatly admired as hangings in alcoves of tea rooms.

I myself have two specimens of Ikkyū's calligraphy. One of them is a single line: "It is easy to enter the world of the Buddha, it is hard to enter the world of the devil." Much drawn to these words, I frequently make use of them when asked for a specimen of my own calligraphy. They can be read in any number of ways, as difficult as one chooses, but in that world of the devil added to the world of the Buddha, Ikkyū of Zen comes home to me with great immediacy. The fact that for an artist, seeking truth, good, and beauty, the fear and petition even as a prayer in those words about the world of the devil—the fact that it should be there apparent on the surface, hidden behind, perhaps speaks with the inevitability of fate. There can be no world of the Buddha without the world of the devil. And the world of the devil is the world difficult of entry. It is not for the weak heart.

> "If you meet a Buddha, kill him.
> If you meet a patriarch of the law, kill him."

This is a well-known Zen motto. If Buddhism is divided generally into the sects that believe in salvation by faith and those that believe in salvation by one's own efforts, then, of course, there must be such violent utterances in Zen, which insists upon salvation by one's own efforts. On the other side, the side of salvation by faith, Shinran (1173–1262), the founder of the Shin sect, once said: "The good shall be reborn in paradise, and how much more shall it be so with the bad." This view of things has something in common with Ikkyū's world of the Buddha and world of the devil, and yet at heart the two have their different inclinations. Shinran also said: "I shall take not a single disciple."

"If you meet a Buddha, kill him. If you meet a patriarch of the law, kill him." "I shall take not a single disciple." In these two statements, perhaps, is the rigorous fate of art.

In Zen there is no worship of images. Zen does have images, but in the hall where the regimen of meditation is pursued, there are neither images nor pictures of Buddhas, nor are there scriptures. The Zen disciple sits for long hours silent and motionless, with his eyes closed. Presently he enters a state of impassivity, free from all ideas and all thoughts. he departs from the self and enters the realm of nothingness. This is not the nothingness or the emptiness of the West. It is rather the reverse, a universe of the spirit in which everything communicates freely with everything, transcending bonds, limitless. There are of course masters of Zen, and the disciple is brought toward enlightenment by exchanging questions and answers with his master, and he studies the scriptures. The disciple must, however, always be lord of his own thoughts, and must attain enlightenment through his own efforts. And the emphasis is less upon reason and argument than upon intuition, immediate feeling. Enlightenment comes not from teaching but through the eye awakened inwardly. Truth is in "the discarding of words," it lies "outside words." And so we have the extreme of "silence like thunder," in the *Vimalakirti Nirdesa Sutra*. Tradition has it that Bodhidharma, a southern Indian prince who lived in about the sixth century and was the founder of Zen in China, sat for nine years in silence facing the wall of a cave, and finally attained enlightenment. The Zen practice of silent mediation in a seated posture derives from Bodhidharma.

Here are two religious poems by Ikkyū:

> "When I ask you answer. When I do not you do not.
> What is there then in your heart, O Lord Bodhidharma."

> "And what is it, the heart?
> It is the sound of the pine breeze in the ink painting."

Here we have the spirit of Zen in Oriental painting. The heart of the ink painting is in space, abbreviation, what is left undrawn. In the words of the Chinese painter Zhin Nong: "You paint the branch well, and you hear the sound of the wind." And the priest Dōgen once more: "Are there not these cases? Enlightenment in the voice of the bamboo. Radiance of heart in the peach blossom."

Ikenōbo Sen-o, a master of flower arranging, once said (the remark is to be found in his Sayings): "With a spray of flowers, a bit of water, one evokes the vastness of rivers and mountains." The Japanese garden, too, of course, symbolizes the vastness of nature. The Western garden tends to be symmetrical, the Japanese garden asymmetrical, and this is because the asymmetrical has the greater power to symbolize multiplicity and vastness. The asymmetry, of course, rests upon a balance imposed by delicate sensibilities. Nothing is more complicated, varied, attentive to detail, than the Japanese art of landscape gardening. Thus there is the form called the dry landscape, composed entirely of rocks, in which the arrangement of stones gives expression to mountains and rivers that are not present, and even suggests the waves of the great ocean breaking in upon cliffs. Compressed to the ultimate, the Japanese garden becomes the *bonsai* dwarf garden, or the *bonseki,* its dry version.

In the Oriental word for landscape, literally "mountain water," with its related implications in landscape painting and landscape gardening, there is contained the concept of the serene and wasted, and even of the sad and the threadbare. Yet in the sad, austere, autumnal qualities so valued by the tea ceremony, itself summarized in the expression "gently respectful, cleanly quiet," there lies concealed a great richness of spirits; and the tea room, so rigidly confined and simple, contains boundless space and unlimited elegance. The single flower contains more brightness than a hundred flowers. The great sixteenth-century master of the tea ceremony and flower arranging, Rikyū, taught that it was wrong to use fully opened flowers. Even in the tea ceremony today the general practice is to have in the alcove of the tea room but a single flower, and that a flower in bud. In winter a special flower of winter, let us say a camellia, bearing some such name as White Jewel or *Wabisuke,* which might be translated literally as "Helpmate in Solitude," is chosen, a camellia remarkable among camellias for its whiteness and the smallness of its blossoms; and but a single bud is set out in the alcove. White is the cleanest of colors, it contains in itself all the other colors. And there must always be dew on the bud. The bud is moistened with a few drops of water. The most splendid of arrangements for the tea ceremony comes in May, when a peony is put in a celadon vase; but here again there is but a single white bud, always with dew upon it. Not only are there drops of water upon the flower, the vase too is frequently moistened.

Among flower vases, the ware that is given the highest rank is old Iga, from the sixteenth and seventeenth centuries, and it commands the highest price. When old Iga has been dampened, its colors and its glow take on a beauty such as to awaken one afresh. Iga was fired at very high temperatures. The straw ash and the smoke from the fuel fell and flowed against the surface, and, as the temperature dropped, became a sort of glaze, because the colors were not fabricated but were rather the result of nature at work in the kiln, color patterns emerged in such varieties as to be called quirks and freaks of the kiln. The rough, austere, strong surfaces of old Iga take on a voluptuous glow when dampened. It breathes to the rhythm of the dew of the flowers. The taste of the tea ceremony also asks that the tea bowl be moistened before using, to give it its own soft glow.

Ikenobō Sen-o remarked on another occasion (this too is in his Sayings) that "the mountains and strands should appear in their own forms." Bringing a new spirit into his school of flower arranging, therefore, he found "flowers" in broken vessels and withered branches, and in them too the enlightenment. Here we see an awakening to the heart of the Japanese spirit, under the influence of Zen. And in it too, perhaps, is the heart of a man living in the devastation of long civil wars. The *Tales of Ise,* compiled in the tenth century, is the oldest Japanese collection of lyrical episodes, numbers of which might be called short stories. In one of them we learn that the poet Ariwara no Yukihira, having invited guests, put out flowers:

> Being a man of feeling, he had in a large jar a most unusual wisteria. The trailing spray of flowers was upwards of three and a half feet long.

A spray of wisteria of such length is indeed so unusual as to make one have doubts about the credibility of the writer; and yet I can feel in this great spray a symbol of Heian culture. The wisteria is a very Japanese flower, and it has a feminine elegance. Wisteria sprays, as they trail in the breeze, suggest softness, gentleness, reticence. Disappearing and then appearing again in the early-summer greenery, they have in them that feeling for the poignant beauty of things long characterized by the Japanese as *mono no aware.* No doubt there was a particular splendor in that spray upwards of three and a half feet long. The splendor of Heian culture a millennium ago and the emergence of a peculiarly Japanese beauty were as wondrous as this most unusual wisteria, for the culture of Tang China had at length been absorbed and Japanized. In poetry there came, early in the tenth century, the first of the imperially commissioned anthologies, the *Kokinshū,* and in fiction the *Tales of Ise,* followed by the supreme masterpieces of classical Japanese prose, *The Tale of Genji* of Lady Murasaki and the *Pillow Book* of Sei Shōnagon, both of whom lived from the late tenth century into the early eleventh. So was established a tradition that influenced and even controlled Japanese literature for eight hundred years. *The Tale of Genji* in particular is the highest pinnacle of Japanese literature. Even down to our day there has not been a piece of fiction to compare with it. That such a modern work should have been written in the eleventh century is a miracle, and as a miracle the work is widely known abroad. Although my grasp of classical Japanese was uncertain, the Heian classics were my principal boyhood reading, and it is the *Genji,* I think, that has meant the most to me. For centuries after it was written, fascination with the *Genji* persisted, and imitations and reworkings did homage to it. The *Genji* was a wide and deep source of nourishment for poetry, of course, and for the fine arts and handicrafts as well, and even for landscape gardening.

Murasaki and Sei Shonagon, and such famous poets as Izumi Shikibu, who probably died early in the eleventh century, and Akazome Emon, who probably died in the mid-eleventh century, were all ladies-in-waiting in the Imperial Court. Japanese culture was court culture, and court culture was feminine. The day of the *Genji* and the *Pillow Book* was its finest, when court culture ripeness was moving into decay. One feels in it the sadness at the end of glory, the high tide of Japanese court culture. The court went into its decline, power moved from the court nobility to the military aristocracy, in whose hands it remained through almost seven centuries from the founding of the Kamakura Shogunate in 1192 to the Meiji Restoration in 1867 and 1868. It is not to be thought, however, that either the Imperial institution or court culture vanished. In the eighth of the Imperial anthologies, the *Shinkokinshū* of the early thirteenth century, the technical dexterity of the *Kokinshū* was pushed yet a step further, and sometimes fell into mere verbal dalliance; but there were added elements of the mysterious, the suggestive, the evocative and inferential elements of sensuous fantasy that have something in common with modern symbolist poetry. Saigyō, who has been mentioned earlier, was a representative poet spanning the two ages, Heian and Kamakura.

"I dreamt of him because I was thinking of him.
Had I known it was a dream, I should not have wished to awaken."

"In my dreams I go to him each night without fail.
But this is less than a single glimpse in the waking."

These are by Ono no Komachi, the leading poetess of the *Kokinshū*, who sings of dreams, even, with a straightforward realism. But when we come to the following poems of the Empress Eifuku, who lived at about the same time as Ikkyū, in the Muromachi Period, somewhat later than the *Shinkokinshū*, we have a subtle realism that becomes a melancholy symbolism, delicately Japanese, and seems to me more modern:

"Shining upon the bamboo thicket where the sparrows twitter,
the sunlight takes on the color of the autumn."

"The autumn wind, scattering the bush clover in the garden,
sinks into one's bones. Upon the wall, the evening sun disappears."

Dōgen, whose poem about the clear, cold snow I have quoted and Myōe, who wrote of the winter moon as his companion, were of generally the *Shinkokinshū* period. Myōe exchanged poems with Saigyō and they discussed poetry together. The following is from the biography of Myōe by his disciple Kikai:

Saigyō frequently came and talked of poetry. His own attitude towards poetry, he said, was far from the ordinary. Cherry blossoms, the cuckoo, the moon, snow: confronted with all the manifold forms of nature, his eyes and his ears were filled with emptiness. And were not all the words that came forth true words. When he sang of the blossoms the blossoms were not on his mind. When he sang of the moon he did not think of the moon. As the occasion presented itself, as the urge arose, he wrote poetry. The red rainbow across the sky was as the sky taking on color. The white sunlight was as the sky growing bright. It was not something to take on color. With a spirit like the empty sky he gave color to all the manifold scenes, but not a trace remained. In such poetry was the Buddha, the manifestation of the ultimate truth.

Here we have the emptiness, the nothingness, of the Orient. My own works have been described as works of emptiness, but it is not to be taken for the nihilism of the West. The spiritual foundation would seem to be quite different. Dōgen entitled his poem about the seasons "Innate Reality," and even as he sang of the beauty of the seasons he was deeply immersed in Zen.

FROM EXOTICISM TO UNIVERSALITY

Ōe Kanzaburo was known to the West through a number of his works translated into English, including The Catch *(1959),*[2] A Personal Matter *(1968),* The Silent Cry *(1974), and* The Clever Rain Tree *(1985). At home he was well known, but his works were not necessarily well read. Thus when his Nobel Prize in Literature was announced, it came as a surprise to a large number of the Japanese public. Some critics even suggested that it was Ōe's proclivity to play to the taste of the Western audience that had earned him the prize, insinuating that there were many worthier genuine Japanese writers who should have been the recipients. Katō Shūichi (b. 1919) took exception to these views and redefined the terms of debate. According to Kato, Ōe's works symbolized "liberation from exoticism" and were universal as they were linked to the works of contemporary writers elsewhere. His rebuttal is reproduced as Document 2. Dr. Katō once practiced medicine and engaged in medical research. He has taught Japanese intellectual history at a number of universities both in Japan and abroad. Among his works available in English is his major work,* A History of Japanese Literature, *in three volumes.*

2 **Kawabata and Ōe: From Exoticism to Universality, 1994**[3] During the almost half century since the end of the Pacific War, the Western world became acquainted with modern Japanese literature in translation and gradually came to appreciate it. For the most part, what Westerners savored were those features perceived as being "purely Japanese," as reflecting little Western influ-

---

[2]The dates given are those dates in which the translated works appeared, not the original publication dates of the same works in Japan.

[3]Katō Shūichi, *"Kawabata Yasunari kara Ōe Kenzaburō e"* (From Kawabata to Ōe), *Asahi Shimbun*, evening edition, October 20, 1994, as translated in *Japan Echo* 22, no. 1 (Spring 1995): pp. 78–79.

ence, as being far removed from Western literature in both style and content.

In other words, the appeal of modern Japanese literature lay in its exoticism, as symbolized by the selection of Kawabata Yasunari for the 1968 Nobel Prize in Literature. To be sure, Kawabata's novels were not only widely read in Japan but also epitomized a sensuous "beautiful Japan," from the texture of Shino-ware pottery to the delicate feel of a woman's skin. At the time of the Vietnam War and a surging student movement, however, that sort of thing was not the major concern of Japan's intellectuals.

The quarter century since then has seen an increase in both the number of foreign students of Japanese literature and the number of works translated. Fascination with the exotic aspects of Japanese culture has not disappeared from Western society, but a new kind of interest in Japanese literature and new criteria for evaluating it have appeared. This approach focuses on not how distant Japan is but how close; not what a different world Japanese literature depicts but how the Japanese deal with situations and problems common to all humanity.

Of course, great historical and cultural differences do exist. But this is true not just of Japan and the West. Just as Palermo is distant from New York, so is Mexico City far from Tokyo. And just as the legends of the Albanian mountains differ from the folktales of the Auvergne, so do village customs in the Shikoku Mountains differ from those in the Deccan. Ismail Kadare[4] has written about Albanian mountain villages, and his contemporary Ōe Kenzaburo has written about Shikoku mountain villages. The works of both writers are part of the body of modern world literature, and that is the way they are read—an approach diametrically opposed to exoticism. This "unexotic" approach to literature has gradually strengthened in some Western circles, a trend symbolized by the choice of Ōe for the 1994 Nobel Prize in Literature.

What has this Japanese writer done? Through the format of the modern novel, he has consistently explored and expressed the basic issues of postwar Japanese society. The modern novel is consciously organized (unlike Kawabata's works) and emphasizes overlapping time frames, the crossing of imaginary and actual worlds, and characters' inner unfolding (unlike nineteenth-century Western novels). These features characterize the work of most writers of Ōe's generation, from Italo Calvino[5] to Günter Grass.[6] Of course this type of novel is closely

---

[4]Kadare (b. 1936) is an Albanian writer who has been in exile in Paris since 1990. His semiautobiographical *Chronicle in Stone* (1976) depicts his childhood during the wartime fascist occupation. Another work, *The Great Winter* (1977), describes the worsening of relations between the Soviet Union and Albania since 1961.

[5]A Cuban-born Italian journalist, Calvino (1923–85) joined the Italian resistance during World War II. *The Path to the Nest of Spiders* views the resistance from the perspective of a helpless adolescent. He once edited a left-wing magazine, but his chief fame comes from a number of imaginative fables and fantasies.

[6]Through his first novel, *The Tin Drum* (1959), Grass (b. 1927) clearly established himself as the spokesman for the generation that survived the war under Nazi Germany.

bound up with the writer's view of humanity (or the world), and is what makes Ōe's view "contemporary," reflecting a universality that is in no way "Japanese."

Ōe's themes, however, are peculiar to postwar Japanese society. They are linked to the collective memory pervading the soil of his birthplace, and are also inseparable from the individual, concrete circumstances of his own family. In short, they spring from the "personal matter" of his war experience. They include Hiroshima and Okinawa, the myths of Japanese village society, life with a disabled son. Writing about these things means, for the writer and thus for the reader, forging a connection between specific circumstances and a universal outlook. Through this linkage, specificity is transformed into universality. More precisely, the individual, concrete, specific world opens out toward a universal horizon.

The Hiroshima experience belongs to the only people in the world to have undergone atomic bombing. But the threat of nuclear weapons belongs to the entire human race. Even today, almost fifty years after the war, Okinawa contains the biggest military base in Asia and is also the target of large-scale tourism-development projects. It thus epitomizes the disparity between the industrialized North and the developing South and the North's exploitation of that disparity. The relationship between mountain villages and the central government, throughout the world as on the island of Shikoku, has led not only to environmental despoliation but also to the tragic despoliation of traditional society and culture. Living with a disabled son means recognizing his dignity as a human being and leads inevitably to deep personal involvement with human rights in general.

In postwar Japanese literature, Kawabata created a self-contained space of sensuous beauty; Ōe opened up Japan's literary space by giving it a universal horizon. Kawabata wrote of "beautiful Japan"; Ōe writes of Japan's anguish, and thus of the anguish of all contemporary humanity.

Ōe, however, is not the only postwar Japanese writer to have done so, or at least to have aspired to do so, as attested by the work of Ōoka Shōhei,[7] Noma Hiroshi,[8] Kinoshita Junji,[9] and Hotta Yoshie.[10] Nor are writers the only people to have

---

His 1980 novel, *Headbirths, or, the Germans Are Dying Out,* depicts the agony faced by a young couple whether or not to have a child because the threats of nuclear war and population explosion are too real to them. His political writings include *Two States One Nation?* (1990).

[7]Ōoka (1909–88) wrote about his war experiences in *Prisoner of War* (1967) (*Furyoki,* 1948) and *Fires on the Plane* (1967) (*Nobi,* 1951). In his other works, he has shown the abiding influence of Stendhal, about whom he wrote a critical work before being drafted into the army.

[8]Noma (1915–91) was once an employee of the Osaka City Welfare Department working with the *burakumin* minority. Most of his works, such as *Seinen no Wa* (*Ring of Youth,* 1971), show his deep personal involvement with and compassion for the *burakumin.* An activist in the Japan Communist Party from 1947, he was expelled from it in 1964.

[9]Kinoshita (b. 1914) is one of Japan's foremost playwrights. Aside from a complete

618 JAPAN: A DOCUMENTARY HISTORY

taken this approach. Many Japanese who have lived through the war and its aftermath have maintained a critical stance—in their workplaces, their university offices, their homes—toward Japanese society and state power. In regard to many issues, the critical voices do not necessarily represent a majority. But is democracy possible without critics of the powers that be? Is an intelligentsia possible without a critical spirit? It is these critics, taken as a whole, who have ensured democracy and the existence of intellectual Japan.

Honoring Ōe's literary accomplishments is especially significant at this time. In addition to symbolizing liberation from exoticism, it means recognition of the many postwar writers who have striven to expand the literary horizon, and of the critical spirit in modern Japan. In short, it confirms the existence of intellectual Japan.

(Note 9 continued) translation of Shakespeare's plays, he is known for an indelible mark he has left on postwar shingeki (new theater), and for establishing a new type of modern play called minwageki (folktale play). A number of his plays portray an individual's struggle against the tide of history and against the all powerful outside world.

[10]Hotta (b. 1918) is known for his sensitive handling of an individual's conflict with society, and of irreconcilable foreign and native ways. He was an army propagandist in China during World War II. That experience is recorded in his *Sokoku sōshitsu* (*Loss of the Motherland,* 1950) and other works.

Weights and Measures—
Metric and U.S. Equivalents

Linear Measure

1 *sun*	3.03 centimeters	1.193 inches
1 *shaku* (10 *sun*)	0.303 meter	0.995 foot
1 *ken* (6 *shaku*)	1.818 meters	1.987 yards
1 *jō* (10 *shaku*)	3.030 meters	3.316 yards
1 *chō* (60 *ken*)	109.1 meters	0.542 furlong
1 *ri* (36 *chō*)	3.927 kilometers	2.439 miles
1 traditional *ri* (6 *chō*)	654.6 meters	3.252 furlongs

Square Measure

1 *gō*	0.330 square meter	1.083 square feet
1 *bu* (or *tsubo*, 10 *gō*)	3.306 square meters	3.615 square yards
1 *se* (30 *bu* or *tsubo*)	99.17 square meters	19,726 square rods
1 *tan* (10 *se* or 300 *bu*)	9.92 ares	0.245 acre
1 *chō* (10 *tan*)	99.17 ares	2.45 acres

Prior to Hideyoshi's decree of 1598

1 *tan* (360 *bu*)	11.904 ares	0.294 acre
1 *chō* (10 *tan*)	119.04 ares	2.94 acres

Weights

1 *momme*	3.750 grams	2.115 drams
1 *kin* (160 *momme*)	0.600 kilogram	1.322 pounds
1 *kan* (1,000 *momme*)	3.750 kilograms	8.26 pounds

Liquid and Dry Measures

1 *gō*	0.180 liter	1.525 gills	0.328 pint
1 *shō* (10 *gō*)	1.804 liters	3.81 pints	1.638 quarts
1 *to* (10 *shō*)	18.04 liters	19.06 quarts	2.048 pecks
1 *koku* (10 *to*)	180.4 liters	47.6 gallons	5.12 bushels
1 *koku* of brown rice	150 kilograms		5.01 bushels

Note: the term *masu* may at times be used in place of the term *shō* (1.805 liters). Rice and other grains are often measured by *hyō*, which means a bag or bale. One *hyō* normally contains four *to* (1 *to* equals 2.048 pecks) of rice. The term *ryō* represents a unit of gold currency and must not be confused with terms of weights and measures.

Appendix 2

Glossary of Japanese Terms

ando no kudashibumi: A writ of assurance given to military households, temples, and shrines by the Kamakura and Muromachi *bakufu,* confirming their rights to hold lands in fief (*chigyō-chi*).

bakufu: Headquarters of the *shōgun*: or the shogunate.

baku-han: A term describing the Tokugawa system of government in which the *bakufu* exercised authority over *han.*

bodhisattva: (Buddhism) One who has attained enlightenment, but postpones entering Nirvana in order to help others attain enlightenment.

bugyō: An official of the *bakufu* charged with specific administrative functions: commissioner.

bummei kaika: "Civilization and enlightenment," a primary slogan of Meiji intellectuals promoting Westernization.

bunkoku: (1) In the Heian period, the term referred to provinces over which court nobles were given the functions of governor; (2) in the Sengoku period, territories held by *sengoku daimyō.*

buke shohatto: "Laws for military households," first issued in 1615.

chigyō: To have right over land and hold it in fief; in the Tokugawa period, the term also referred to land granted by the *bakufu* or *han* as stipend.

chokkatsuryō: See *tenryō.*

chokunin: Under the system established by the Meiji constitution, those civil servants of first and second ranks were technically appointed to their posts by an imperial command (*chokunin*), and were so called.

chōnin: Townspeople, urban dwellers who were not samurai; merchants and artisans.

chū: Loyalty.

daijōkan: (1) The Council of State under the *ritsu-ryō* system. It supervised eight ministries under it; (2) the highest organ of state in the Meiji government from 1868 to 1885.

daikan: (1) One who performs on behalf of his master, deputy; (2) an official of a *daimyō* in charge of collecting taxes; (3) a *bakufu* official responsible for collecting taxes and civil administration in *tenryō.*

daimyō: (1) During the Tokugawa period, those fief holders who had territories producing 10,000 *koku* or more of rice; (2) in the later Heian period and the Kamakura period, holders of large *myōden.* See also *shugo daimyō* and *sengoku daimyō.*

dangō: Consultation among participants before making bids for large construction projects.

detchi: An apprentice in a commercial establishment.

dōmin: (1) People who were native to certain localities; (2) also used as a pejorative term for farmers.

dōri: Propriety or practical reason; the correct way in which man must act; the way consistent with the nature of things.

fudai: "Hereditary" *daimyō,* comprising the descendants of those men who, almost without exception, recognized Ieyasu as their overlord on or before 1600.

fukoku kyōhei: "Rich nation, strong army," one of the primary slogans of Meiji leaders to strengthen the nation.

genrō: Elder statesmen, men who served collectively and individually as the Emperor's closest advisers from the 1890s through the 1930s. Only nine men received the designation to this extraconstitutional but extremely powerful position.

genrōin: Council of Elders, or Senate: an early Meiji legislative organ established in 1875, which was disbanded in 1890 prior to the convening of the Diet under the Meiji constitution.

gō: An administrative unit under the *ritsu-ryō* system, normally comprising several villages (*ri*); county.

gokenin: "Men of the household," direct or close vassals of the *shōgun.*

goningumi: A group of five who shared collective responsibility.

gun: District, (1) a subdivision of a province, also rendered *kōri* in traditional Japan; (2) from 1879 to 1921, the *gun* was an administrative subdivision of a prefecture.

haihan chiken: Replacing the *han* with prefectures.

hakkō ichiu: Literally, "all under heaven under one roof," hence to spread the benevolent rule of the emperor throughout the world, a slogan used by the militarists in the 1930s.

han: A domain belonging to a *daimyō,* with its own administrative structure.

hanseki hōkan: Return of feudal domains and census registers.

hatamoto: "Bannermen," enfeoffed vassals of the Tokugawa *shōgun* with stipends ranging from 500 *koku* to 10,000 *koku* with the privilege of audience with the *shōgun.*

honke: "Main family," patron of *shōen*; main family as against branch families (*bunke*).

hyakusho: Farmers; also collectively common people.

ichi: Market, or marketplace.

ikki: Uprising.

ishin: Restoration, also used specifically to refer to the Meiji Restoration.

jinsei: Benevolent rule, found in Confucian writings.

jiriki: (Buddhism) Dependence on one's own power to attain enlightenment.

JIT: Just-in-time method of manufacturing.

jitō: Stewards; (1) in the Heian period, officials appointed by the *ryōshu* to facilitate *shōen* administration; (2) in the Kamakura and Muromachi periods, the term stood for "military land stewards," who were placed in *shōen* and territories directly held by the *bakufu.* (3) In the Tokugawa period, those *hatamoto* who had their own *chigyō* or those retainers of *daimyō* who had the right to collect their own land revenue were also called *jitō.*

jitō-uke: An arrangement under which the *jitō* pledged to pay a set amount of annual rent to the *ryōshu* in return for the right to manage or control the *shōen.* Practiced in the Kamakura period.

jōi: Expelling barbarians (foreigners).

kaikoku: "Opening the country" to end the seclusion policy.

kalpa: (Buddhism) A general term for a long period that cannot be defined by months or years.

karma: (Buddhism) Action bringing upon oneself the inevitable results either in this life or in reincarnation; the law of cause and effect.

karō: "House elders," important retainers of a *daimyō* who exercised administrative control over other retainers on his behalf.

kashindan: Corps of retainers of a *daimyō*.

kebiishi: Police officers, constables.

keichō: Tax register.

Keidanren: Federation of Economic Organizations

keiretsu: Enterprise groups; Each group of affiliated business enterprises is normally centered around a major city bank. A trading company in the group may also serve a coordinating function.

Keizai Dōyūkai: Japan Association of Corporate Executives

ken: Prefecture, an administrative division established in 1871 signifying the implementation of direct rule by the central government.

kirishitan: Japanese rendition for "Christian."

ko: Households.

kō: Filial piety.

kōan: (Buddhism) Public themes devised for Zen meditation.

kōgi: Deliberation openly arrived, or "public opinion."

kōri: District, see *gun* above.

kōron: Public matters openly discussed, consensus reached.

koseki: Population register.

ku: (1) In the early Meiji period, it referred to an administrative subdivision that replaced previous townships and villages; (2) currently, the term refers to a ward, which is an administrative subdivision of major cities.

kubunden: Allotment land.

kuge: Court noble.

kuji: Lawsuits.

kuni: Province.

kuni no miyatsuko: Title of territorial aristocracy prior to the Taika reform of 645.

kuni no tsukasa: Provincial governor.

kyūnin: Samurai receiving stipends from a *daimyō.*

machi-bugyō: Town commissioner.

machi-doshiyori: Town elders.

mappō: (Buddhism) The latter degenerate days.

metsuke: A public censor or spy.

meyasu: Legal briefs, petitions, or written complaints.

minbu: Ministry of Popular Affairs.

myōshu: Holders of rights to *myōden.*

myōden: First accepted by provincial governors as basic taxable units within their domains, and later by the *ryōshu* as basic rent-paying units in their *shōen.*

nanushi: In the Tokugawa period, (1) a *hyakushō* appointed to become village head to engage in civil administration of a village; (2) or a *chōnin* who engaged in civil administration under the supervision of *machi-doshiyori.*

nemawashi: Prior consultation; touching base with interested parties before decisions are made to avoid conflict.

nembutsu: (Buddhism) To recite the name of Amida Buddha in the formula, *Namu Ami Dabutsu.*

nengu: Annual rent or tax. The term rent is used when the *nengu* was collected by *shōen* or other private and semiprivate authorities, and tax is used when the *nengu* was collected by *bakufu* or *han* or other duly constituted public authorities.

Nikkeiren: Japan Federation of Employers' Associations

ōdō: Kingly way, found in Confucian writings.

ōjō: (Buddhism) To go to the other shore to live, hence to attain enlightenment or Nirvana.

onchi: Land given to samurai for meritorious service.

QC: Quality control.

rakuichi: Free market.

rakuza: Abolition of the *za.*

ri: The smallest administrative unit under the *ritsu-ryō* system; village.

ri: Principle(s), found in Confucian writings.

ritsu-ryō: Penal and administrative codes; and when used in conjunction with the term *"kokka"* (state or nation), it refers to a country governed by *ritsu* and *ryō,* as under the Taihō-Yōrō codes.

rōjū "Elders," or senior counsellors in the Tokugawa *bakufu* administration.

ryōshu: Lord of *shōen.*

sakoku: Closing the country to foreign commerce and intercourse.

sankin-kōtai: Alternate attendance.

satori: (Buddhism) Sudden enlightenment in Zen Buddhism.

seikanron: An opinion expressed by Saigō Takamori and his followers in the early 1870s advocating the dispatch of expeditionary forces to Korea.

sengoku daimyō: *Daimyō* who replaced *shugo daimyō* in the Sengoku period, each having his own domain, the first true *daimyō.*

seirei toshi: Administratively designated cities. Large cities which are given some of the legislative and administrative powers normally reserved for prefectural government. As of the fall of 1996, the following cities were so designated: Yokohama, Osaka, Nagoya, Sapporo, Kobe, Kyoto, Fukuoka, Kawasaki, Hiroshima, Kita Kyushu, Sendai, and Chiba.

shiki: Rights to recompense for performing certain functions under the *shōen* system.

shikimoku: Formulary; written codes in the medieval period.

shikken: The position held by the Hōjō family during the Kamakura period as *shōgun*'s regent.

shimbun: Newspaper.

shimpan: Daimyō who were collaterally related to the main Tokugawa *shōgun* family.

shō: A short form for *shōen.*

Shinkansen: New trunk line, the high-speed lines using "bullet trains."

shōen: Private estate that was exempted from central government control; see introduction to Chapter IV.

shōgun: A short form for *Sei-i tai shōgun,* or barbarian-subduing generalissimo. From 1192 to 1867, this title was assumed by the head of a *bakufu* who exercised both military and civil authorities.

shokubun: Obligations, functions, or callings, found in Confucian writings.

shokusan kōgyō: Encouragement of industries, a policy adopted by the early Meiji government.

shōmyō: In the medieval period, those who held relatively small *myōden;* during the Tokugawa period, those fief holders who had smaller territories than *daimyō.*

shōya: A *hyakushō* appointed to become village head to engage in civil administration of a village. This term was used in the Kansai region, whereas the term *nanushi* was used mainly in the Kantō region.

shugo: "Protector," a post created in 1185 by Minamoto no Yoritomo, which at first had limited functions. However, it extended its functions to include those normally exercised by provincial governors through the Muromachi period.

shugo daimyō: A term describing those *shugo* who, during the Muromachi period, converted territories under their jurisdiction as their own domains.

shugo-uke: The practice of permitting the *shugo* to submit only a set amount of annual rent in return for the actual control of the *shōen.*

sō: A village organization, which during the period of *shōen's* disintegration, attempted to express the will of the village community or to take joint action.

sōnin: Under the system established by the Meiji constitution, those civil servants of third rank or lower were technically recommended for appointment by the prime minister (*sōnin*) and were thus so called.

sōryō: The heir, later also used to signify oldest son or daughter.

sukiya: A building in which tea ceremony is performed.

tahata: Fields and gardens; paddy fields and dry fields.

tariki: (Buddhism) Dependence on the original vow of Amida Buddha to attain rebirth in the Western paradise.

tatemae: A "principle" or stated reason which may differ from the real intention (*honne*).

tato: Farmers who exercised some of the rights of landlords in the *shōen* system during the Heian period.

tedai: (1) Minor officials in the Tokugawa period engaged in tax collection and other duties; (2) clerks in a commercial establishment.

tenryō: The territory directly held by the Tokugawa *bakufu.*

toiya or *tonya:* A wholesale merchant.

tokusei: Act of grace, hence forgiveness of debts.

tozama: "Outer" *daimyō,* comprising the descendants of those men who pledged allegiance to Ieyasu on or after 1600.

wabi: Enjoyment of an austere type of beauty, and finding fulfillment in poverty. A state of mind as well a moral principle.

yin-yang: In Chinese naturalist philosophy, *yin* is female, dark and negative, and *yang* is male, light and positive. The two principles complement and balance each other.

za: Medieval Japanese trade or craft guilds that attempted to establish local monopoly rights.

zaibatsu: The "financial clique" or the great conglomerates, such as Mitsui and Mitsubishi, which exercised profound influence over the Japanese economy from late Meiji to early 1940s.

zaikai: the financial world, financial circles.

zasshō: Officials of governmental bureaus, *shōen,* or *bakufu,* who engaged in miscellaneous functions.

zazen: (Buddhism) To sit in Zen meditation.

zukuri: the style of architecture that comprises a small space, uses natural wood, with little or no ornamentation.

Chronology of Modern Japanese History

Late Tokugawa Period (1800–1867)

1804	Russian envoy Rezanov reaches Nagasaki
1808	British frigate *Pheton* successfully enters Nagasaki Harbor
1809	Mamiya Rinzō's exploration proves that Sakhalin is an island
1823	von Siebold arrives in Japan as physician to the Dutch factory
1825	An edict to drive off foreign vessels is issued
1833–37	The Tempō famine
1837	Insurrection of Ōshio Heihachirō
1841	Rōju Mizuno Tadakuni's Tempō reforms
1853	Arrival of Commodore Perry in Uraga
1854	The Treaty of Kanagawa signed with the United States
1858	Ii Naosuke becomes *tairō*. Signing of a commercial treaty with United States
1859	The Ansei purge
1860	First Japanese mission to the United States
	Assassination of Ii Naosuke
	Kōbu gattai, as symbolized in Kazunomiya's marriage to shōgun Iemochi
1866	Satsuma-Chōshū alliance
1867	Keiki restores political power to the Imperial Court

Meiji Period (1868–1912)

1868	Establishment of a new government. Tokyo becomes the capital
1869	Return of feudal domains (*han*) to the Emperor
1870	Telegraph line links Tokyo and Yokohama
	Commoners (*heimin*) are permitted to assume surnames
1871	First daily newspaper, *Yokohama Mainichi,* begins publication
	The *han* replaced by prefectures
	Elimination of the Tokugawa class distinction
	Introduction of the postal system
	Dispatch of the Iwakura mission to America and Europe (returned 1873)
1872	Opening of the Tokyo-Yokohama railroad
	Compulsory elementary education instituted
	Granting of the freedom to buy and sell land
1873	Adoption of the Gregorian calendar (12/3 becomes 1/1/1873)
	New land tax law instituted
	Beginning of the universal military conscription
1874	Expedition to Taiwan
1875	Mitsubishi begins the Yokohama-Shanghai line
1876	Population of Japan as of January 1 stands at 34,338,400
	Wearing of swords by former samurai forbidden
1877	The Satsuma rebellion
1878	Assassination of Home Minister Ōkubo Toshimichi
1879	The Ryukyu islands become Okinawa prefecture
1881	Expulsion of Ōkuma Shigenobu from the government
	A national assembly is promised for 1890
1882	Establishment of the Bank of Japan
1884	The peerage is created
1885	The Cabinet system is adopted, Itō Hirobumi the first prime minister
1886	Tokyo Imperial University is established
1887	Electric lighting introduced in Tokyo
	Masquerade party at the Rokumeikan
	Peace Preservation Law is issued to suppress political agitation

1888	The Privy Council is established
1889	Promulgation of the Meiji constitution
	Opening of the Imperial Museums in Tokyo, Kyoto, and Nara
1890	The first Diet convenes
	The Imperial rescript on education
	"Japan Labor Union" formed
1894	Treaty revision agreed upon between Japan and England
1894–95	The Sino-Japanese War
1895	Triple intervention, but Taiwan becomes a Japanese colony
1897	Ashio copper mine pollution incident
1898	Kenseitō (Constitutional Party) formed
1899	First automobile imported from the United States
1900	Rikken Seiyūkai formed with Itō Hirobumi as its first president
	Boxer Rebellion in China ended
1901	Death of Fukuzawa Yukichi (b. 1834)
	Social Democratic Party formed
1902	The Anglo-Japanese Alliance
1904–05	The Russo-Japanese War
1905	Natsume Sōseki begins serialization of his novel *I Am a Cat*
1906	Shimazaki Tōson's novel *The Broken Commandment* about *burakumin*
1910	Annexation of Korea
	Execution of Kōtoku Shūsui
1911	Factory law enacted to protect workers
	Seitōsha (Blue Stocking Society), a feminist organization, is formed
	Nishida Kitarō publishes *Zen no Kenkyu (A Study of Good)*

Taishō Period (1912–26)

1914	Japan enters World War I
1915	The twenty-one demands presented to China
1916	Rabindranath Tagore, the Indian Nobel laureate in literature, visits Japan
1918	Beginning of the Siberian intervention
	Rice riots spread across the country

1922	The Washington naval disarmament treaty
1923	The great Kantō earthquake
1925	Universal manhood suffrage enacted
	Peace preservation law
	Radio broadcasting begins
	Establishment of diplomatic relations with the Soviet Union

Early Shōwa Period (1926–1945)

1927	Financial panic in Japan
1928	First election under universal suffrage
1929	Beginning of worldwide panic
1930	London naval conference
1931	The Manchurian Incident
1932	Prime Minister Inukai is assassinated, end of party Cabinet.
1933	Japan's withdrawal from the League of Nations
1936	Attempted coup d'etat, February 26 incident
1937	Beginning of the Sino-Japanese War
1938	Passage of the national mobilization law
	Suzuki Daisetsu publishes *Zen Buddhism and Its Influence on Japanese Culture*
1939	Hostilities between USSR and Japan at Nomonhan
	Outbreak of World War II in Europe
1940	Japanese troops move into northern French Indochina
	Tripartite alliance with Germany and Italy
1941	Japan–USSR neutrality pact
	Japanese troops move into Southern French Indochina
	U.S. economic sanctions against Japan
	Konoye replaced by General Tōjo as prime minister
	Japan attacks Pearl Harbor
1942	The Battle of Midway (June)
1944	Fall of Saipan, shift in the tide of war
1945	U.S. troops land in the Philippines and Okinawa
	Atomic bombs dropped on Hiroshima and Nagasaki
	Japan surrenders to the Allied powers

Postwar Shōwa period (1945–89)

1945	Allied occupation of Japan begins
1946	A new constitution is promulgated
	The SCAP-sponsored land reform law goes into effect
1948–49	The Dodge line—economic stabilization ordered
1949	Nobel Prize in physics to Dr. Yukawa Hideki
1951	San Francisco peace treaty
	Concurrent signing of mutual security agreement with the United States
1952	Japan regains independence
1953	Television broadcasting begins
1955	Japan Productivity Center is organized
	Economic Planning Agency is formed
	Japan Socialist Party formed through merger
	Liberal Democratic Party formed through merger
1956	Restoration of diplomatic relations with USSR
	Japan's admission to the United Nations
1957	Completion of the nuclear reactor at Tōkaimura
1958	Undersea Shimonoseki-Moji tunnel is completed
1959	Marriage of crown prince with a commoner
1960	New U.S.–Japan mutual security treaty concluded amid demonstrations
	"Plan to double individual's income" is initiated
1964	New bullet train between Tokyo and Osaka opens
	Tokyo Olympics
1967	Rapprochement with South Korea following Prime Minister Satō's visit
1968	Yawata and Fuji are merged to form New Japan Steel
	Nobel Prize in literature to Kawabata Yasunari
1969	Student activists occupy Tokyo University
1970	Japan signs nuclear nonproliferation treaty
	Expo 70 opens in Osaka
1971	Merger of Kangyō and Daiichi, making it the largest bank in Japan
	Environment Agency established
1972	Winter Olympics open in Sapporo
	Okinawa formally returned to Japan

1972 (continued)	Normalization of relations with Beijing
1973–74	The first oil crisis
1974	President Ford visits Japan, first visit by a sitting American president.
	Satō Eisaku receives Nobel Peace Prize
1975	The bullet train is extended to Hakata in Kyushu
	Emperor Hirohito visits the United States
1976	The Lockheed bribery scandal implicating former Prime Minister Tanaka
1976	Narita International Airport (Tokyo) opens
	Life expectancy exceeds that of Sweden
	Japan-China treaty of friendship is signed
1979	The Tokyo summit of advanced industrial nations
1980	Japanese automobile production exceeds that of America
1981	Voluntary restriction of car exports at 1.68 million units to the United States
	Administrative reform movement is spearheaded by Dokō Toshio, former president of Keidanren
1982	Northeast bullet train line opens to Morioka
	Bullet train line reaches Niigata on the Japan sea coast
1983	National debt reaches 100 trillion yen
	Tokyo Disneyland opens
1985	The Plaza accord to deflate the value of the dollar against the Japanese yen.
	Equal employment opportunity law for men and women enacted
1987	The Japan National Railway is made into seven separate private companies
	Crisis in stock market (October 20) an average of 14.9 percent loss in price in one day
1988	Opening of the Hokkaido-Honshu tunnel
	Opening of the Seto bridge linking Honshu and Shikoku
	General sales tax instituted, going into effect April 1, 1989
1989	Death of Emperor Hirohito and accession of Akihito

Heisei Period (1989–   )

1989	The Recruit scandal forces the resignation of Prime Minister Takeshita

1989 (continued)	LDP suffers its first major defeat in the House of Councillors election (July 23)
1991	Japan pledges a total of $13 billion to the Gulf crisis
	Severe stock market loss, disclosure of illegal refunds by Nomura Securities
1992	Participation in UN sponsored peacekeeping operations [PKO] approved
	Emperor Akihito and Empress Michiko make their first official visit to China
1993	End of LDP's consecutive one-party rule since 1955
	Trade surplus reaches $132.6 billion and U.S. dollar hits the 100 yen mark
1994	Modified single-seat constituency for the House of Representatives passes
	New Osaka international airport opens
	The New Frontier Party (NFP, Shinshintō) is formed
1995	The Kobe earthquake
	Poison gas attack on civilians in Tokyo subways by the Aum Shinrikyō sect
1996	Merger of Mitsubishi and Tokyo creates the largest bank in the world
	First election under modified single constituency election law

List of Prewar and Postwar Prime Ministers

Prewar and Wartime Prime Ministers

Itō Hirobumi	December 22, 1885	35[1]
Kuroda Kiyotaka	April 30, 1888	44
Yamagata Aritomo	December 24, 1889	35
Matsukata Masayoshi	May 6, 1891	44
Itō Hirobumi	August 8, 1892	35
Matsukata Masayoshi	September 18, 1896	44
Itō Hirobumi	January 12, 1898	35
Ōkuma Shigenobu	June 30, 1898	45
Yamagata Aritomo	November 8, 1898	35
Itō Hirobumi	October 19, 1900	35
Katsura Tarō	June 2, 1901	35
Saionji Kinmochi	January 7, 1906	26
Katsura Tarō	July 14, 1911	35
Saionji Kinmochi	August 30, 1911	26
Katsura Tarō	December 21, 1912	35
Yamamoto Gonnohyōe	February 20, 1913	44
Ōkuma Shigenobu	April 16, 1914	45
Terauchi Masatake	October 9, 1916	35

[1]The number given corresponds to the legal domicile of each prime minister. It is keyed to the number given in appendix 5, the administrative map of Japan.

Hara Takashi	September 29, 1918	4
Takahashi Korekiyo	November 13, 1921	8
Katō Tomosaburō	June 12, 1922	34
Yamamoto Gonnohyōe	September 2, 1923	44
Kiyoura Keigo	January 7, 1924	43
Katō Takaaki	June 11, 1924	21
Wakatsuki Reijirō	January 30, 1926	33
Tanaka Giichi	April 20, 1927	35
Hamaguchi Osachi	July 2, 1929	38
Inukai Tsuyoshi	December 13, 1931	32
Saitō Makoto	May 26, 1932	4
Okada Keisuke	July 8, 1934	23
Hirota Kōki	March 9, 1936	42
Hayashi Senjūrō	February 2, 1937	22
Konoye Fumimaro	June 4, 1937	8
Hiranuma Kiichirō	January 5, 1939	32
Abe Nobuyuki	August 30, 1939	22
Yonai Mitsumasa	January 16, 1940	4
Konoye Fumimaro	July 22, 1940	8
Tōjō Hideki	October 18, 1941	8
Koiso Kuniaki	July 22, 1944	5
Suzuki Kantarō	April 7, 1945	13

Postwar Prime Ministers

Prince Higashikuni	August 17, 1945	26
Shidehara Kijūrō	October 9, 1945	28
Yoshida Shigeru	May 22, 1946	8
Katayama Tetsu	May 22, 1947	29
Ashida Hitoshi	March 10, 1948	26
Yoshida Shigeru	October 15, 1948	38
Hatoyama Ichirō	December 10, 1954	8
Ishibashi Tanzan	December 23, 1956	17
Kishi Nobusuke	February 25, 1957	35
Ikeda Hayato	July 19, 1960	34
Satō Eisaku	November 9, 1964	35
Tanaka Kakuei	July 7, 1972	15

Miki Takeo	December 9, 1974	37
Fukuda Takeo	December 24, 1976	9
Ōhira Masayoshi	December 7, 1978	36
Suzuki Zenkō	July 17, 1980	4
Nakasone Yasuhiro	November 27, 1982	9
Takeshita Noboru	November 6, 1987	33
Uno Sōsuke	June 3, 1989	24
Kaifu Toshiki	August 9, 1989	21
Miyazawa Kiichi	November 5, 1991	34
Hosokawa Morihiro	August 9, 1993	43
Hata Tsutomu	April 28, 1994	16
Murayama Tomiichi	June 30, 1994	40
Hashimoto Ryūtarō	January 11, 1996	32

Appendix 5

Administrative Map
of Japan

Legends for Administrative Map of Japan

The boundaries shown in the map are boundaries of the present-day prefectures. Each prefecture is given a number which corresponds to the name given below. These numbers may also be used to identify traditional names of areas occupied by these prefectures. A present-day prefecture may contain a number of traditional administrative divisions. When that occurs, these place names are given sequentially from north to south, and east to west.

Macron signs to indicate long vowels are utilized in this section, even though such signs are normally omitted from place names.

Prefectures in Present-Day Japan	*Traditional Names in Use Prior to 1868*
Hokkaidō Region	
1. Hokkaidō	1. Ezo
Tōhoku Region	
2. Aomori	2. Mutsu
3. Akita	3. Dewa (Ugo)[1]
4. Iwate	4. Mutsu (Rikuchū)
5. Yamagata	5. Dewa (Uzen)
6. Miyagi	6. Mutsu (Rikuzen)
7. Fukushima	7. Mutsu (Iwashiro, Iwaki)
Kantō Region	
8. Tōkyō	8. Edo, Musashi
9. Gumma	9. Kōzuke
10. Tochigi	10. Shimotsuke
11. Ibaraki	11. Hitachi, Shimousa
12. Saitama	12. Musashi
13. Chiba	13. Shimousa, Kazusa, Awa
14. Kanagawa	14. Musashi, Sagami
Chūbu Region	
15. Niigata	15. Echigo, Sado
16. Nagano	16. Shinano
17. Yamanashi	17. Kai

---

[1]The Tōhoku region traditionally consisted of two provinces of Mutsu and Dewa. In 1869, the Meiji government divided these two provinces into seven separate administrative entities. Their names are shown in parentheses from 3 through 7. The present-day Aomori prefecture inherited the name Mutsu under this plan.

18. Shizuoka	18. Izu, Suruga, Tōtōmi
19. Toyama	19. Ecchū
20. Gifu	20. Hida, Mino
21. Aichi	21. Mikawa, Owari
22. Ishikawa	22. Noto, Kaga
23. Fukui	23. Echizen, Wakasa

Kinki Region

24. Shiga	24. Ōmi
25. Mie	25. Ise, Iga, Shima, Kii
26. Kyōto	26. Yamashiro, Tango, Tanba
27. Nara	27. Yamato
28. Ōsaka	28. Kawachi, Settsu, Izumi
29. Wakayama	29. Kii
30. Hyōgo	30. Tanba, Settsu, Tajima, Harima

Chūgoku Region

31. Tottori	31. Inaba, Hōki
32. Okayama	32. Mimasaka, Bizen, Bicchū
33. Shimane	33. Izumo, Iwami
34. Hiroshima	34. Bingo, Aki
35. Yamaguchi	35. Suō, Nagato (Chōshū)

Shikoku Region

36. Kagawa	36. Sanuki
37. Tokushima	37. Awa
38. Kōchi	38. Tosa
39. Ehime	39. Iyo

Kyushu Region

40. Ōita	40. Bungo, Buzen
41. Miyazaki	41. Hyūga
42. Fukuoka	42. Buzen, Chikuzen, Chikugo
43. Kumamoto	43. Higo
44. Kagoshima	44. Ōsumi, Satsuma
45. Saga	45. Hizen
46. Nagasaki	46. Hizen, Iki, Tsushima

Okinawa Region

47. Okinawa[2]	47. Ryūkyū

---

[2]Officially became part of Japan in 1872.

Index to Present-Day Place Names

Prefectures and their capital cities often share same names. Those names appearing in *italics* represent cities which are not administrative capitals of their respective prefectures.

Index to Traditional Place Names

Aki	34	Kazusa	13
Awa (安房)	13	Kii	25, 29
Awa (阿波)	37	Kōzuke	9
Bicchu	32	Mikawa	21
Bingo	34	Mimasaka	32
Bizen	32	Mino	20
Bungo	40	Musashi	8, 12, 14
Buzen	40, 42	Mutsu	2, 4, 6, 7
Chikugo	42	Nagato	35
Chikuzen	42	Noto	22
Chōshū	35	Ōmi	24
Dewa	3	Ōsumi	44
Ecchū	19	Owari	21
Echigo	15	Rikuchū	4
Echizen	23	Rikuzen	6
Edo	8	Ryūkyū	47
Ezo	1	Sado	15
Harima	30	Sagami	14
Hida	20	Sanuki	36
Higo	43	Satsuma	44
Hitachi	11	Settsu	28, 30
Hizen	45, 46	Shima	25
Hōki	31	Shimotsuke	10
Hyūga	41	Shimousa	11, 13
Iga	25	Shinano	16
Iki	46	Suō	35
Inaba	31	Suruga	18
Ise	25	Tajima	30
Iwaki	7	Tanba	26, 30
Iwami	33	Tango	26
Iwashiro	7	Tosa	38
Iyo	39	Tōtōmi	18
Izu	18	Tsushima	46
Izumi	28	Ugo	3
Izumo	33	Uzen	5
Kaga	22	Wakasa	23
Kai	17	Yamashiro	26
Kawachi	28	Yamato	27

Index

David J. Lu is professor emeritus of history and Japanese studies at Bucknell University. He has maintained close contact with Japanese political and business leaders and the scholarly community through his frequent visits to Japan, including a year as a Fulbright scholar and a year as resident director of the Associated Kyoto Program at Doshisha University. His works reflect his desire to be a bridge builder. He writes in English about Japanese history and business practices, and in Japanese about American history and society. The latter includes writing regularly for the *Sekai to Nippon* (The World and Japan), a Japanese weekly journal of opinion.

This book is compiled to share with the readers his wide-ranging interest in Japan developed over his thirty-five-year teaching career and his lifelong contact with Japan. It combines the perspectives of an insider with those of an outsider. He is an insider because of his birth in Taiwan which was then a Japanese colony, of his Japanese education through Higher School (*kotō gakkō*), and of his position as a respected columnist in Japan. Yet he is an outsider because of his American graduate education, long academic career, and citizenship. This combination has earned praise from Japanese readers for his earlier works: "Professor Lu is one of the very few Americans who can see the reality beneath the obvious surface," commented a former Minister of Justice. "He does not hesitate to criticize Japan, but does it without malice. His books can be respected and trusted." That even-handed approach is also evident in this work.

David Lu lives in Milton, Pennsylvania, the birthplace of Dr. J.C. Hepburn, the first American Protestant missionary to Japan, and creator of the Hepburn system of Romanization. With his wife, Annabelle, he does some gardening, but is also busily at work on a three-volume history of Japan.

Books by David Lu

From the Marco Polo Bridge to Pearl Harbor (1961), Japanese edition (1967)
Sources of Japanese History, two volumes (1974)
Perspectives on Japan's External Affairs: Views from America (1982)
Inside Corporate Japan: The Art of Fumble-Free Management (1987)

Published in Japanese in Japan

*The Great Society That the Pioneers Built: A Bicentennial History of the
    United States* (1976)
The Life and Times of Foreign Minister Matsuoka Yōsuke, 1880–1946 (1981).

Translated works

Usui Katsumi and Hata Ikuhiko, *The China Quagmire: Japan's Expansion on
    the Asian Continent, 1933–1941* (1983)
Ishikawa Kaoru, *What Is Total Quality Control? The Japanese Way* (1985)
Japan Management Association, *Kanban and Just-In-Time at Toyota* (1986)
Nemoto Masao, *Total Quality Control for Management* (1987)
Karatsu Hajime, *TQC: Wisdom of Japan* (1988)